FAIRY TAIL 100 YEARS QUEST

11

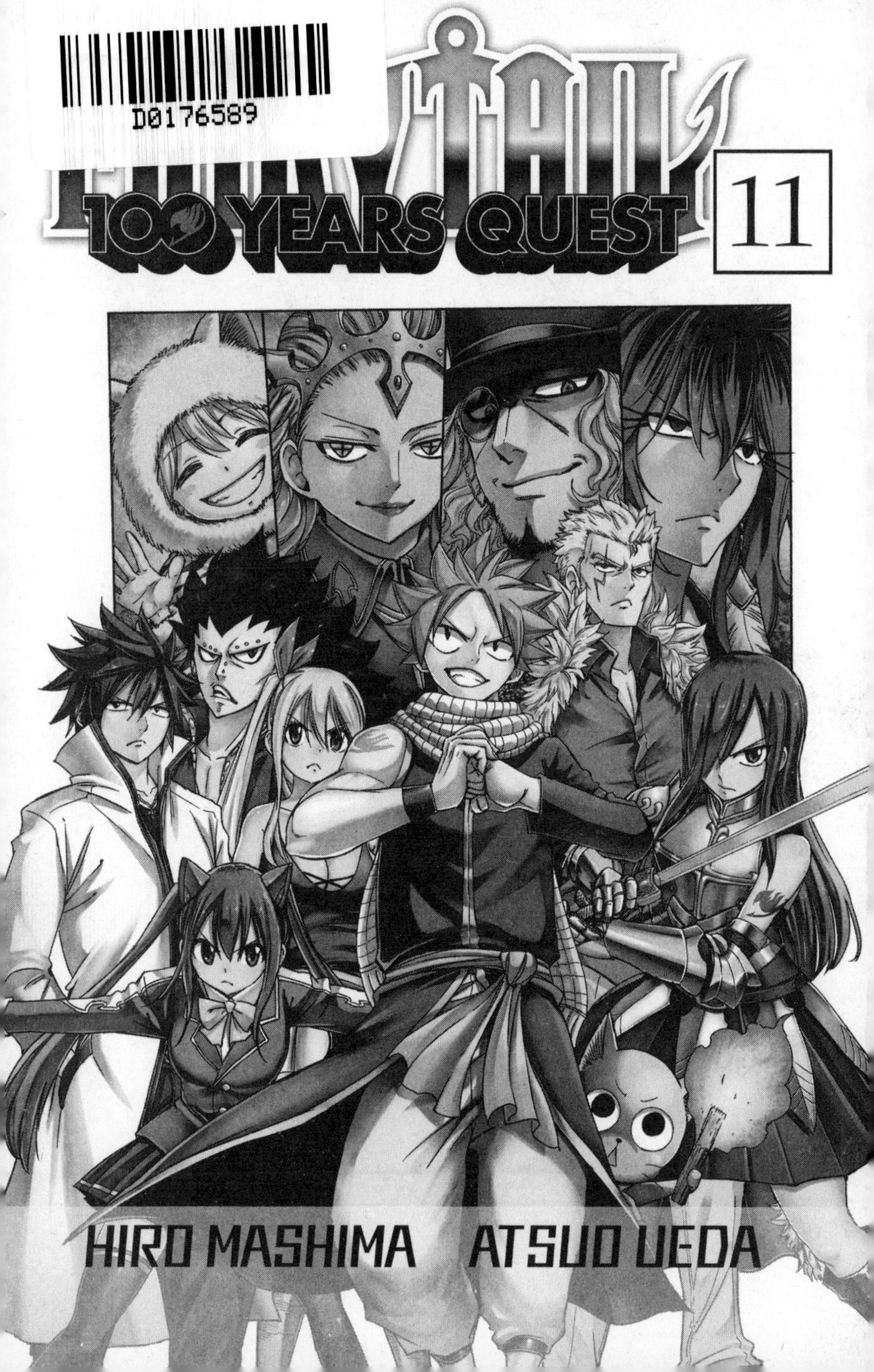

HIRO MASHIMA ATSUO UEDA

FAIRY TAIL 100 YEARS QUEST 11 CONTENTS

FAIRY TAIL 100 YEARS QUEST

Chapter 91: My World

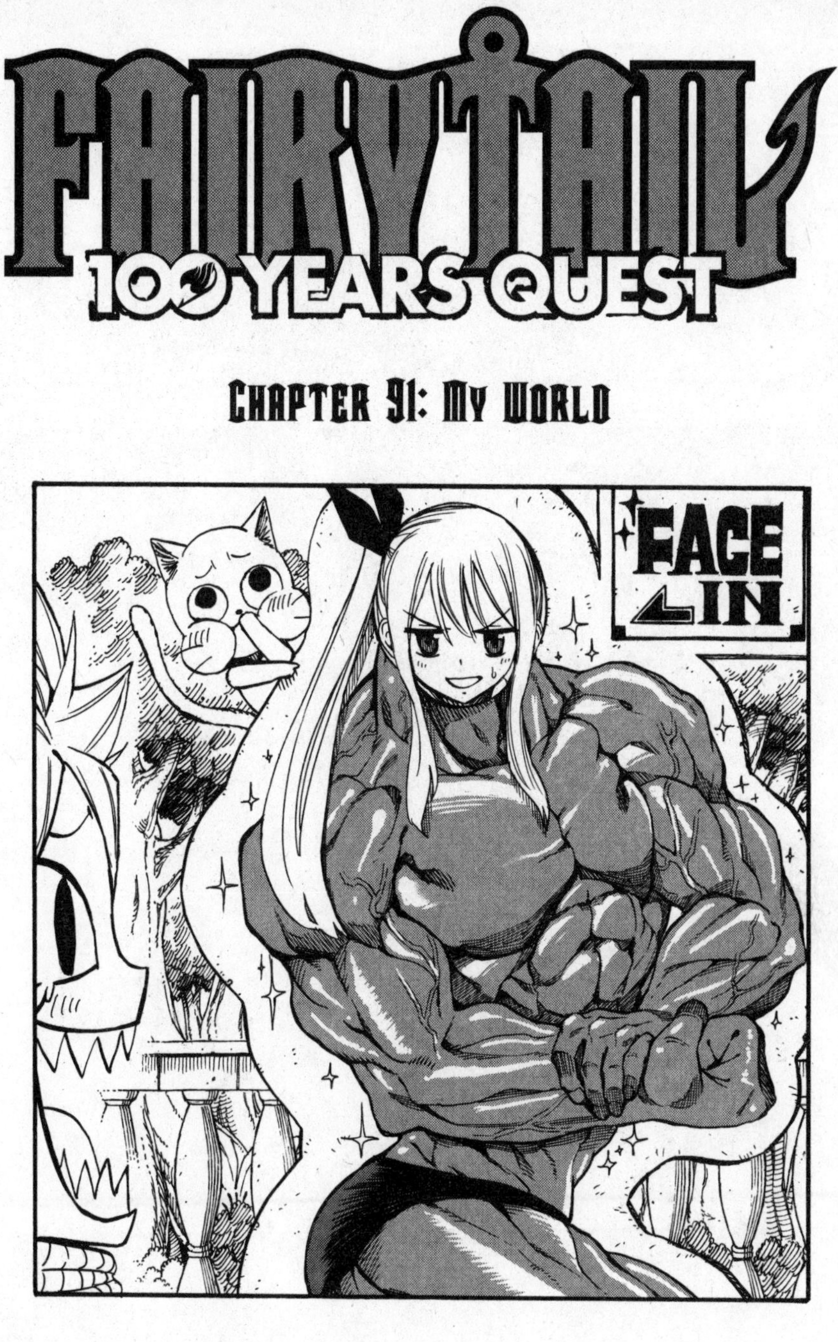
FACE IN

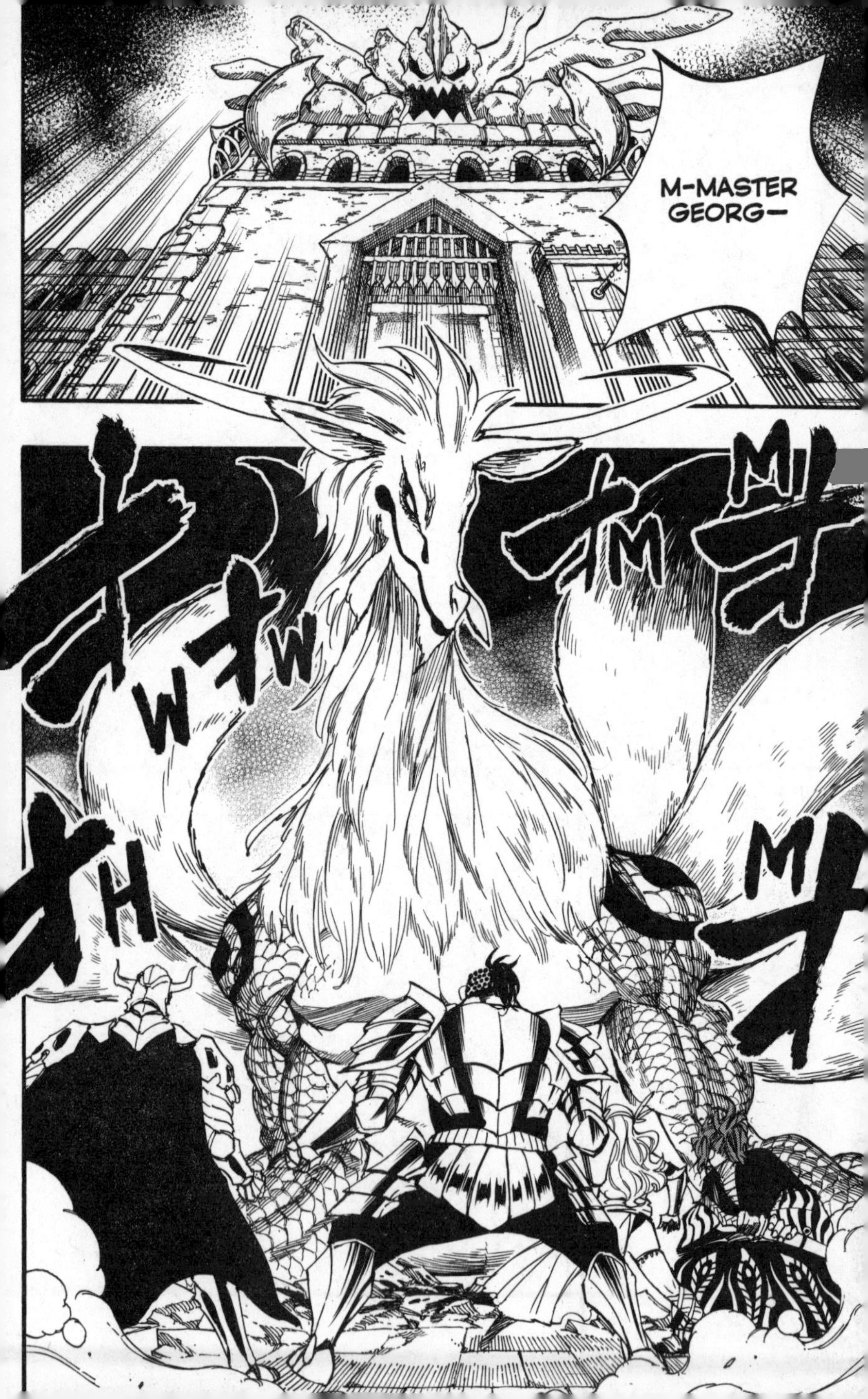
M-MASTER GEORG—

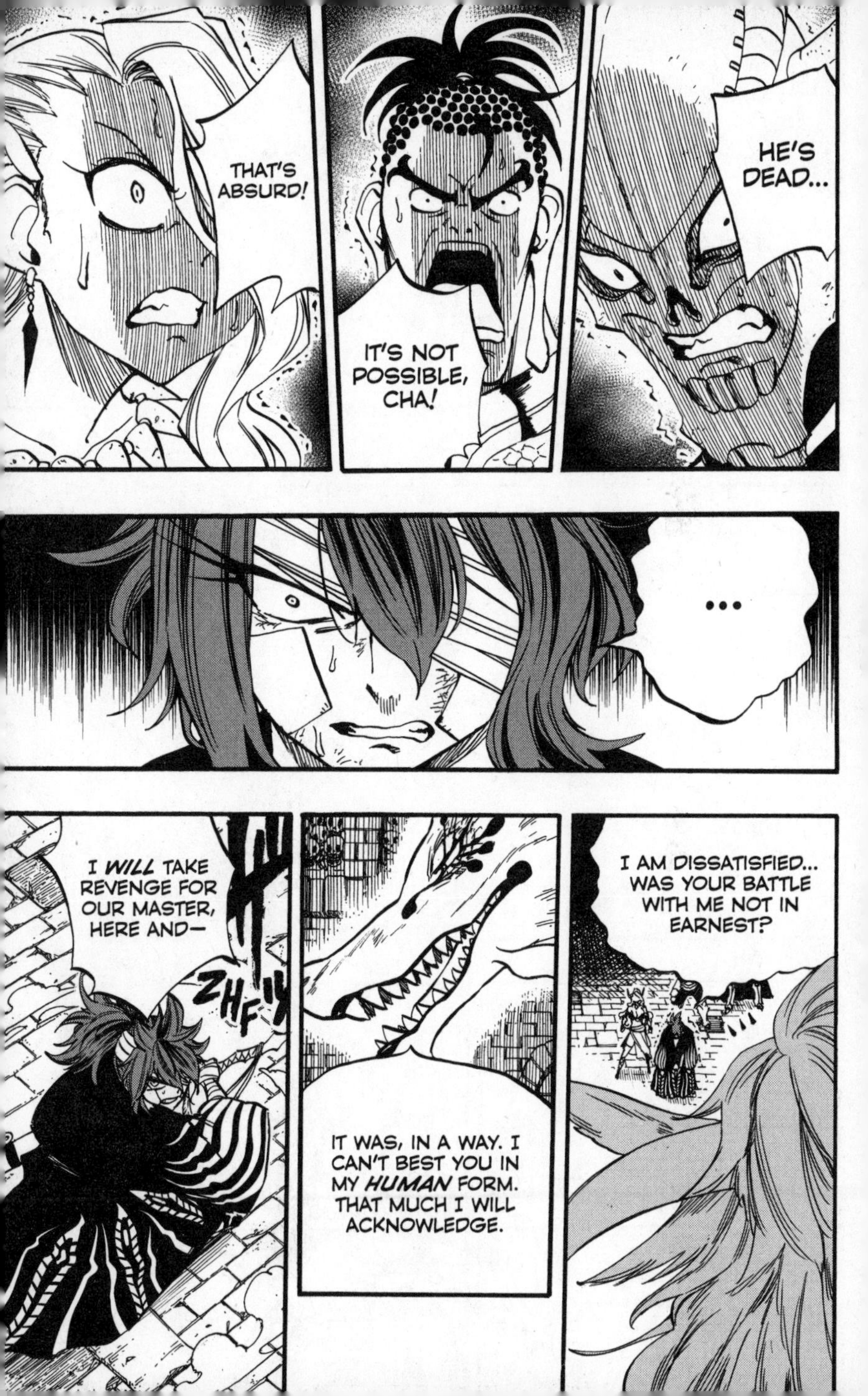
HE'S DEAD...
IT'S NOT POSSIBLE, CHA!
THAT'S ABSURD!
...
I AM DISSATISFIED... WAS YOUR BATTLE WITH ME NOT IN EARNEST?
IT WAS, IN A WAY. I CAN'T BEST YOU IN MY *HUMAN* FORM. THAT MUCH I WILL ACKNOWLEDGE.
I *WILL* TAKE REVENGE FOR OUR MASTER, HERE AND—

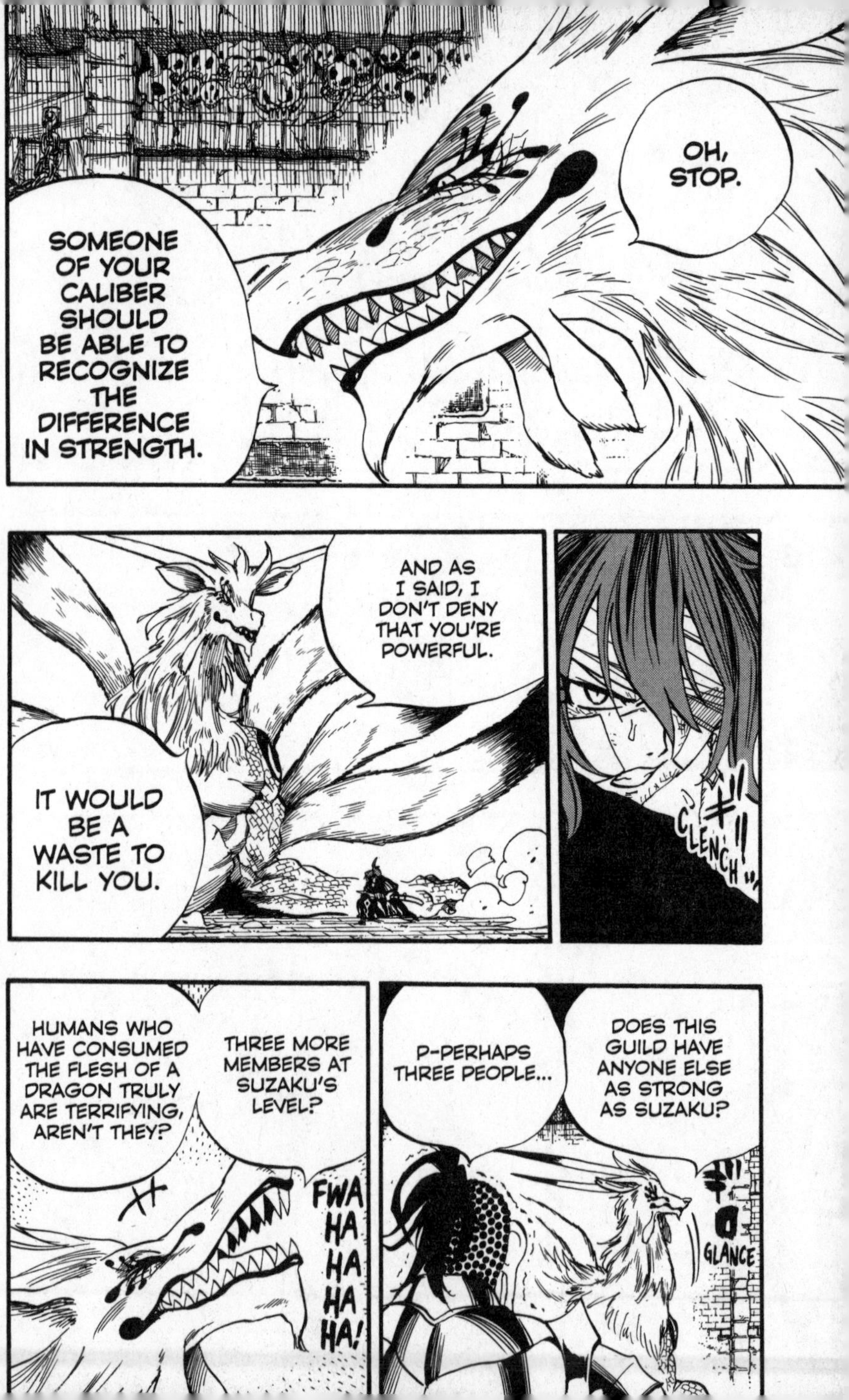
OH, STOP.
SOMEONE OF YOUR CALIBER SHOULD BE ABLE TO RECOGNIZE THE DIFFERENCE IN STRENGTH.
CLENCH!!
AND AS I SAID, I DON'T DENY THAT YOU'RE POWERFUL.
IT WOULD BE A WASTE TO KILL YOU.
DOES THIS GUILD HAVE ANYONE ELSE AS STRONG AS SUZAKU?
P-PERHAPS THREE PEOPLE...
GLANCE
THREE MORE MEMBERS AT SUZAKU'S LEVEL?
HUMANS WHO HAVE CONSUMED THE FLESH OF A DRAGON TRULY ARE TERRIFYING, AREN'T THEY?
FWA HA HA HA HA HA!

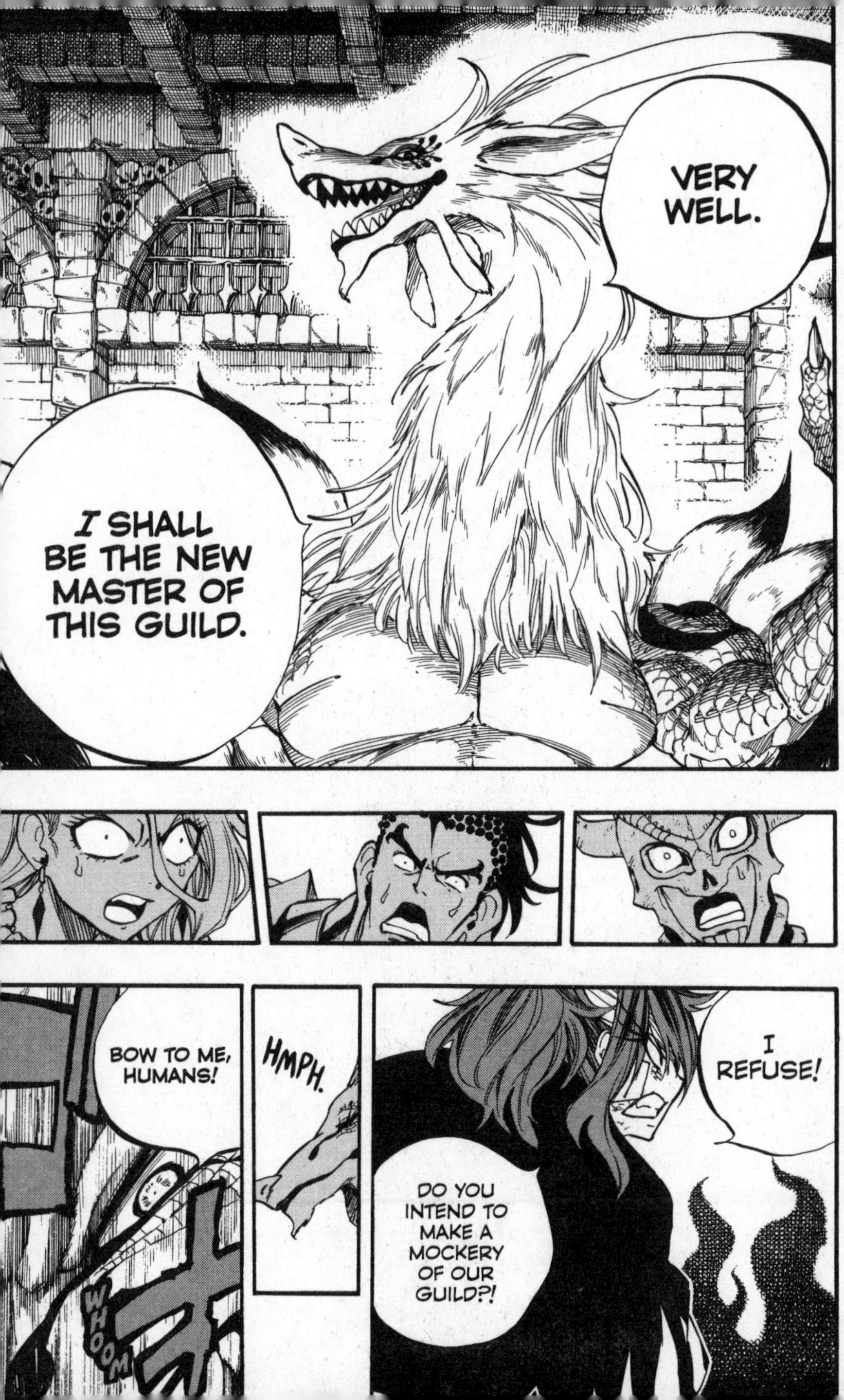
VERY WELL.
I SHALL BE THE NEW MASTER OF THIS GUILD.
I REFUSE!
DO YOU INTEND TO MAKE A MOCKERY OF OUR GUILD?!
HMPH.
BOW TO ME, HUMANS!
WHOOM

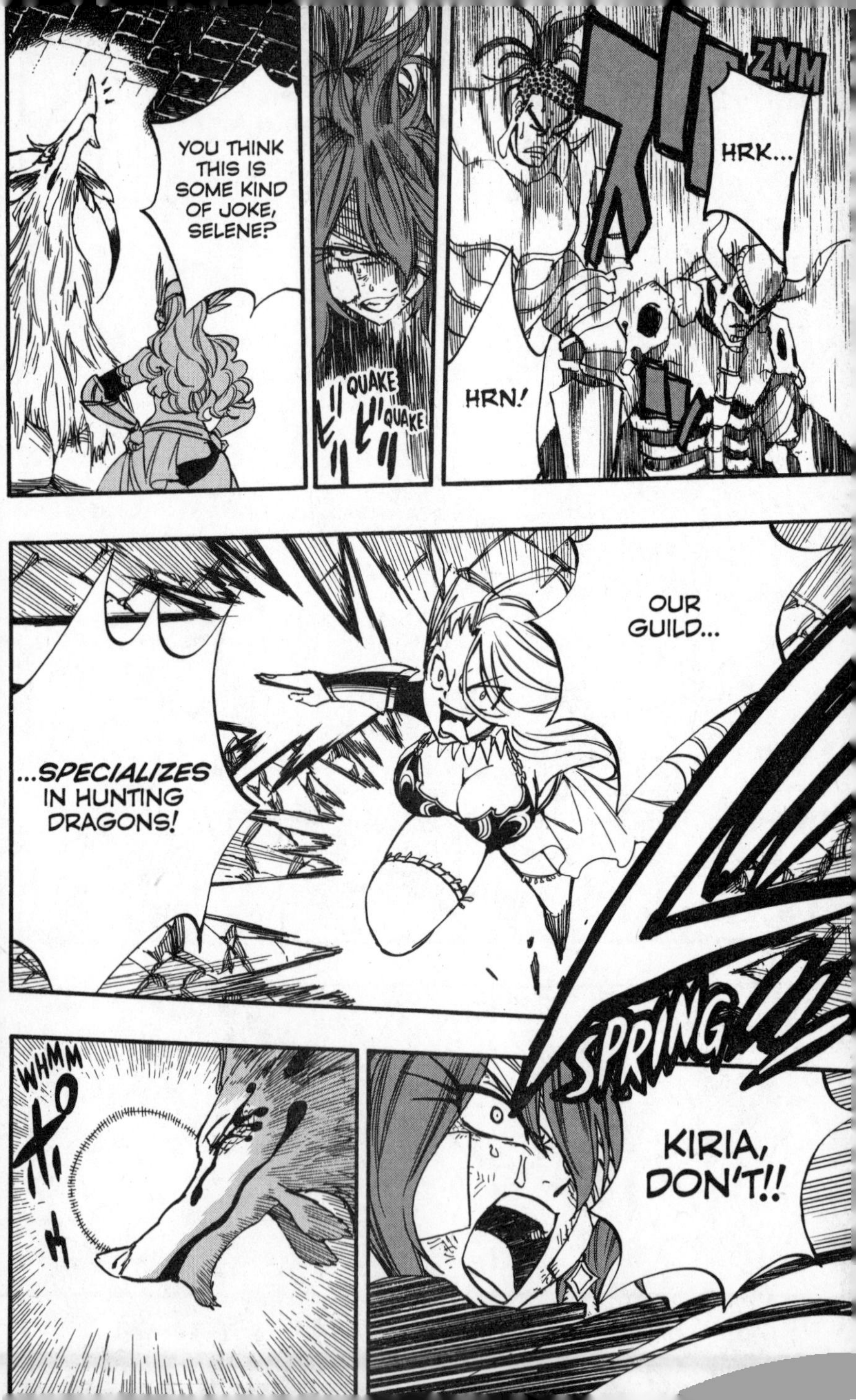
ZMM
HRK...
HRN!
QUAKE
QUAKE
YOU THINK THIS IS SOME KIND OF JOKE, SELENE?
OUR GUILD...
...SPECIALIZES IN HUNTING DRAGONS!
SPRING
KIRIA, DON'T!!
WHMM

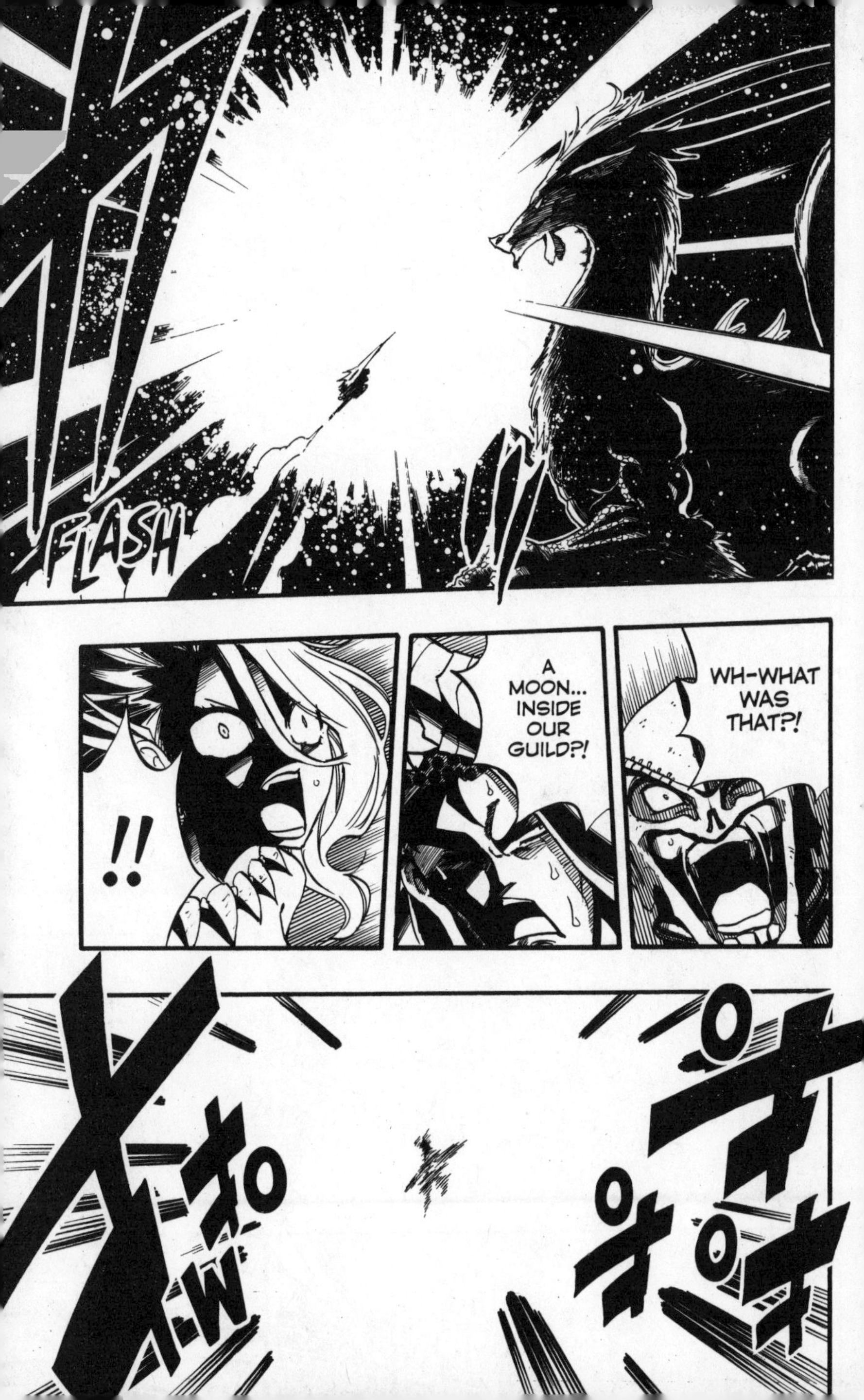
FLASH
WH-WHAT WAS THAT?!
A MOON... INSIDE OUR GUILD?!
!!

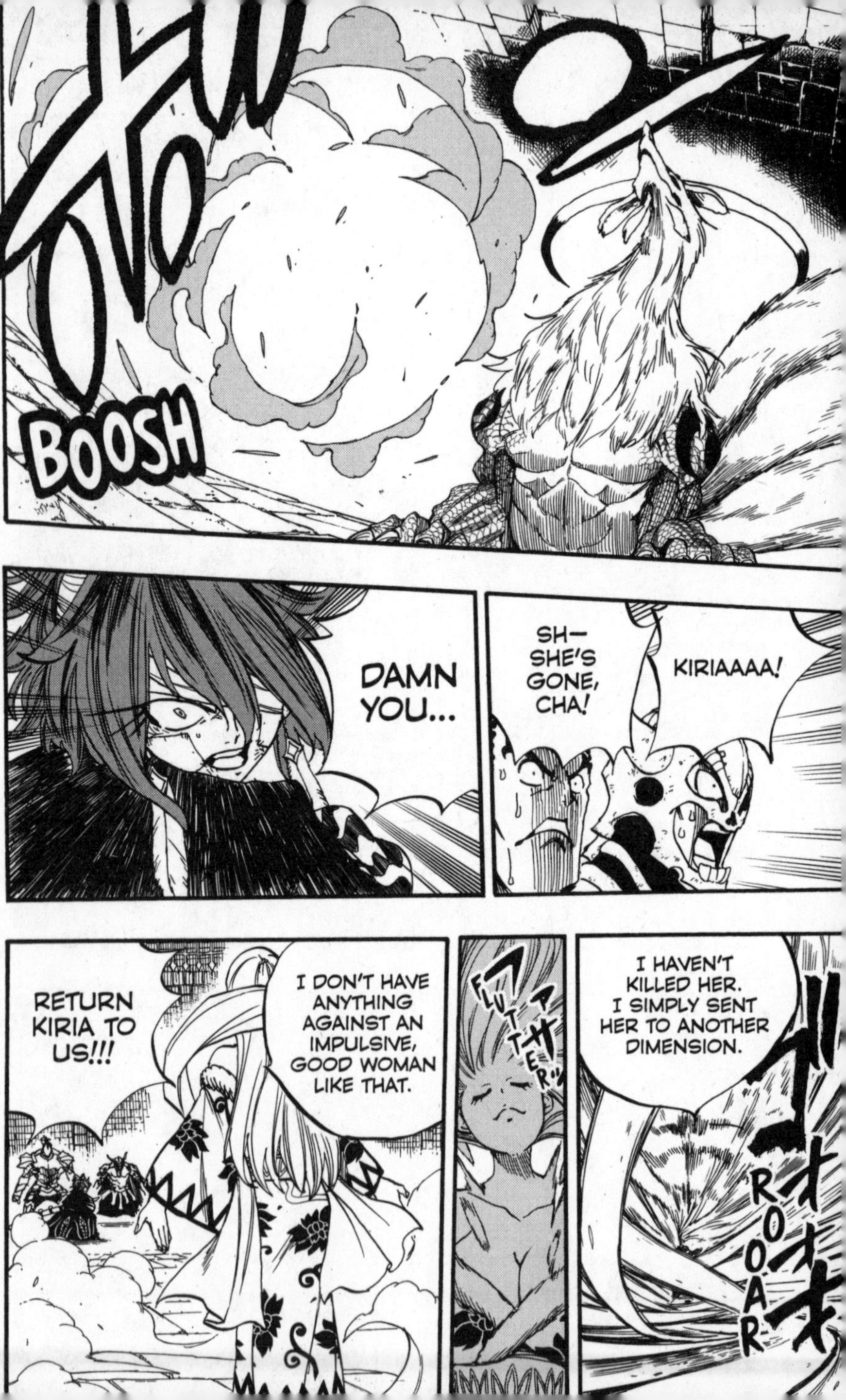
BOOSH
KIRIAAAA!
SH— SHE'S GONE, CHA!
DAMN YOU...
I HAVEN'T KILLED HER. I SIMPLY SENT HER TO ANOTHER DIMENSION.
ROOAR
FLUTTER
PATTER
I DON'T HAVE ANYTHING AGAINST AN IMPULSIVE, GOOD WOMAN LIKE THAT.
RETURN KIRIA TO US!!!

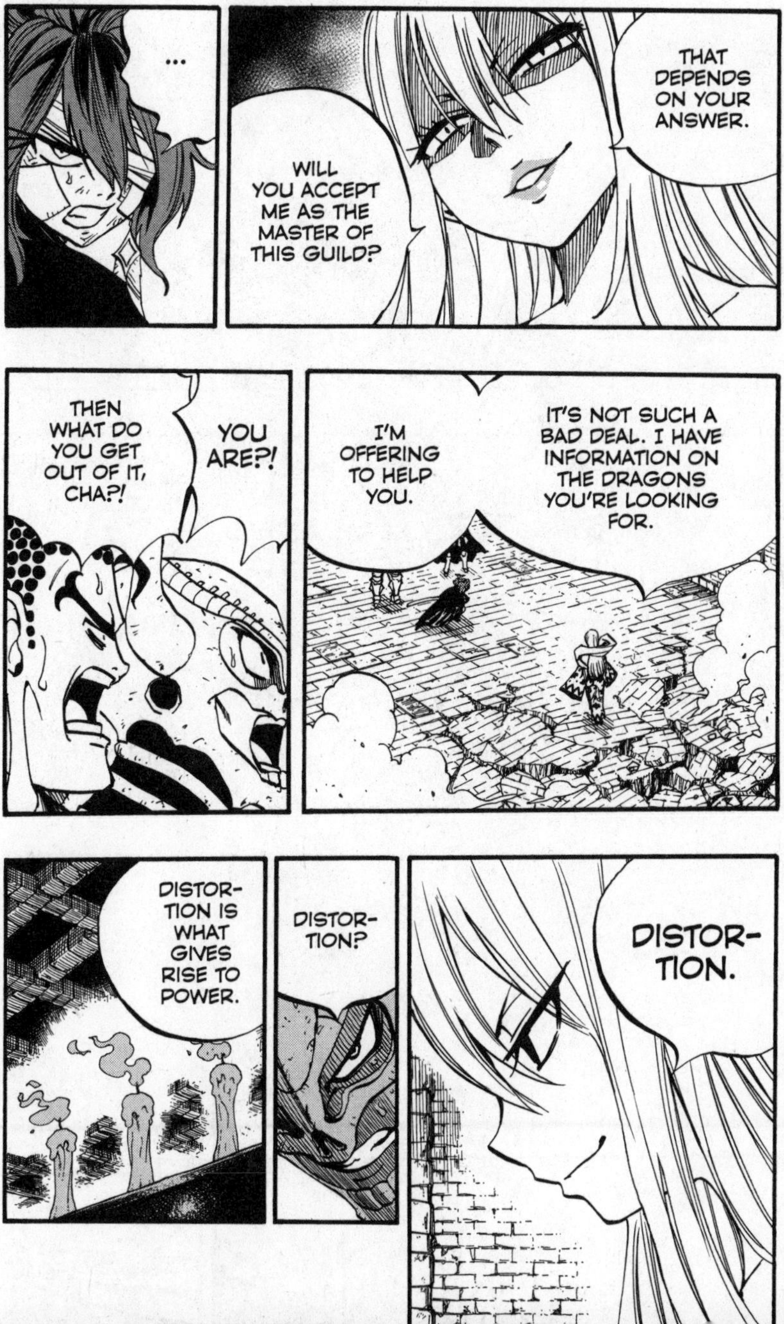
THAT DEPENDS ON YOUR ANSWER.
WILL YOU ACCEPT ME AS THE MASTER OF THIS GUILD?
...
IT'S NOT SUCH A BAD DEAL. I HAVE INFORMATION ON THE DRAGONS YOU'RE LOOKING FOR.
I'M OFFERING TO HELP YOU.
YOU ARE?!
THEN WHAT DO YOU GET OUT OF IT, CHA?!
DISTOR-TION.
DISTOR-TION?
DISTOR-TION IS WHAT GIVES RISE TO POWER.

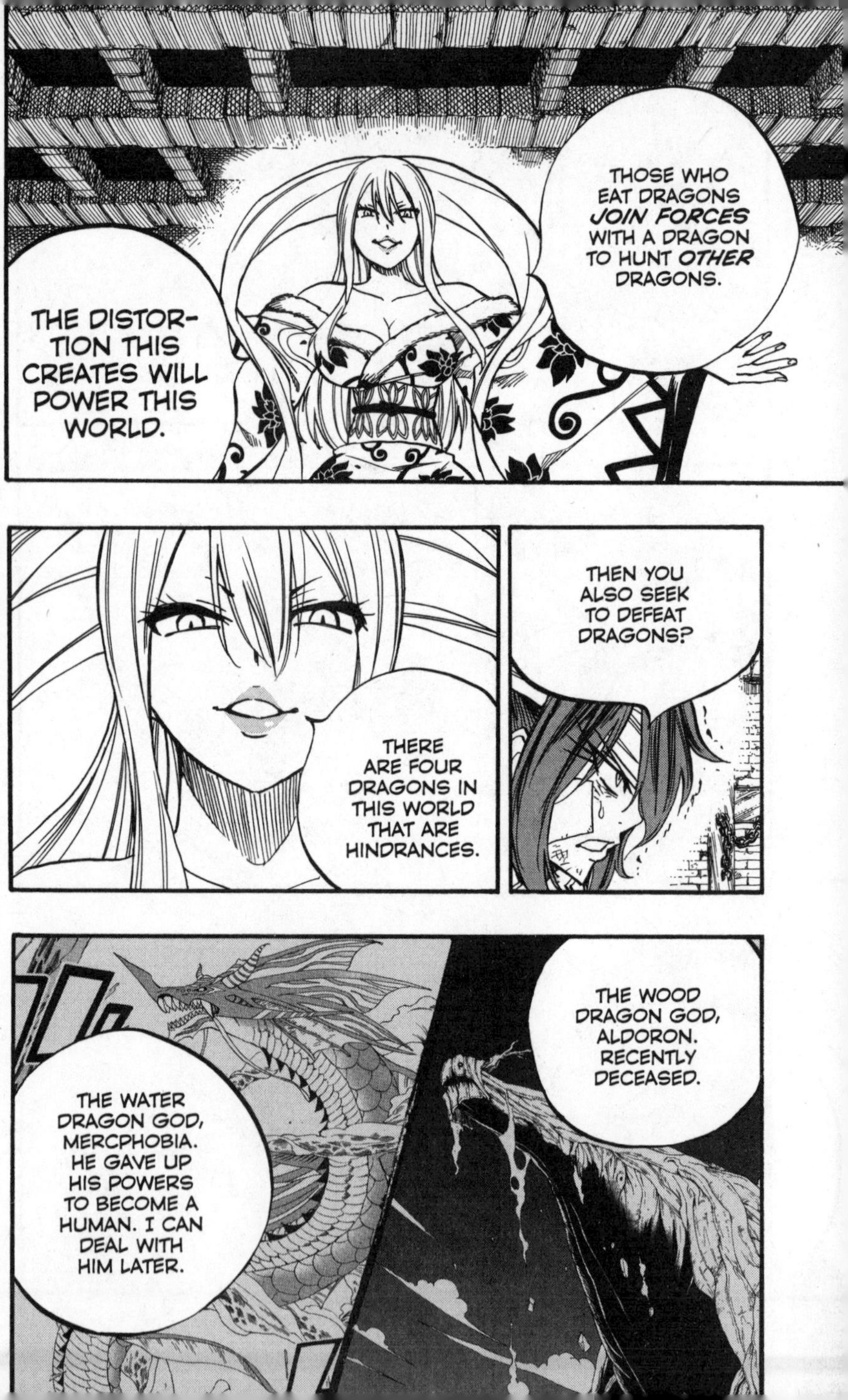
THOSE WHO EAT DRAGONS JOIN FORCES WITH A DRAGON TO HUNT OTHER DRAGONS.
THE DISTORTION THIS CREATES WILL POWER THIS WORLD.
THEN YOU ALSO SEEK TO DEFEAT DRAGONS?
THERE ARE FOUR DRAGONS IN THIS WORLD THAT ARE HINDRANCES.
THE WOOD DRAGON GOD, ALDORON. RECENTLY DECEASED.
THE WATER DRAGON GOD, MERCPHOBIA. HE GAVE UP HIS POWERS TO BECOME A HUMAN. I CAN DEAL WITH HIM LATER.

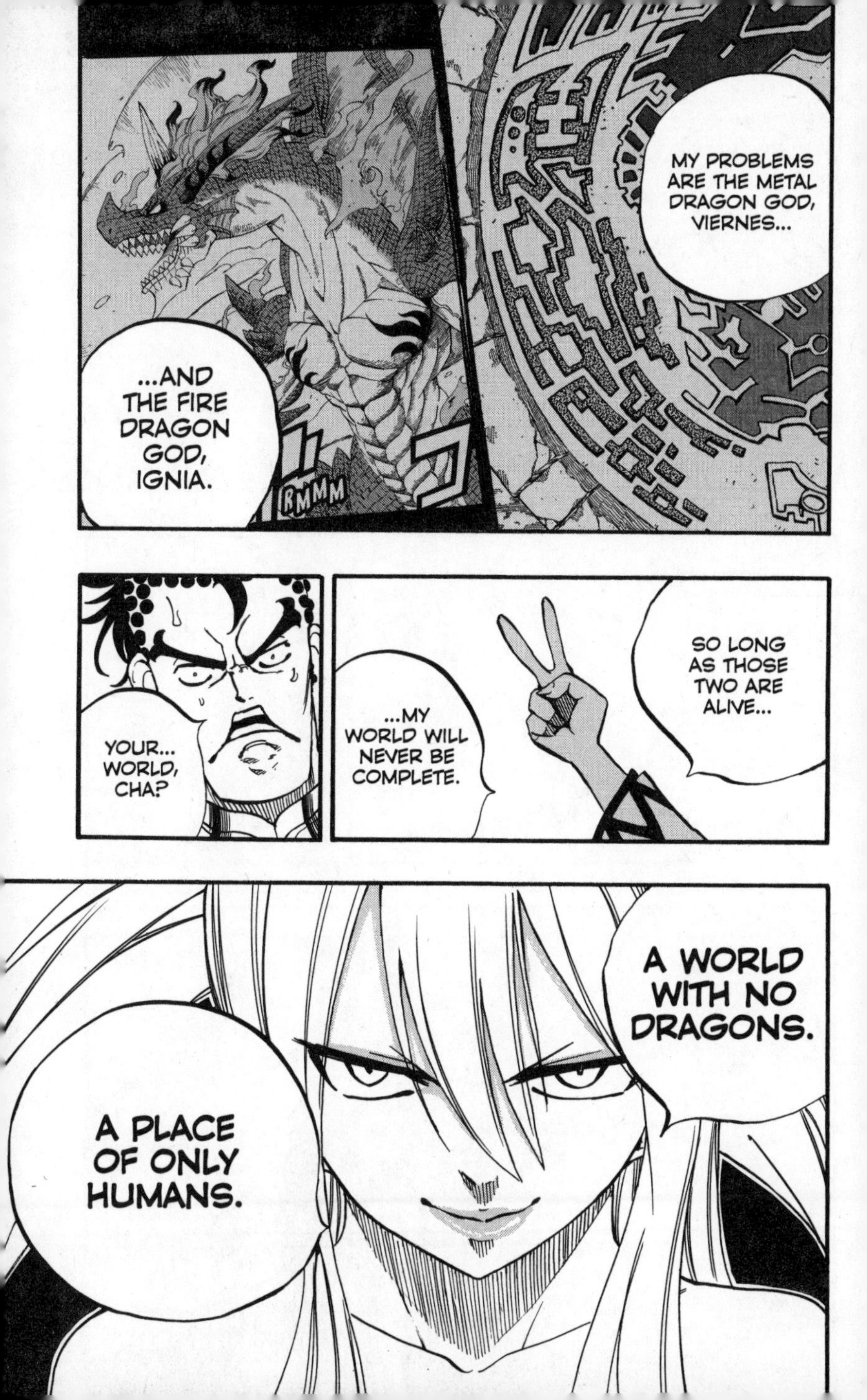
MY PROBLEMS ARE THE METAL DRAGON GOD, VIERNES...
...AND THE FIRE DRAGON GOD, IGNIA.
RMMM
SO LONG AS THOSE TWO ARE ALIVE...
...MY WORLD WILL NEVER BE COMPLETE.
YOUR... WORLD, CHA?
A WORLD WITH NO DRAGONS.
A PLACE OF ONLY HUMANS.

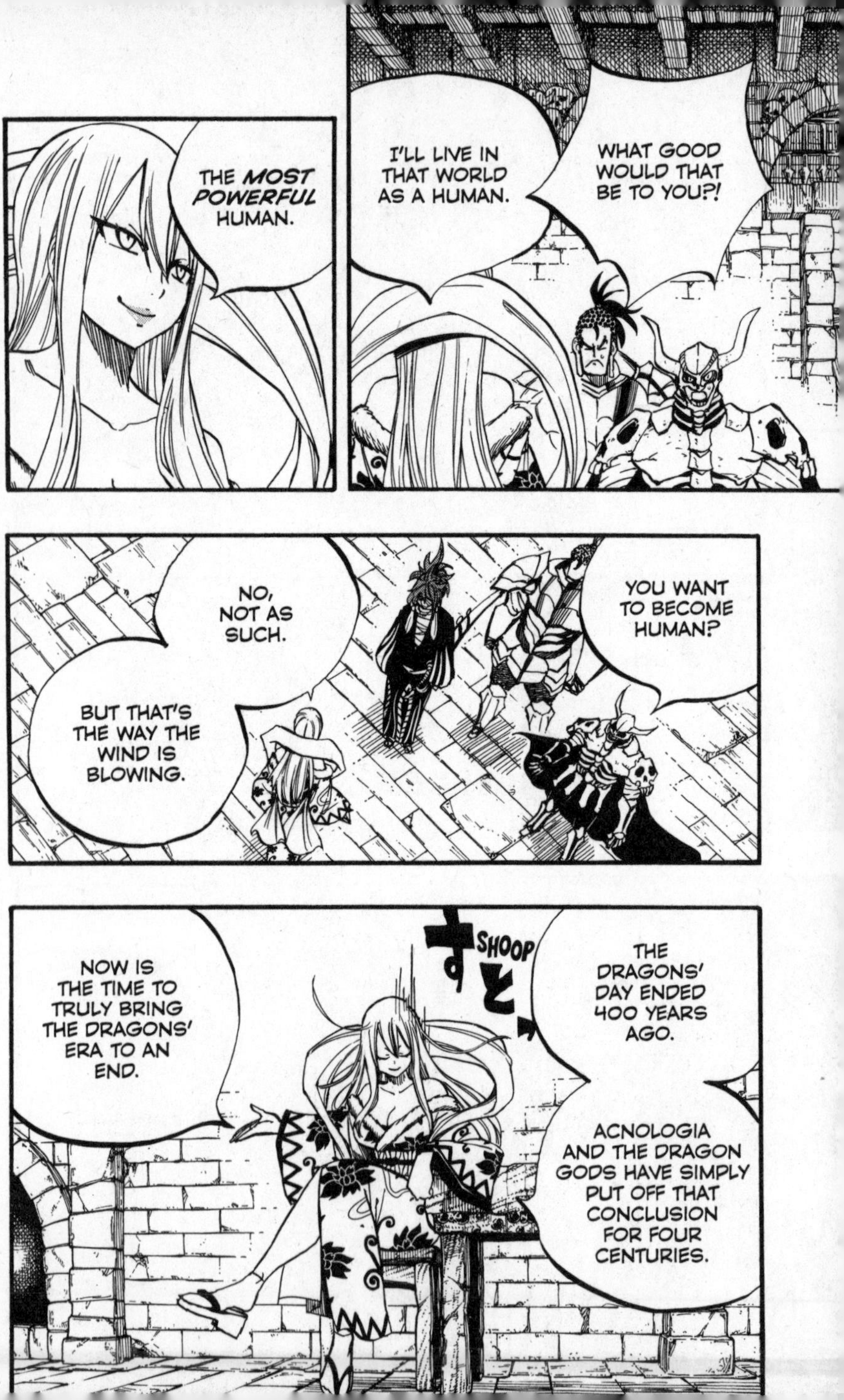
WHAT GOOD WOULD THAT BE TO YOU?!
I'LL LIVE IN THAT WORLD AS A HUMAN.
THE *MOST POWERFUL* HUMAN.
YOU WANT TO BECOME HUMAN?
NO, NOT AS SUCH.
BUT THAT'S THE WAY THE WIND IS BLOWING.
すと SHOOP
THE DRAGONS' DAY ENDED 400 YEARS AGO.
ACNOLOGIA AND THE DRAGON GODS HAVE SIMPLY PUT OFF THAT CONCLUSION FOR FOUR CENTURIES.
NOW IS THE TIME TO TRULY BRING THE DRAGONS' ERA TO AN END.

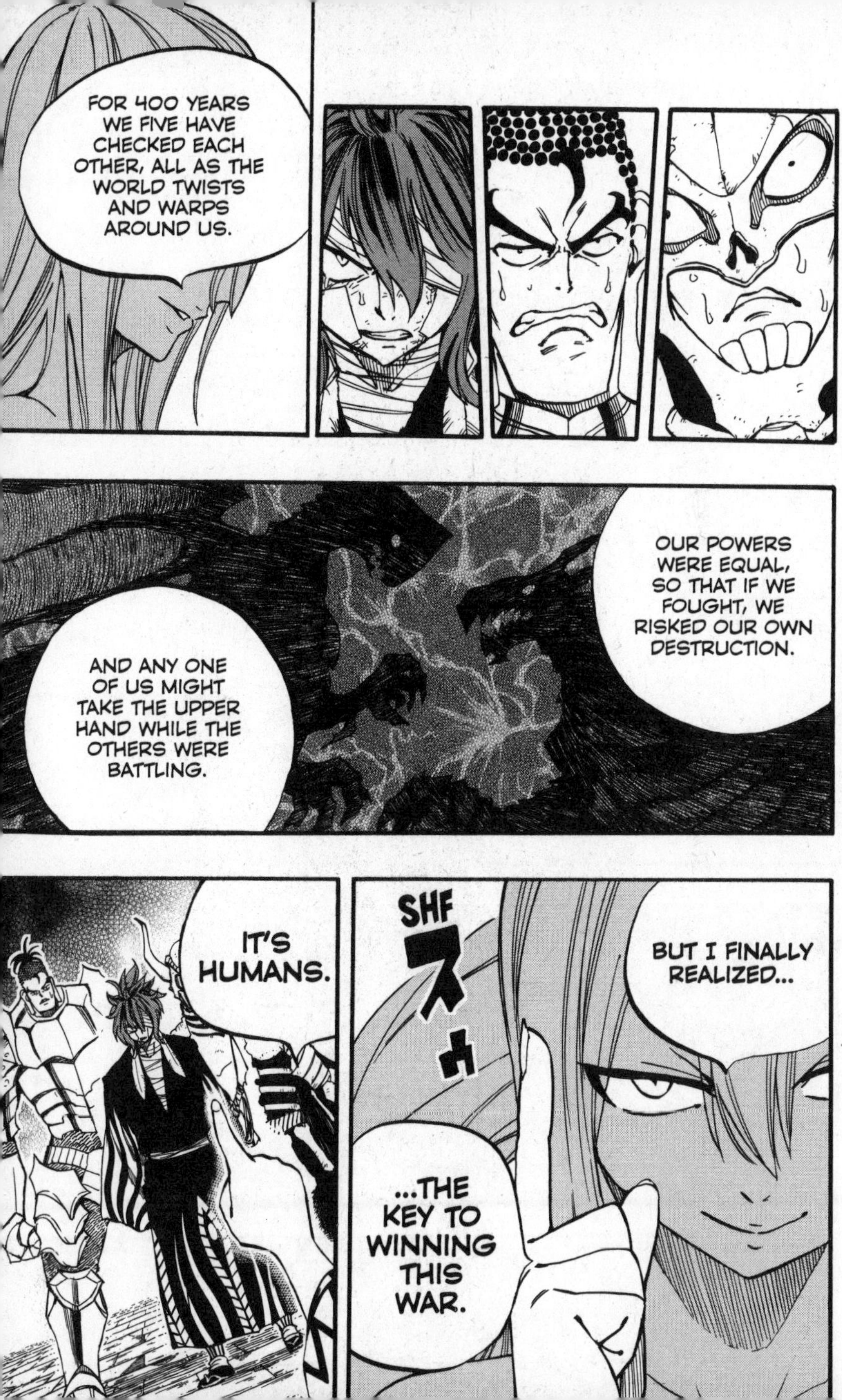
FOR 400 YEARS WE FIVE HAVE CHECKED EACH OTHER, ALL AS THE WORLD TWISTS AND WARPS AROUND US.
OUR POWERS WERE EQUAL, SO THAT IF WE FOUGHT, WE RISKED OUR OWN DESTRUCTION.
AND ANY ONE OF US MIGHT TAKE THE UPPER HAND WHILE THE OTHERS WERE BATTLING.
SHF
BUT I FINALLY REALIZED...
...THE KEY TO WINNING THIS WAR.
IT'S HUMANS.

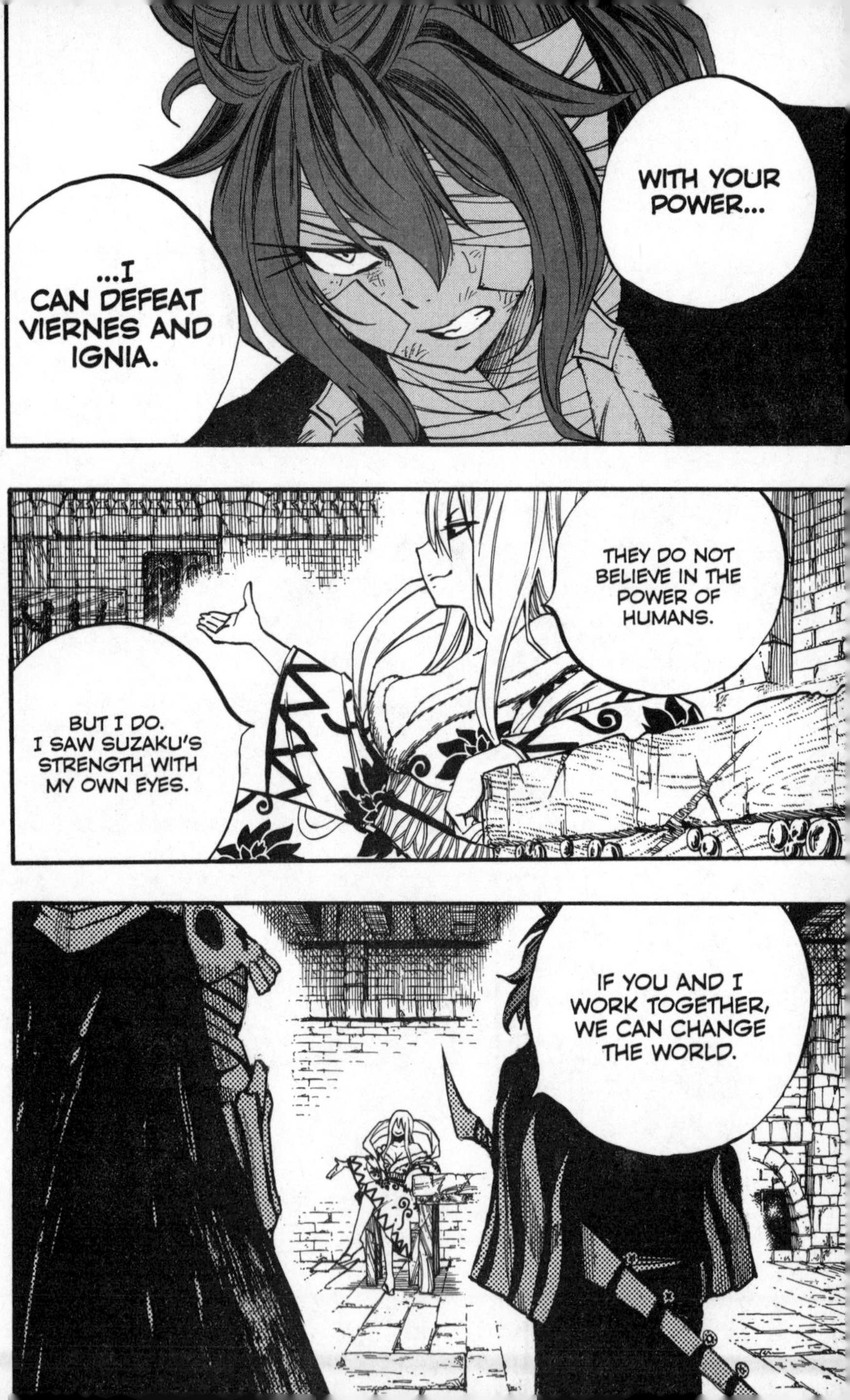
WITH YOUR POWER...
...I CAN DEFEAT VIERNES AND IGNIA.
THEY DO NOT BELIEVE IN THE POWER OF HUMANS.
BUT I DO. I SAW SUZAKU'S STRENGTH WITH MY OWN EYES.
IF YOU AND I WORK TOGETHER, WE CAN CHANGE THE WORLD.

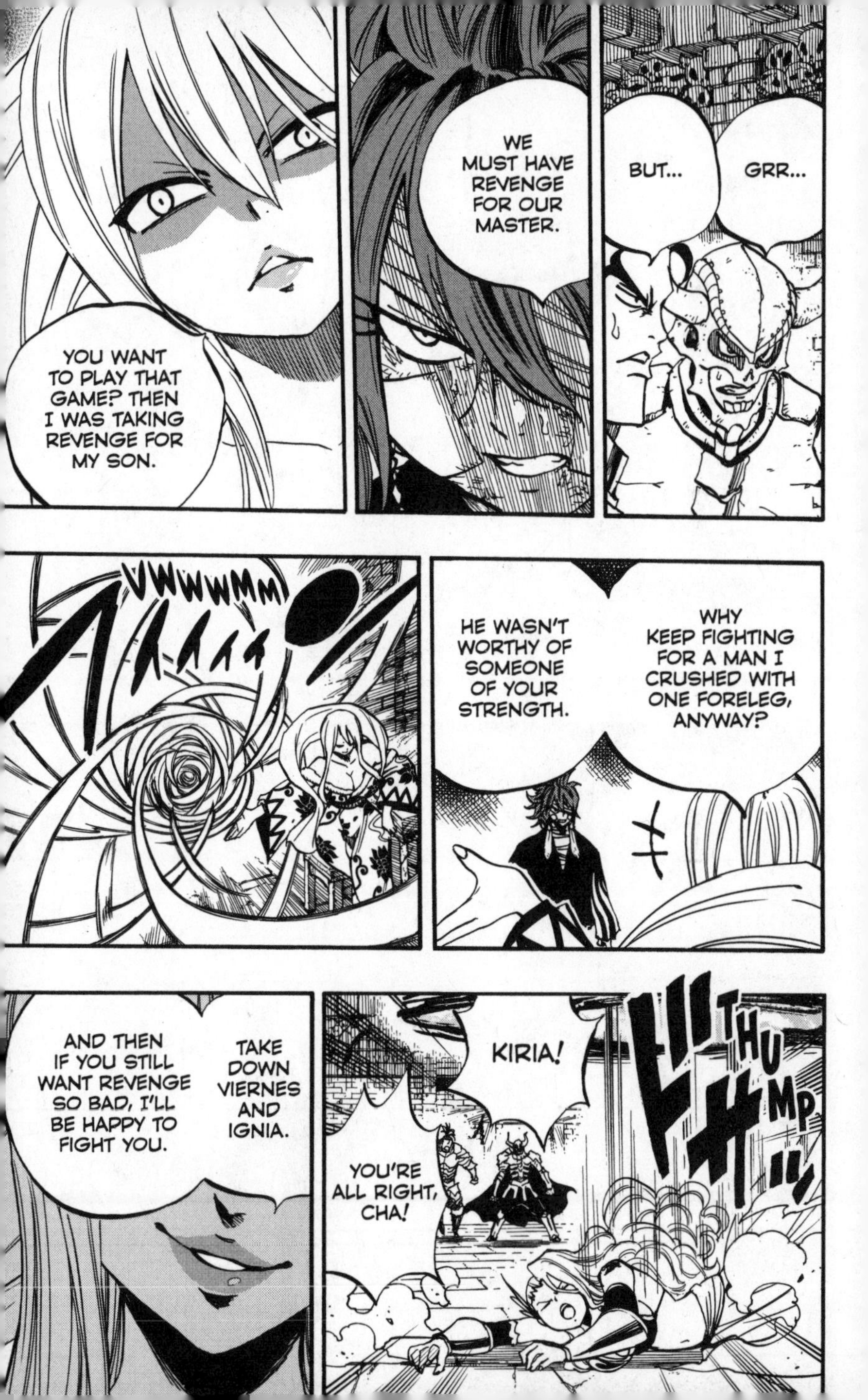
GRR...
BUT...
WE MUST HAVE REVENGE FOR OUR MASTER.
YOU WANT TO PLAY THAT GAME? THEN I WAS TAKING REVENGE FOR MY SON.
WHY KEEP FIGHTING FOR A MAN I CRUSHED WITH ONE FORELEG, ANYWAY?
HE WASN'T WORTHY OF SOMEONE OF YOUR STRENGTH.
VWWWMM
THUMP
KIRIA!
YOU'RE ALL RIGHT, CHA!
TAKE DOWN VIERNES AND IGNIA.
AND THEN IF YOU STILL WANT REVENGE SO BAD, I'LL BE HAPPY TO FIGHT YOU.

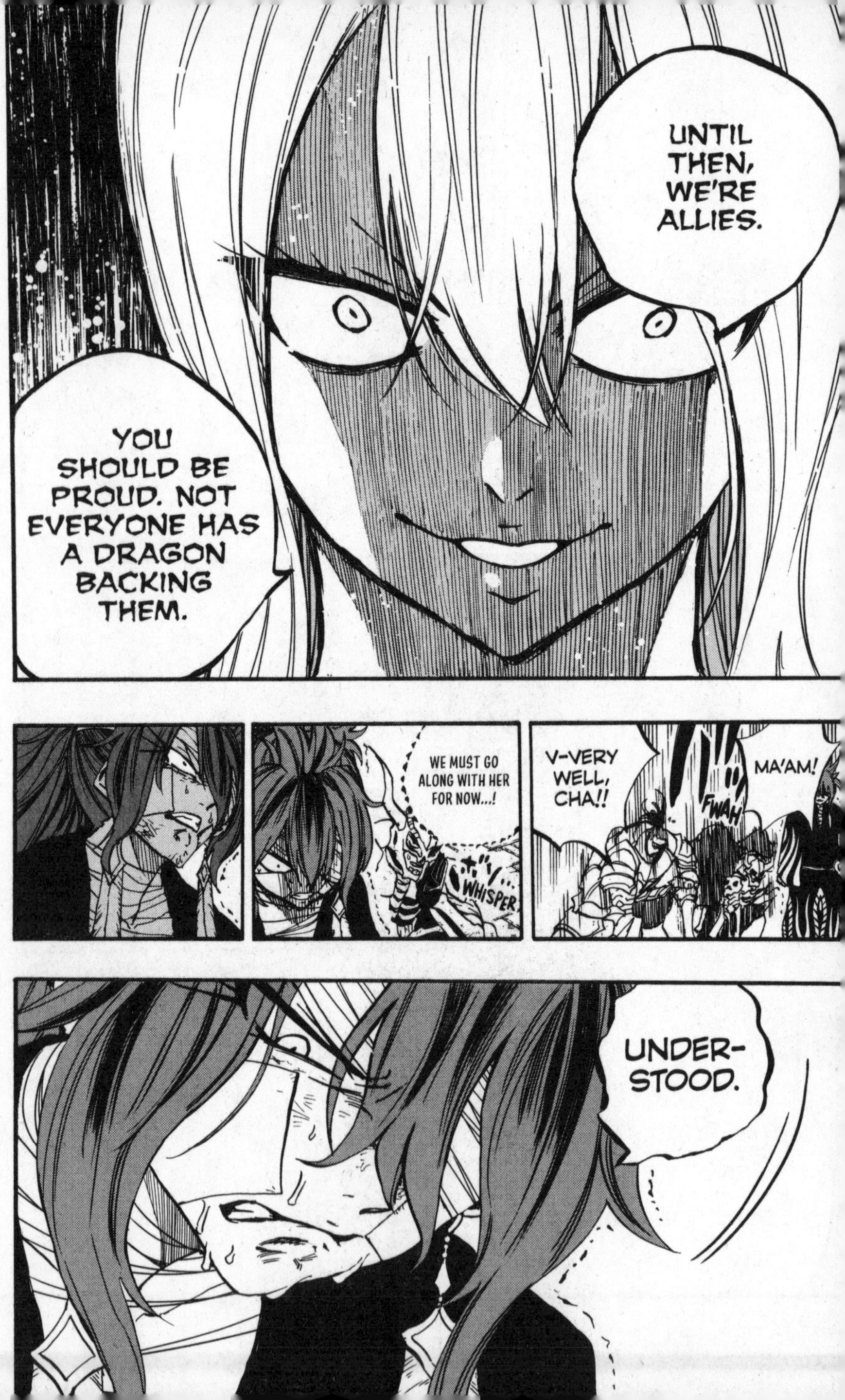
UNTIL THEN, WE'RE ALLIES.
YOU SHOULD BE PROUD. NOT EVERYONE HAS A DRAGON BACKING THEM.
MA'AM!
V-VERY WELL, CHA!!
FWAH
WE MUST GO ALONG WITH HER FOR NOW...!
WHISPER
UNDER-STOOD.

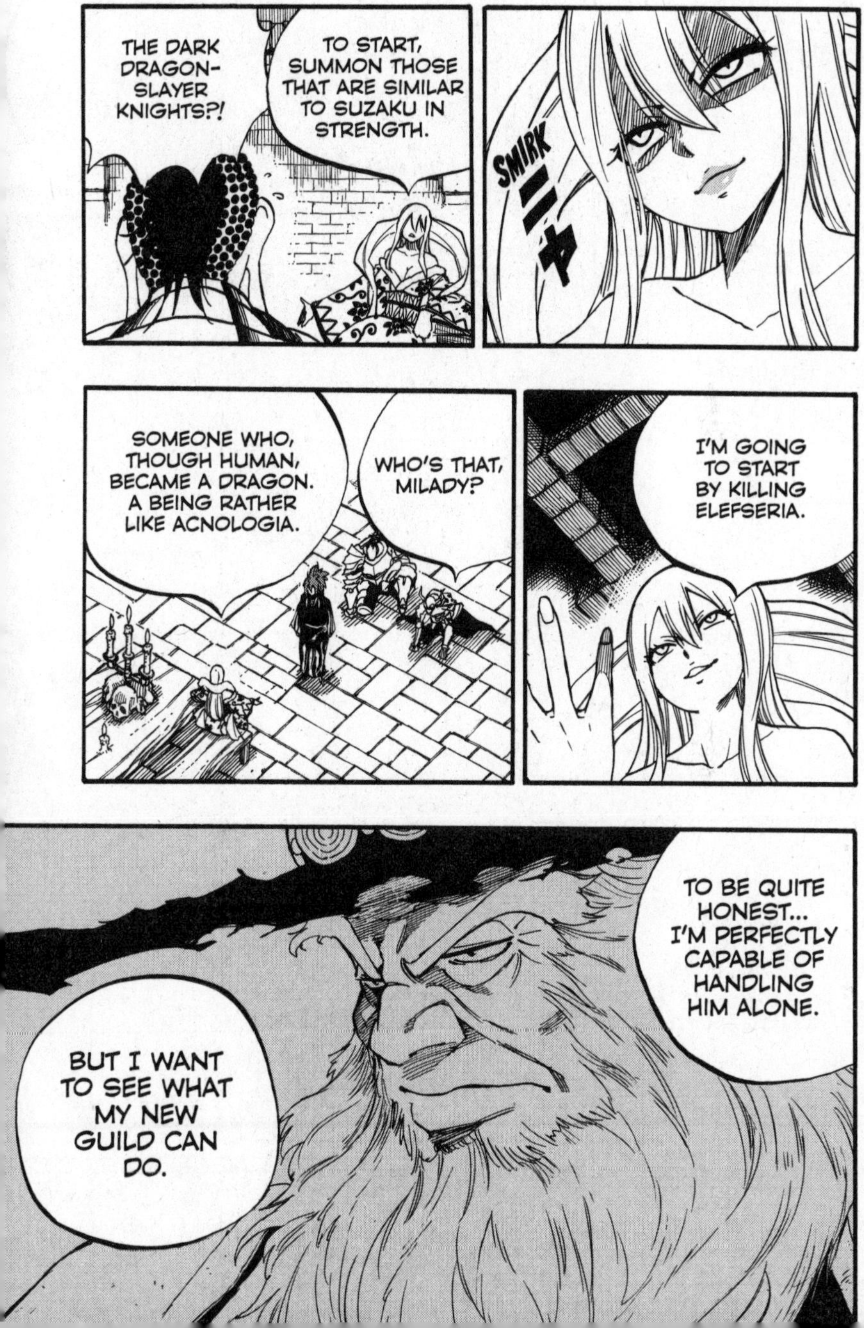
SMIRK
ニヤ
TO START, SUMMON THOSE THAT ARE SIMILAR TO SUZAKU IN STRENGTH.
THE DARK DRAGON-SLAYER KNIGHTS?!
I'M GOING TO START BY KILLING ELEFSERIA.
WHO'S THAT, MILADY?
SOMEONE WHO, THOUGH HUMAN, BECAME A DRAGON. A BEING RATHER LIKE ACNOLOGIA.
TO BE QUITE HONEST... I'M PERFECTLY CAPABLE OF HANDLING HIM ALONE.
BUT I WANT TO SEE WHAT MY NEW GUILD CAN DO.

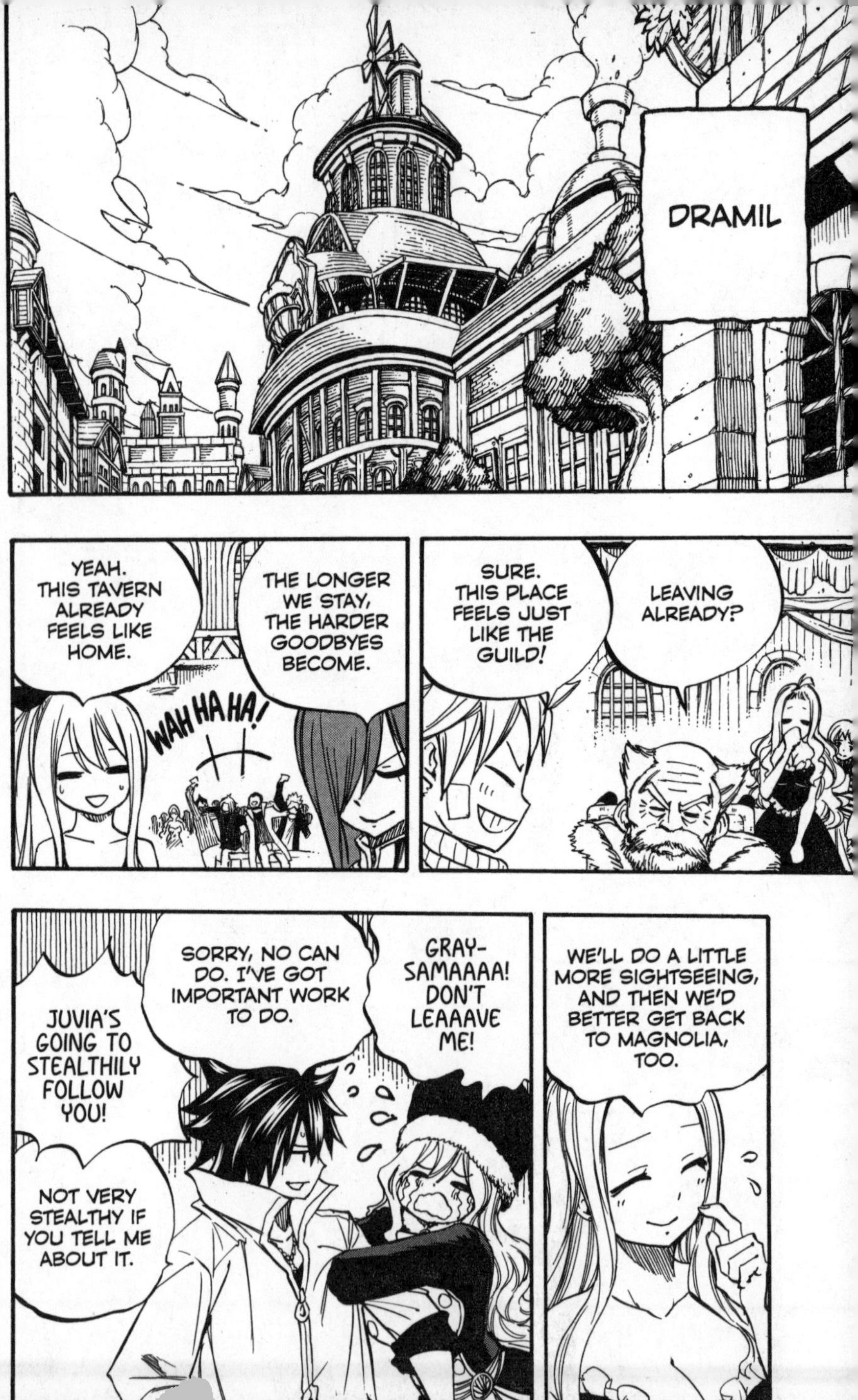
DRAMIL
LEAVING ALREADY?
SURE. THIS PLACE FEELS JUST LIKE THE GUILD!
THE LONGER WE STAY, THE HARDER GOODBYES BECOME.
YEAH. THIS TAVERN ALREADY FEELS LIKE HOME.
WAH HA HA!
WE'LL DO A LITTLE MORE SIGHTSEEING, AND THEN WE'D BETTER GET BACK TO MAGNOLIA, TOO.
GRAY-SAMAAAA! DON'T LEAAAVE ME!
SORRY, NO CAN DO. I'VE GOT IMPORTANT WORK TO DO.
JUVIA'S GOING TO STEALTHILY FOLLOW YOU!
NOT VERY STEALTHY IF YOU TELL ME ABOUT IT.

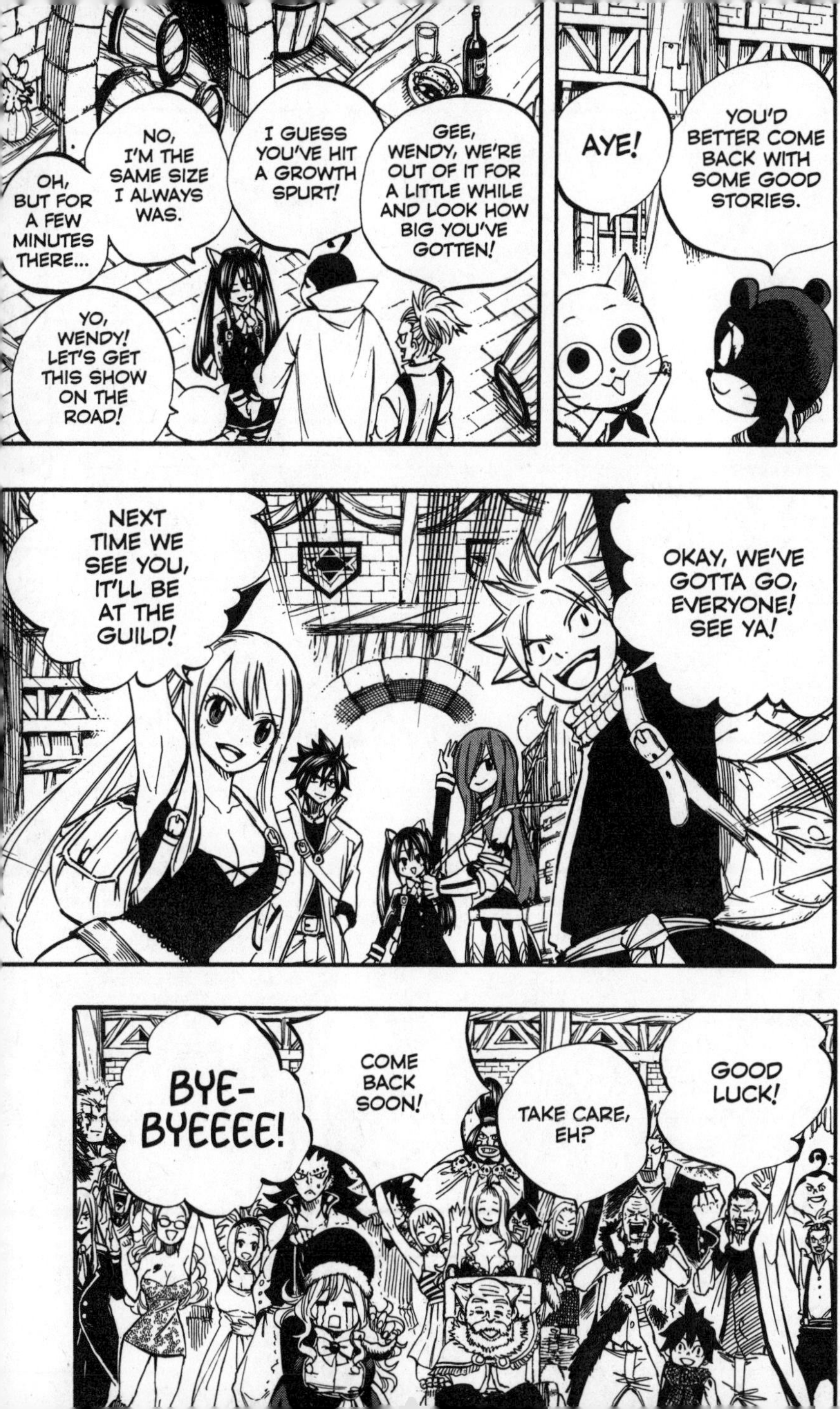
YOU'D BETTER COME BACK WITH SOME GOOD STORIES.
AYE!
GEE, WENDY, WE'RE OUT OF IT FOR A LITTLE WHILE AND LOOK HOW BIG YOU'VE GOTTEN!
I GUESS YOU'VE HIT A GROWTH SPURT!
NO, I'M THE SAME SIZE I ALWAYS WAS.
OH, BUT FOR A FEW MINUTES THERE...
YO, WENDY! LET'S GET THIS SHOW ON THE ROAD!
OKAY, WE'VE GOTTA GO, EVERYONE! SEE YA!
NEXT TIME WE SEE YOU, IT'LL BE AT THE GUILD!
GOOD LUCK!
TAKE CARE, EH?
COME BACK SOON!
BYE-BYEEEEE!

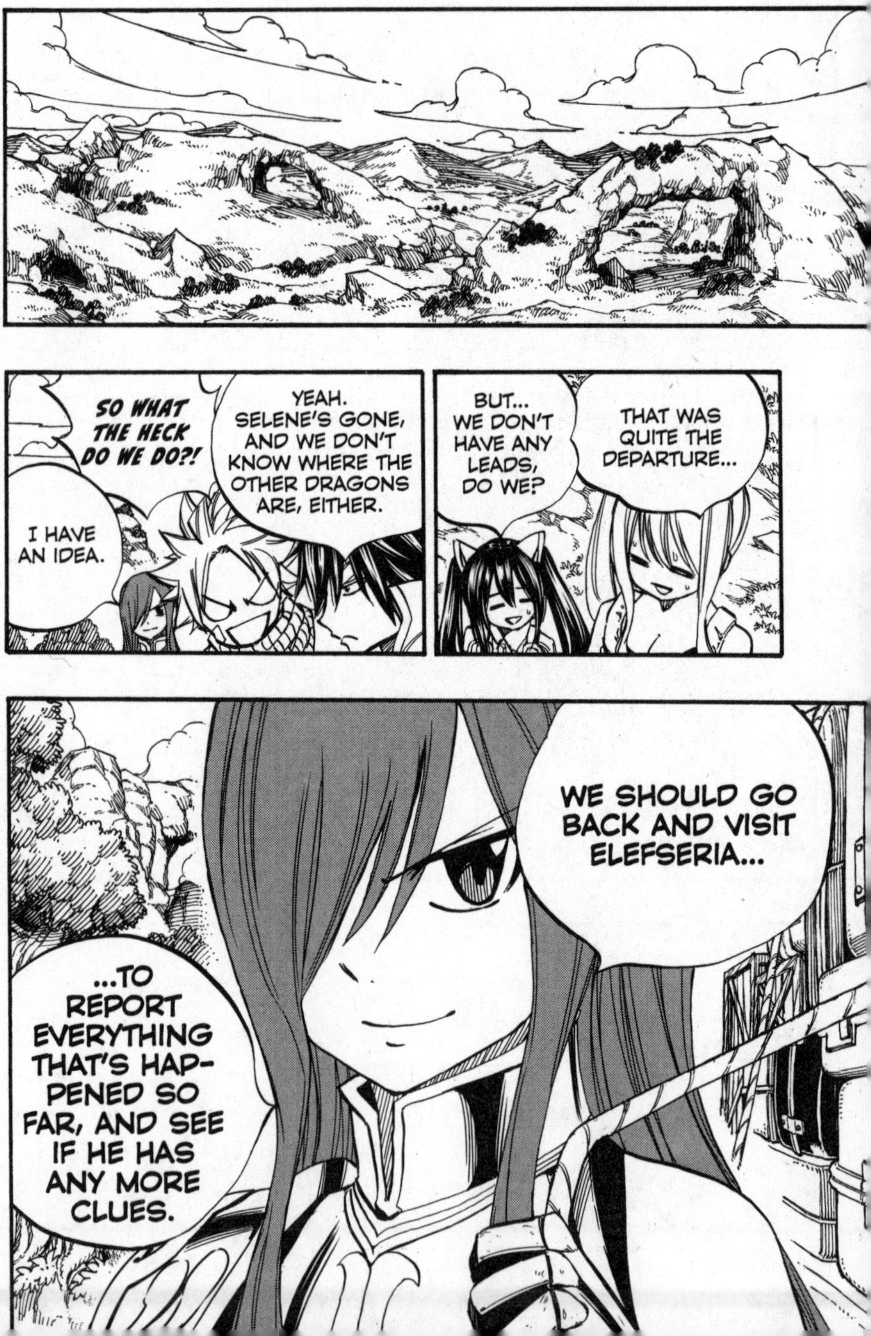
THAT WAS QUITE THE DEPARTURE...
BUT... WE DON'T HAVE ANY LEADS, DO WE?
YEAH. SELENE'S GONE, AND WE DON'T KNOW WHERE THE OTHER DRAGONS ARE, EITHER.
SO WHAT THE HECK DO WE DO?!
I HAVE AN IDEA.
WE SHOULD GO BACK AND VISIT ELEFSERIA...
...TO REPORT EVERYTHING THAT'S HAP-PENED SO FAR, AND SEE IF HE HAS ANY MORE CLUES.

FAIRY TAIL 100 YEARS QUEST

Chapter 92: The Great Labyrinth

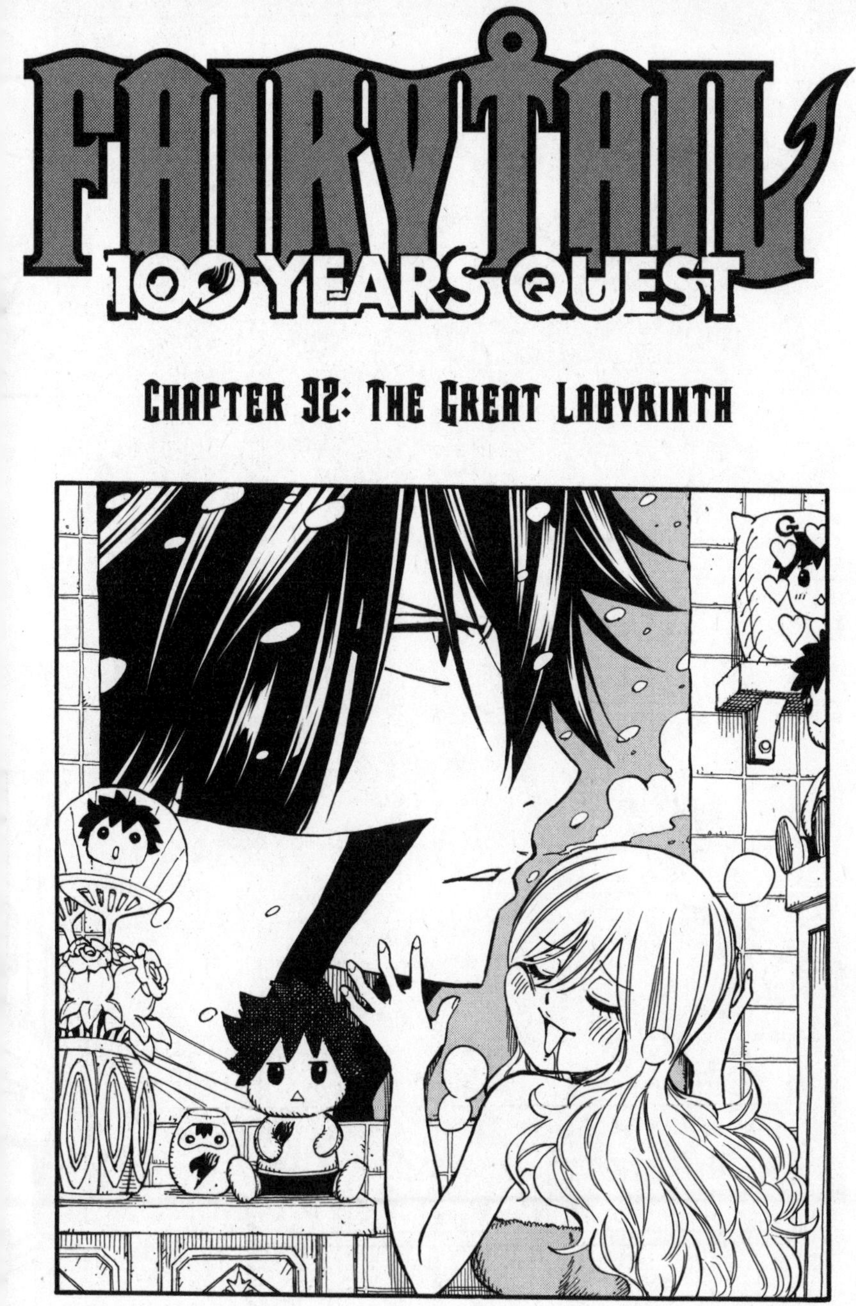

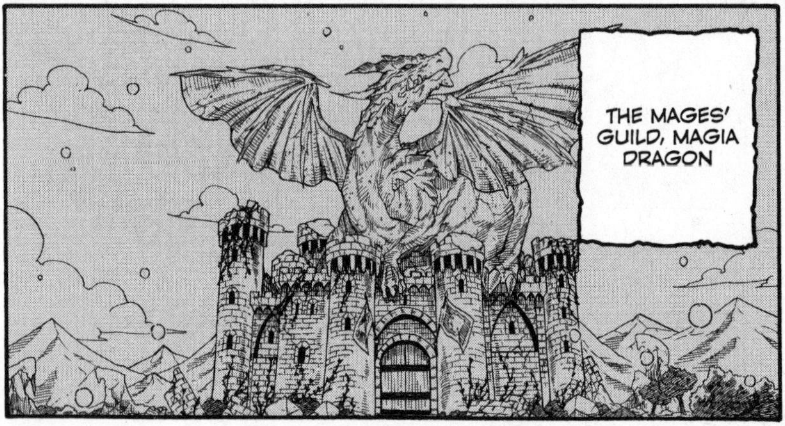
THE MAGES' GUILD, MAGIA DRAGON

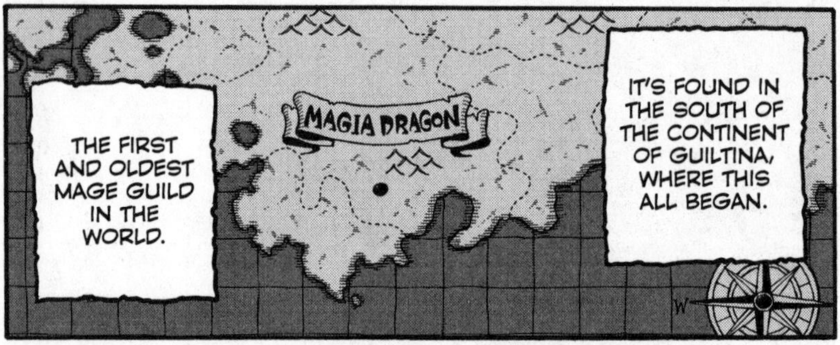
IT'S FOUND IN THE SOUTH OF THE CONTINENT OF GUILTINA, WHERE THIS ALL BEGAN.
MAGIA DRAGON
THE FIRST AND OLDEST MAGE GUILD IN THE WORLD.

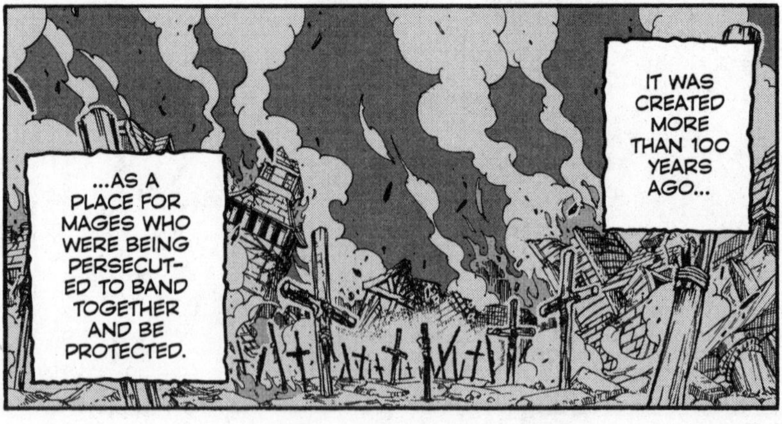
IT WAS CREATED MORE THAN 100 YEARS AGO...
...AS A PLACE FOR MAGES WHO WERE BEING PERSECUT-ED TO BAND TOGETHER AND BE PROTECTED.

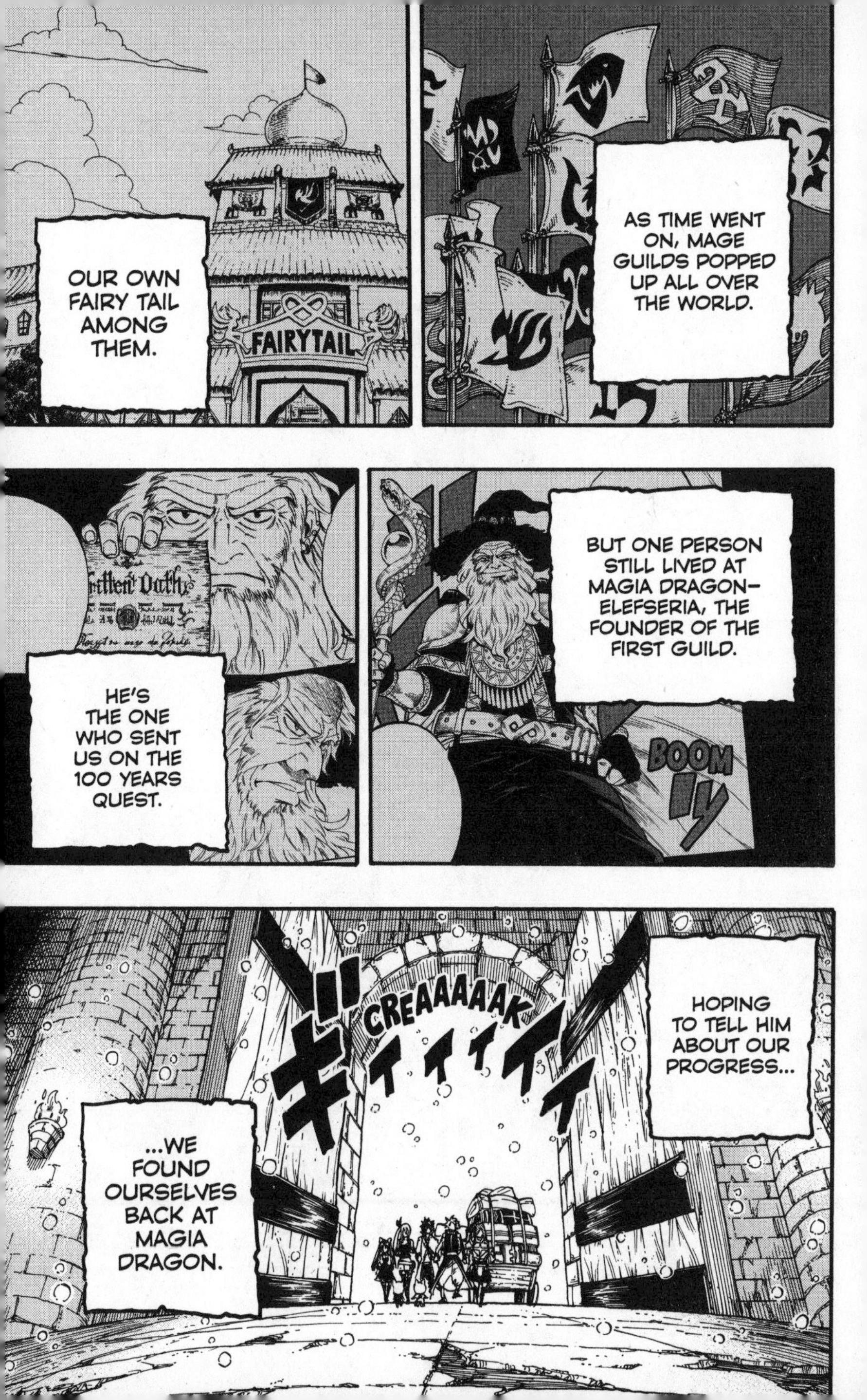
AS TIME WENT ON, MAGE GUILDS POPPED UP ALL OVER THE WORLD.
OUR OWN FAIRY TAIL AMONG THEM.
FAIRYTAIL
BUT ONE PERSON STILL LIVED AT MAGIA DRAGON—ELEFSERIA, THE FOUNDER OF THE FIRST GUILD.
BOOM
HE'S THE ONE WHO SENT US ON THE 100 YEARS QUEST.
HOPING TO TELL HIM ABOUT OUR PROGRESS...
CREAAAAAK
...WE FOUND OURSELVES BACK AT MAGIA DRAGON.

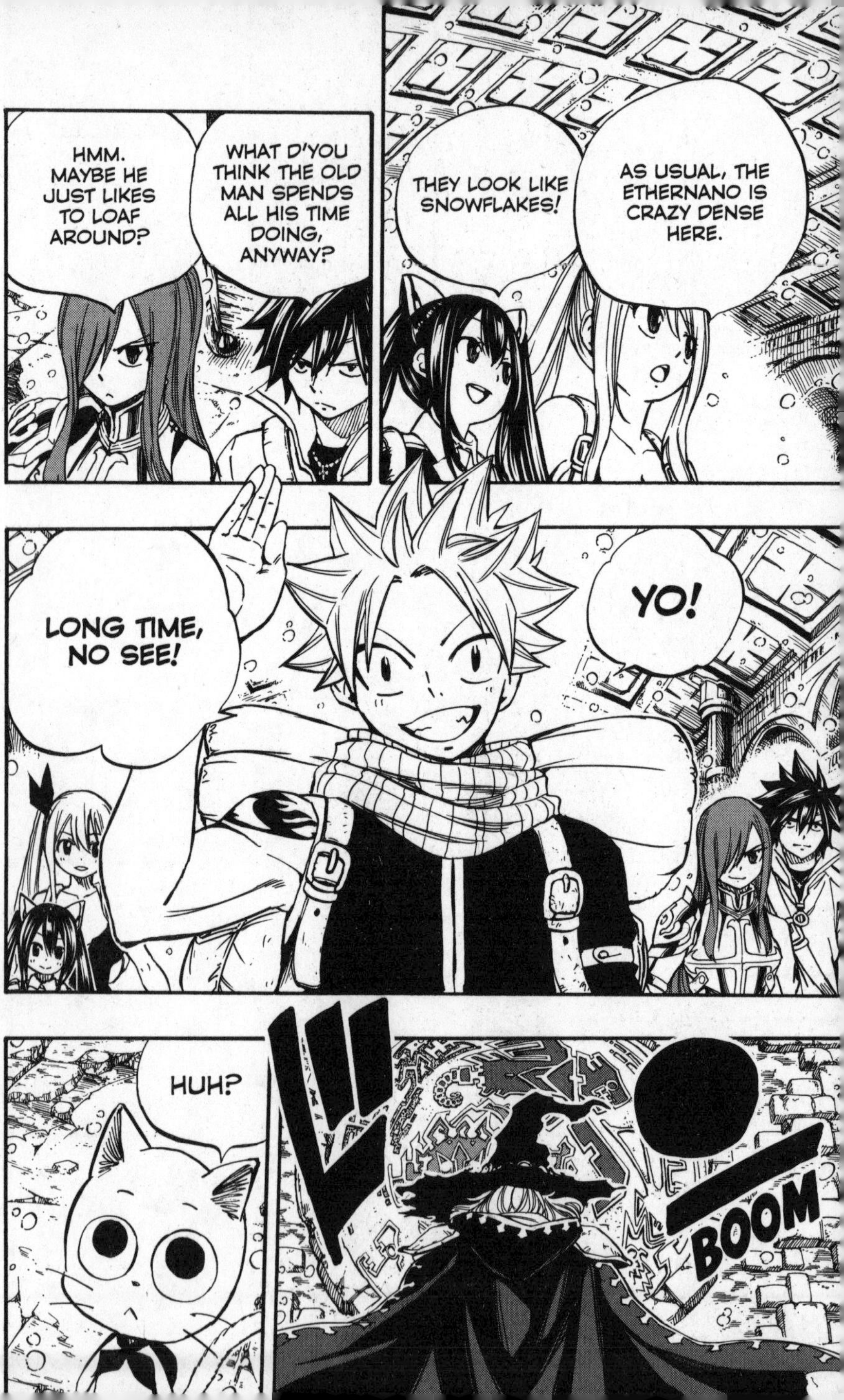
AS USUAL, THE ETHERNANO IS CRAZY DENSE HERE.
THEY LOOK LIKE SNOWFLAKES!
WHAT D'YOU THINK THE OLD MAN SPENDS ALL HIS TIME DOING, ANYWAY?
HMM. MAYBE HE JUST LIKES TO LOAF AROUND?
YO!
LONG TIME, NO SEE!
BOOM
HUH?

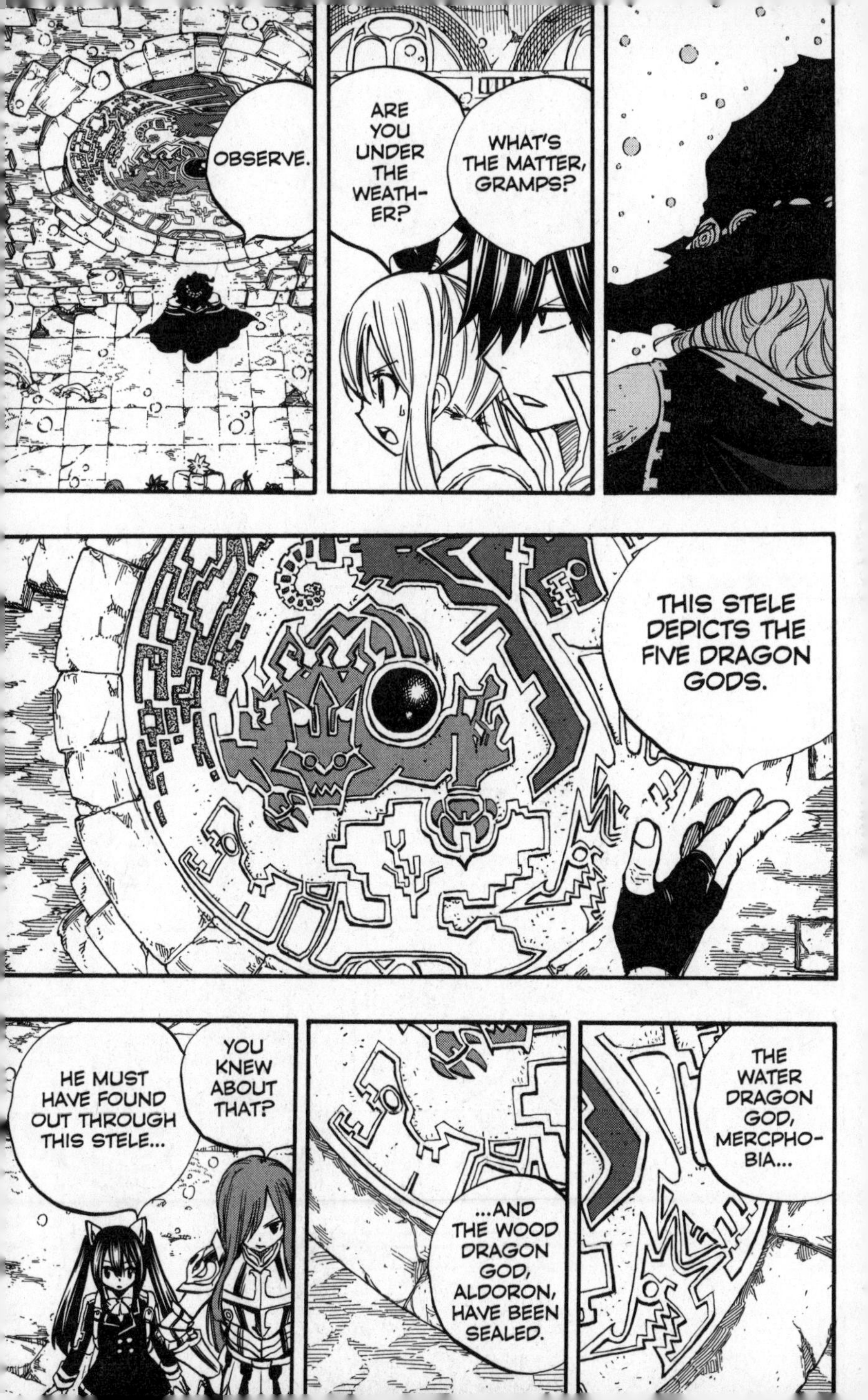
WHAT'S THE MATTER, GRAMPS?
ARE YOU UNDER THE WEATHER?
OBSERVE.
THIS STELE DEPICTS THE FIVE DRAGON GODS.
THE WATER DRAGON GOD, MERCPHOBIA...
...AND THE WOOD DRAGON GOD, ALDORON, HAVE BEEN SEALED.
YOU KNEW ABOUT THAT?
HE MUST HAVE FOUND OUT THROUGH THIS STELE...

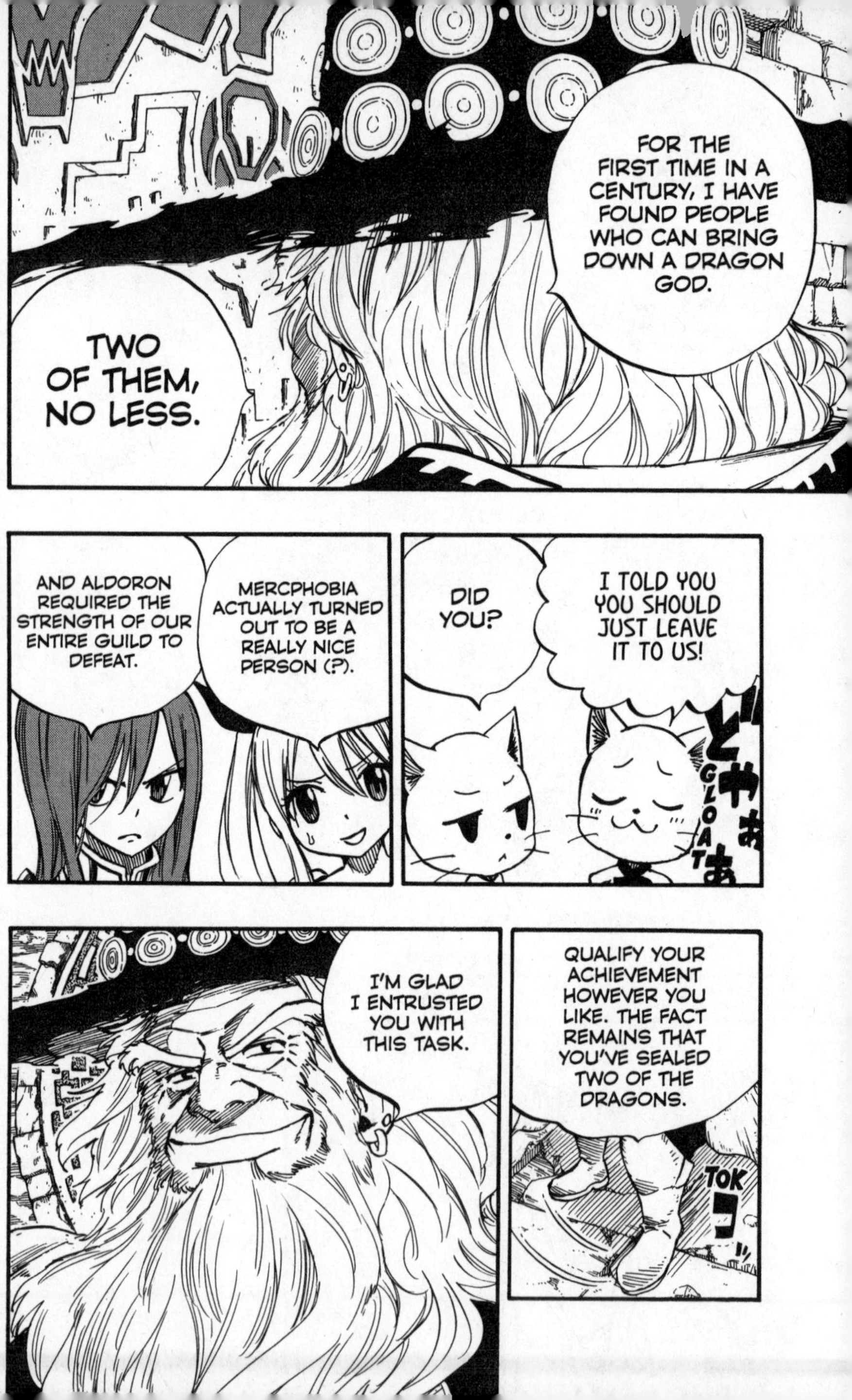

FOR THE FIRST TIME IN A CENTURY, I HAVE FOUND PEOPLE WHO CAN BRING DOWN A DRAGON GOD.
TWO OF THEM, NO LESS.
I TOLD YOU YOU SHOULD JUST LEAVE IT TO US!
GLOAT
DID YOU?
MERCPHOBIA ACTUALLY TURNED OUT TO BE A REALLY NICE PERSON (?).
AND ALDORON REQUIRED THE STRENGTH OF OUR ENTIRE GUILD TO DEFEAT.
QUALIFY YOUR ACHIEVEMENT HOWEVER YOU LIKE. THE FACT REMAINS THAT YOU'VE SEALED TWO OF THE DRAGONS.
TOK
I'M GLAD I ENTRUSTED YOU WITH THIS TASK.

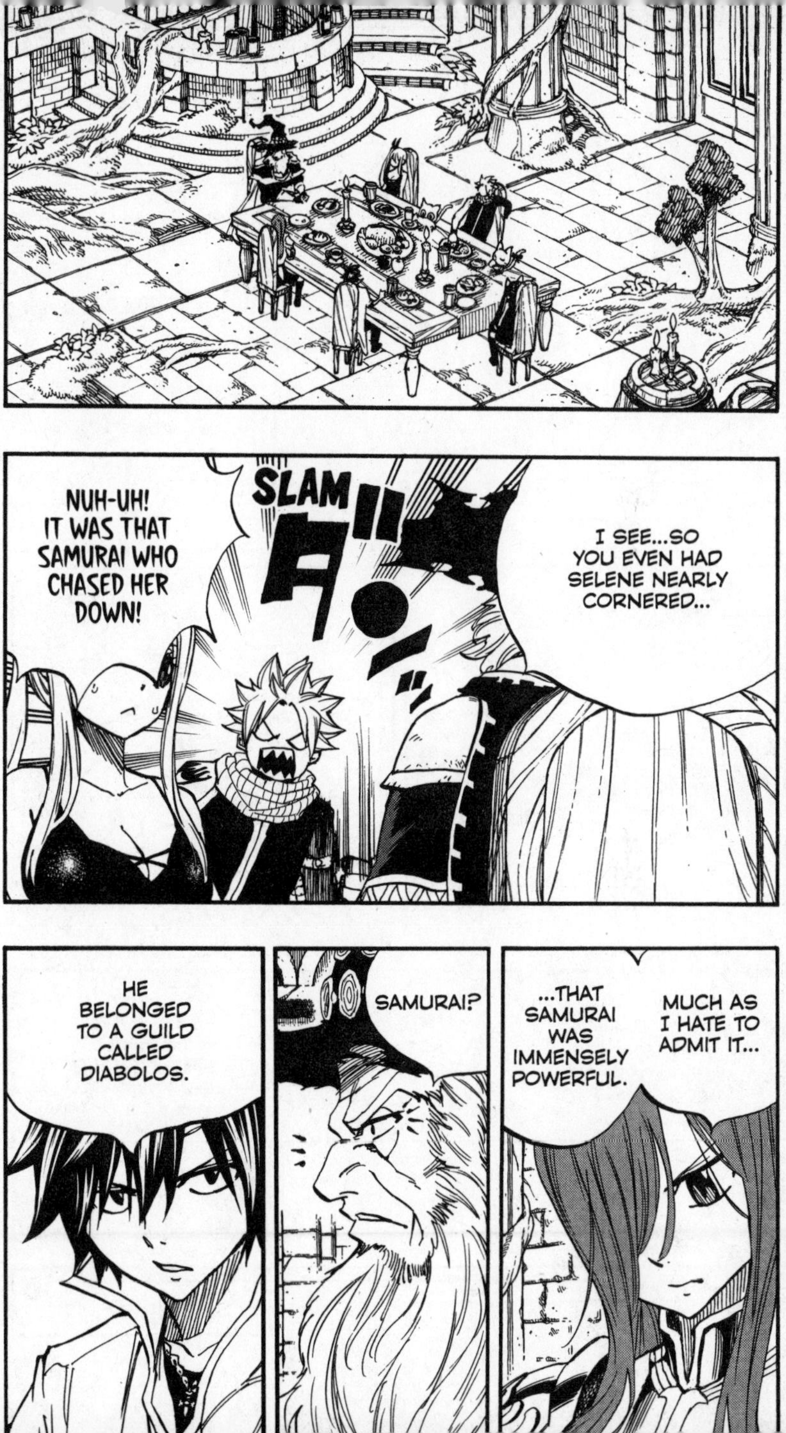
I SEE...SO YOU EVEN HAD SELENE NEARLY CORNERED...
SLAM
NUH-UH! IT WAS THAT SAMURAI WHO CHASED HER DOWN!
MUCH AS I HATE TO ADMIT IT...
...THAT SAMURAI WAS IMMENSELY POWERFUL.
SAMURAI?
HE BELONGED TO A GUILD CALLED DIABOLOS.

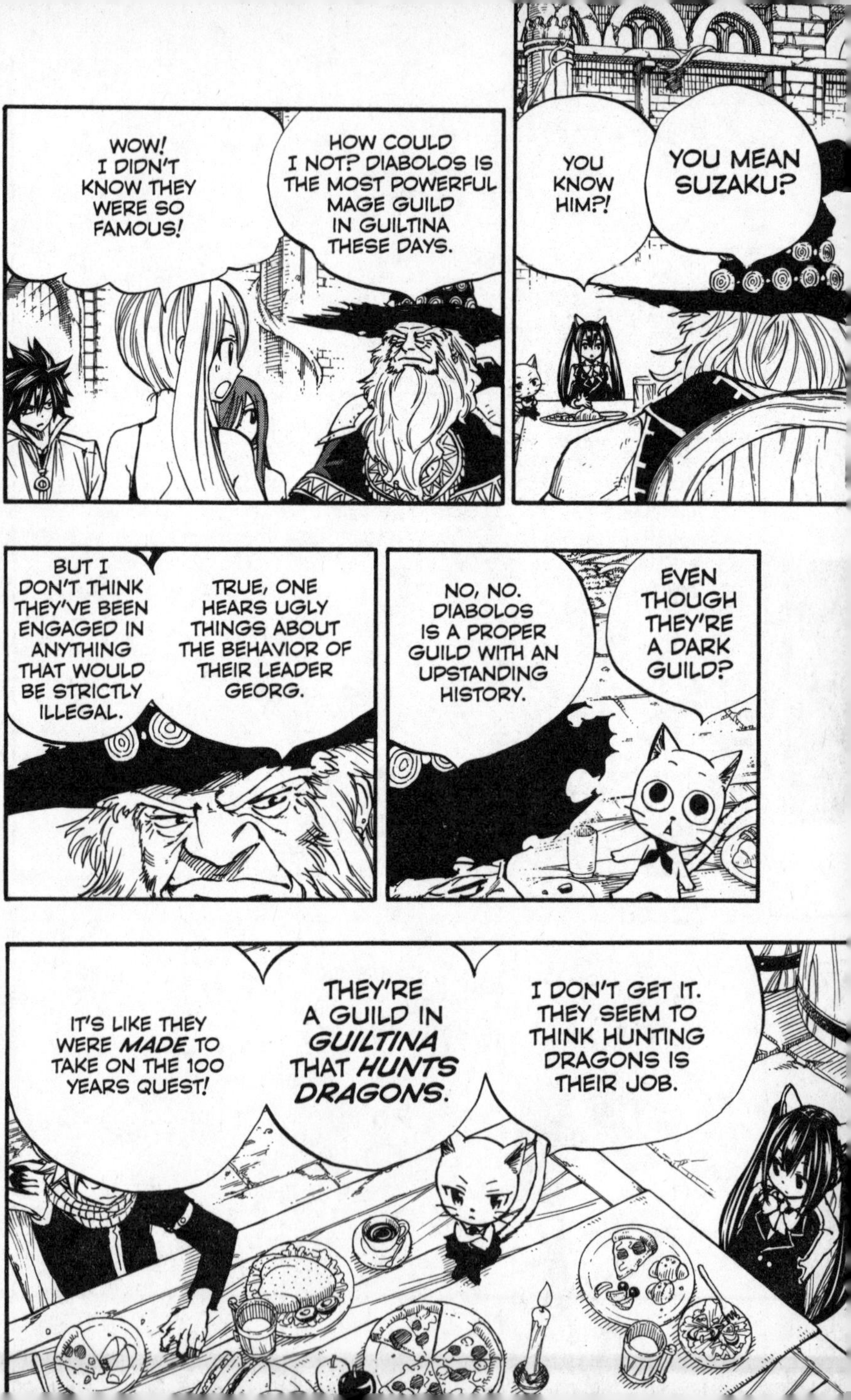
YOU MEAN SUZAKU?
YOU KNOW HIM?!
HOW COULD I NOT? DIABOLOS IS THE MOST POWERFUL MAGE GUILD IN GUILTINA THESE DAYS.
WOW! I DIDN'T KNOW THEY WERE SO FAMOUS!
EVEN THOUGH THEY'RE A DARK GUILD?
NO, NO. DIABOLOS IS A PROPER GUILD WITH AN UPSTANDING HISTORY.
TRUE, ONE HEARS UGLY THINGS ABOUT THE BEHAVIOR OF THEIR LEADER GEORG.
BUT I DON'T THINK THEY'VE BEEN ENGAGED IN ANYTHING THAT WOULD BE STRICTLY ILLEGAL.
I DON'T GET IT. THEY SEEM TO THINK HUNTING DRAGONS IS THEIR JOB.
THEY'RE A GUILD IN *GUILTINA* THAT *HUNTS DRAGONS*.
IT'S LIKE THEY WERE *MADE* TO TAKE ON THE 100 YEARS QUEST!

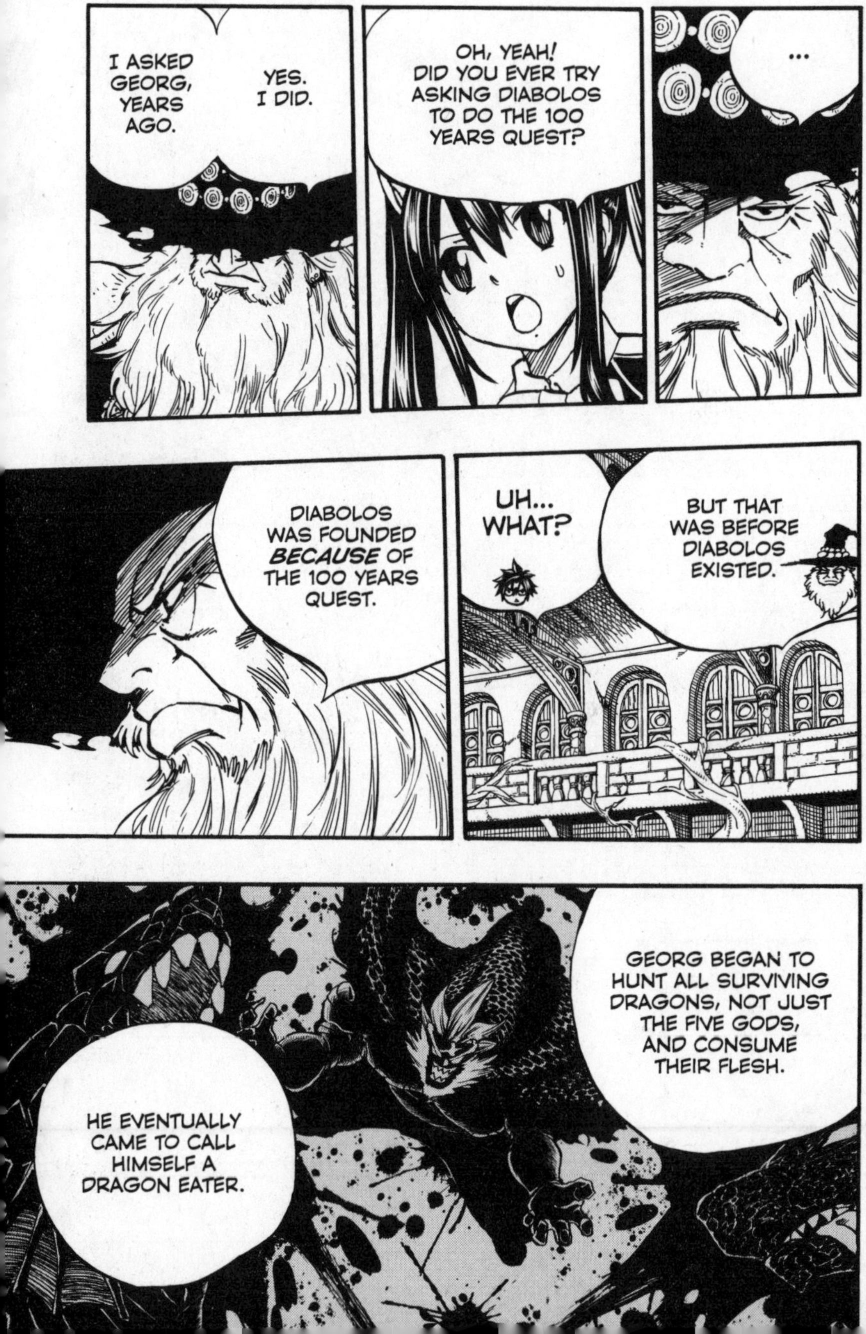
...
OH, YEAH! DID YOU EVER TRY ASKING DIABOLOS TO DO THE 100 YEARS QUEST?
YES. I DID.
I ASKED GEORG, YEARS AGO.
BUT THAT WAS BEFORE DIABOLOS EXISTED.
UH... WHAT?
DIABOLOS WAS FOUNDED *BECAUSE* OF THE 100 YEARS QUEST.
GEORG BEGAN TO HUNT ALL SURVIVING DRAGONS, NOT JUST THE FIVE GODS, AND CONSUME THEIR FLESH.
HE EVENTUALLY CAME TO CALL HIMSELF A DRAGON EATER.

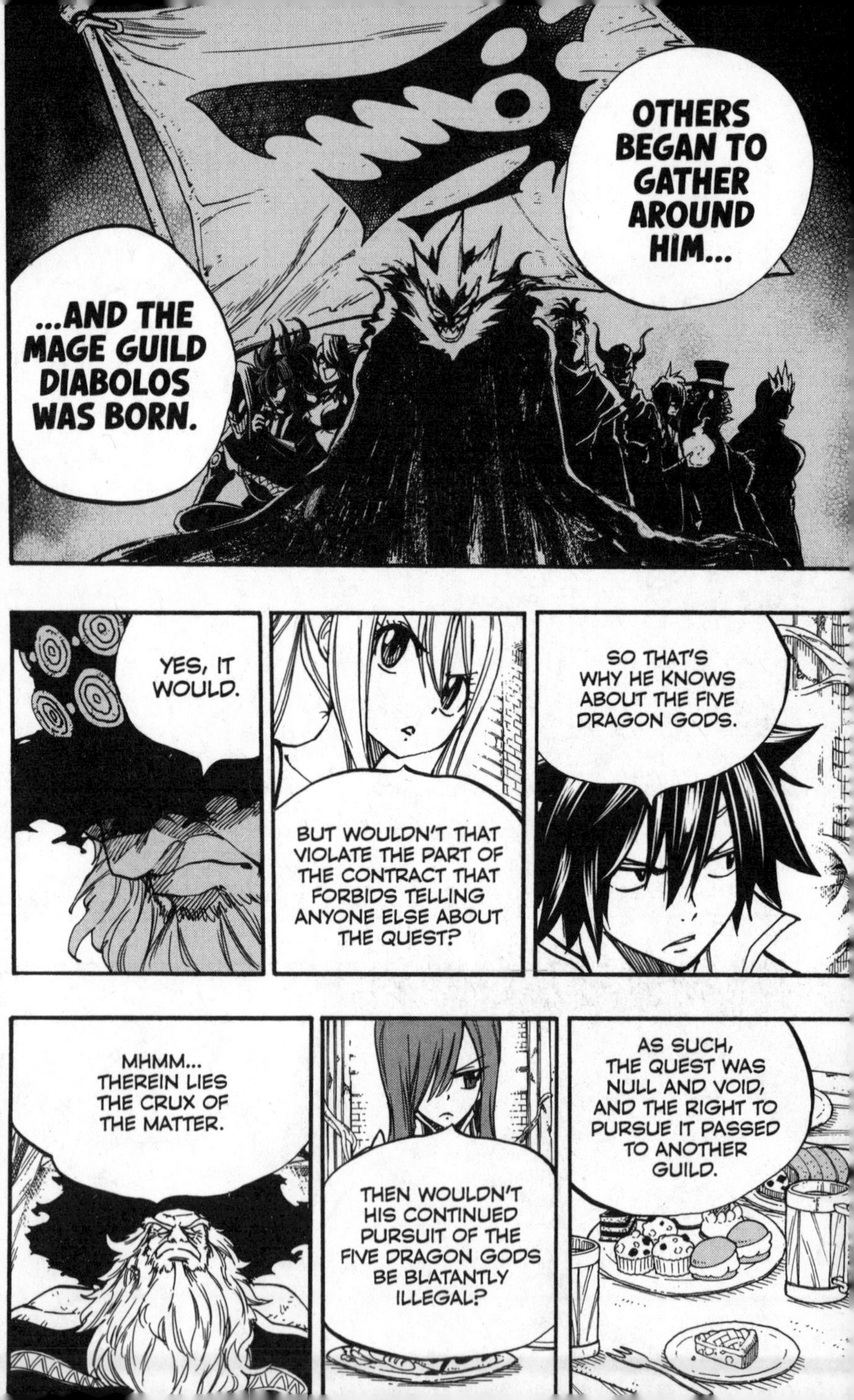
OTHERS BEGAN TO GATHER AROUND HIM...
...AND THE MAGE GUILD DIABOLOS WAS BORN.
SO THAT'S WHY HE KNOWS ABOUT THE FIVE DRAGON GODS.
BUT WOULDN'T THAT VIOLATE THE PART OF THE CONTRACT THAT FORBIDS TELLING ANYONE ELSE ABOUT THE QUEST?
YES, IT WOULD.
AS SUCH, THE QUEST WAS NULL AND VOID, AND THE RIGHT TO PURSUE IT PASSED TO ANOTHER GUILD.
THEN WOULDN'T HIS CONTINUED PURSUIT OF THE FIVE DRAGON GODS BE BLATANTLY ILLEGAL?
MHMM... THEREIN LIES THE CRUX OF THE MATTER.

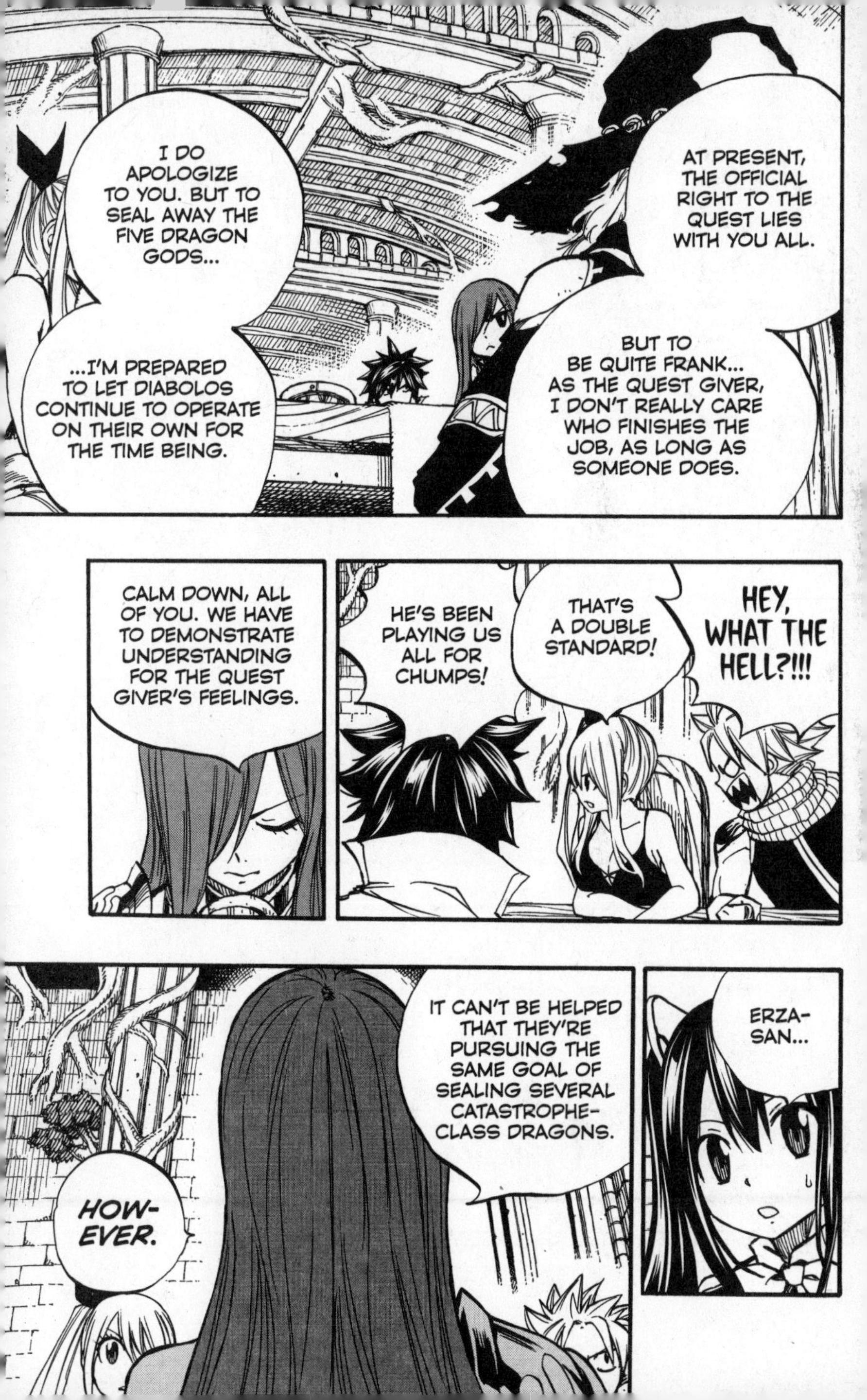
AT PRESENT, THE OFFICIAL RIGHT TO THE QUEST LIES WITH YOU ALL.
BUT TO BE QUITE FRANK... AS THE QUEST GIVER, I DON'T REALLY CARE WHO FINISHES THE JOB, AS LONG AS SOMEONE DOES.
I DO APOLOGIZE TO YOU. BUT TO SEAL AWAY THE FIVE DRAGON GODS...
...I'M PREPARED TO LET DIABOLOS CONTINUE TO OPERATE ON THEIR OWN FOR THE TIME BEING.
HEY, WHAT THE HELL?!!!
THAT'S A DOUBLE STANDARD!
HE'S BEEN PLAYING US ALL FOR CHUMPS!
CALM DOWN, ALL OF YOU. WE HAVE TO DEMONSTRATE UNDERSTANDING FOR THE QUEST GIVER'S FEELINGS.
ERZA-SAN...
IT CAN'T BE HELPED THAT THEY'RE PURSUING THE SAME GOAL OF SEALING SEVERAL CATASTROPHE-CLASS DRAGONS.
HOW-EVER.

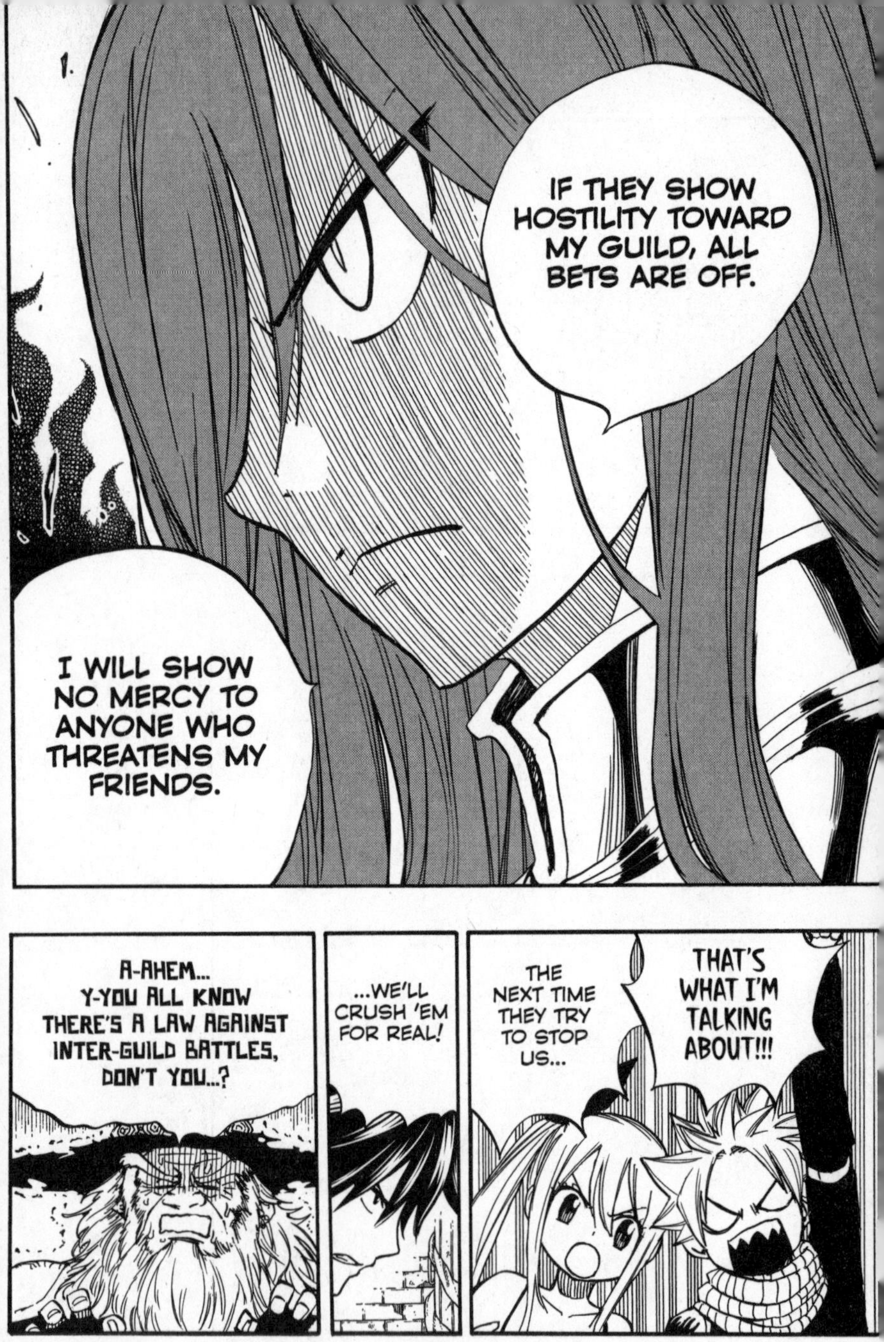
IF THEY SHOW HOSTILITY TOWARD MY GUILD, ALL BETS ARE OFF.
I WILL SHOW NO MERCY TO ANYONE WHO THREATENS MY FRIENDS.
THAT'S WHAT I'M TALKING ABOUT!!!
THE NEXT TIME THEY TRY TO STOP US...
...WE'LL CRUSH 'EM FOR REAL!
A-AHEM... Y-YOU ALL KNOW THERE'S A LAW AGAINST INTER-GUILD BATTLES, DON'T YOU...?

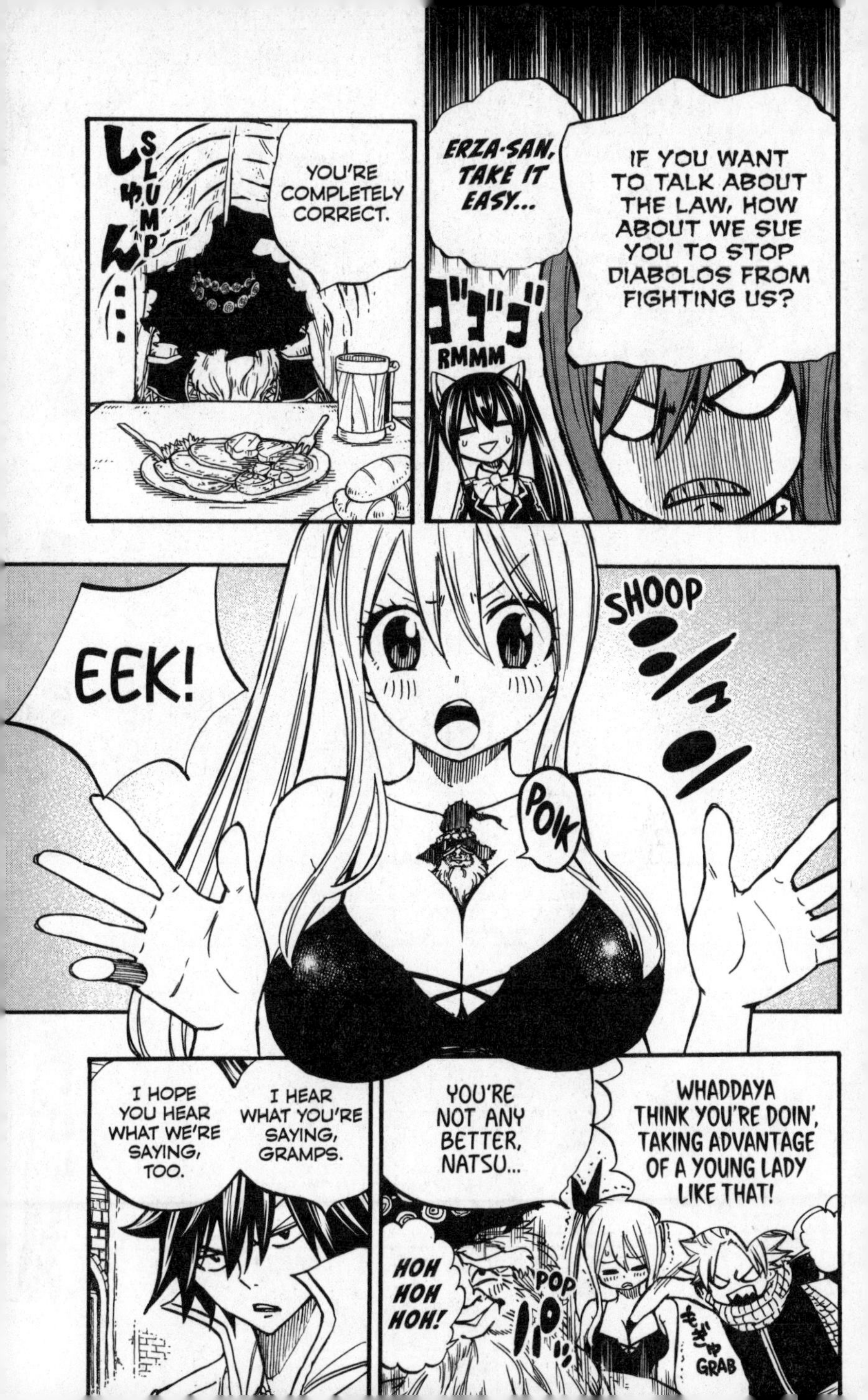
IF YOU WANT TO TALK ABOUT THE LAW, HOW ABOUT WE SUE YOU TO STOP DIABOLOS FROM FIGHTING US?
ERZA-SAN, TAKE IT EASY...
RMMM
YOU'RE COMPLETELY CORRECT.
SLUMP
SHOOP
POIK
EEK!
WHADDAYA THINK YOU'RE DOIN', TAKING ADVANTAGE OF A YOUNG LADY LIKE THAT!
YOU'RE NOT ANY BETTER, NATSU...
HOH HOH HOH!
POP
GRAB
I HEAR WHAT YOU'RE SAYING, GRAMPS.
I HOPE YOU HEAR WHAT WE'RE SAYING, TOO.

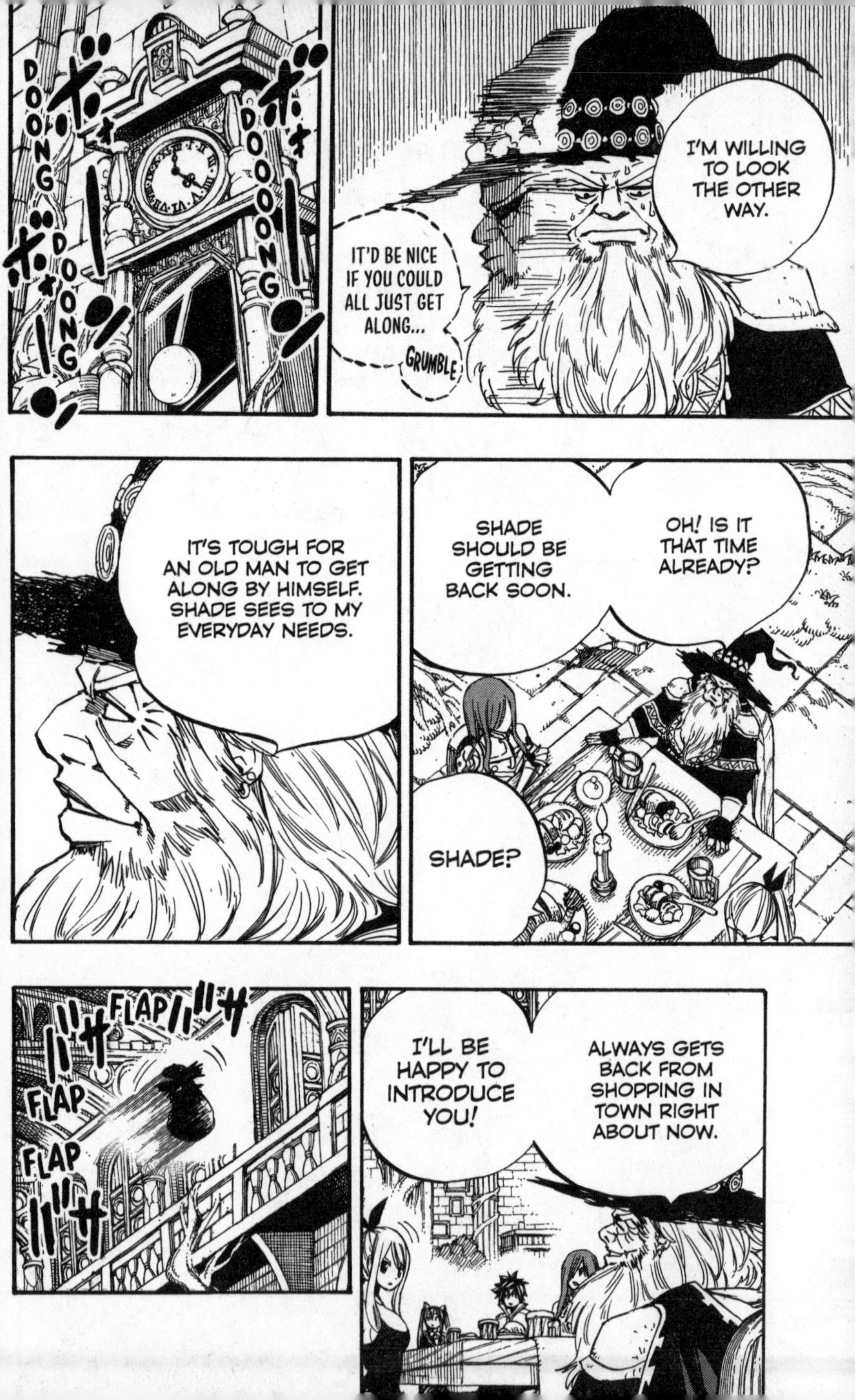
I'M WILLING TO LOOK THE OTHER WAY.
IT'D BE NICE IF YOU COULD ALL JUST GET ALONG...
GRUMBLE
DOOOOONG
DOONG
DOONG
OH! IS IT THAT TIME ALREADY?
SHADE SHOULD BE GETTING BACK SOON.
SHADE?
IT'S TOUGH FOR AN OLD MAN TO GET ALONG BY HIMSELF. SHADE SEES TO MY EVERYDAY NEEDS.
ALWAYS GETS BACK FROM SHOPPING IN TOWN RIGHT ABOUT NOW.
I'LL BE HAPPY TO INTRODUCE YOU!
FLAP
FLAP
FLAP

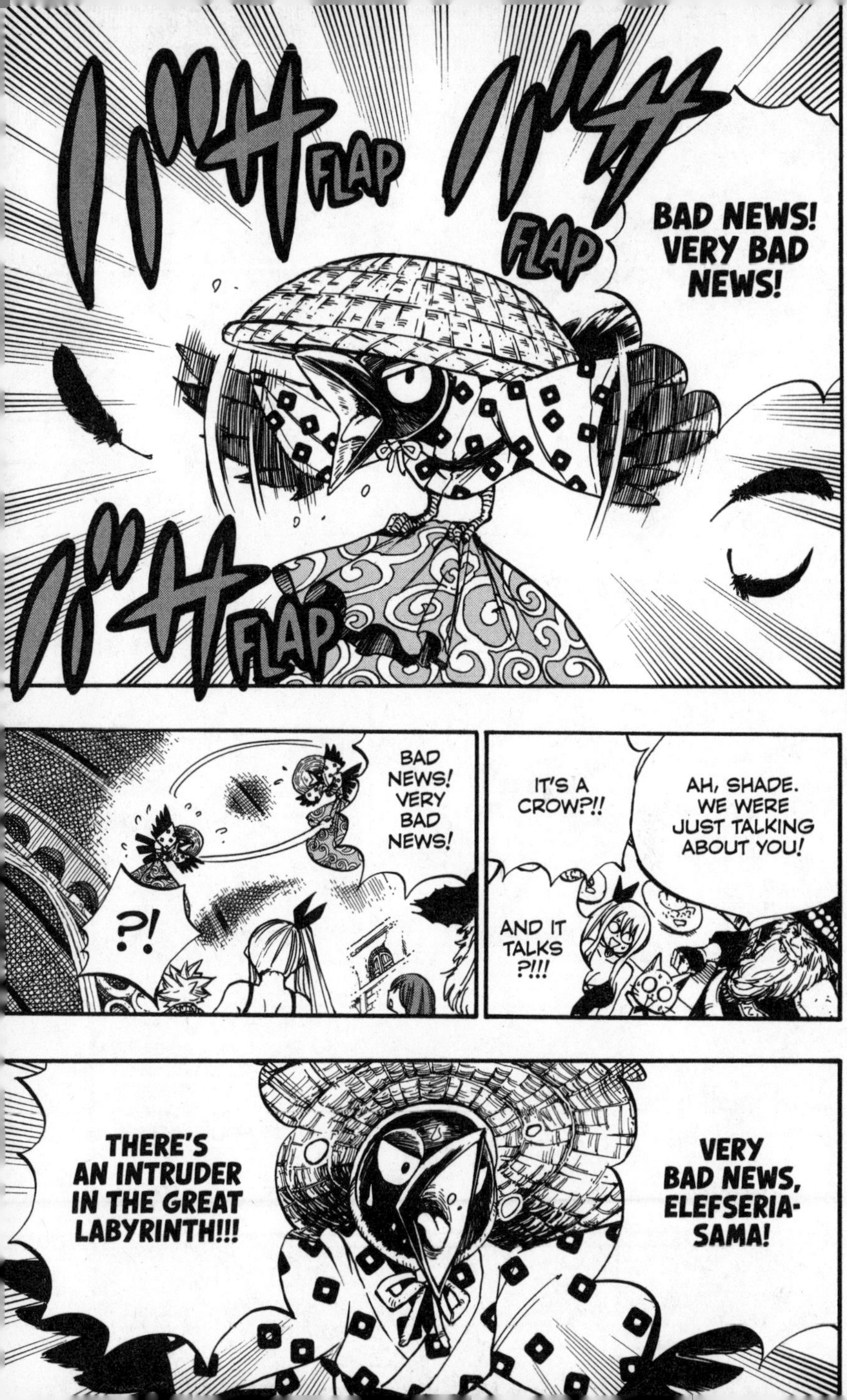
BAD NEWS! VERY BAD NEWS!
FLAP
FLAP
FLAP
AH, SHADE. WE WERE JUST TALKING ABOUT YOU!
IT'S A CROW?!!
AND IT TALKS ?!!!
BAD NEWS! VERY BAD NEWS!
?!
VERY BAD NEWS, ELEFSERIA-SAMA!
THERE'S AN INTRUDER IN THE GREAT LABYRINTH!!!

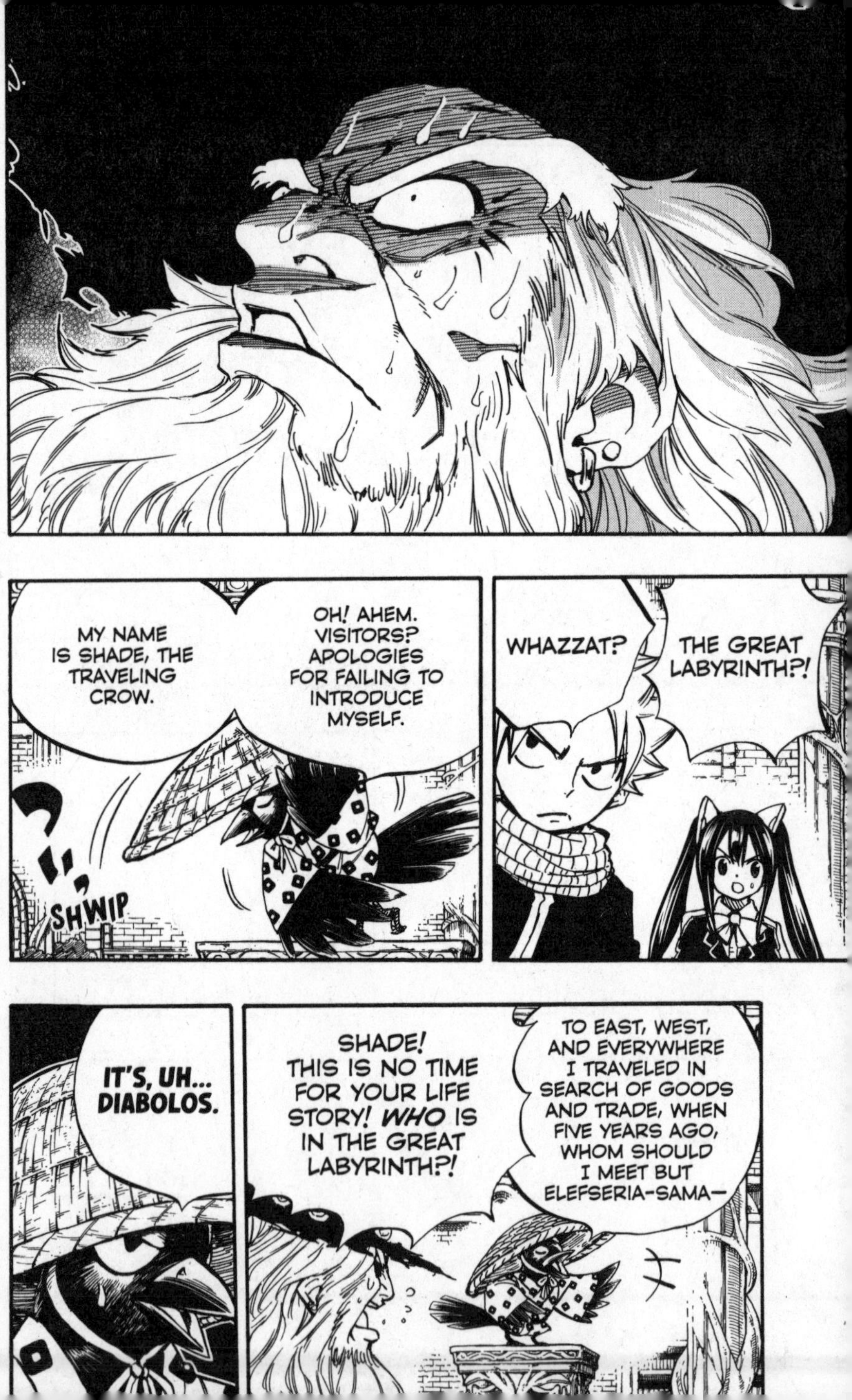
THE GREAT LABYRINTH?!
WHAZZAT?
OH! AHEM. VISITORS? APOLOGIES FOR FAILING TO INTRODUCE MYSELF.
MY NAME IS SHADE, THE TRAVELING CROW.
SHWIP
TO EAST, WEST, AND EVERYWHERE I TRAVELED IN SEARCH OF GOODS AND TRADE, WHEN FIVE YEARS AGO, WHOM SHOULD I MEET BUT ELEFSERIA-SAMA—
SHADE! THIS IS NO TIME FOR YOUR LIFE STORY! WHO IS IN THE GREAT LABYRINTH?!
IT'S, UH... DIABOLOS.

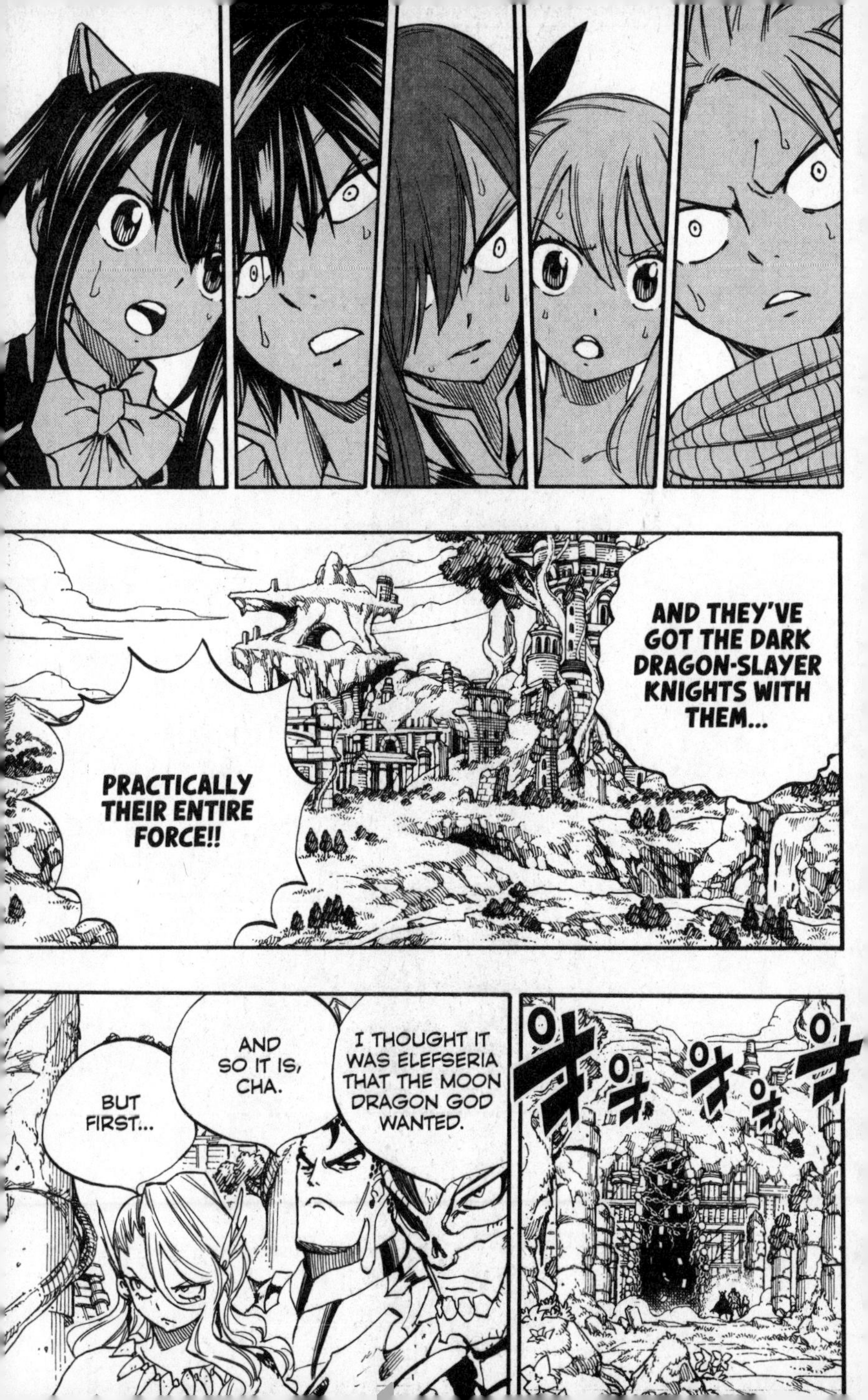
AND THEY'VE GOT THE DARK DRAGON-SLAYER KNIGHTS WITH THEM...
PRACTICALLY THEIR ENTIRE FORCE!!
I THOUGHT IT WAS ELEFSERIA THAT THE MOON DRAGON GOD WANTED.
AND SO IT IS, CHA.
BUT FIRST...

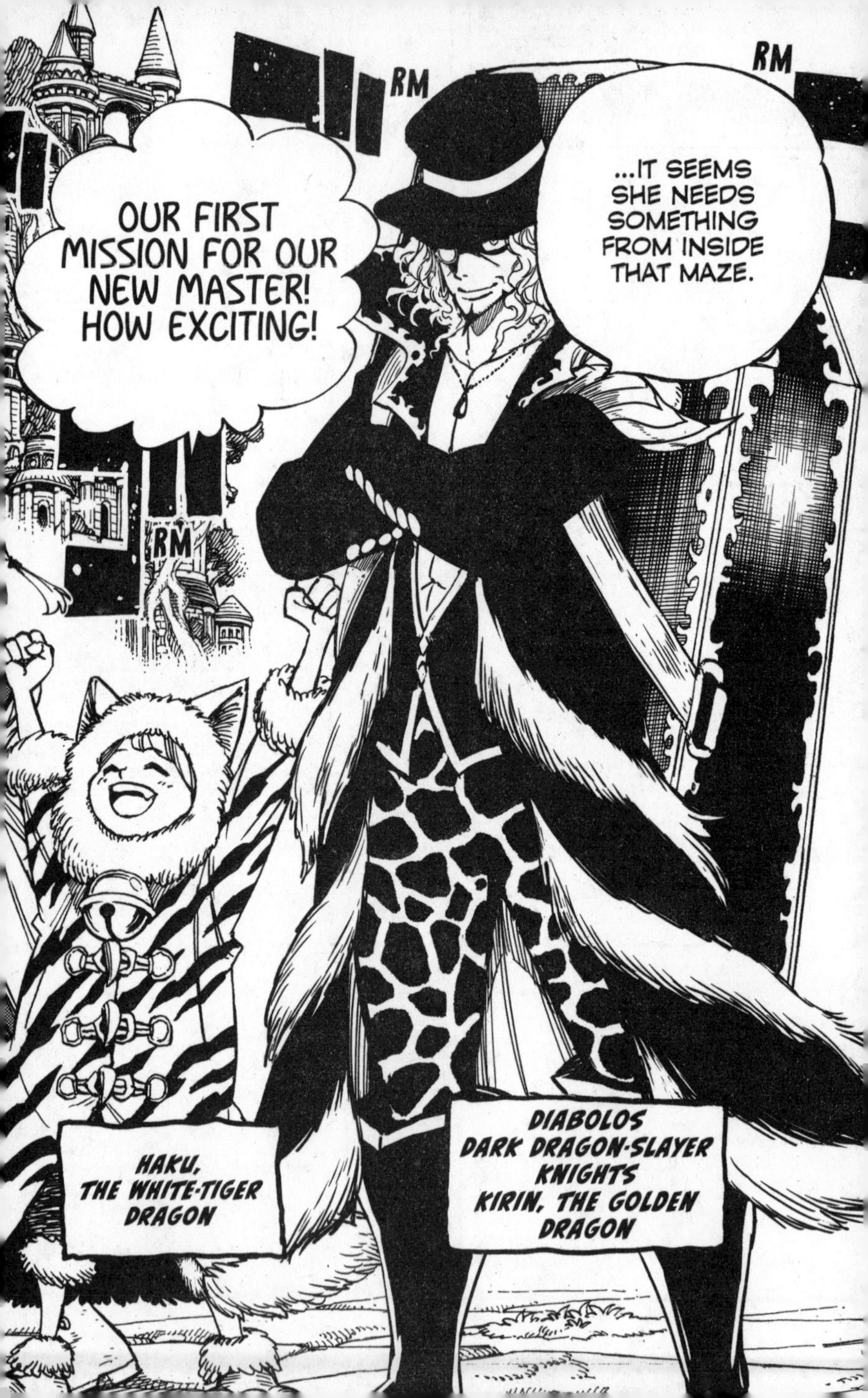
RM
...IT SEEMS SHE NEEDS SOMETHING FROM INSIDE THAT MAZE.
RM
OUR FIRST MISSION FOR OUR NEW MASTER! HOW EXCITING!
RM
DIABOLOS DARK DRAGON-SLAYER KNIGHTS KIRIN, THE GOLDEN DRAGON
HAKU, THE WHITE-TIGER DRAGON

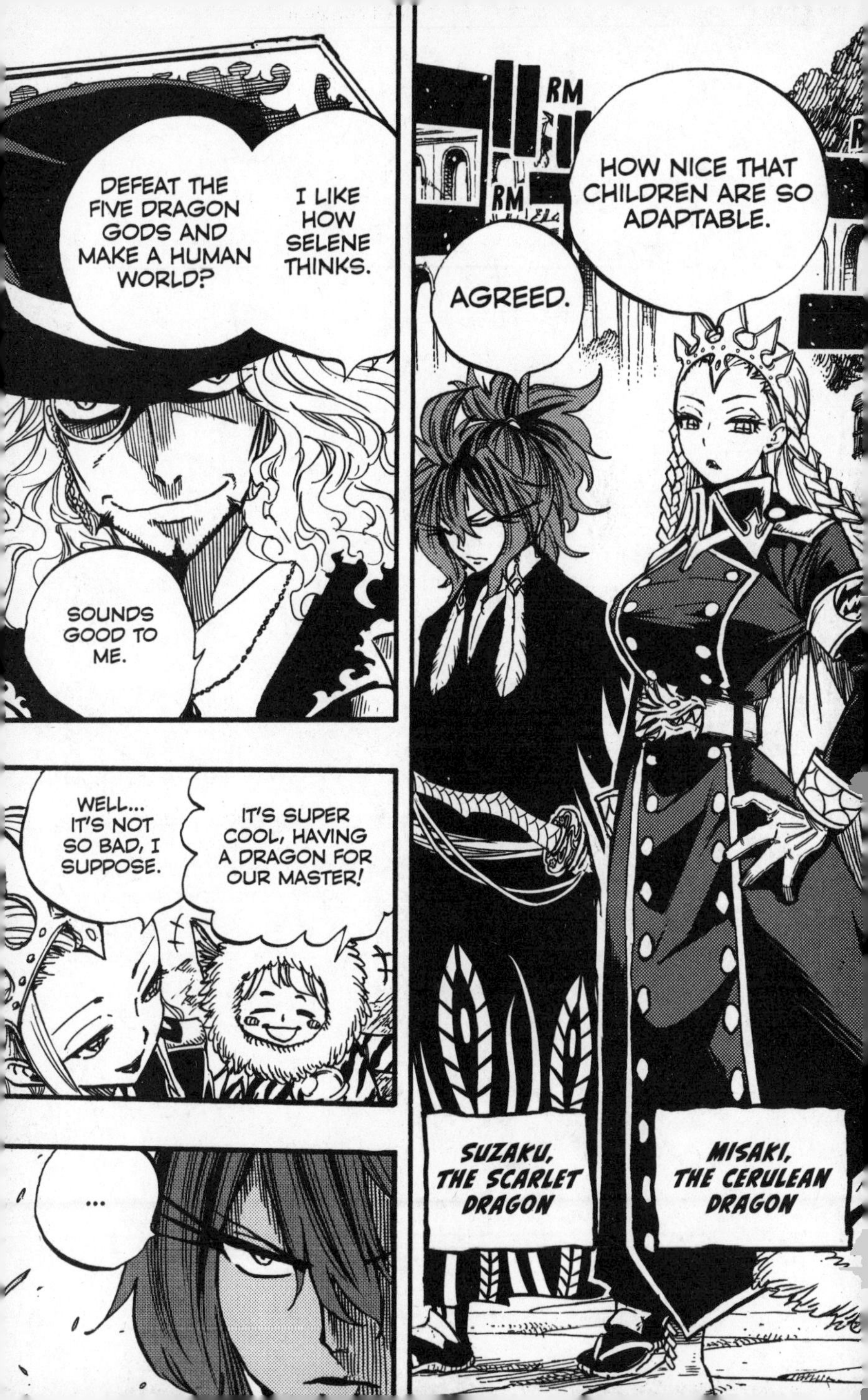
RM
RM
HOW NICE THAT CHILDREN ARE SO ADAPTABLE.
AGREED.
MISAKI, THE CERULEAN DRAGON
SUZAKU, THE SCARLET DRAGON
I LIKE HOW SELENE THINKS.
DEFEAT THE FIVE DRAGON GODS AND MAKE A HUMAN WORLD?
SOUNDS GOOD TO ME.
IT'S SUPER COOL, HAVING A DRAGON FOR OUR MASTER!
WELL... IT'S NOT SO BAD, I SUPPOSE.
...

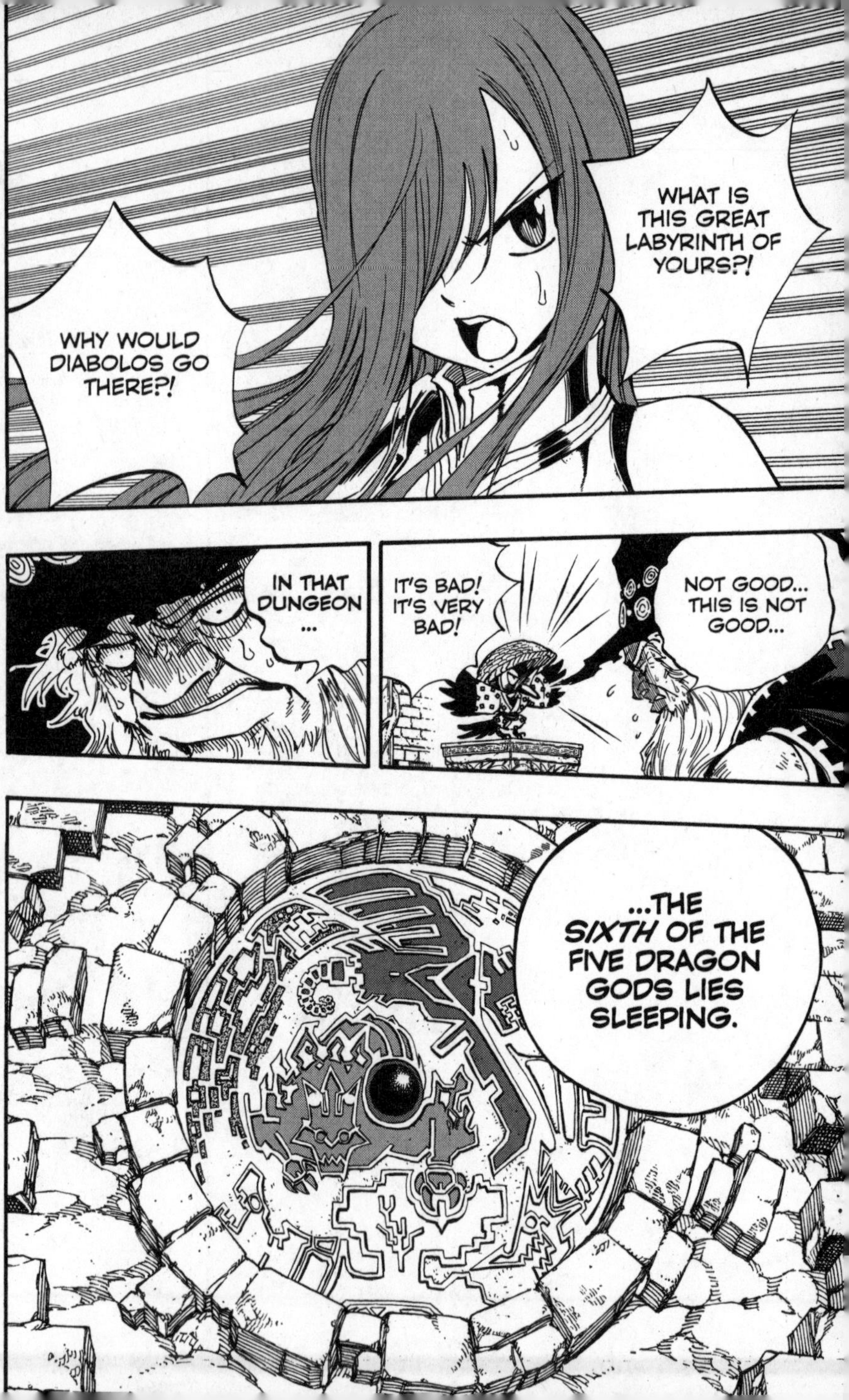
WHAT IS THIS GREAT LABYRINTH OF YOURS?!
WHY WOULD DIABOLOS GO THERE?!
NOT GOOD... THIS IS NOT GOOD...
IT'S BAD! IT'S VERY BAD!
IN THAT DUNGEON ...
...THE *SIXTH* OF THE FIVE DRAGON GODS LIES SLEEPING.

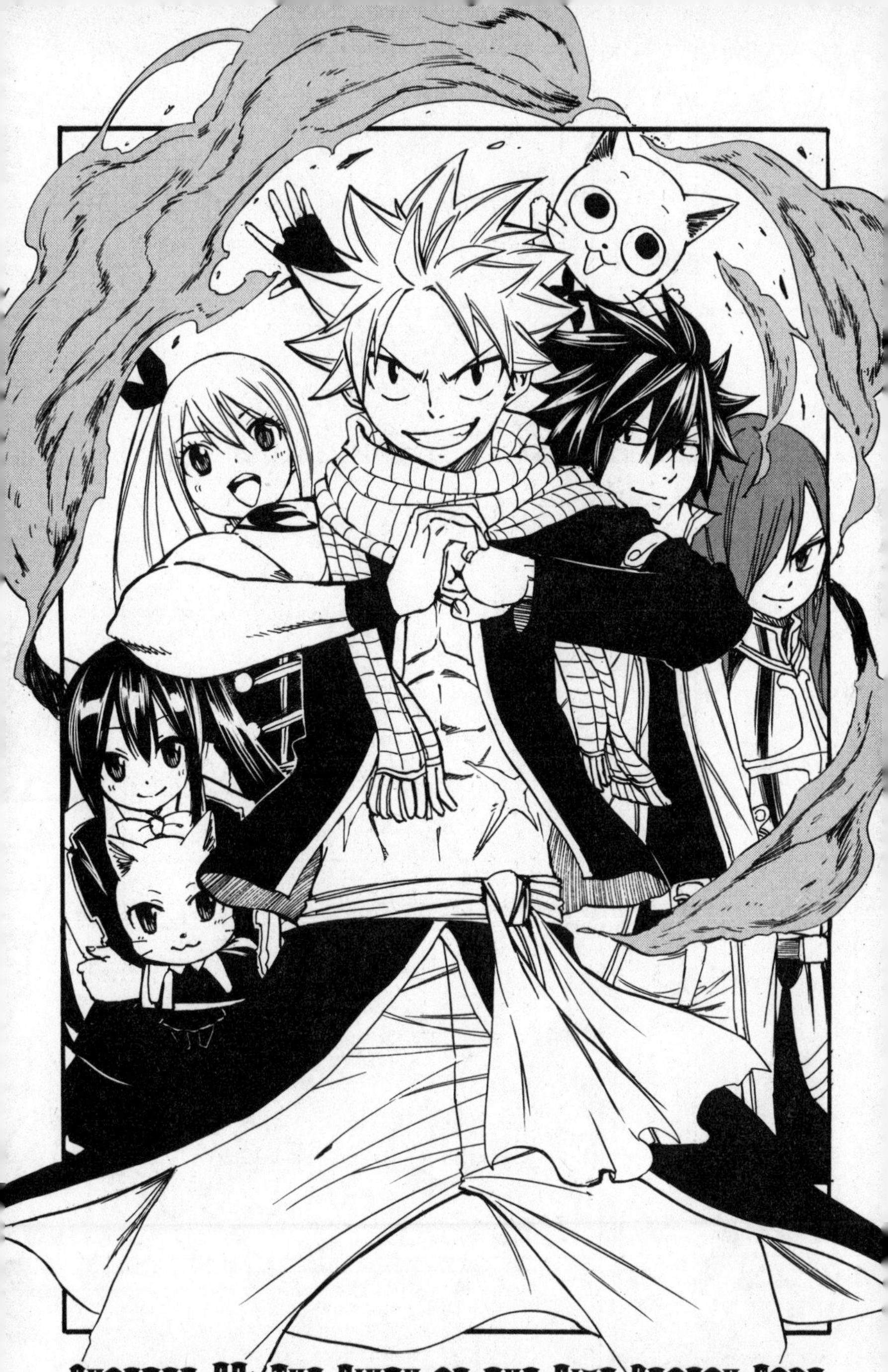

Chapter 93: The Sixth of the Five Dragon Gods

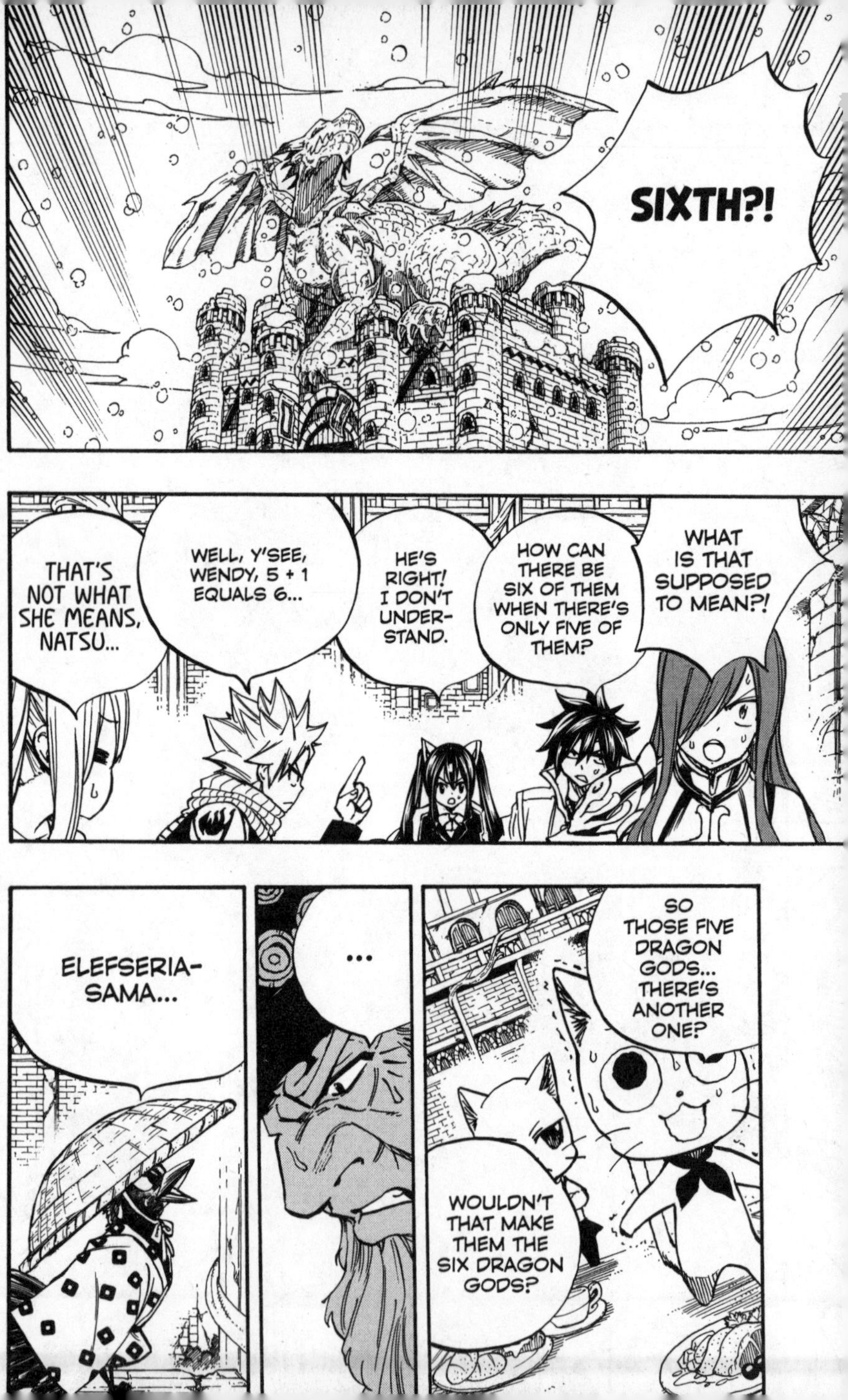
SIXTH?!
WHAT IS THAT SUPPOSED TO MEAN?!
HOW CAN THERE BE SIX OF THEM WHEN THERE'S ONLY FIVE OF THEM?
HE'S RIGHT! I DON'T UNDER-STAND.
WELL, Y'SEE, WENDY, 5 + 1 EQUALS 6...
THAT'S NOT WHAT SHE MEANS, NATSU...
SO THOSE FIVE DRAGON GODS... THERE'S ANOTHER ONE?
WOULDN'T THAT MAKE THEM THE SIX DRAGON GODS?
...
ELEFSERIA-SAMA...

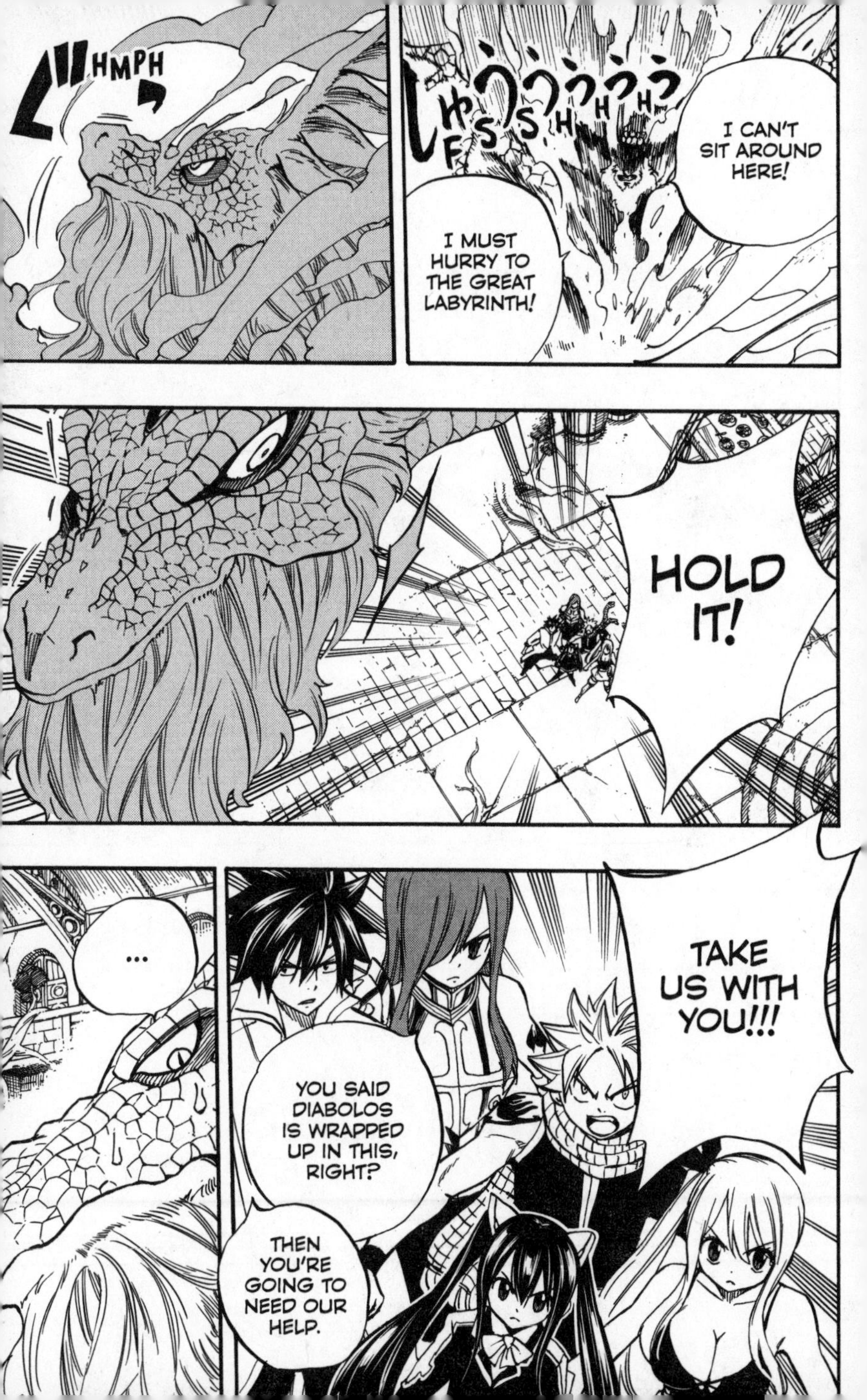

FSSHHH
I CAN'T SIT AROUND HERE!
I MUST HURRY TO THE GREAT LABYRINTH!
HMPH
HOLD IT!
TAKE US WITH YOU!!!
YOU SAID DIABOLOS IS WRAPPED UP IN THIS, RIGHT?
THEN YOU'RE GOING TO NEED OUR HELP.
...

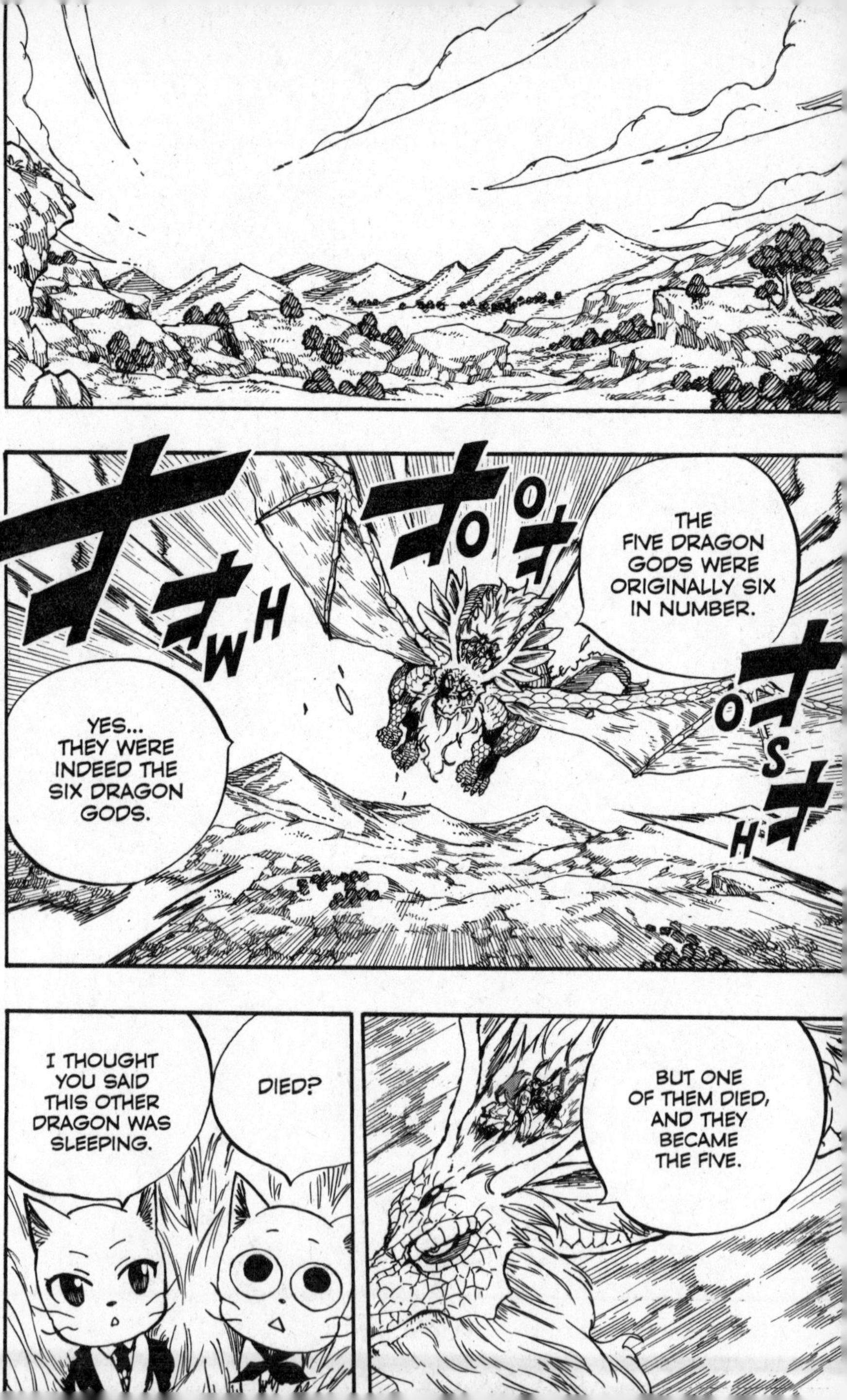
THE FIVE DRAGON GODS WERE ORIGINALLY SIX IN NUMBER.
YES... THEY WERE INDEED THE SIX DRAGON GODS.
BUT ONE OF THEM DIED, AND THEY BECAME THE FIVE.
DIED?
I THOUGHT YOU SAID THIS OTHER DRAGON WAS SLEEPING.

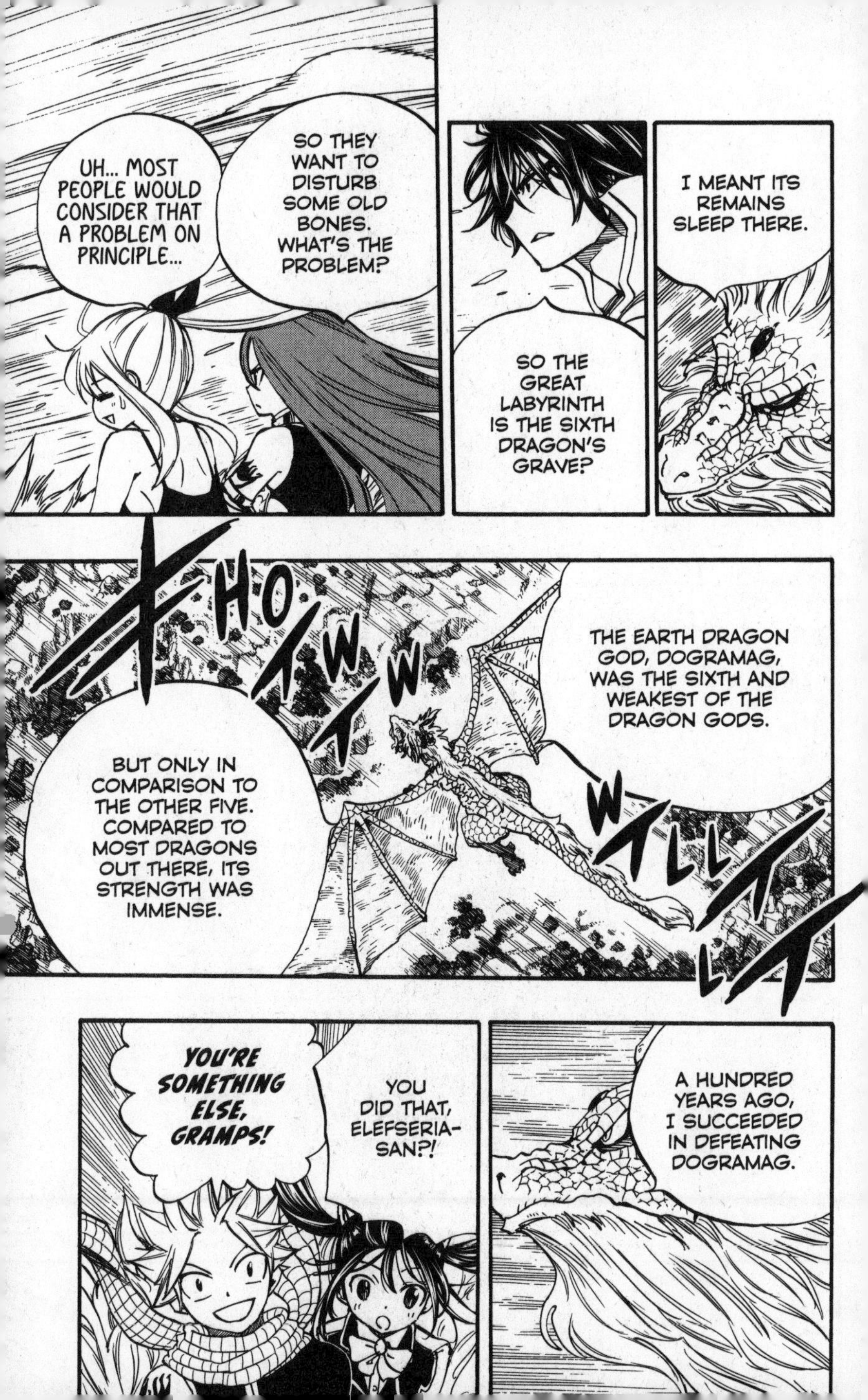
I MEANT ITS REMAINS SLEEP THERE.
SO THE GREAT LABYRINTH IS THE SIXTH DRAGON'S GRAVE?
SO THEY WANT TO DISTURB SOME OLD BONES. WHAT'S THE PROBLEM?
UH... MOST PEOPLE WOULD CONSIDER THAT A PROBLEM ON PRINCIPLE...
THE EARTH DRAGON GOD, DOGRAMAG, WAS THE SIXTH AND WEAKEST OF THE DRAGON GODS.
BUT ONLY IN COMPARISON TO THE OTHER FIVE. COMPARED TO MOST DRAGONS OUT THERE, ITS STRENGTH WAS IMMENSE.
A HUNDRED YEARS AGO, I SUCCEEDED IN DEFEATING DOGRAMAG.
YOU DID THAT, ELEFSERIA-SAN?!
YOU'RE SOMETHING ELSE, GRAMPS!

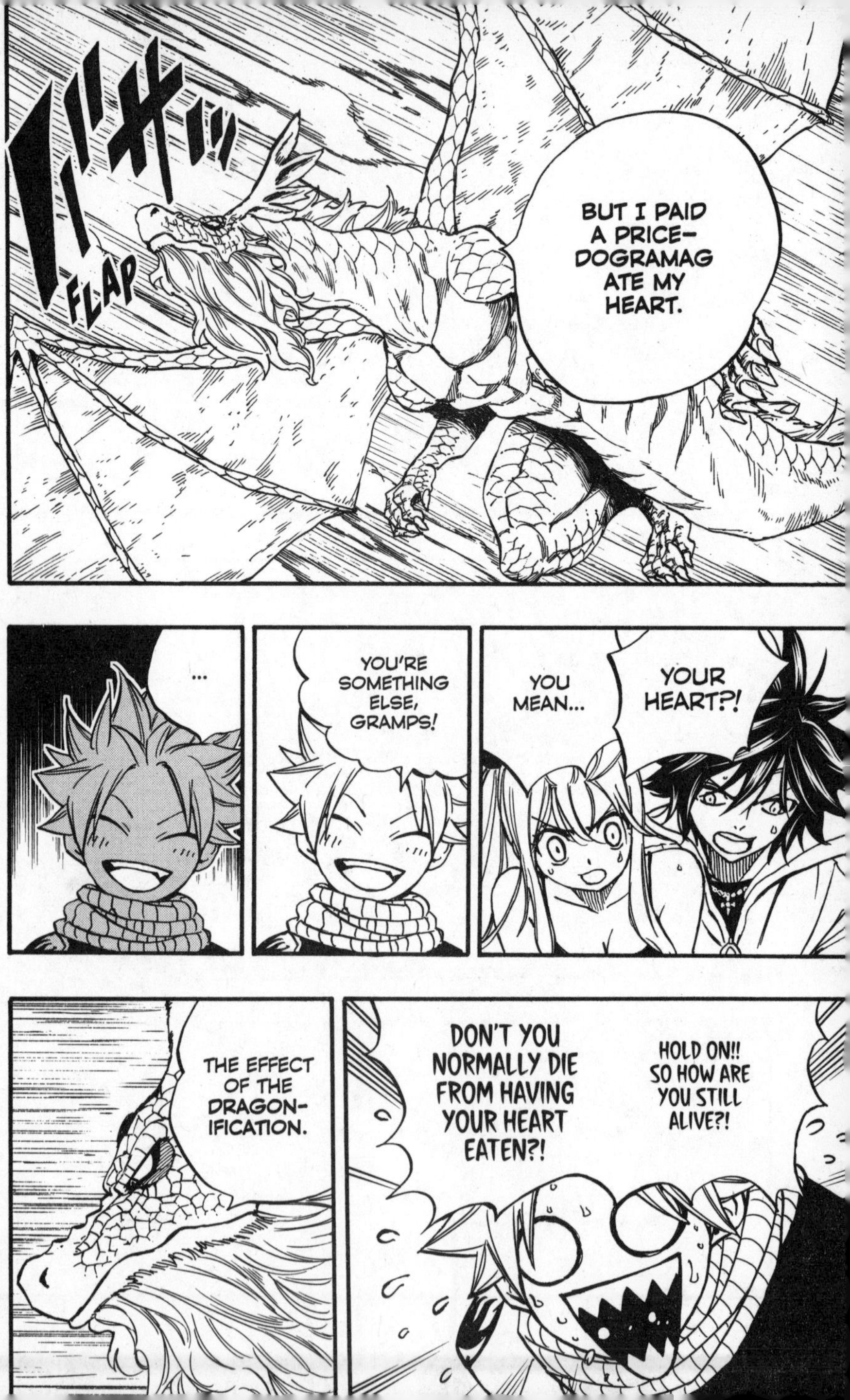
BUT I PAID A PRICE—DOGRAMAG ATE MY HEART.
FLAP
YOUR HEART?!
YOU MEAN...
YOU'RE SOMETHING ELSE, GRAMPS!
...
HOLD ON!! SO HOW ARE YOU STILL ALIVE?!
DON'T YOU NORMALLY DIE FROM HAVING YOUR HEART EATEN?!
THE EFFECT OF THE DRAGON-IFICATION.

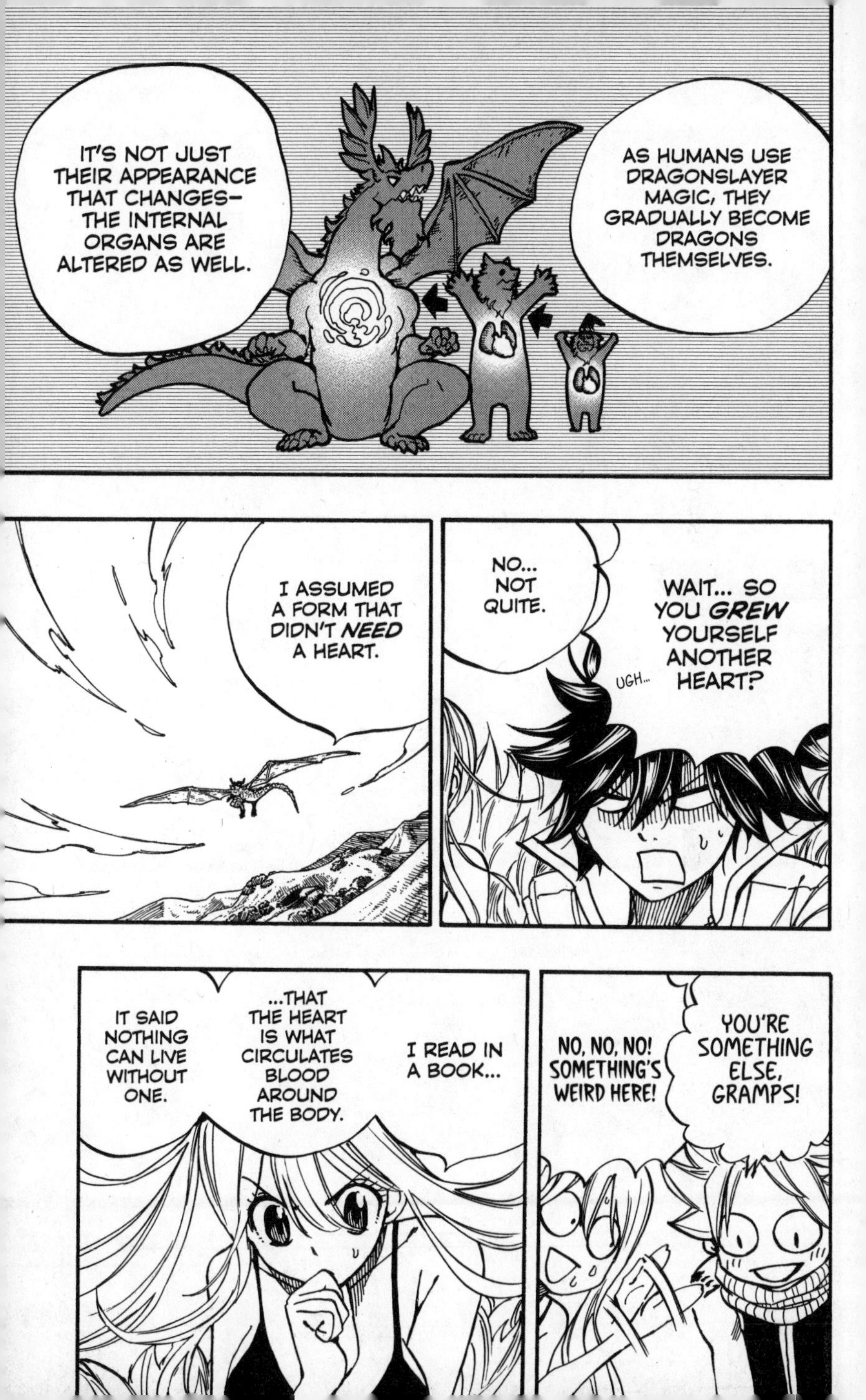
AS HUMANS USE DRAGONSLAYER MAGIC, THEY GRADUALLY BECOME DRAGONS THEMSELVES.
IT'S NOT JUST THEIR APPEARANCE THAT CHANGES— THE INTERNAL ORGANS ARE ALTERED AS WELL.
WAIT... SO YOU GREW YOURSELF ANOTHER HEART?
UGH...
NO... NOT QUITE.
I ASSUMED A FORM THAT DIDN'T NEED A HEART.
YOU'RE SOMETHING ELSE, GRAMPS!
NO, NO, NO! SOMETHING'S WEIRD HERE!
I READ IN A BOOK...
...THAT THE HEART IS WHAT CIRCULATES BLOOD AROUND THE BODY.
IT SAID NOTHING CAN LIVE WITHOUT ONE.

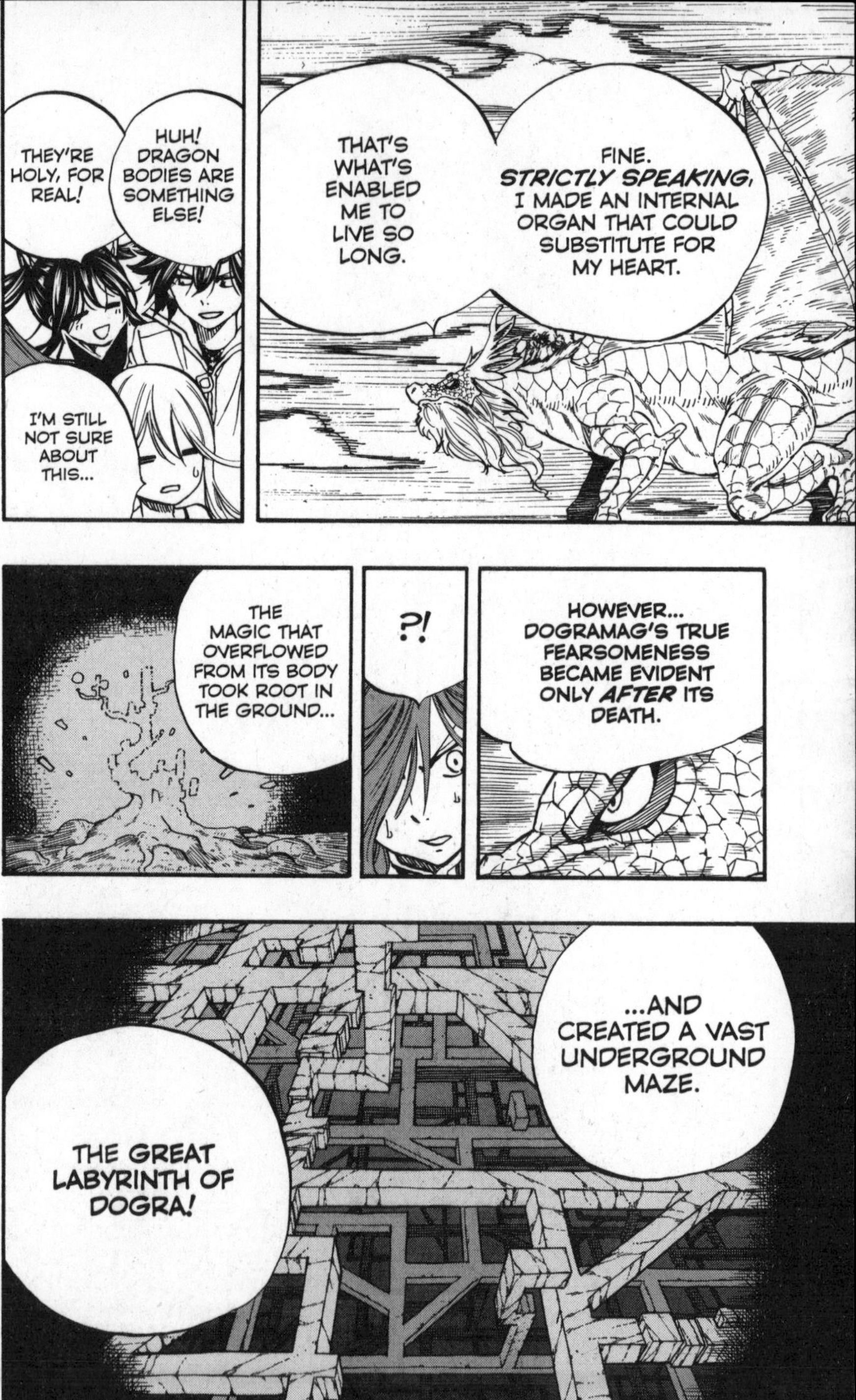
FINE. *STRICTLY SPEAKING*, I MADE AN INTERNAL ORGAN THAT COULD SUBSTITUTE FOR MY HEART.
THAT'S WHAT'S ENABLED ME TO LIVE SO LONG.
HUH! DRAGON BODIES ARE SOMETHING ELSE!
THEY'RE HOLY, FOR REAL!
I'M STILL NOT SURE ABOUT THIS...
HOWEVER... DOGRAMAG'S TRUE FEARSOMENESS BECAME EVIDENT ONLY *AFTER* ITS DEATH.
?!
THE MAGIC THAT OVERFLOWED FROM ITS BODY TOOK ROOT IN THE GROUND...
...AND CREATED A VAST UNDERGROUND MAZE.
THE GREAT LABYRINTH OF DOGRA!

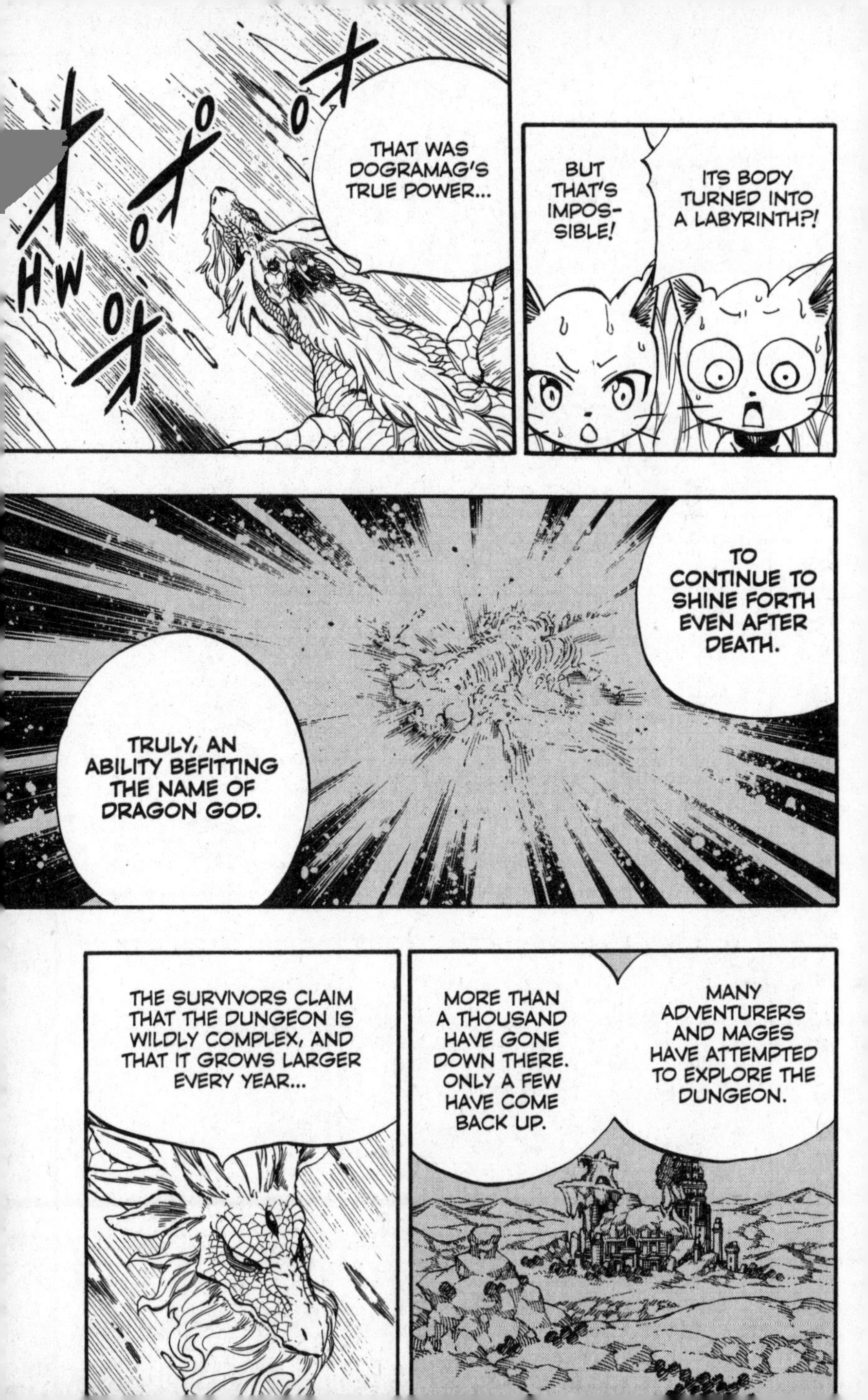
ITS BODY TURNED INTO A LABYRINTH?!
BUT THAT'S IMPOS-SIBLE!
THAT WAS DOGRAMAG'S TRUE POWER...
HWOOOO
TO CONTINUE TO SHINE FORTH EVEN AFTER DEATH.
TRULY, AN ABILITY BEFITTING THE NAME OF DRAGON GOD.
MANY ADVENTURERS AND MAGES HAVE ATTEMPTED TO EXPLORE THE DUNGEON.
MORE THAN A THOUSAND HAVE GONE DOWN THERE. ONLY A FEW HAVE COME BACK UP.
THE SURVIVORS CLAIM THAT THE DUNGEON IS WILDLY COMPLEX, AND THAT IT GROWS LARGER EVERY YEAR...

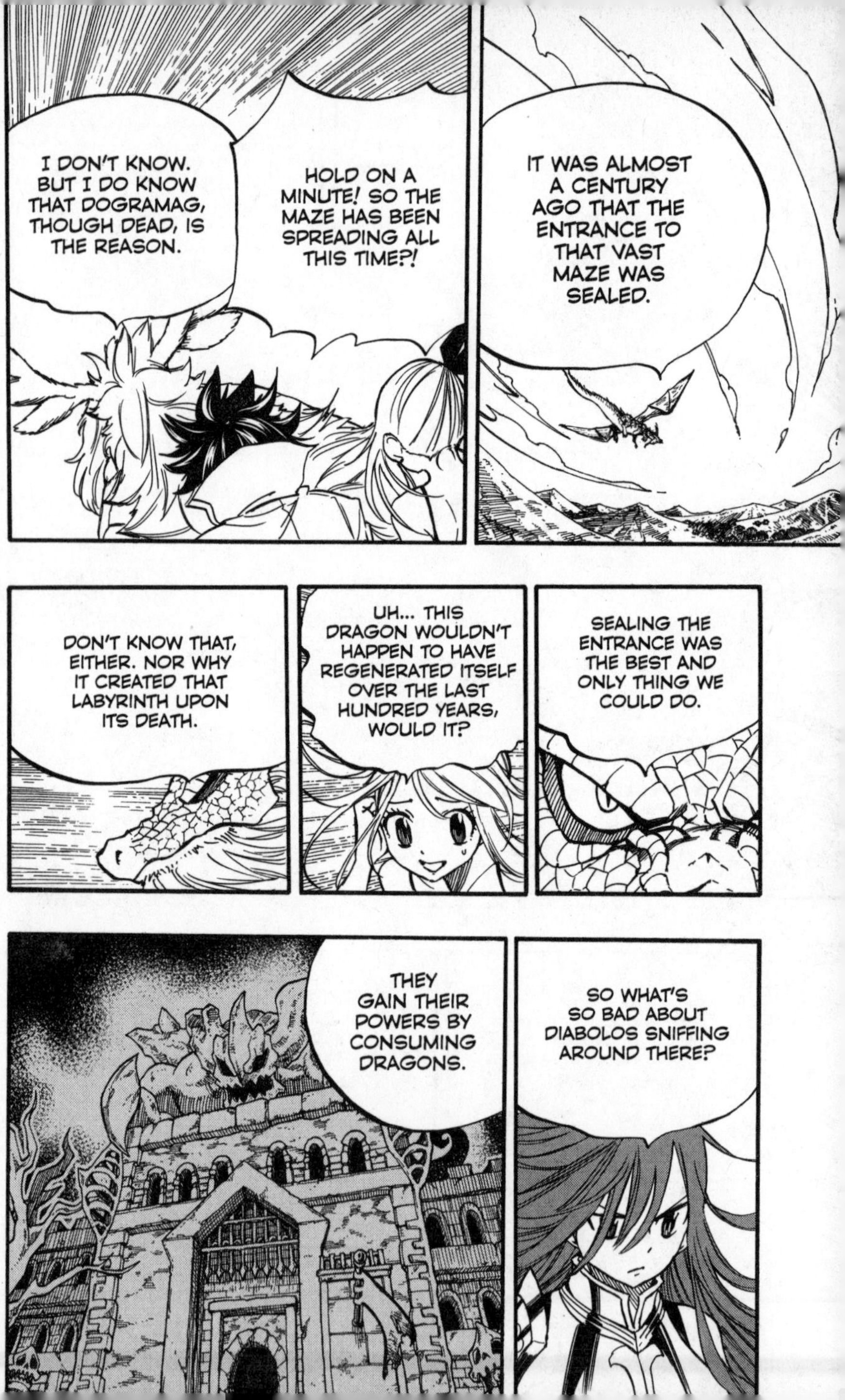
IT WAS ALMOST A CENTURY AGO THAT THE ENTRANCE TO THAT VAST MAZE WAS SEALED.
HOLD ON A MINUTE! SO THE MAZE HAS BEEN SPREADING ALL THIS TIME?!
I DON'T KNOW. BUT I DO KNOW THAT DOGRAMAG, THOUGH DEAD, IS THE REASON.
SEALING THE ENTRANCE WAS THE BEST AND ONLY THING WE COULD DO.
UH... THIS DRAGON WOULDN'T HAPPEN TO HAVE REGENERATED ITSELF OVER THE LAST HUNDRED YEARS, WOULD IT?
DON'T KNOW THAT, EITHER. NOR WHY IT CREATED THAT LABYRINTH UPON ITS DEATH.
SO WHAT'S SO BAD ABOUT DIABOLOS SNIFFING AROUND THERE?
THEY GAIN THEIR POWERS BY CONSUMING DRAGONS.

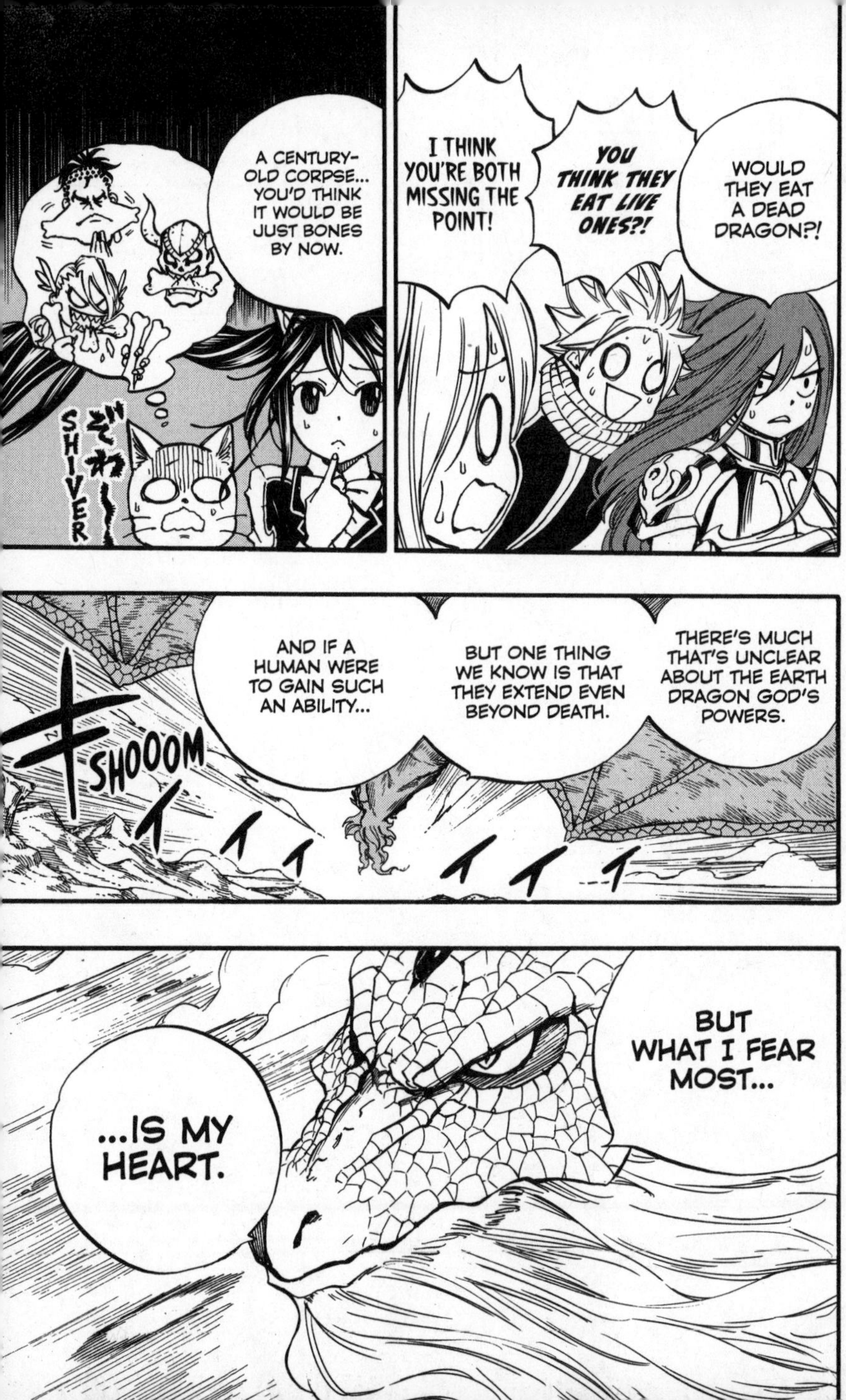
WOULD THEY EAT A DEAD DRAGON?!
YOU THINK THEY EAT LIVE ONES?!
I THINK YOU'RE BOTH MISSING THE POINT!
A CENTURY-OLD CORPSE... YOU'D THINK IT WOULD BE JUST BONES BY NOW.
SHIVER
THERE'S MUCH THAT'S UNCLEAR ABOUT THE EARTH DRAGON GOD'S POWERS.
BUT ONE THING WE KNOW IS THAT THEY EXTEND EVEN BEYOND DEATH.
AND IF A HUMAN WERE TO GAIN SUCH AN ABILITY...
SHOOOM
BUT WHAT I FEAR MOST...
...IS MY HEART.

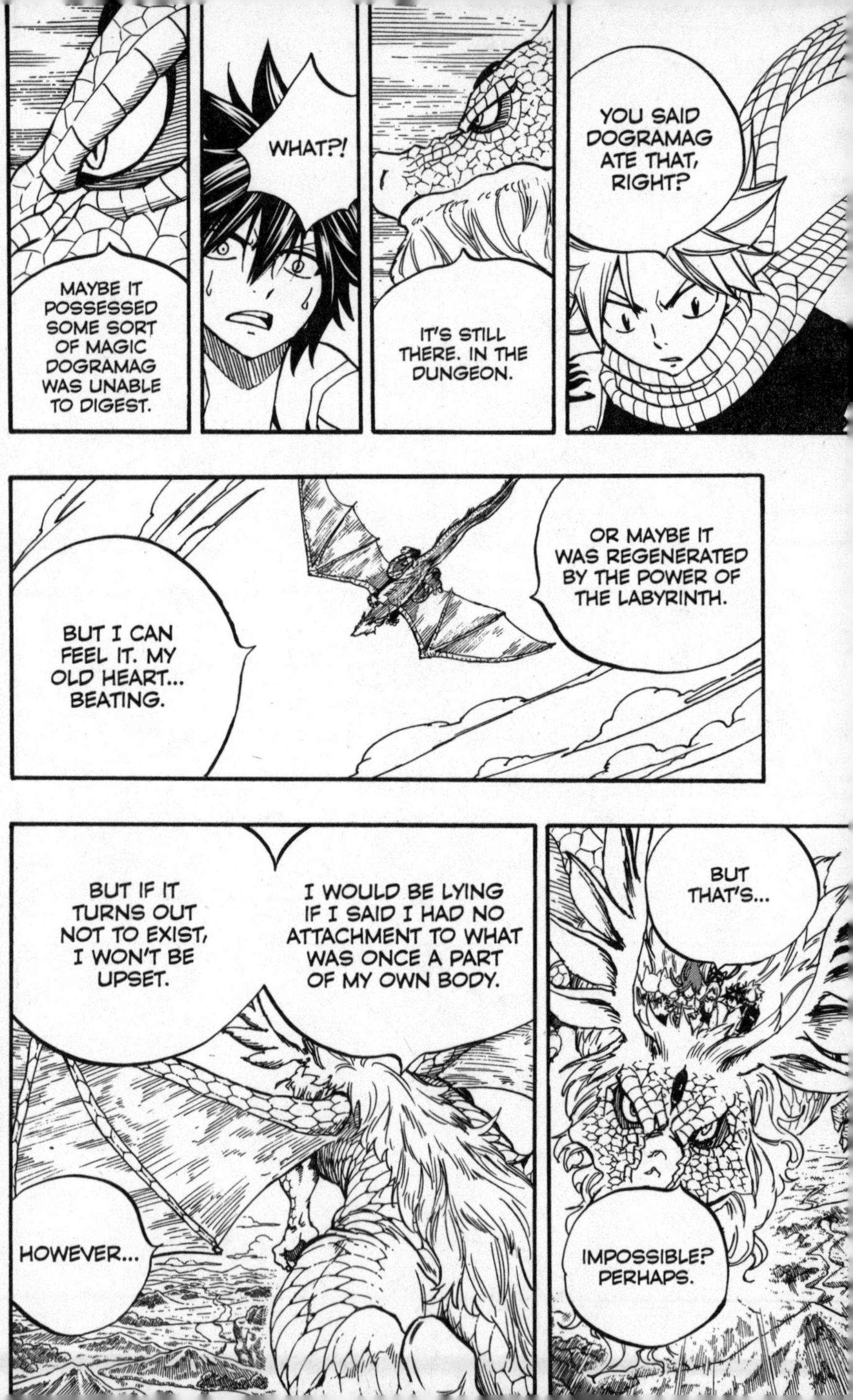
YOU SAID DOGRAMAG ATE THAT, RIGHT?
IT'S STILL THERE. IN THE DUNGEON.
WHAT?!
MAYBE IT POSSESSED SOME SORT OF MAGIC DOGRAMAG WAS UNABLE TO DIGEST.
OR MAYBE IT WAS REGENERATED BY THE POWER OF THE LABYRINTH.
BUT I CAN FEEL IT. MY OLD HEART... BEATING.
BUT THAT'S...
IMPOSSIBLE? PERHAPS.
I WOULD BE LYING IF I SAID I HAD NO ATTACHMENT TO WHAT WAS ONCE A PART OF MY OWN BODY.
BUT IF IT TURNS OUT NOT TO EXIST, I WON'T BE UPSET.
HOWEVER...

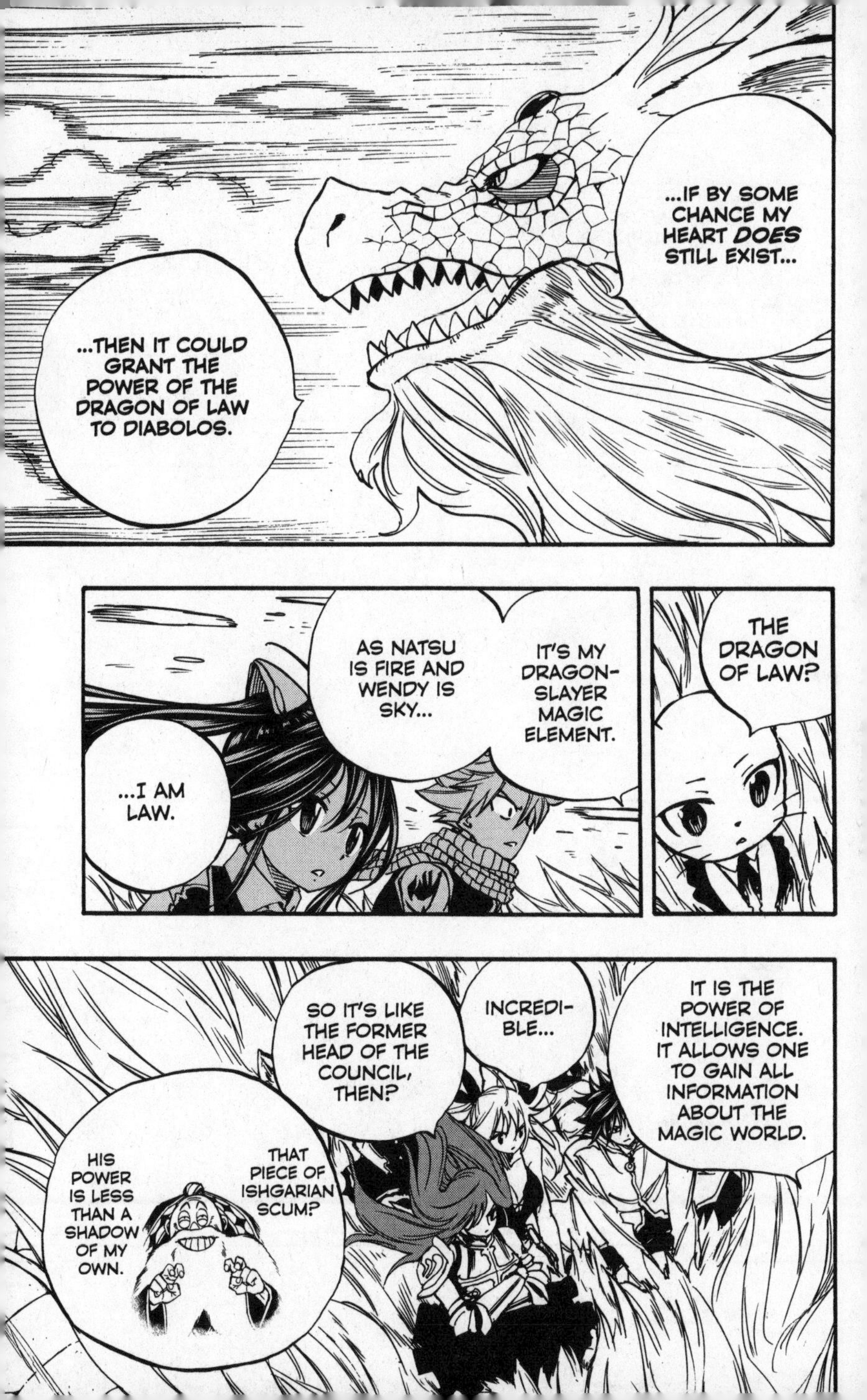
...IF BY SOME CHANCE MY HEART *DOES* STILL EXIST...
...THEN IT COULD GRANT THE POWER OF THE DRAGON OF LAW TO DIABOLOS.
THE DRAGON OF LAW?
IT'S MY DRAGON-SLAYER MAGIC ELEMENT.
AS NATSU IS FIRE AND WENDY IS SKY...
...I AM LAW.
IT IS THE POWER OF INTELLIGENCE. IT ALLOWS ONE TO GAIN ALL INFORMATION ABOUT THE MAGIC WORLD.
INCREDI-BLE...
SO IT'S LIKE THE FORMER HEAD OF THE COUNCIL, THEN?
THAT PIECE OF ISHGARIAN SCUM?
HIS POWER IS LESS THAN A SHADOW OF MY OWN.

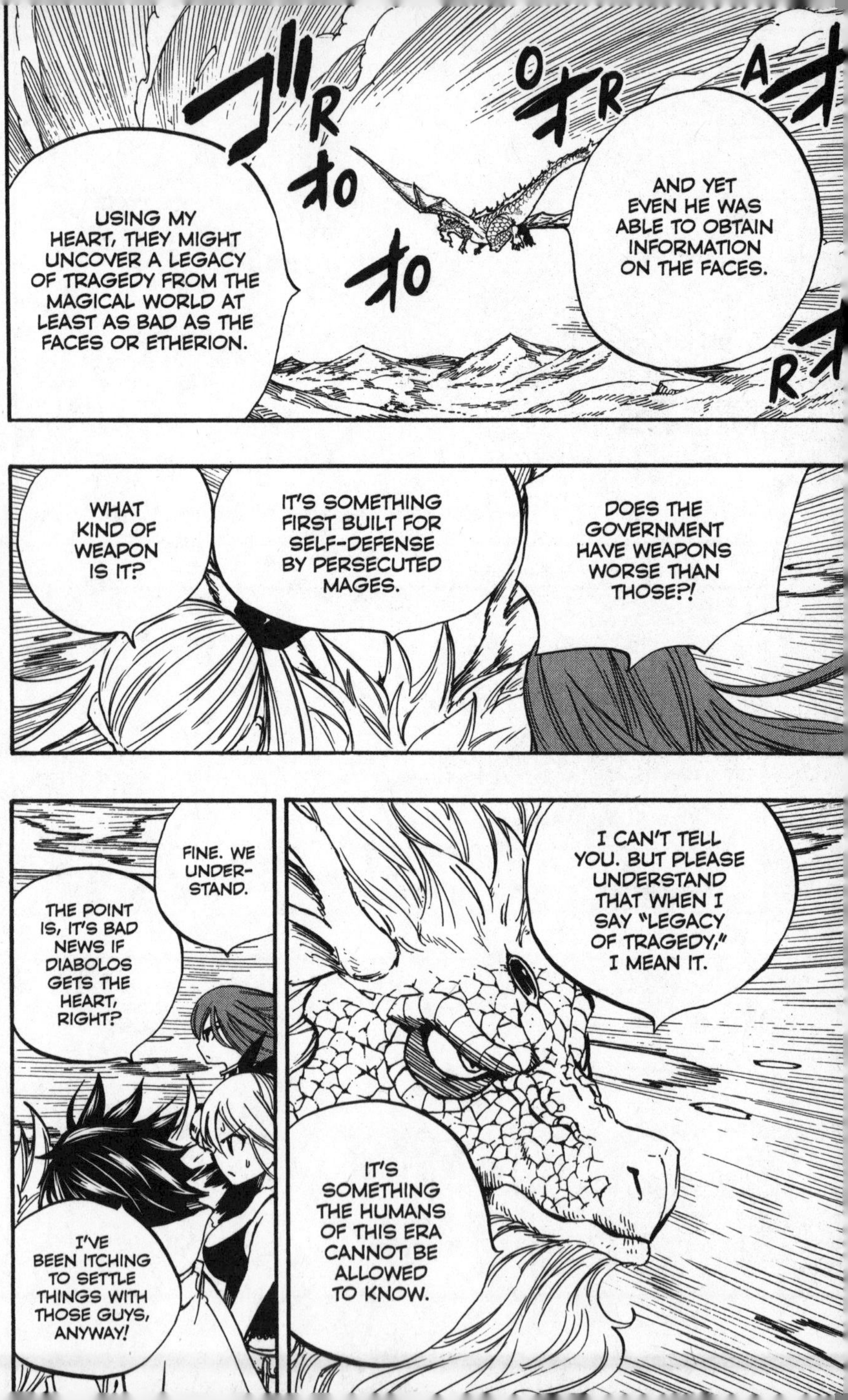
AND YET EVEN HE WAS ABLE TO OBTAIN INFORMATION ON THE FACES.
USING MY HEART, THEY MIGHT UNCOVER A LEGACY OF TRAGEDY FROM THE MAGICAL WORLD AT LEAST AS BAD AS THE FACES OR ETHERION.
DOES THE GOVERNMENT HAVE WEAPONS WORSE THAN THOSE?!
IT'S SOMETHING FIRST BUILT FOR SELF-DEFENSE BY PERSECUTED MAGES.
WHAT KIND OF WEAPON IS IT?
I CAN'T TELL YOU. BUT PLEASE UNDERSTAND THAT WHEN I SAY "LEGACY OF TRAGEDY," I MEAN IT.
IT'S SOMETHING THE HUMANS OF THIS ERA CANNOT BE ALLOWED TO KNOW.
FINE. WE UNDER-STAND.
THE POINT IS, IT'S BAD NEWS IF DIABOLOS GETS THE HEART, RIGHT?
I'VE BEEN ITCHING TO SETTLE THINGS WITH THOSE GUYS, ANYWAY!

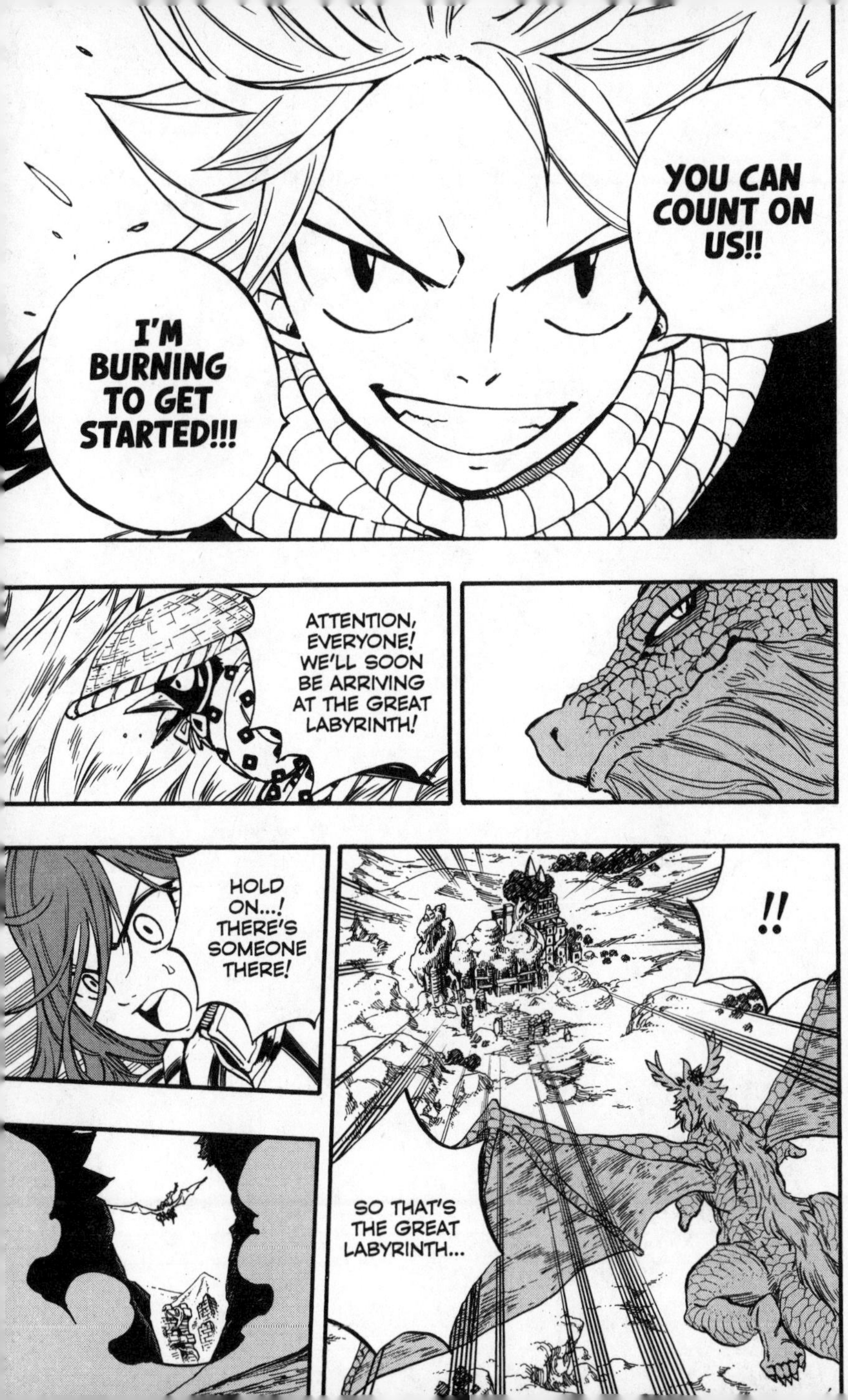
YOU CAN COUNT ON US!!
I'M BURNING TO GET STARTED!!!
ATTENTION, EVERYONE! WE'LL SOON BE ARRIVING AT THE GREAT LABYRINTH!
!!
SO THAT'S THE GREAT LABYRINTH...
HOLD ON...! THERE'S SOMEONE THERE!

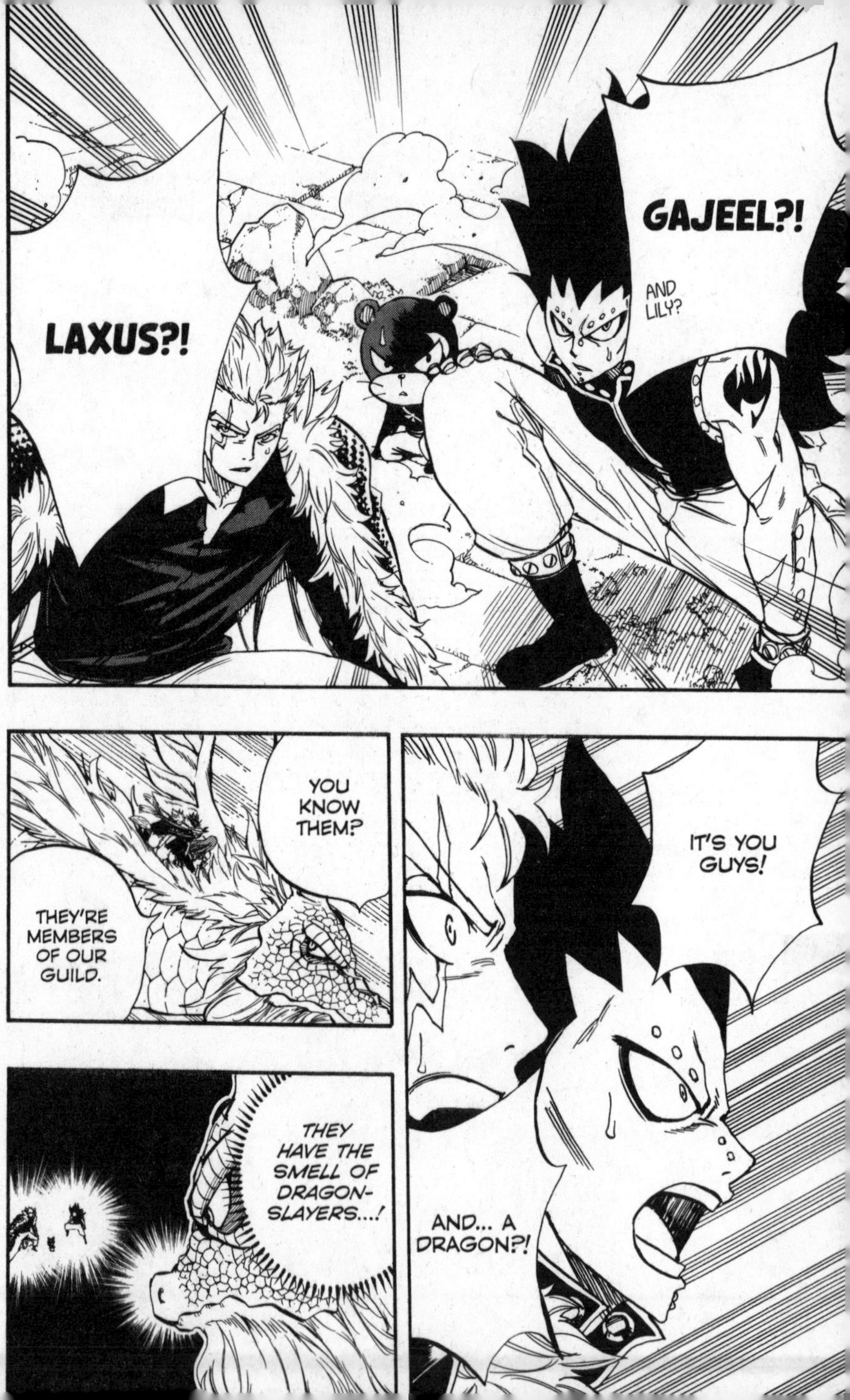
GAJEEL?!
AND LILY?
LAXUS?!
IT'S YOU GUYS!
AND... A DRAGON?!
YOU KNOW THEM?
THEY'RE MEMBERS OF OUR GUILD.
THEY HAVE THE SMELL OF DRAGON-SLAYERS...!

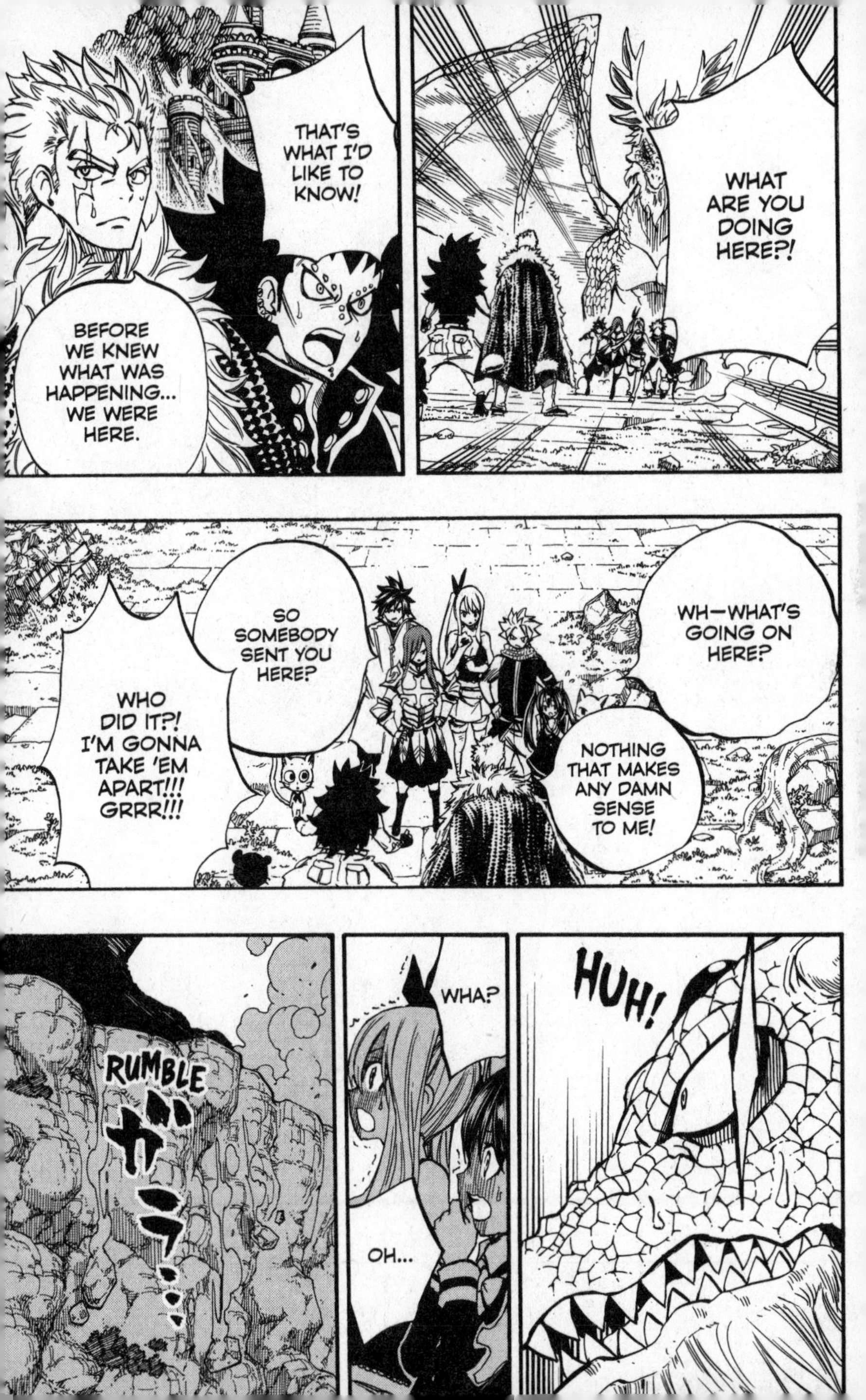
WHAT ARE YOU DOING HERE?!
THAT'S WHAT I'D LIKE TO KNOW!
BEFORE WE KNEW WHAT WAS HAPPENING... WE WERE HERE.
WH—WHAT'S GOING ON HERE?
NOTHING THAT MAKES ANY DAMN SENSE TO ME!
SO SOMEBODY SENT YOU HERE?
WHO DID IT?! I'M GONNA TAKE 'EM APART!!! GRRR!!!
HUH!
WHA?
OH...
RUMBLE

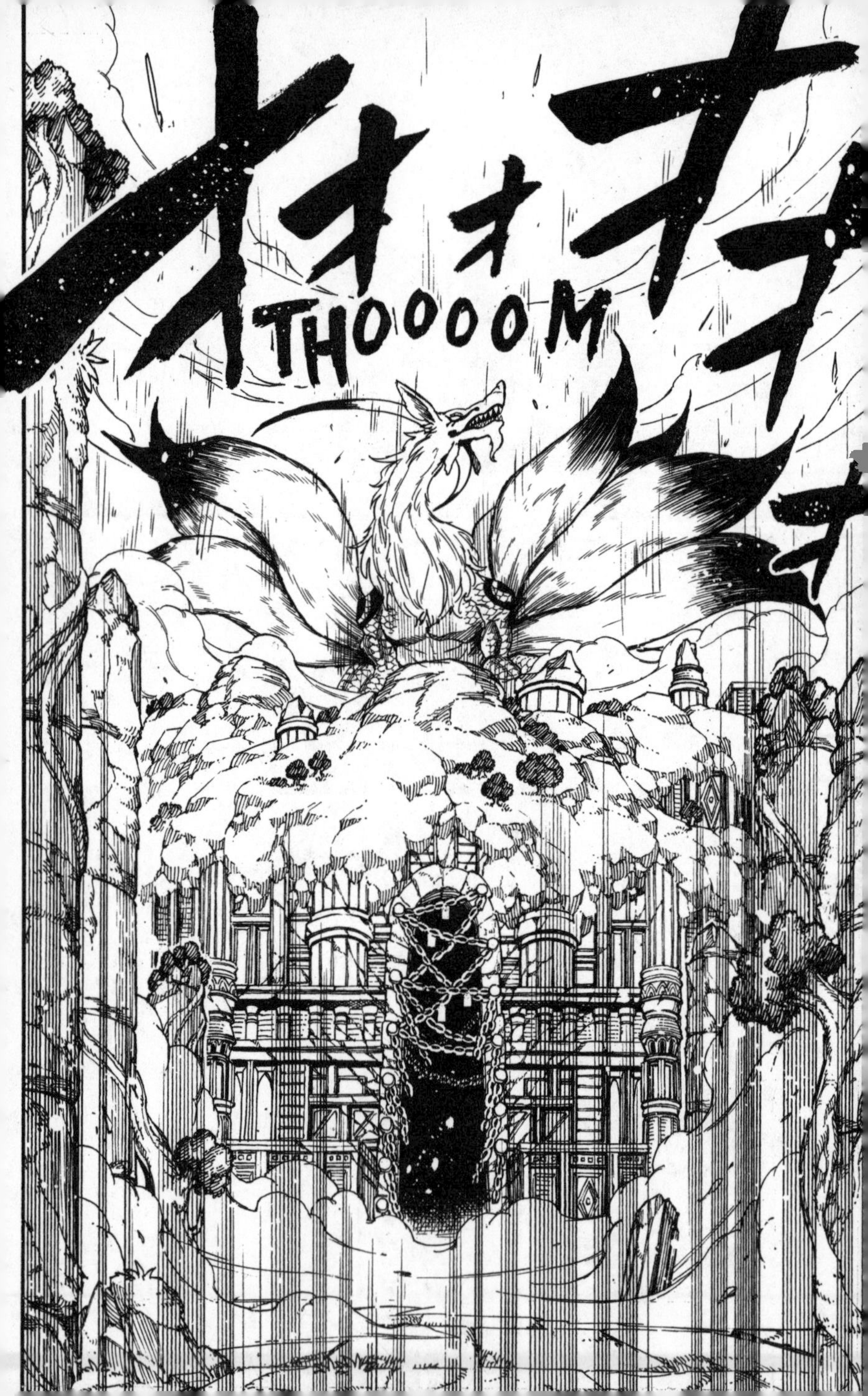

オォォォォ
THOOOOM

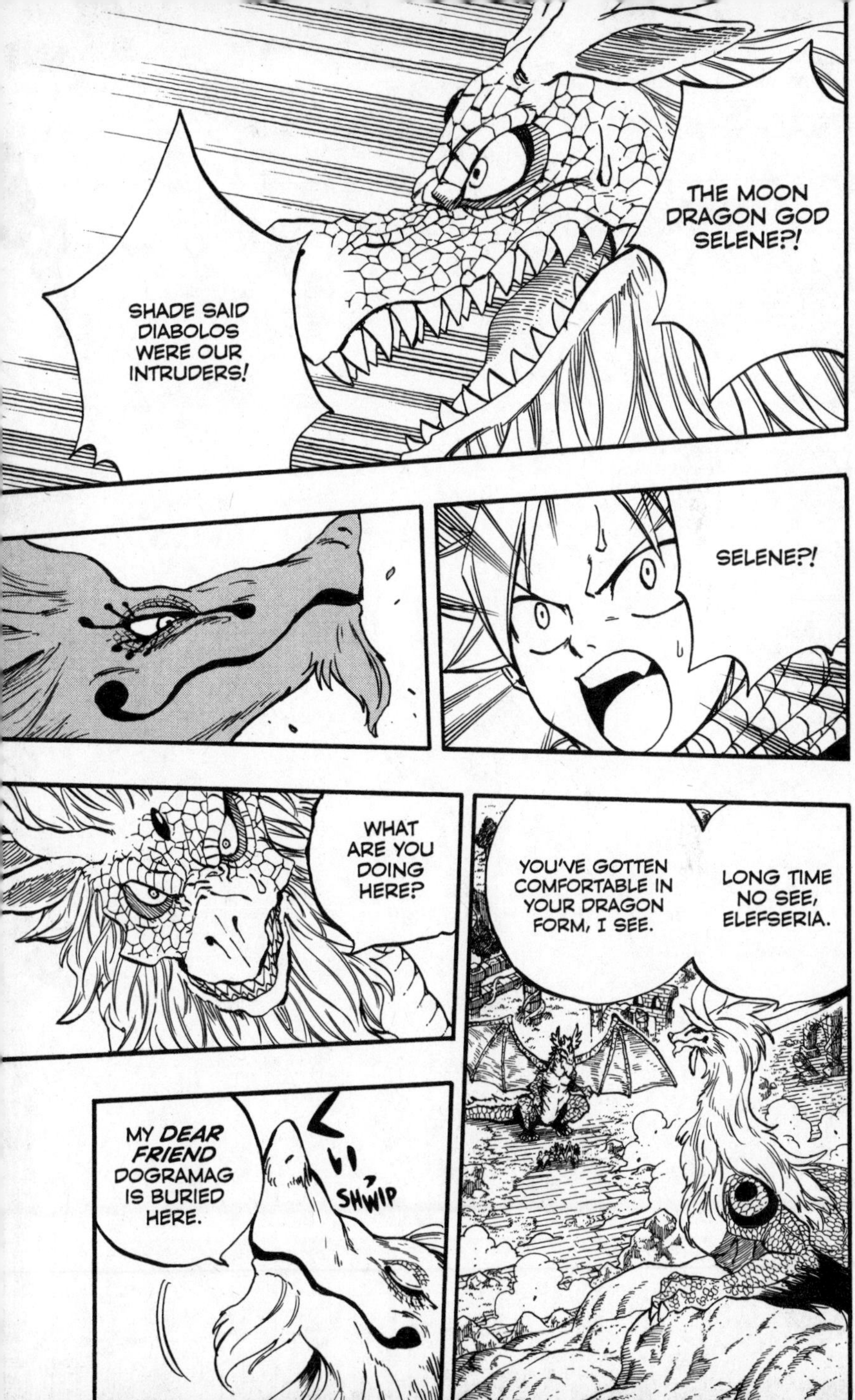
THE MOON DRAGON GOD SELENE?!
SHADE SAID DIABOLOS WERE OUR INTRUDERS!
SELENE?!
LONG TIME NO SEE, ELEFSERIA.
YOU'VE GOTTEN COMFORTABLE IN YOUR DRAGON FORM, I SEE.
WHAT ARE YOU DOING HERE?
MY *DEAR FRIEND* DOGRAMAG IS BURIED HERE.
SHWIP

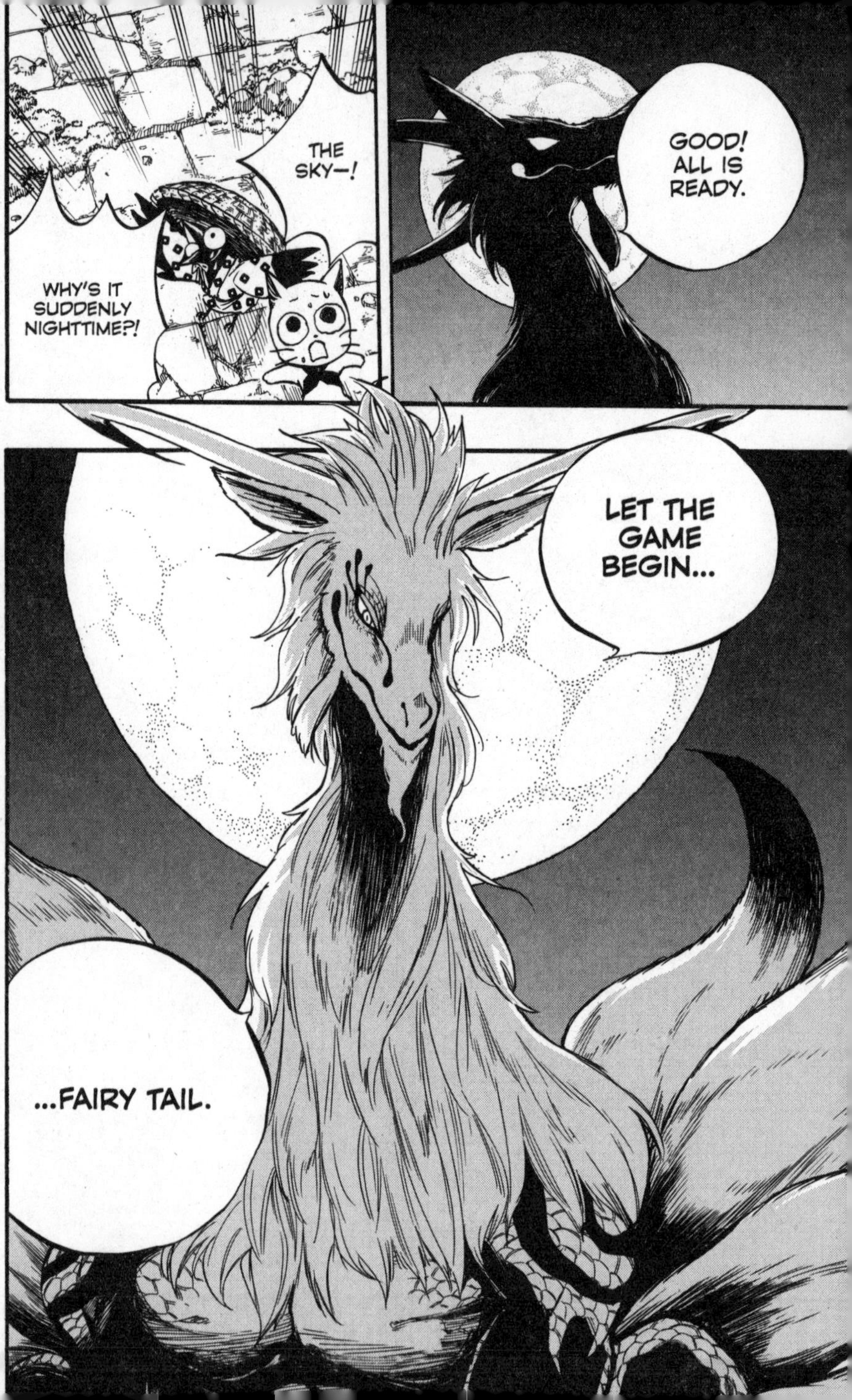
GOOD! ALL IS READY.
THE SKY—!
WHY'S IT SUDDENLY NIGHTTIME?!
LET THE GAME BEGIN...
...FAIRY TAIL.

FAIRY TAIL 100 YEARS QUEST

Chapter 94: Battle Dungeon

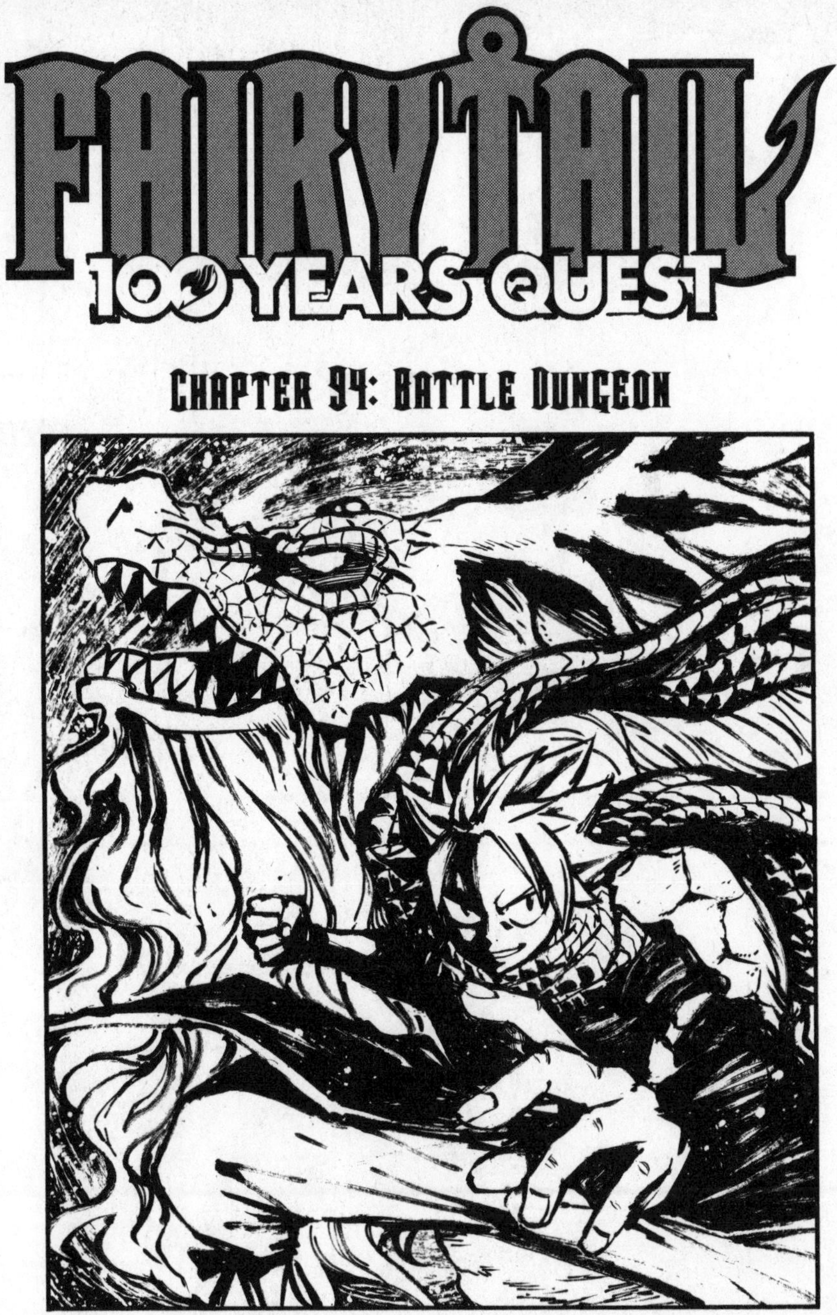

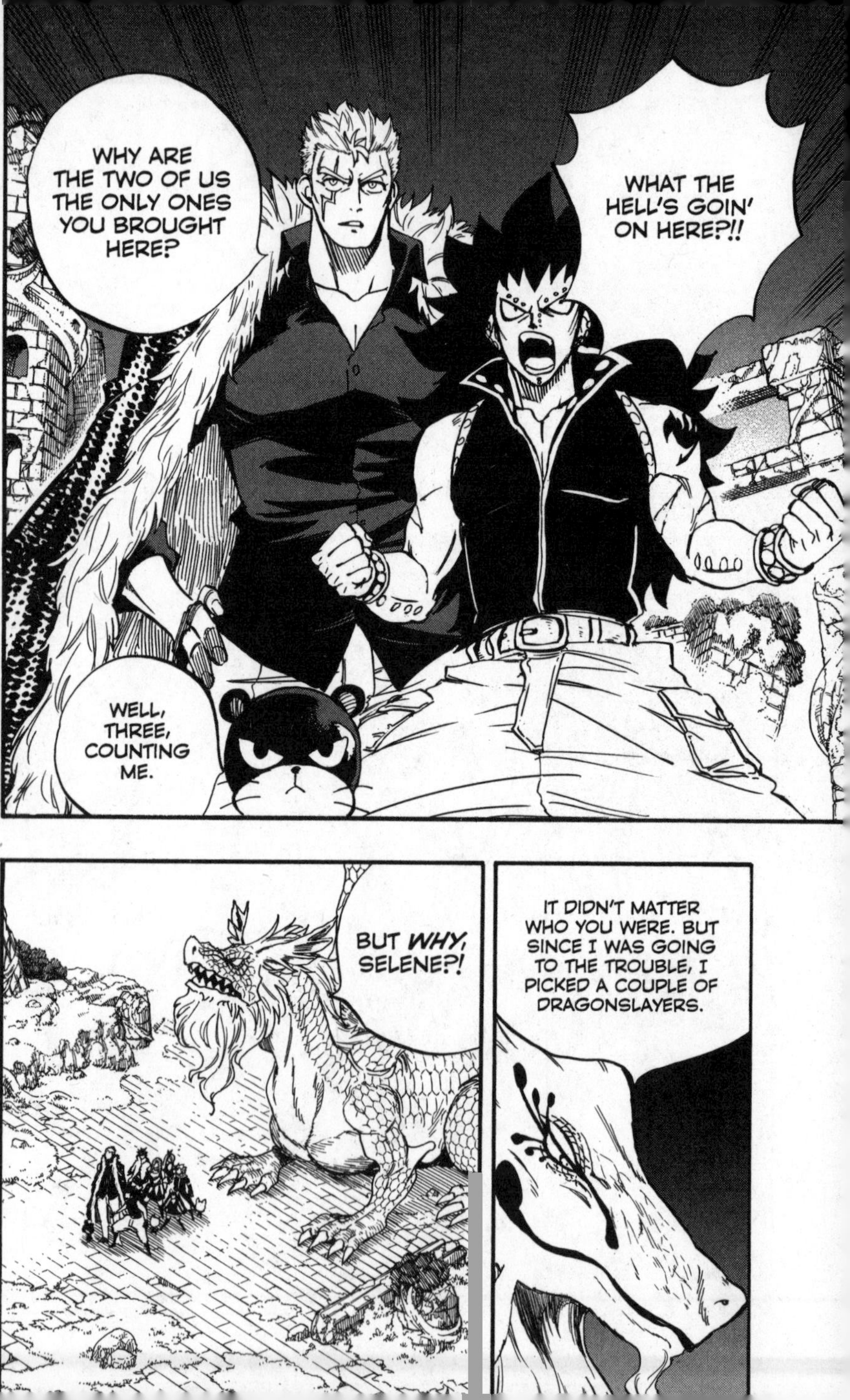
WHY ARE THE TWO OF US THE ONLY ONES YOU BROUGHT HERE?
WHAT THE HELL'S GOIN' ON HERE?!!
WELL, THREE, COUNTING ME.
BUT *WHY*, SELENE?!
IT DIDN'T MATTER WHO YOU WERE. BUT SINCE I WAS GOING TO THE TROUBLE, I PICKED A COUPLE OF DRAGONSLAYERS.

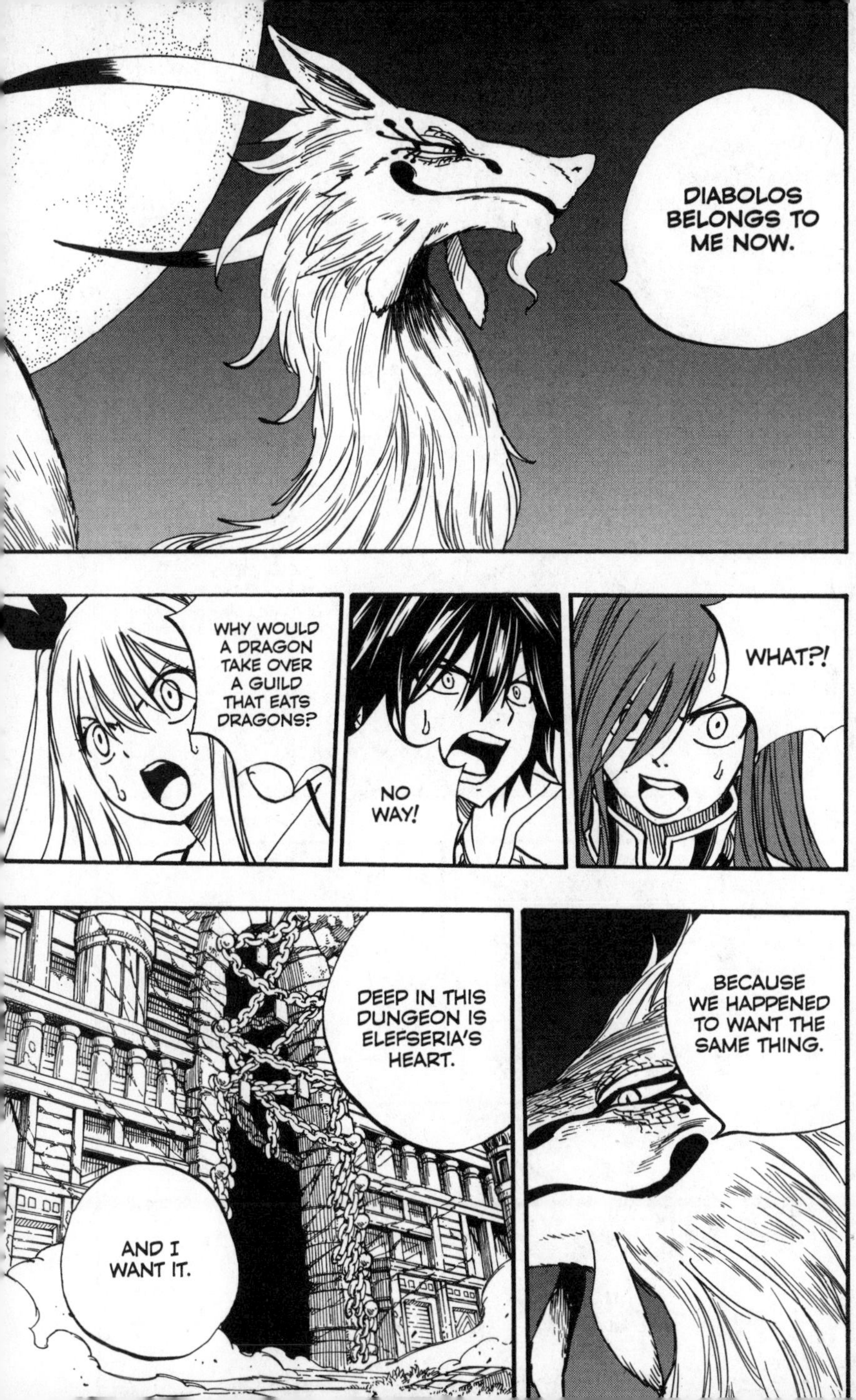
DIABOLOS BELONGS TO ME NOW.
WHAT?!
NO WAY!
WHY WOULD A DRAGON TAKE OVER A GUILD THAT EATS DRAGONS?
BECAUSE WE HAPPENED TO WANT THE SAME THING.
DEEP IN THIS DUNGEON IS ELEFSERIA'S HEART.
AND I WANT IT.

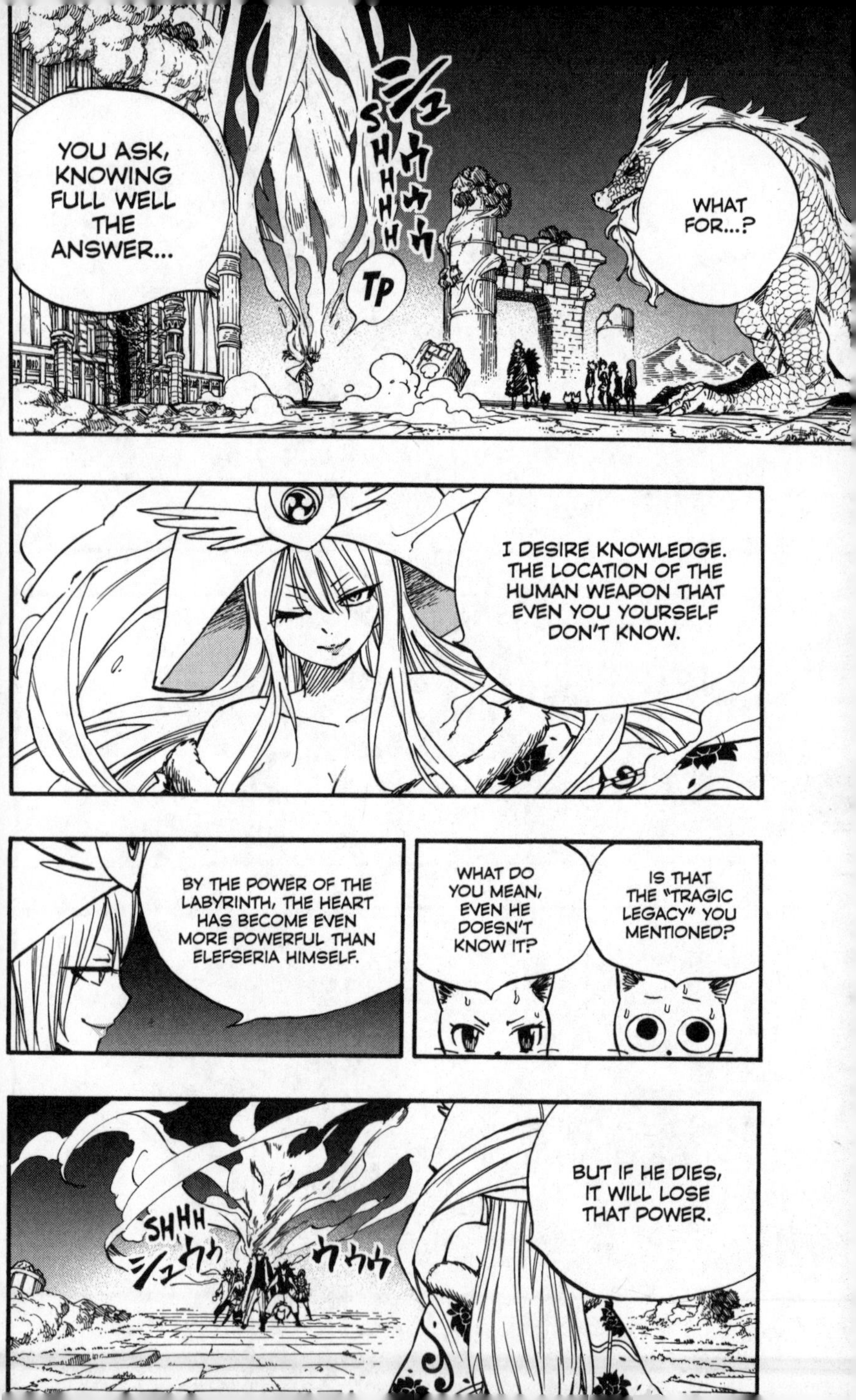
WHAT FOR...?
シュウウウ
SHHHHH
YOU ASK, KNOWING FULL WELL THE ANSWER...
TP
I DESIRE KNOWLEDGE. THE LOCATION OF THE HUMAN WEAPON THAT EVEN YOU YOURSELF DON'T KNOW.
IS THAT THE "TRAGIC LEGACY" YOU MENTIONED?
WHAT DO YOU MEAN, EVEN HE DOESN'T KNOW IT?
BY THE POWER OF THE LABYRINTH, THE HEART HAS BECOME EVEN MORE POWERFUL THAN ELEFSERIA HIMSELF.
BUT IF HE DIES, IT WILL LOSE THAT POWER.
SHHH
シュウウ
ウウウ

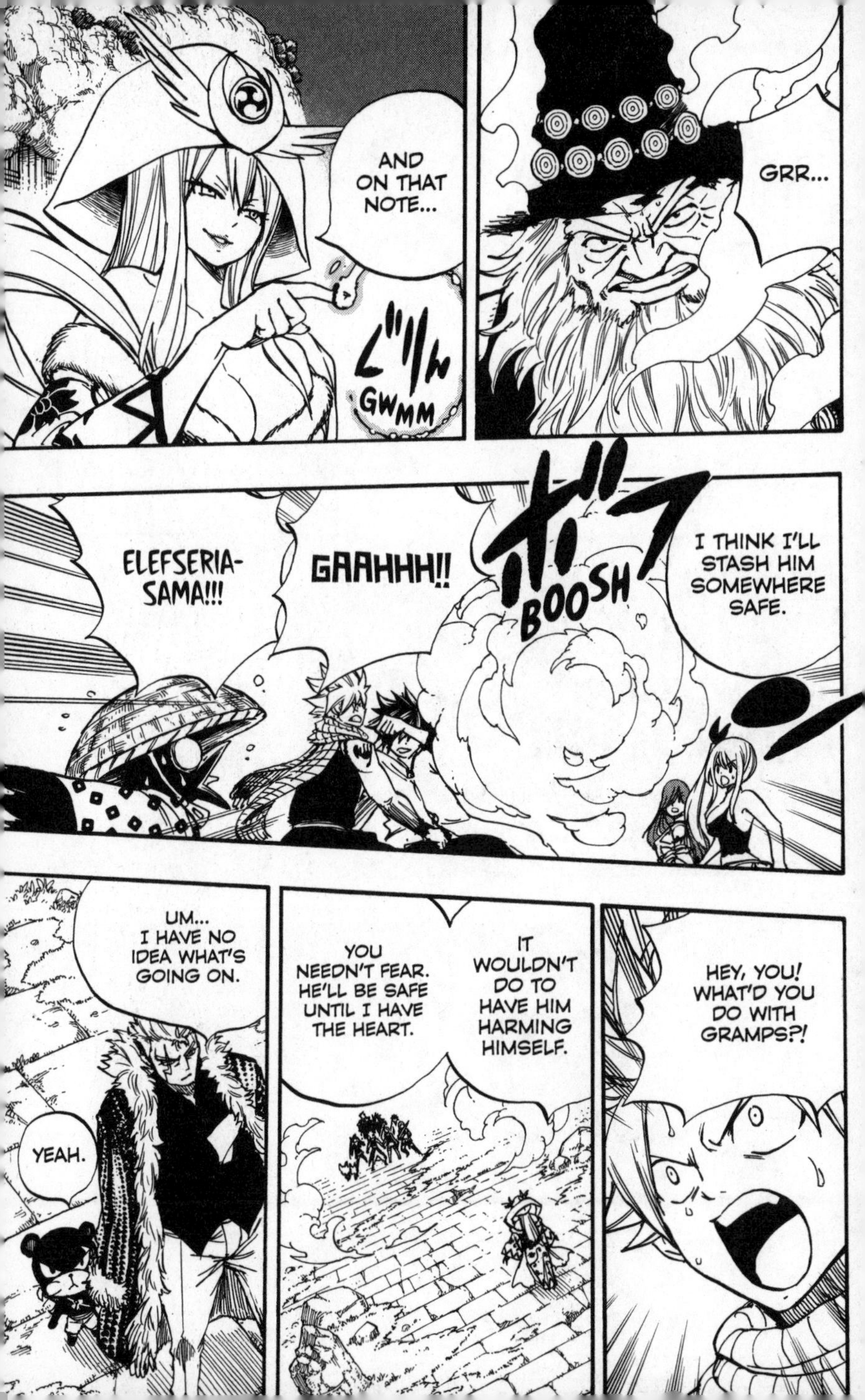
GRR...
AND ON THAT NOTE...
GWMM
I THINK I'LL STASH HIM SOMEWHERE SAFE.
BOOSH
GAAHHH!!
ELEFSERIA-SAMA!!!
HEY, YOU! WHAT'D YOU DO WITH GRAMPS?!
IT WOULDN'T DO TO HAVE HIM HARMING HIMSELF.
YOU NEEDN'T FEAR. HE'LL BE SAFE UNTIL I HAVE THE HEART.
UM... I HAVE NO IDEA WHAT'S GOING ON.
YEAH.

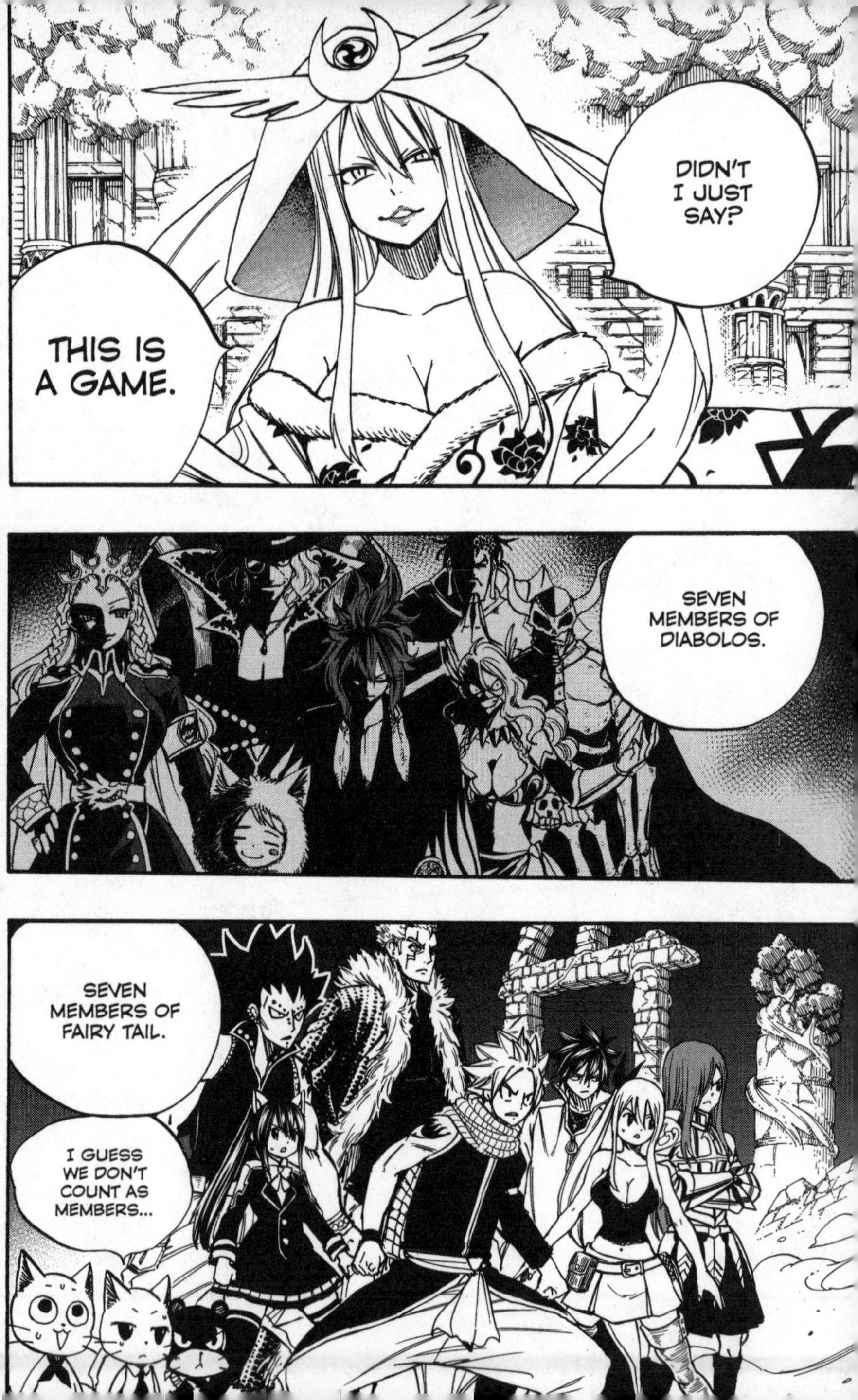
DIDN'T I JUST SAY?
THIS IS A GAME.
SEVEN MEMBERS OF DIABOLOS.
SEVEN MEMBERS OF FAIRY TAIL.
I GUESS WE DON'T COUNT AS MEMBERS...

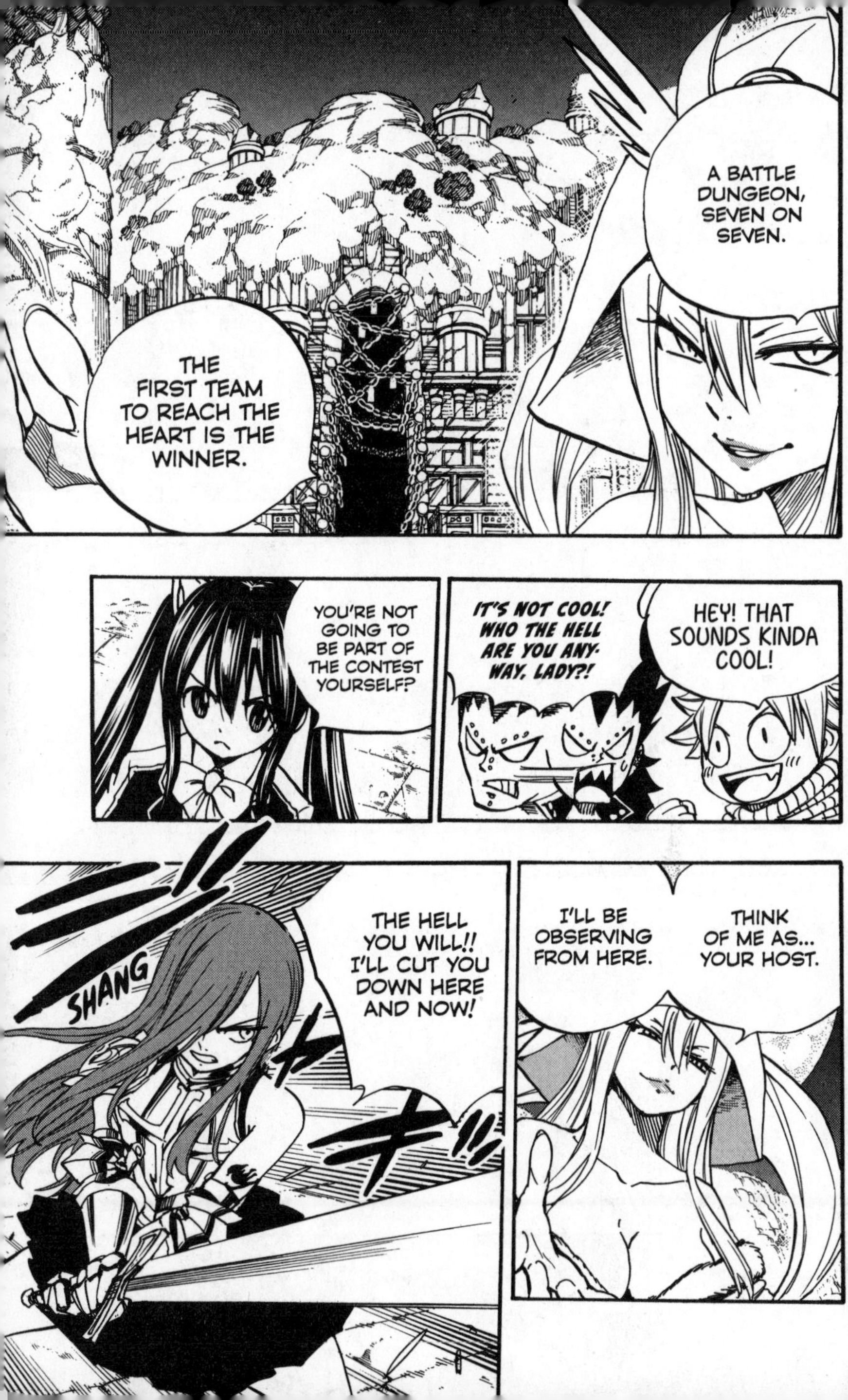
A BATTLE DUNGEON, SEVEN ON SEVEN.
THE FIRST TEAM TO REACH THE HEART IS THE WINNER.
HEY! THAT SOUNDS KINDA COOL!
IT'S NOT COOL! WHO THE HELL ARE YOU ANYWAY, LADY?!
YOU'RE NOT GOING TO BE PART OF THE CONTEST YOURSELF?
THINK OF ME AS... YOUR HOST.
I'LL BE OBSERVING FROM HERE.
THE HELL YOU WILL!! I'LL CUT YOU DOWN HERE AND NOW!
SHANG

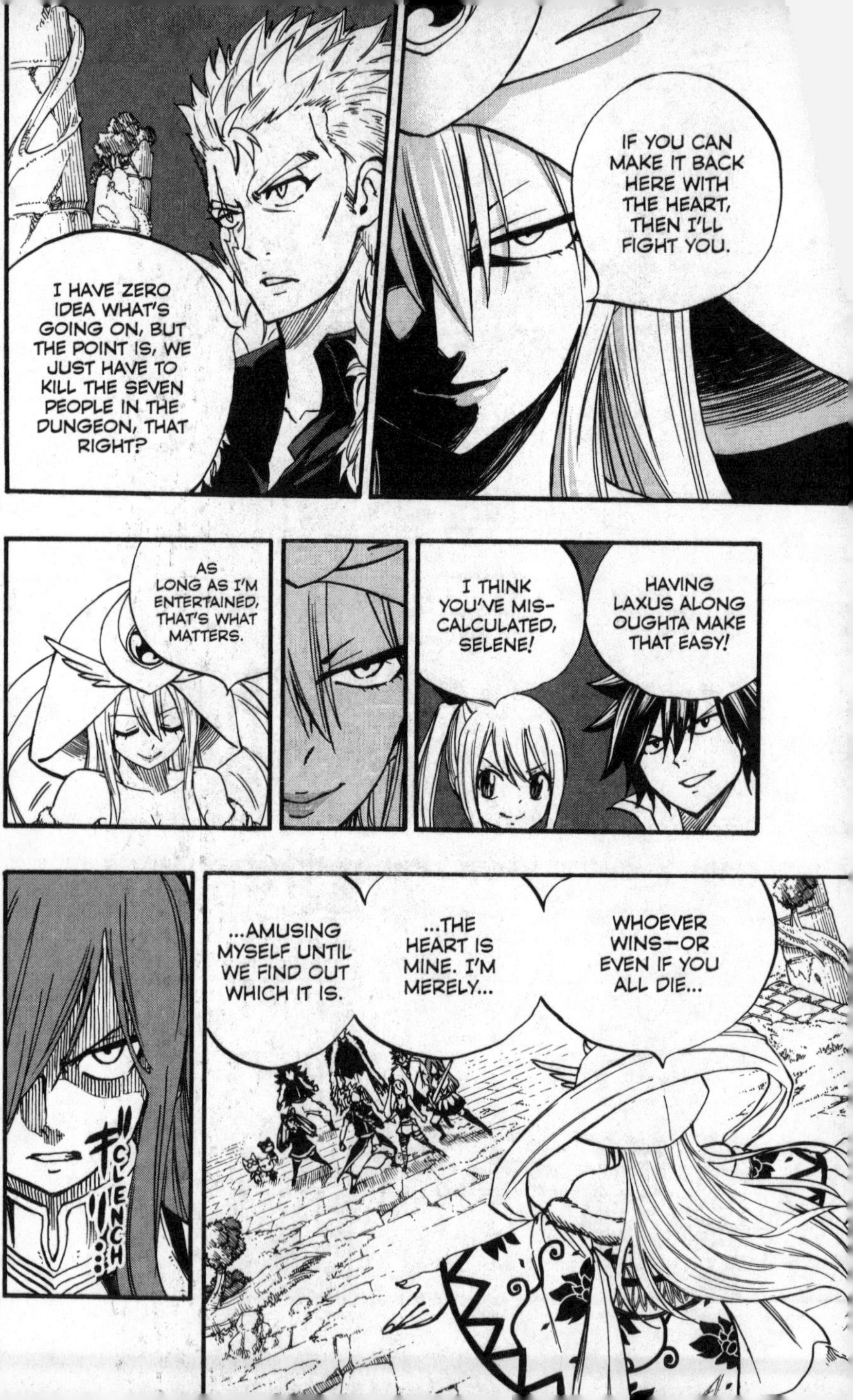
IF YOU CAN MAKE IT BACK HERE WITH THE HEART, THEN I'LL FIGHT YOU.
I HAVE ZERO IDEA WHAT'S GOING ON, BUT THE POINT IS, WE JUST HAVE TO KILL THE SEVEN PEOPLE IN THE DUNGEON, THAT RIGHT?
HAVING LAXUS ALONG OUGHTA MAKE THAT EASY!
I THINK YOU'VE MIS-CALCULATED, SELENE!
AS LONG AS I'M ENTERTAINED, THAT'S WHAT MATTERS.
WHOEVER WINS—OR EVEN IF YOU ALL DIE...
...THE HEART IS MINE. I'M MERELY...
...AMUSING MYSELF UNTIL WE FIND OUT WHICH IT IS.
CLENCH...

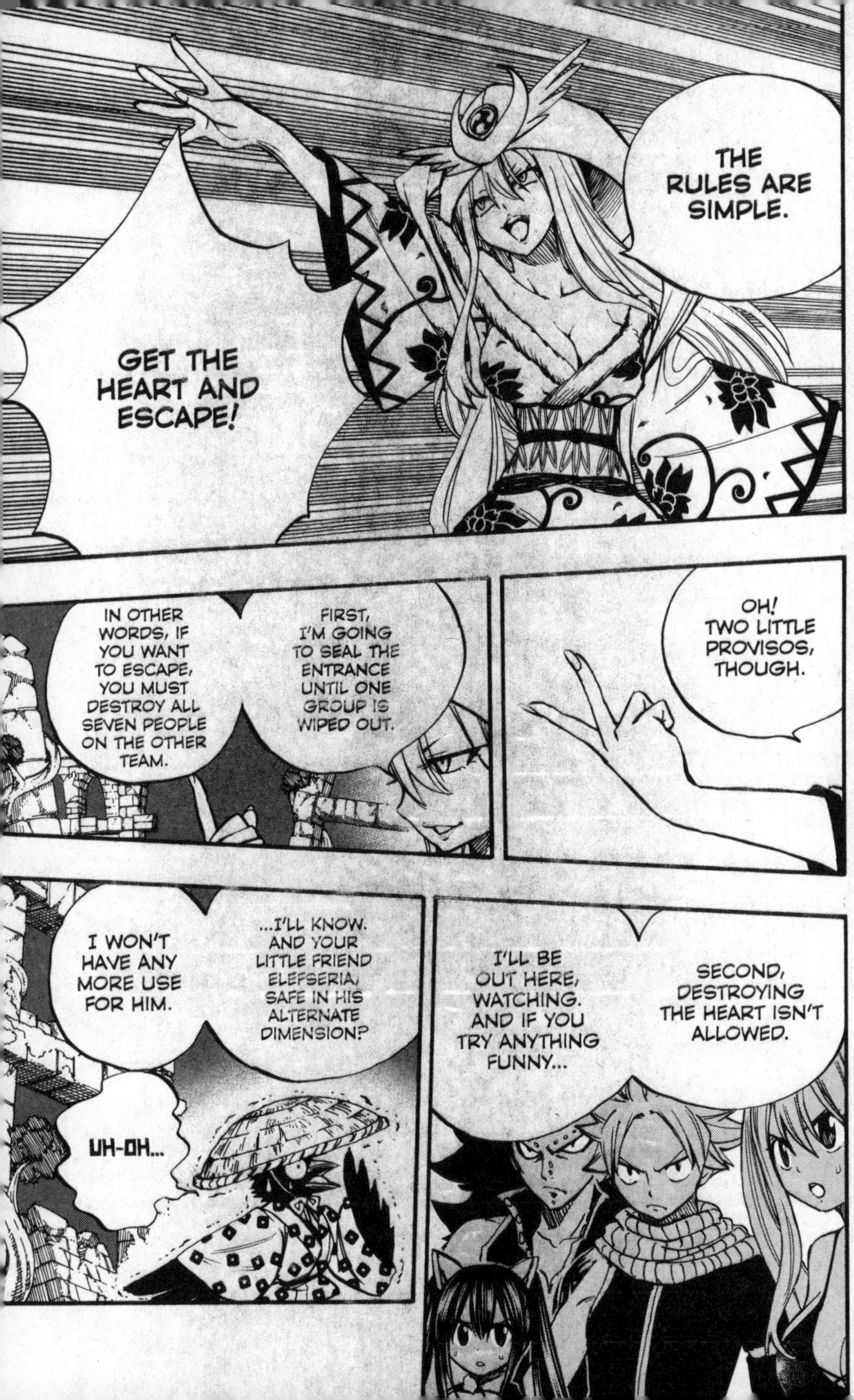
THE RULES ARE SIMPLE.
GET THE HEART AND ESCAPE!
OH! TWO LITTLE PROVISOS, THOUGH.
FIRST, I'M GOING TO SEAL THE ENTRANCE UNTIL ONE GROUP IS WIPED OUT.
IN OTHER WORDS, IF YOU WANT TO ESCAPE, YOU MUST DESTROY ALL SEVEN PEOPLE ON THE OTHER TEAM.
SECOND, DESTROYING THE HEART ISN'T ALLOWED.
I'LL BE OUT HERE, WATCHING. AND IF YOU TRY ANYTHING FUNNY...
...I'LL KNOW. AND YOUR LITTLE FRIEND ELEFSERIA, SAFE IN HIS ALTERNATE DIMENSION?
I WON'T HAVE ANY MORE USE FOR HIM.
UH-OH...

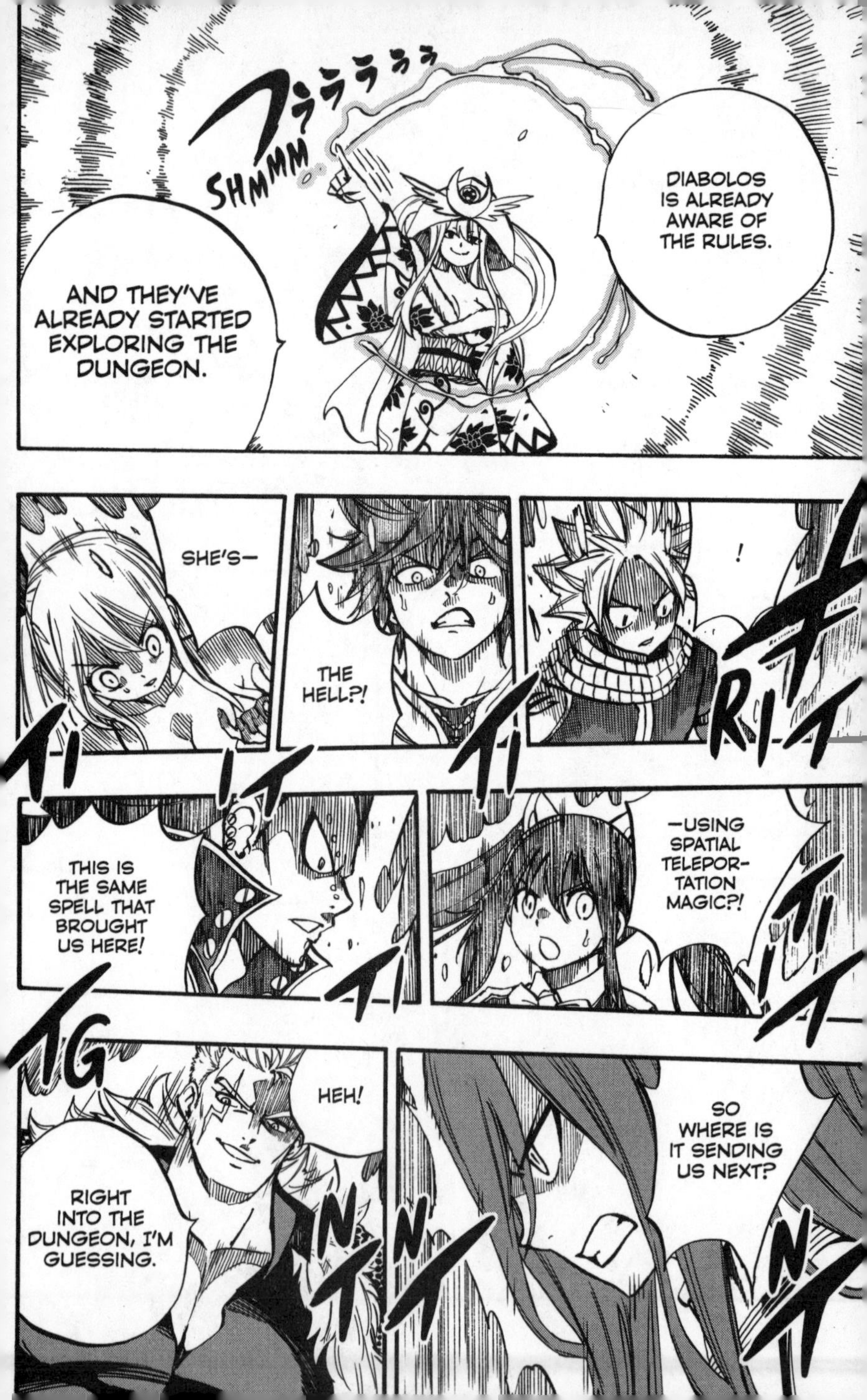

SHMMM
DIABOLOS IS ALREADY AWARE OF THE RULES.
AND THEY'VE ALREADY STARTED EXPLORING THE DUNGEON.
!
THE HELL?!
SHE'S—
—USING SPATIAL TELEPORTATION MAGIC?!
THIS IS THE SAME SPELL THAT BROUGHT US HERE!
SO WHERE IS IT SENDING US NEXT?
HEH!
RIGHT INTO THE DUNGEON, I'M GUESSING.

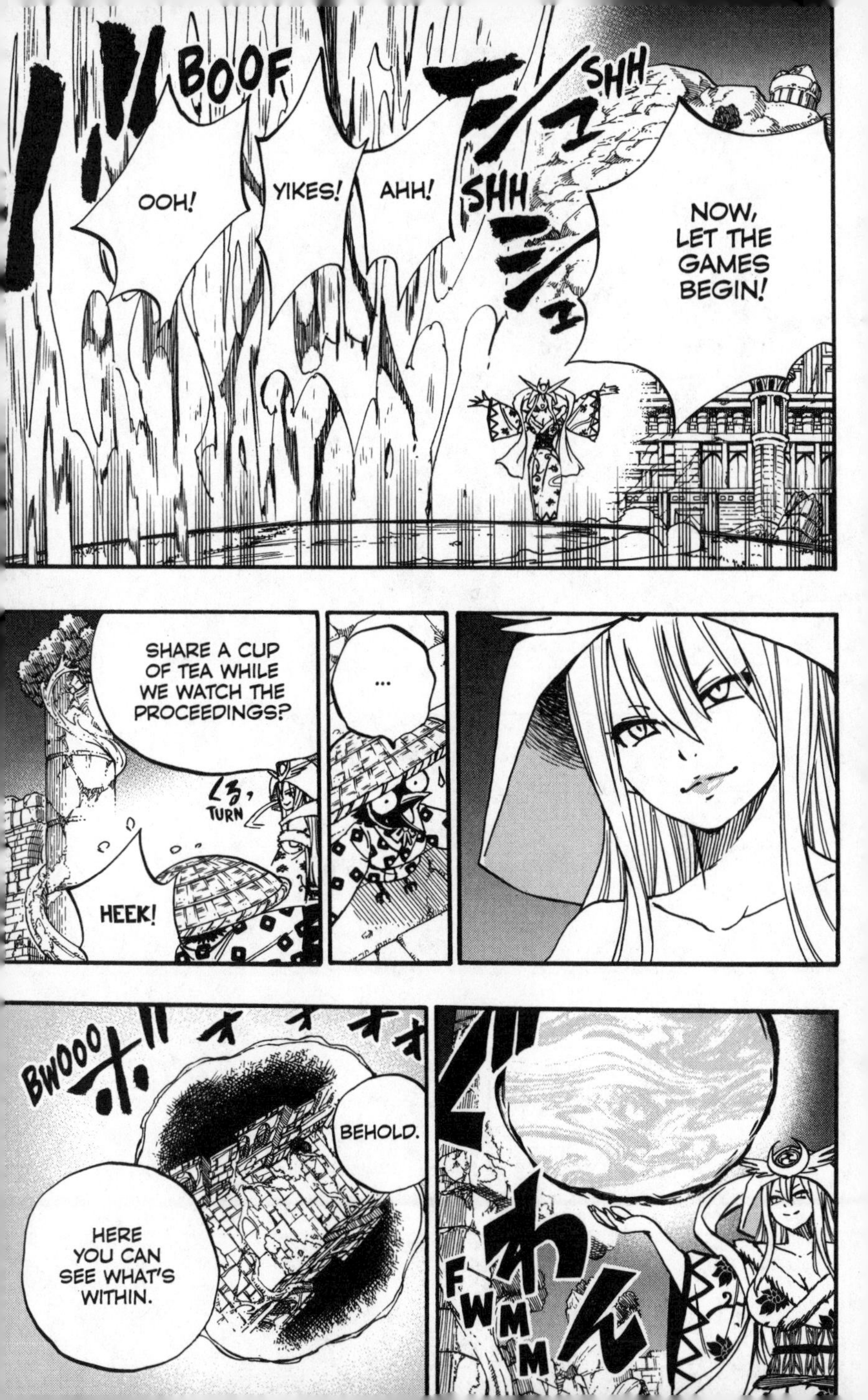
SHH
NOW, LET THE GAMES BEGIN!
SHH
AHH!
YIKES!
BOOF
OOH!
...
SHARE A CUP OF TEA WHILE WE WATCH THE PROCEEDINGS?
くる
TURN
HEEK!
わん
FWMM
BEHOLD.
BWOOO
HERE YOU CAN SEE WHAT'S WITHIN.

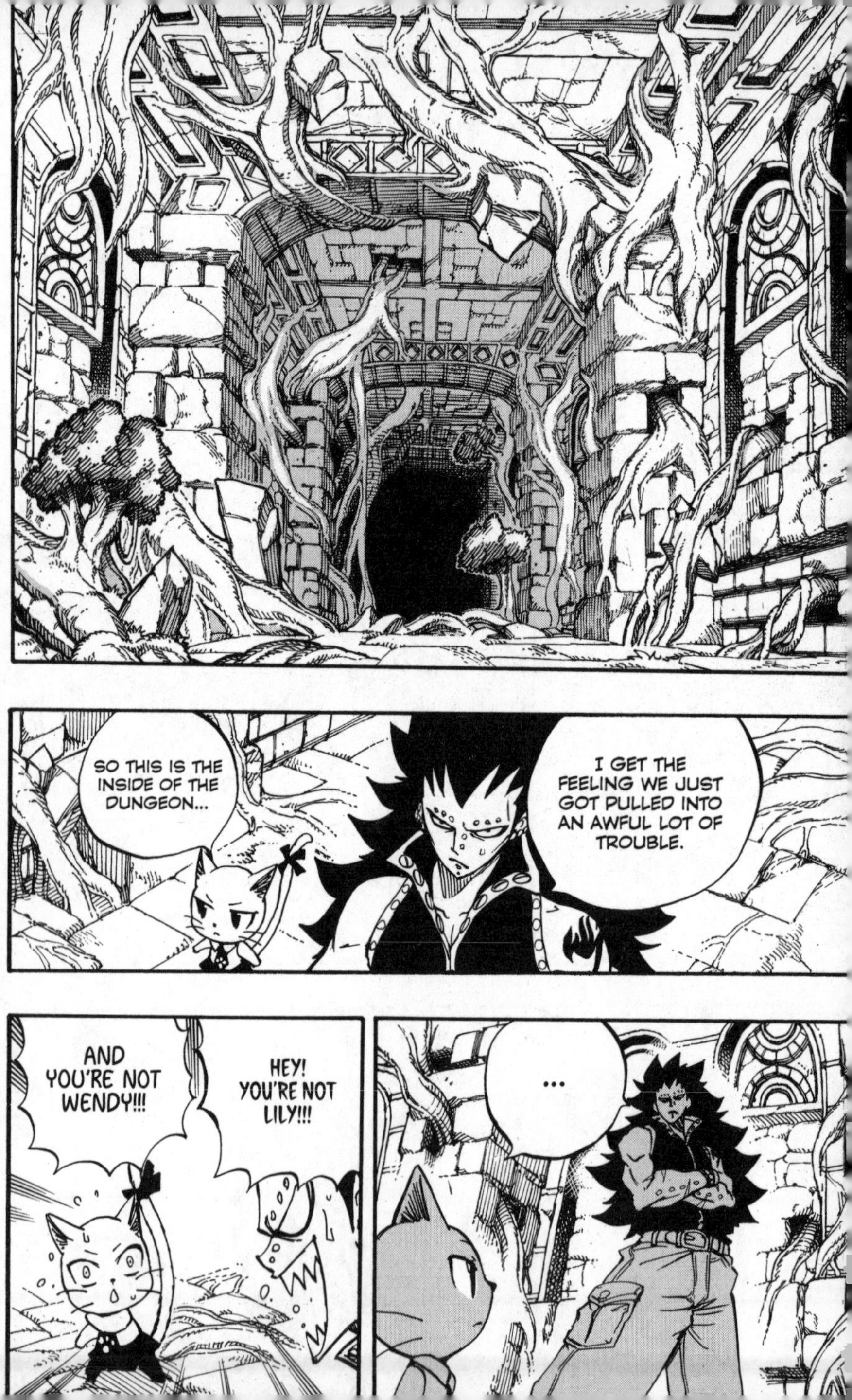
I GET THE FEELING WE JUST GOT PULLED INTO AN AWFUL LOT OF TROUBLE.
SO THIS IS THE INSIDE OF THE DUNGEON...
...
HEY! YOU'RE NOT LILY!!!
AND YOU'RE NOT WENDY!!!

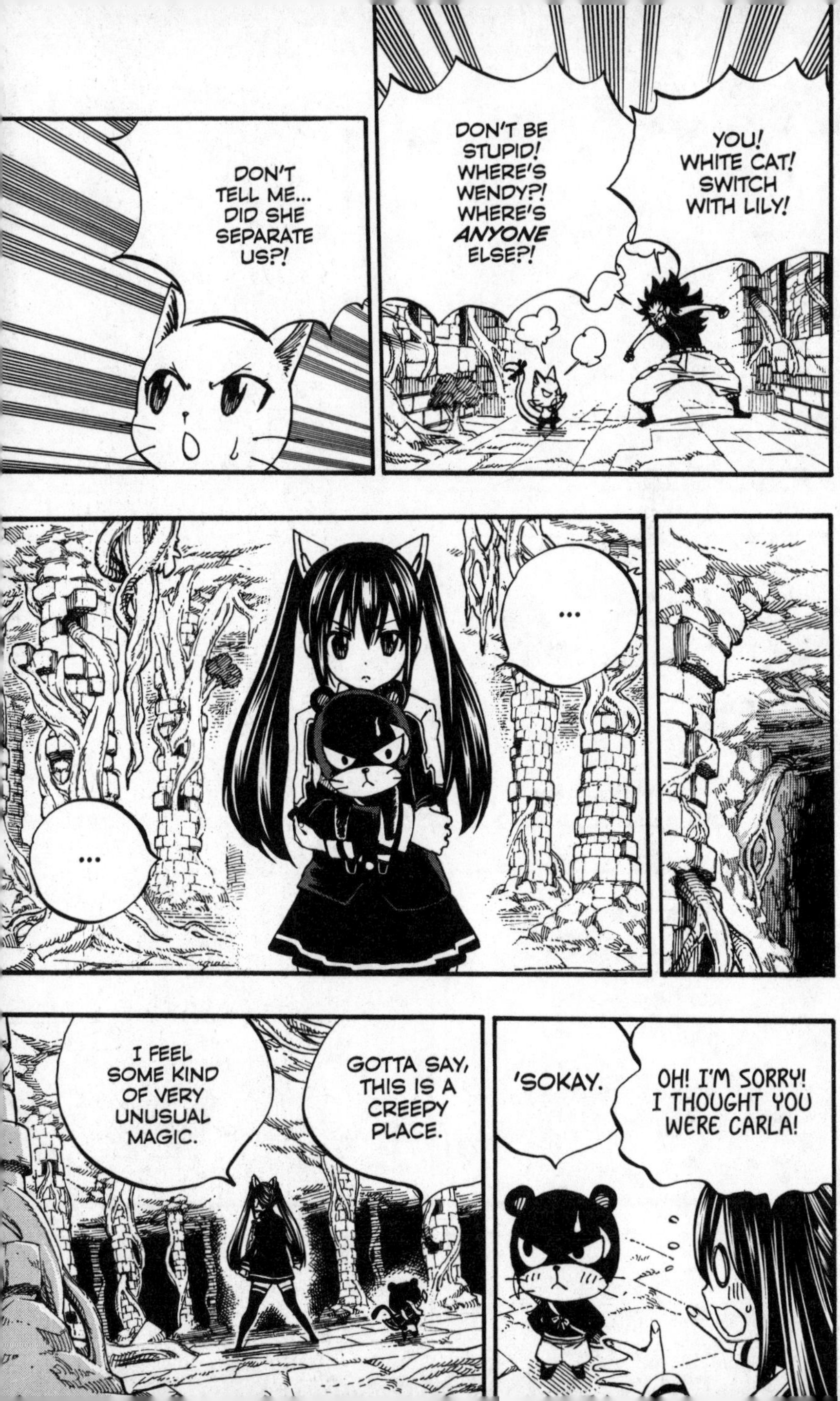
YOU! WHITE CAT! SWITCH WITH LILY!
DON'T BE STUPID! WHERE'S WENDY?! WHERE'S *ANYONE* ELSE?!
DON'T TELL ME... DID SHE SEPARATE US?!
...
...
OH! I'M SORRY! I THOUGHT YOU WERE CARLA!
'SOKAY.
GOTTA SAY, THIS IS A CREEPY PLACE.
I FEEL SOME KIND OF VERY UNUSUAL MAGIC.

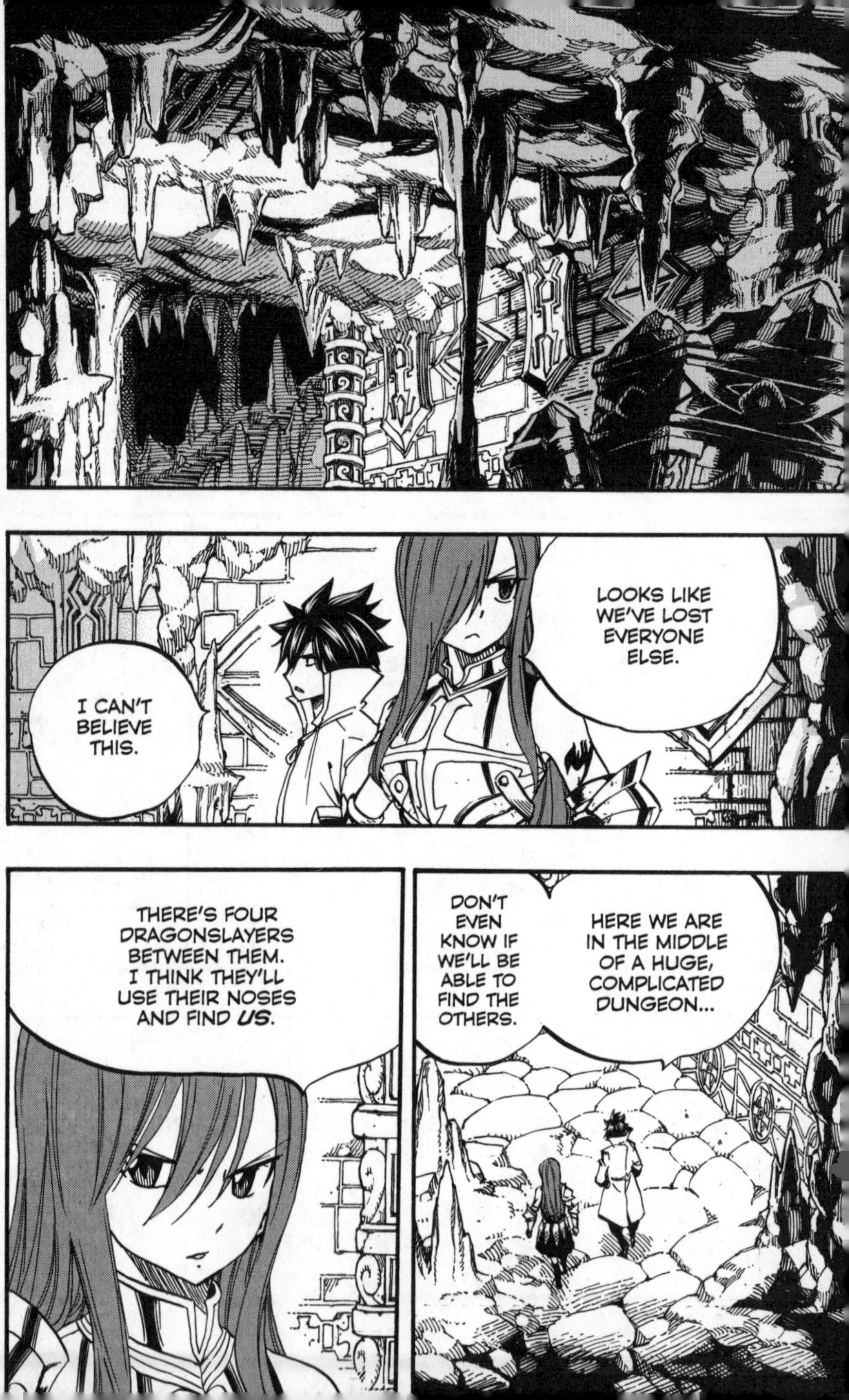
LOOKS LIKE WE'VE LOST EVERYONE ELSE.
I CAN'T BELIEVE THIS.
HERE WE ARE IN THE MIDDLE OF A HUGE, COMPLICATED DUNGEON...
DON'T EVEN KNOW IF WE'LL BE ABLE TO FIND THE OTHERS.
THERE'S FOUR DRAGONSLAYERS BETWEEN THEM. I THINK THEY'LL USE THEIR NOSES AND FIND *US*.

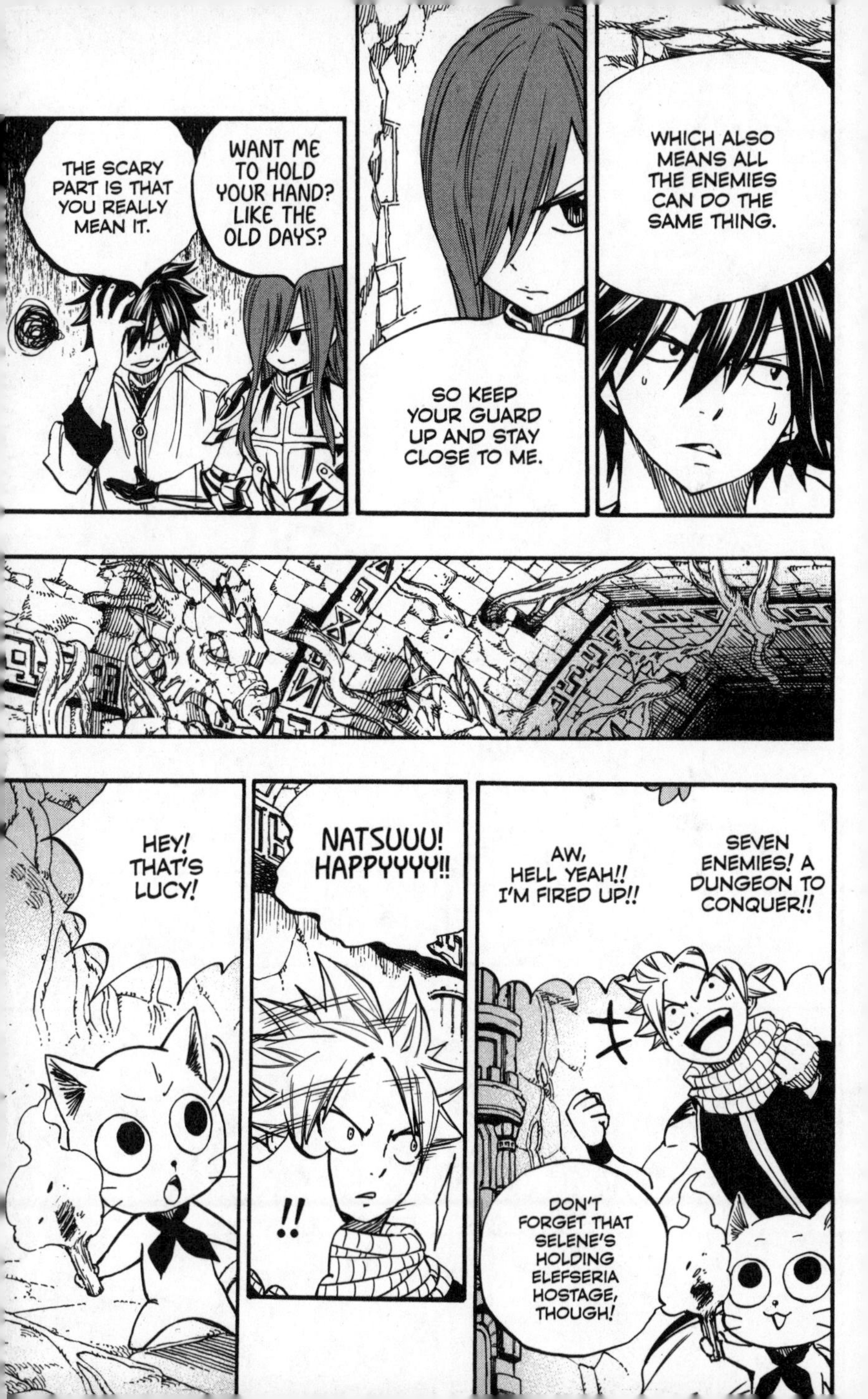
WHICH ALSO MEANS ALL THE ENEMIES CAN DO THE SAME THING.
SO KEEP YOUR GUARD UP AND STAY CLOSE TO ME.
WANT ME TO HOLD YOUR HAND? LIKE THE OLD DAYS?
THE SCARY PART IS THAT YOU REALLY MEAN IT.
SEVEN ENEMIES! A DUNGEON TO CONQUER!!
AW, HELL YEAH!! I'M FIRED UP!!
DON'T FORGET THAT SELENE'S HOLDING ELEFSERIA HOSTAGE, THOUGH!
NATSUUU! HAPPYYYY!!
!!
HEY! THAT'S LUCY!

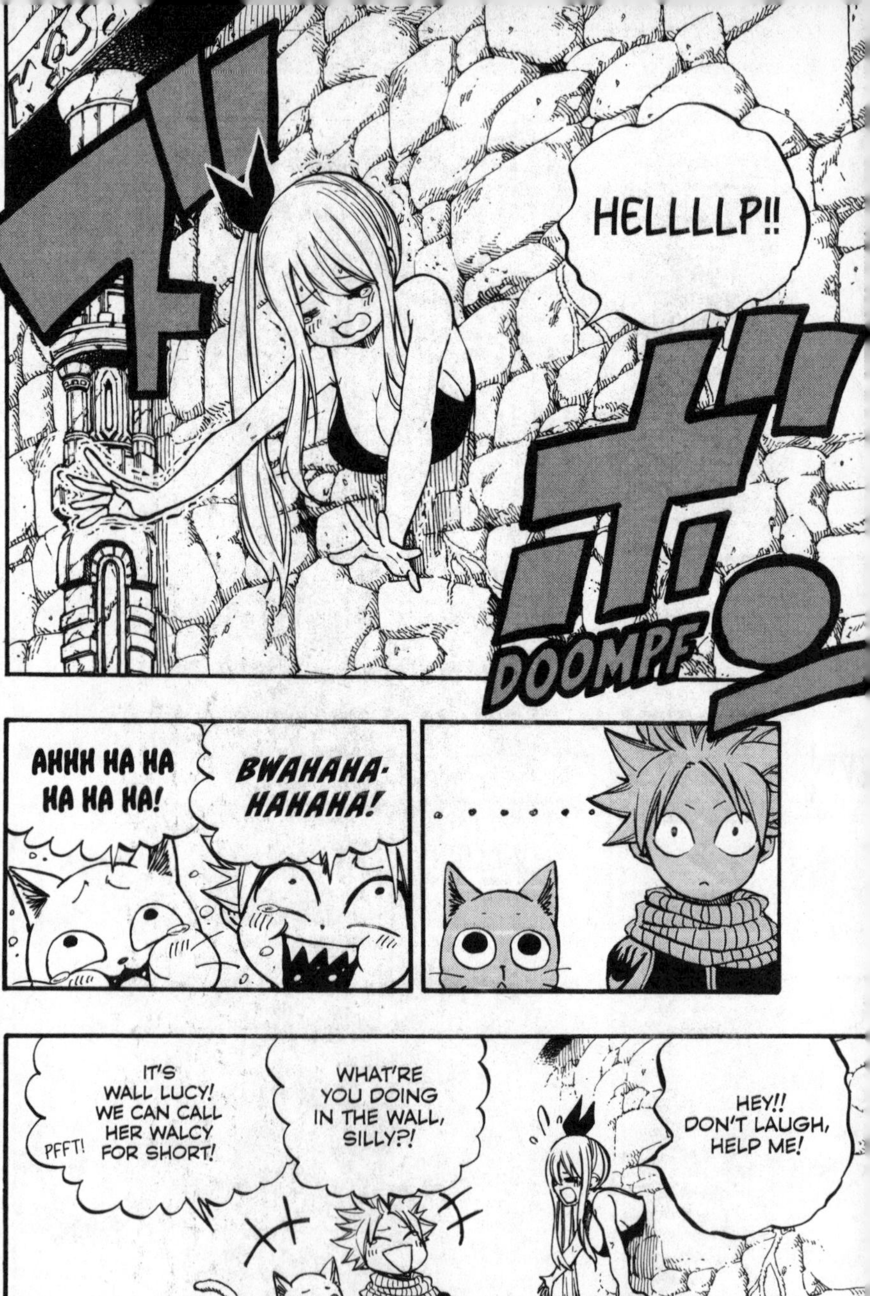
HELLLLP!!
DOOMPF
......
BWAHAHA-HAHAHA!
AHHH HA HA HA HA HA!
HEY!! DON'T LAUGH, HELP ME!
WHAT'RE YOU DOING IN THE WALL, SILLY?!
IT'S WALL LUCY! WE CAN CALL HER WALCY FOR SHORT!
PFFT!

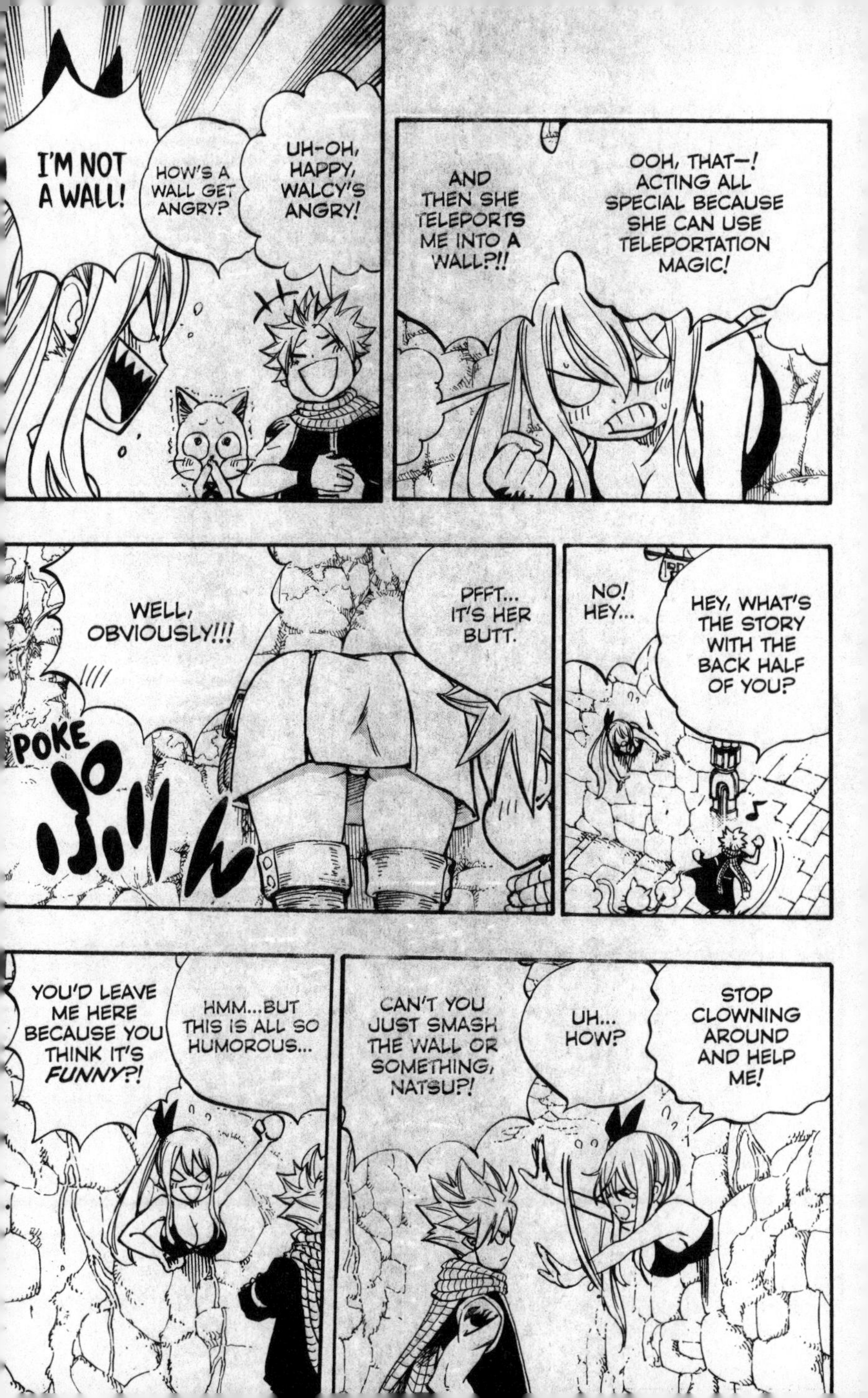

OOH, THAT—! ACTING ALL SPECIAL BECAUSE SHE CAN USE TELEPORTATION MAGIC!
AND THEN SHE TELEPORTS ME INTO A WALL?!!
UH-OH, HAPPY, WALCY'S ANGRY!
HOW'S A WALL GET ANGRY?
I'M NOT A WALL!
HEY, WHAT'S THE STORY WITH THE BACK HALF OF YOU?
NO! HEY...
PFFT... IT'S HER BUTT.
WELL, OBVIOUSLY!!!
POKE
STOP CLOWNING AROUND AND HELP ME!
UH... HOW?
CAN'T YOU JUST SMASH THE WALL OR SOMETHING, NATSU?!
HMM...BUT THIS IS ALL SO HUMOROUS...
YOU'D LEAVE ME HERE BECAUSE YOU THINK IT'S *FUNNY*?!

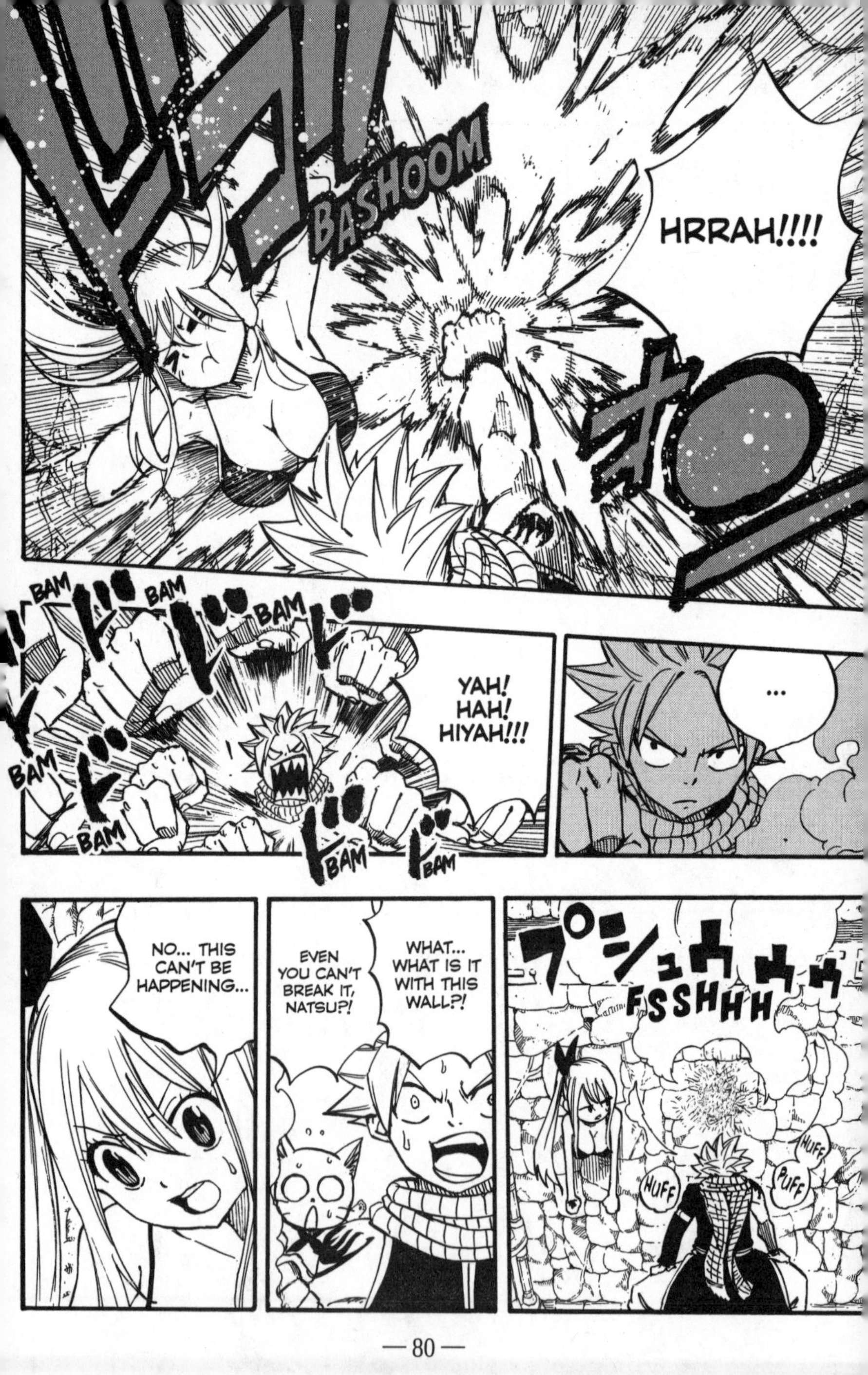
HRRAH!!!!
BASHOOM
...
YAH! HAH! HIYAH!!!
BAM
BAM
BAM
BAM
BAM
BAM
BAM
FSSHHHH
HUFF
PUFF
HUFF
WHAT... WHAT IS IT WITH THIS WALL?!
EVEN YOU CAN'T BREAK IT, NATSU?!
NO... THIS CAN'T BE HAPPENING...

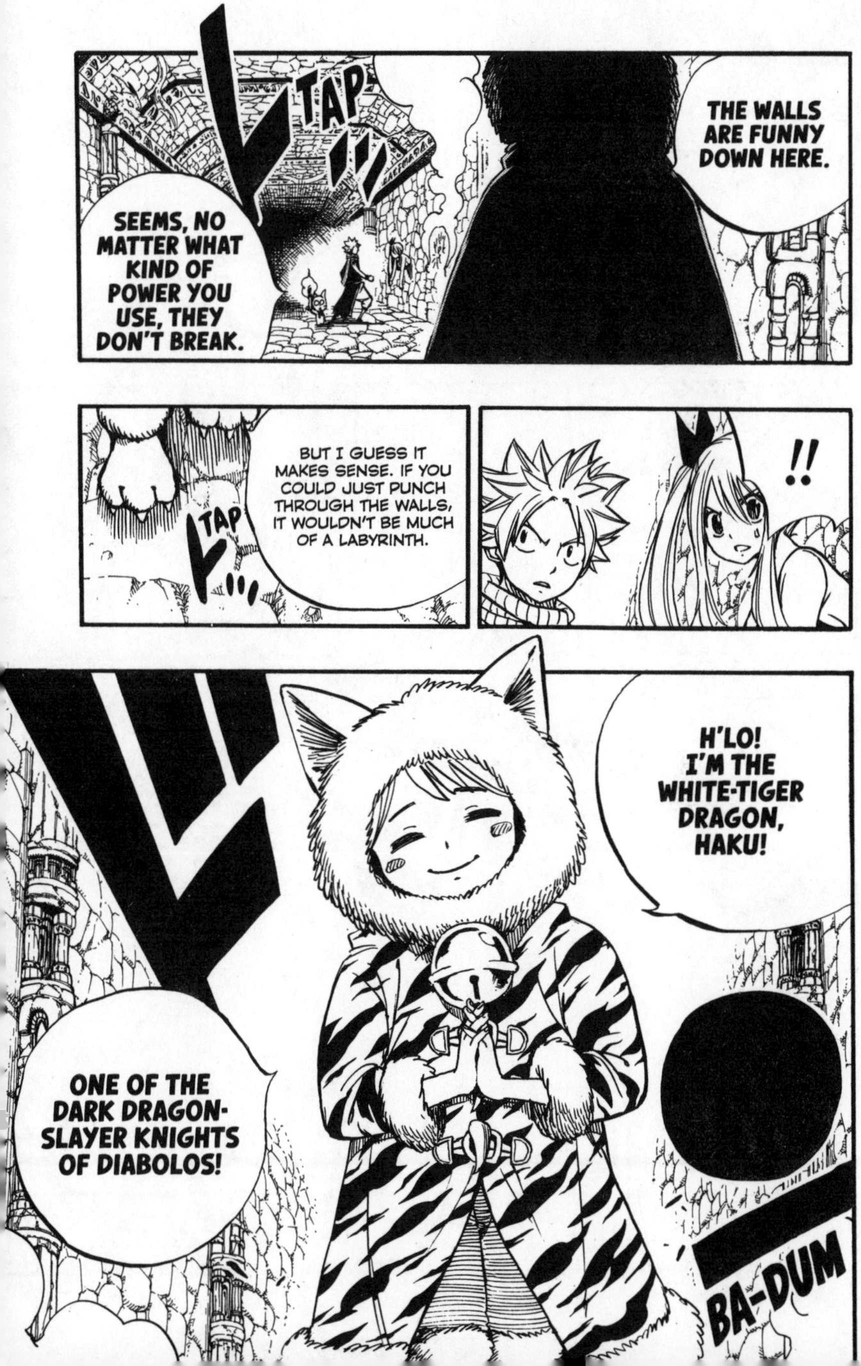
THE WALLS ARE FUNNY DOWN HERE.
TAP...
SEEMS, NO MATTER WHAT KIND OF POWER YOU USE, THEY DON'T BREAK.
!!
BUT I GUESS IT MAKES SENSE. IF YOU COULD JUST PUNCH THROUGH THE WALLS, IT WOULDN'T BE MUCH OF A LABYRINTH.
TAP...
H'LO! I'M THE WHITE-TIGER DRAGON, HAKU!
ONE OF THE DARK DRAGON-SLAYER KNIGHTS OF DIABOLOS!
BA-DUM

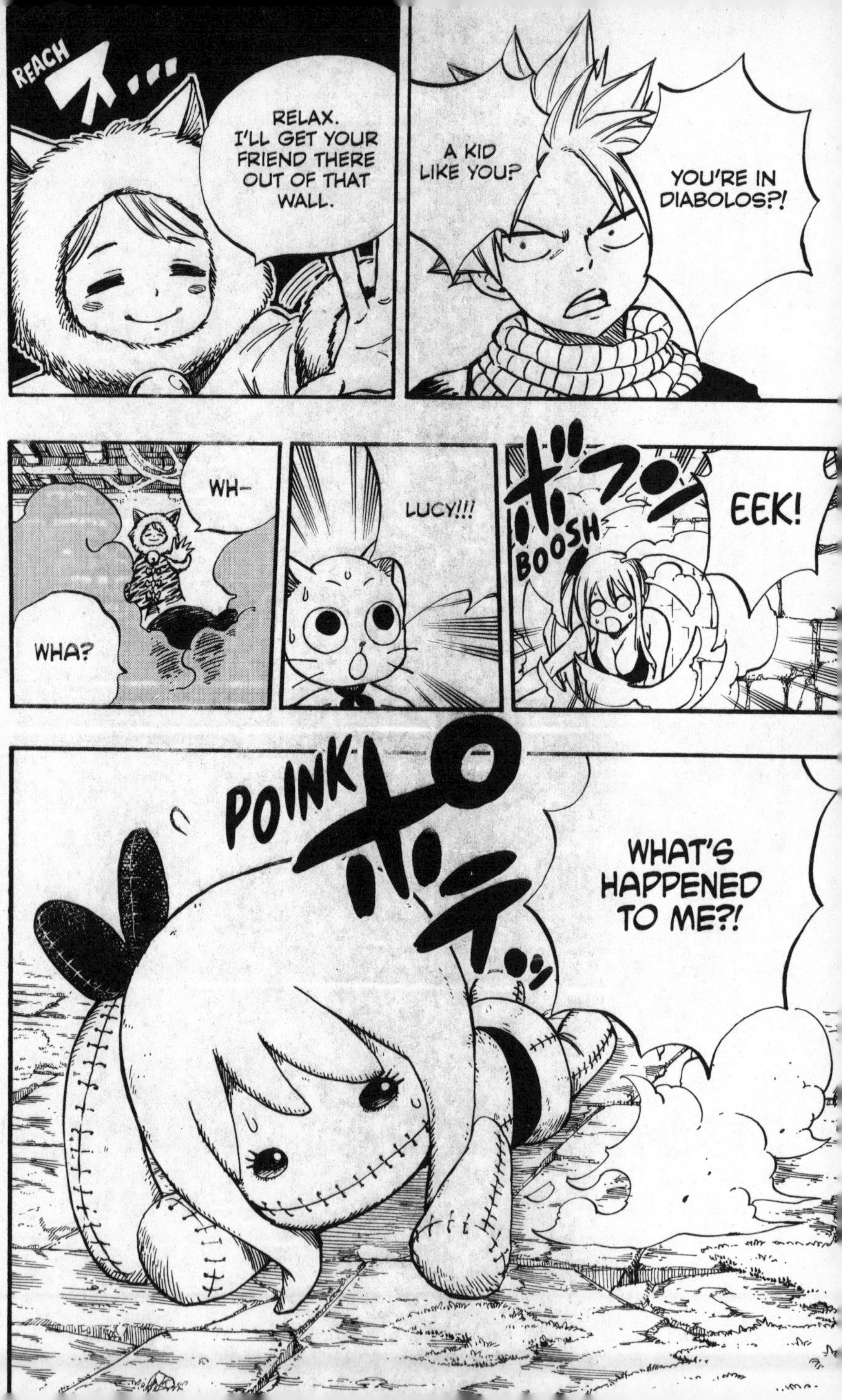
YOU'RE IN DIABOLOS?!
A KID LIKE YOU?
RELAX. I'LL GET YOUR FRIEND THERE OUT OF THAT WALL.
REACH
EEK!
BOOSH
LUCY!!!
WH-
WHA?
WHAT'S HAPPENED TO ME?!
POINK

FAIRY TAIL 100 YEARS QUEST

Chapter 95: Plush Doll

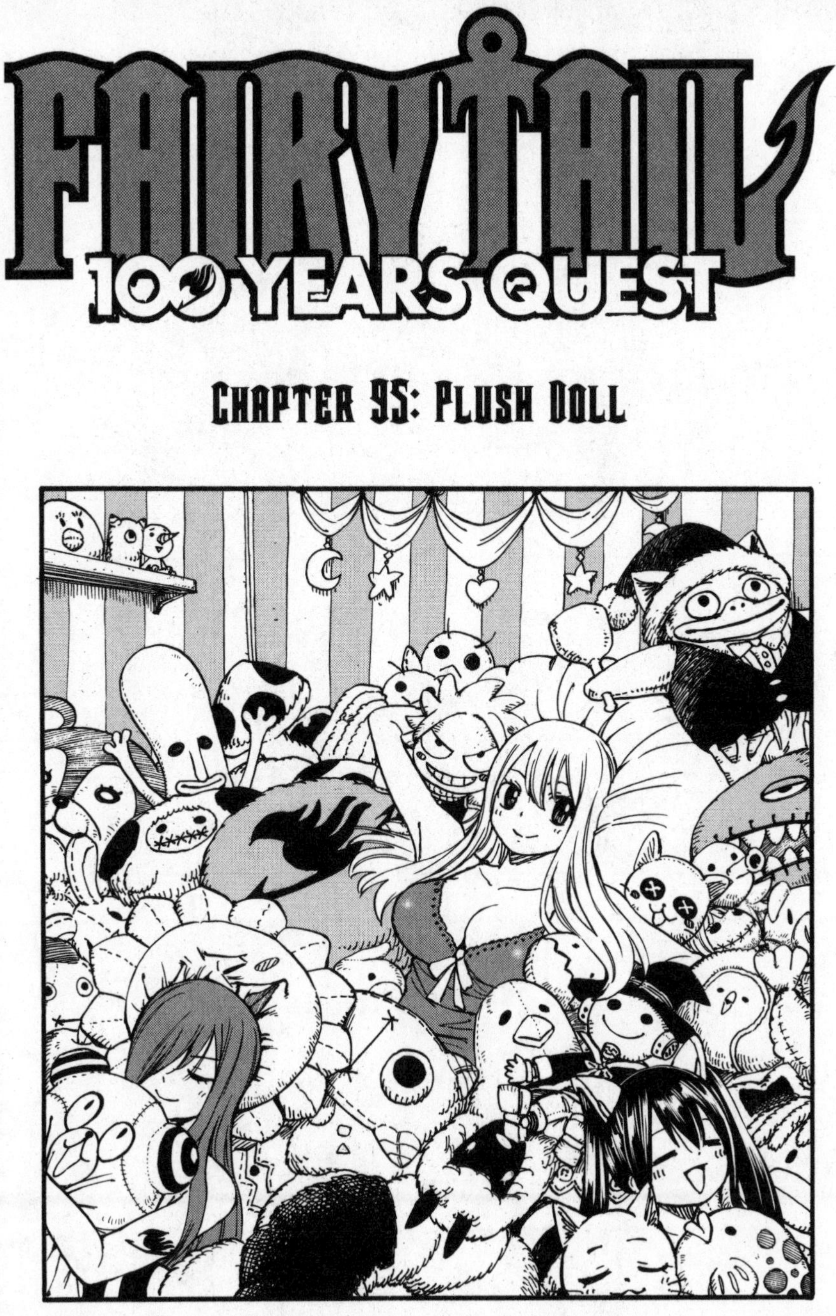

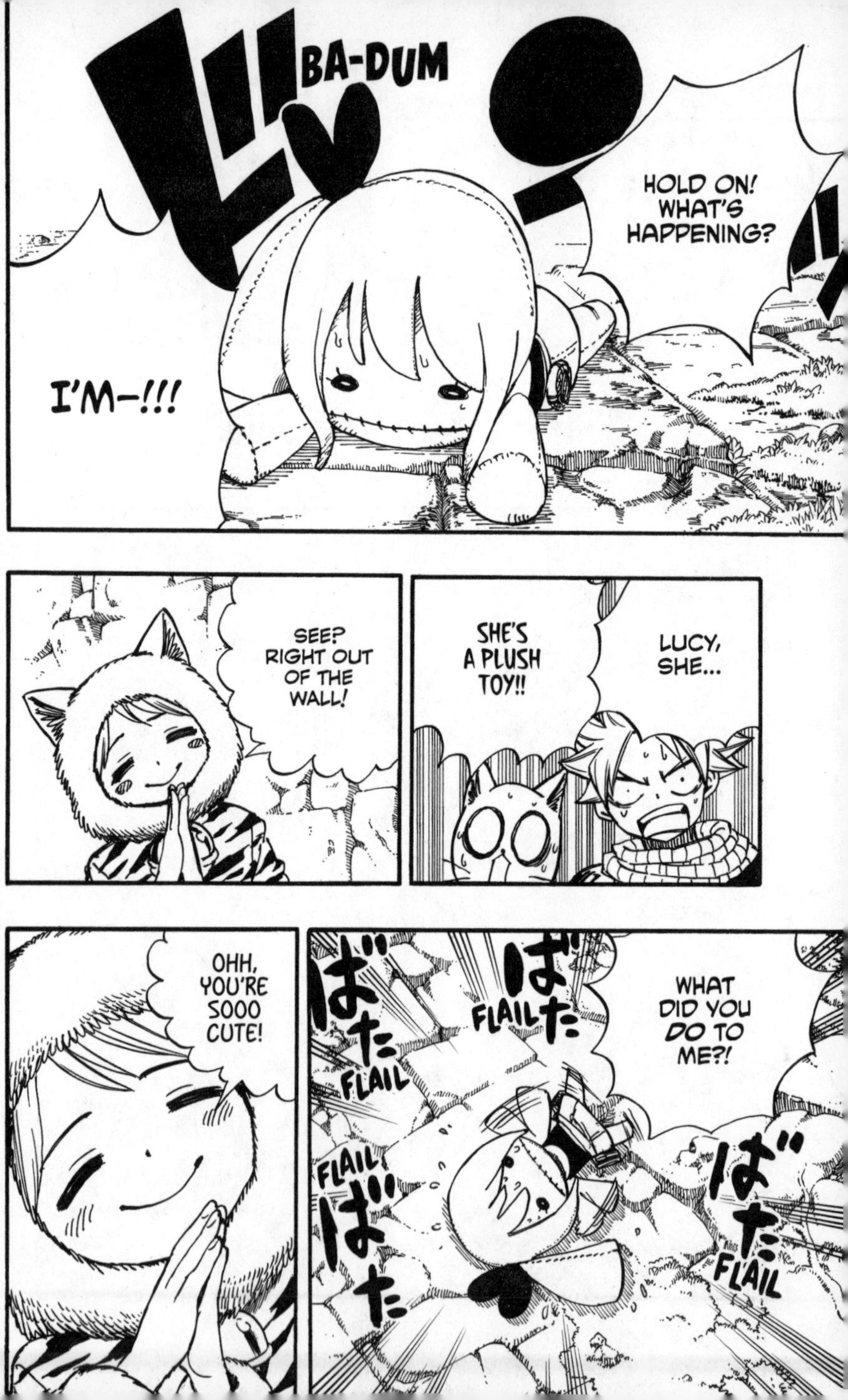
BA-DUM
HOLD ON! WHAT'S HAPPENING?
I'M-!!!
LUCY, SHE...
SHE'S A PLUSH TOY!!
SEE? RIGHT OUT OF THE WALL!
WHAT DID YOU DO TO ME?!
ばた FLAIL
ばた FLAIL
ばた FLAIL
ばた FLAIL
OHH, YOU'RE SOOO CUTE!

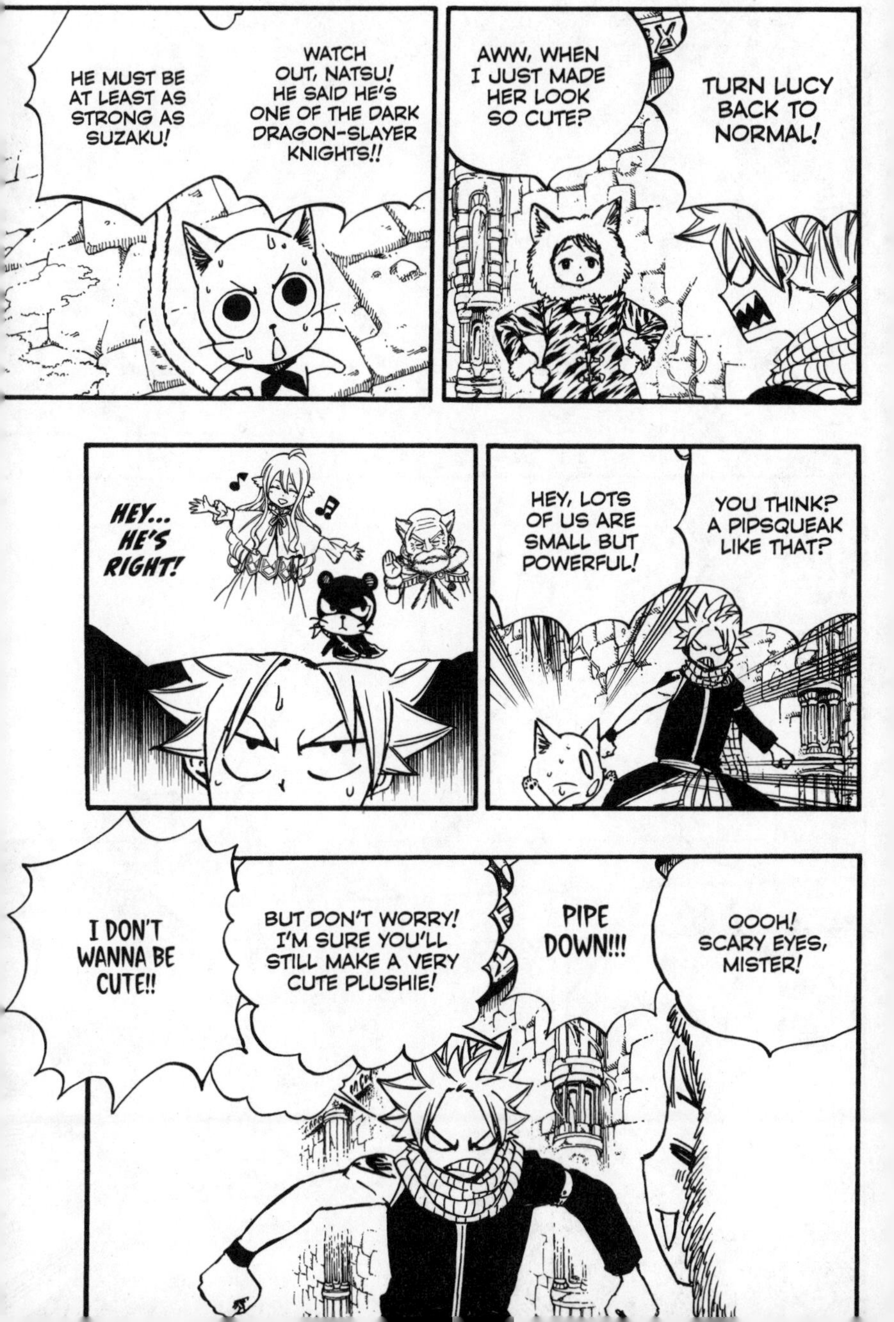
TURN LUCY BACK TO NORMAL!
AWW, WHEN I JUST MADE HER LOOK SO CUTE?
WATCH OUT, NATSU! HE SAID HE'S ONE OF THE DARK DRAGON-SLAYER KNIGHTS!!
HE MUST BE AT LEAST AS STRONG AS SUZAKU!
YOU THINK? A PIPSQUEAK LIKE THAT?
HEY, LOTS OF US ARE SMALL BUT POWERFUL!
HEY... HE'S RIGHT!
OOOH! SCARY EYES, MISTER!
PIPE DOWN!!!
BUT DON'T WORRY! I'M SURE YOU'LL STILL MAKE A VERY CUTE PLUSHIE!
I DON'T WANNA BE CUTE!!

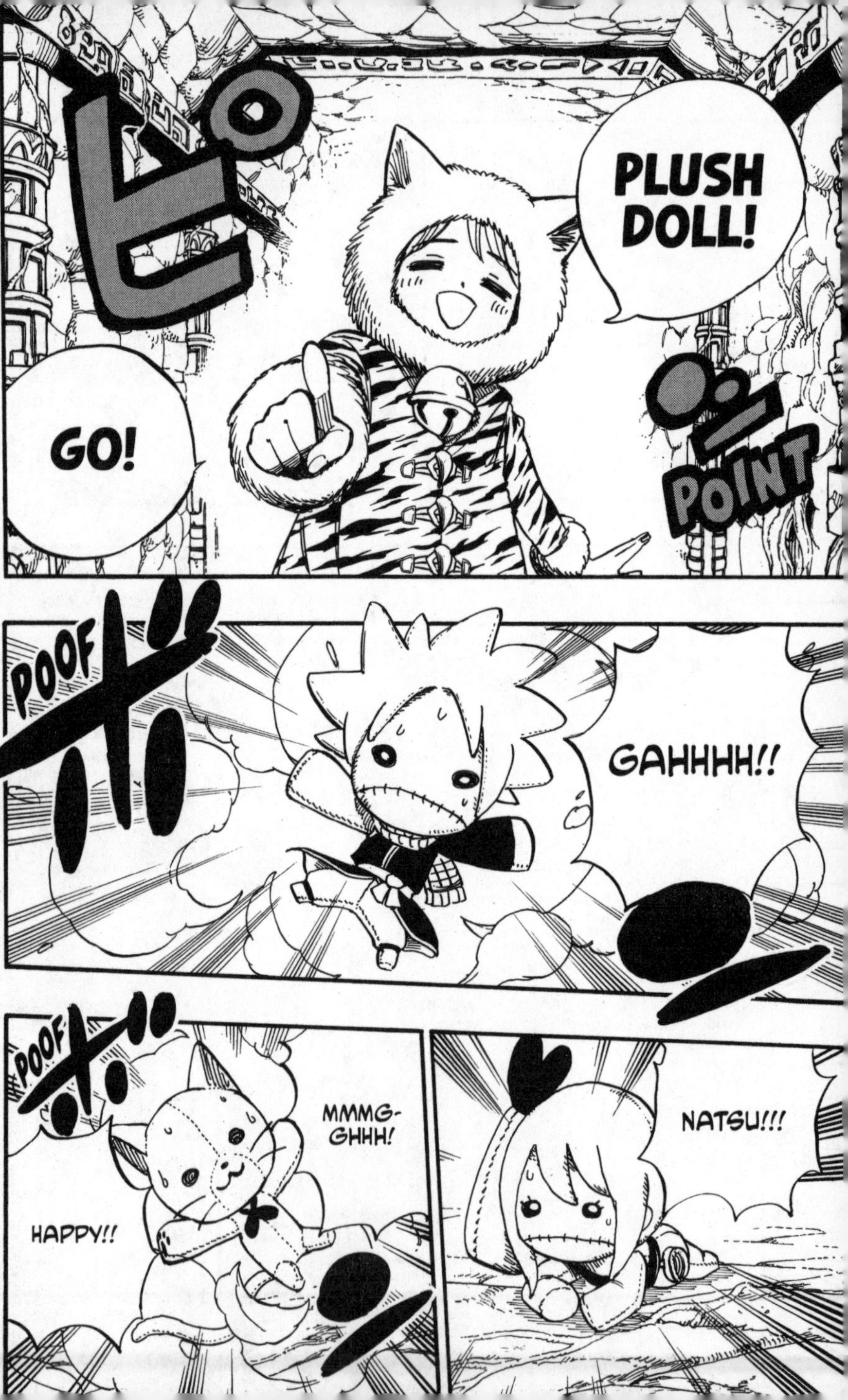
PLUSH DOLL!
POINT
GO!
GAHHHH!!
POOF
NATSU!!!
MMMG-GHHH!
HAPPY!!
POOF

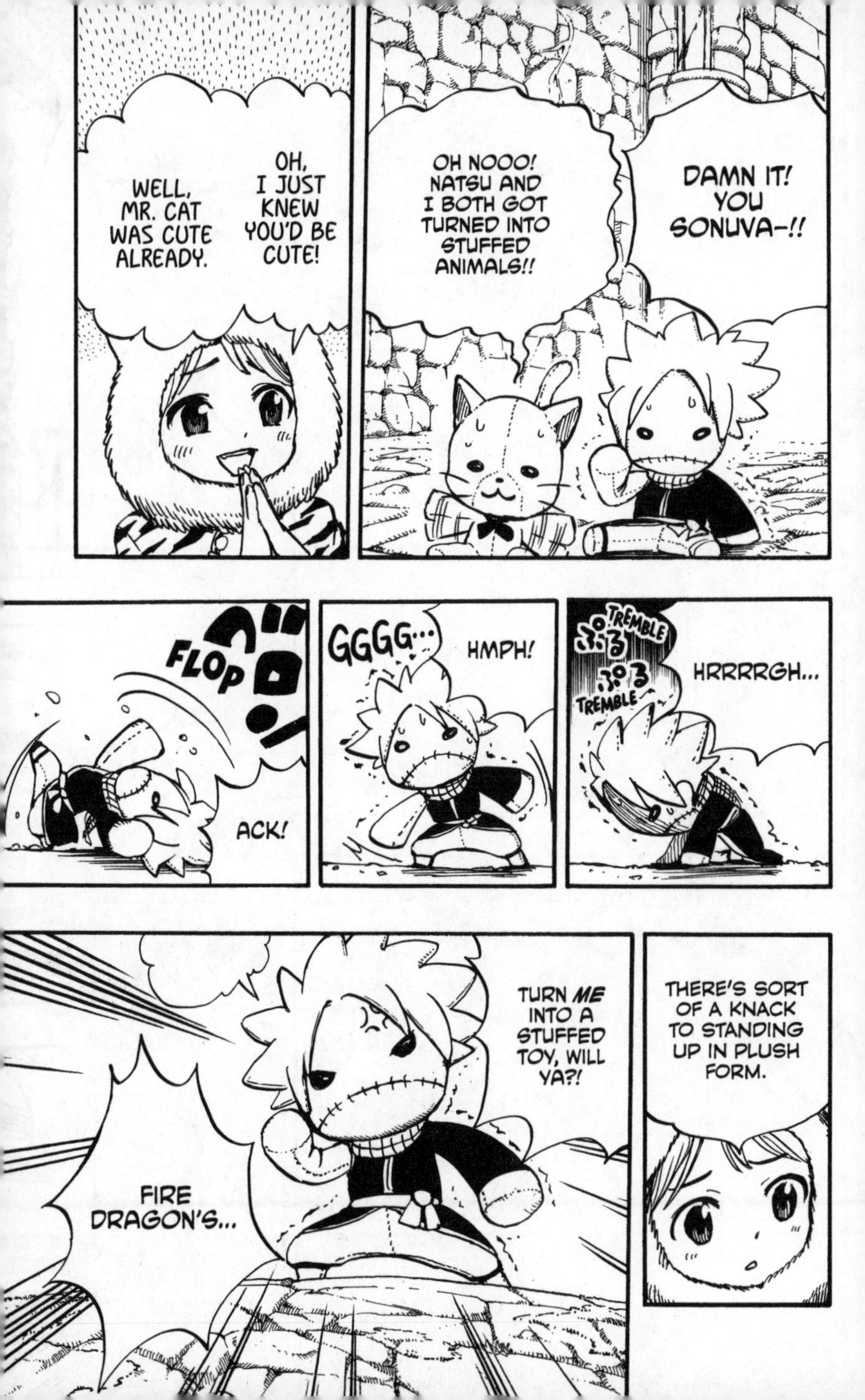
DAMN IT! YOU SONUVA-!!
OH NOOO! NATSU AND I BOTH GOT TURNED INTO STUFFED ANIMALS!!
OH, I JUST KNEW YOU'D BE CUTE!
WELL, MR. CAT WAS CUTE ALREADY.
TREMBLE ぷる ぷる TREMBLE
HRRRRGH...
GGGG...
HMPH!
FLOP
ACK!
THERE'S SORT OF A KNACK TO STANDING UP IN PLUSH FORM.
TURN *ME* INTO A STUFFED TOY, WILL YA?!
FIRE DRAGON'S...

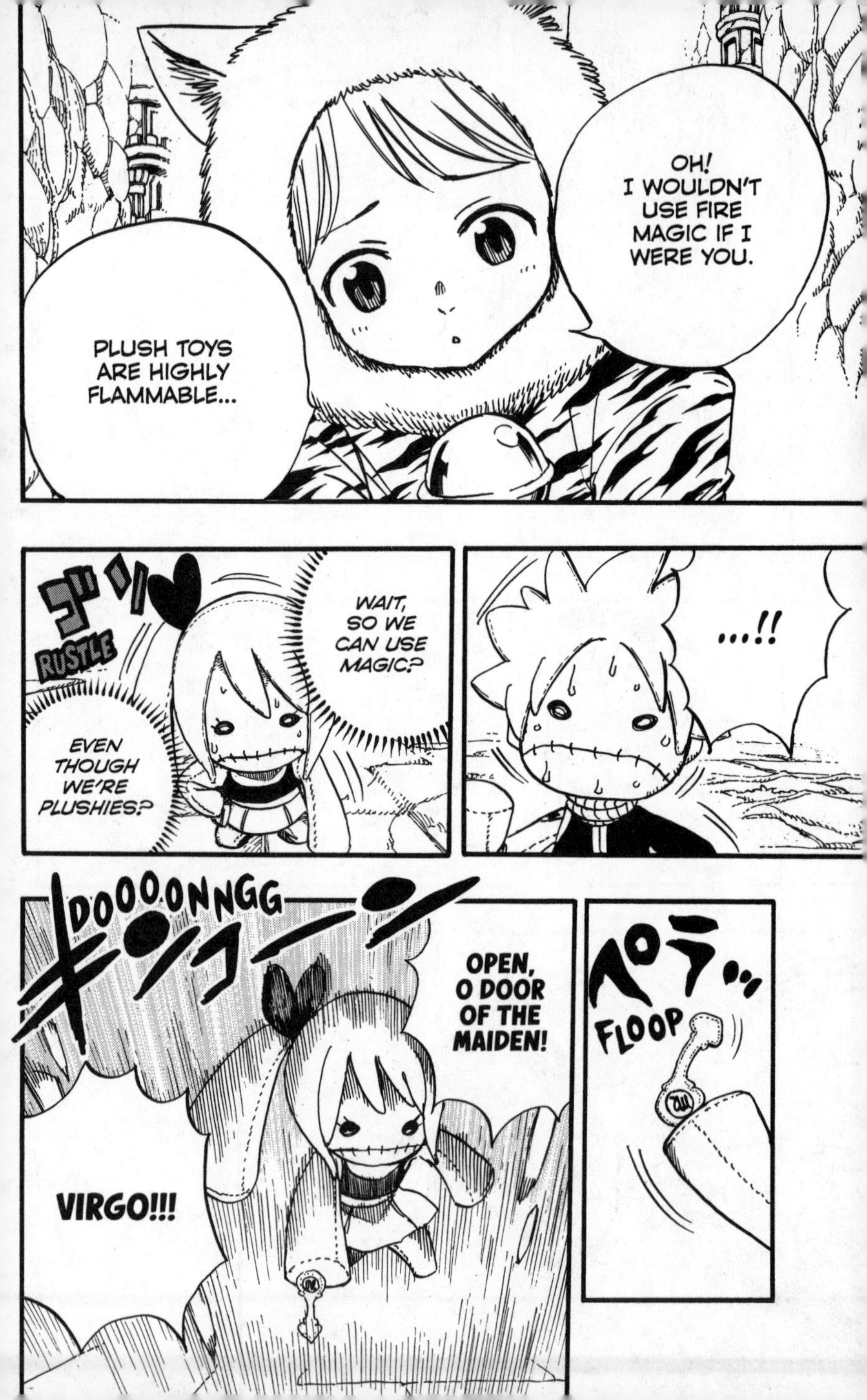
OH! I WOULDN'T USE FIRE MAGIC IF I WERE YOU.
PLUSH TOYS ARE HIGHLY FLAMMABLE...
...!!
RUSTLE
WAIT, SO WE CAN USE MAGIC?
EVEN THOUGH WE'RE PLUSHIES?
FLOOP
DOOOONNGG
OPEN, O DOOR OF THE MAIDEN!
VIRGO!!!

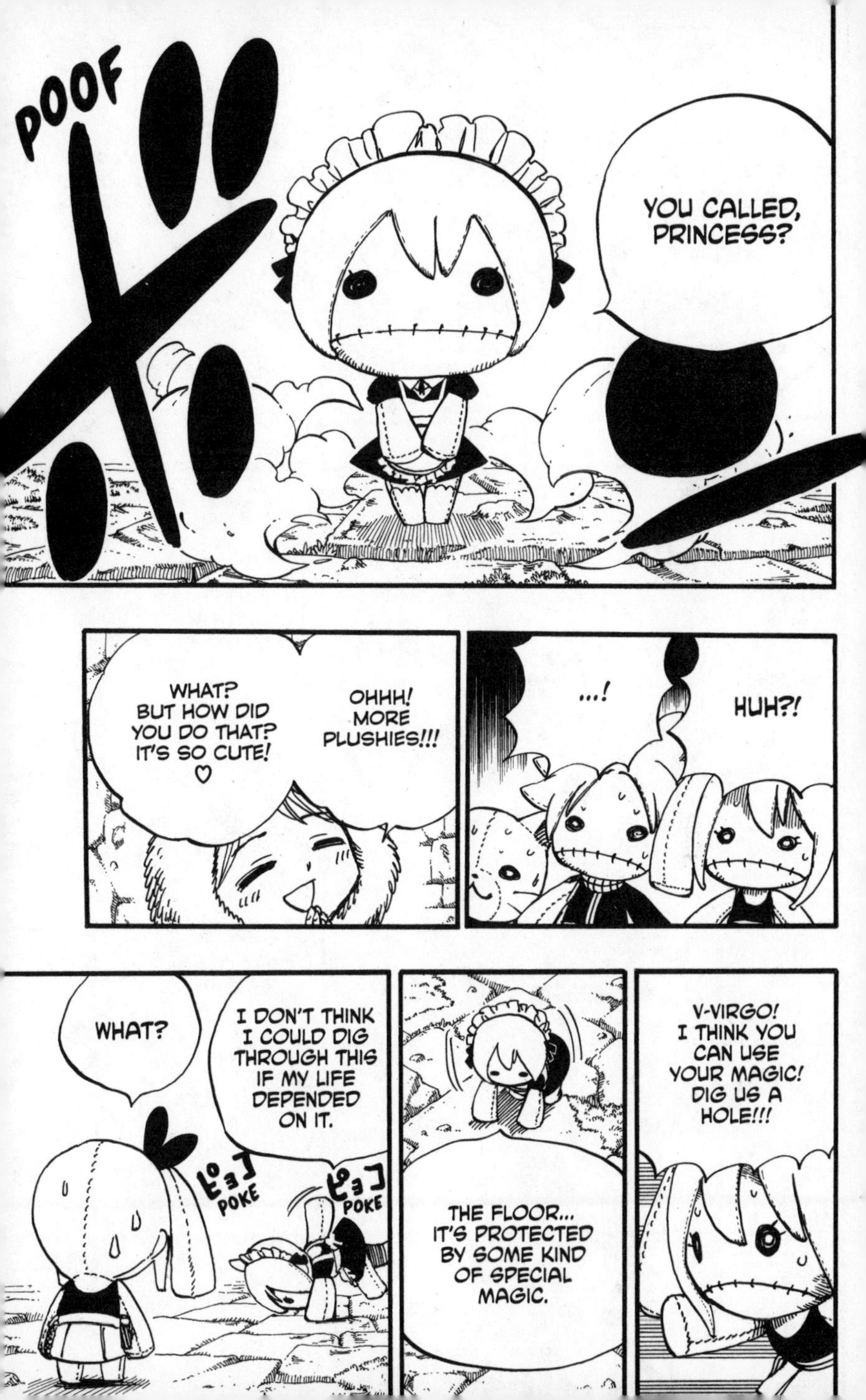
POOF
YOU CALLED, PRINCESS?
HUH?!
...!
OHHH! MORE PLUSHIES!!!
WHAT? BUT HOW DID YOU DO THAT? IT'S SO CUTE! ♡
V-VIRGO! I THINK YOU CAN USE YOUR MAGIC! DIG US A HOLE!!!
THE FLOOR... IT'S PROTECTED BY SOME KIND OF SPECIAL MAGIC.
I DON'T THINK I COULD DIG THROUGH THIS IF MY LIFE DEPENDED ON IT.
WHAT?
ピョコ POKE
ピョコ POKE

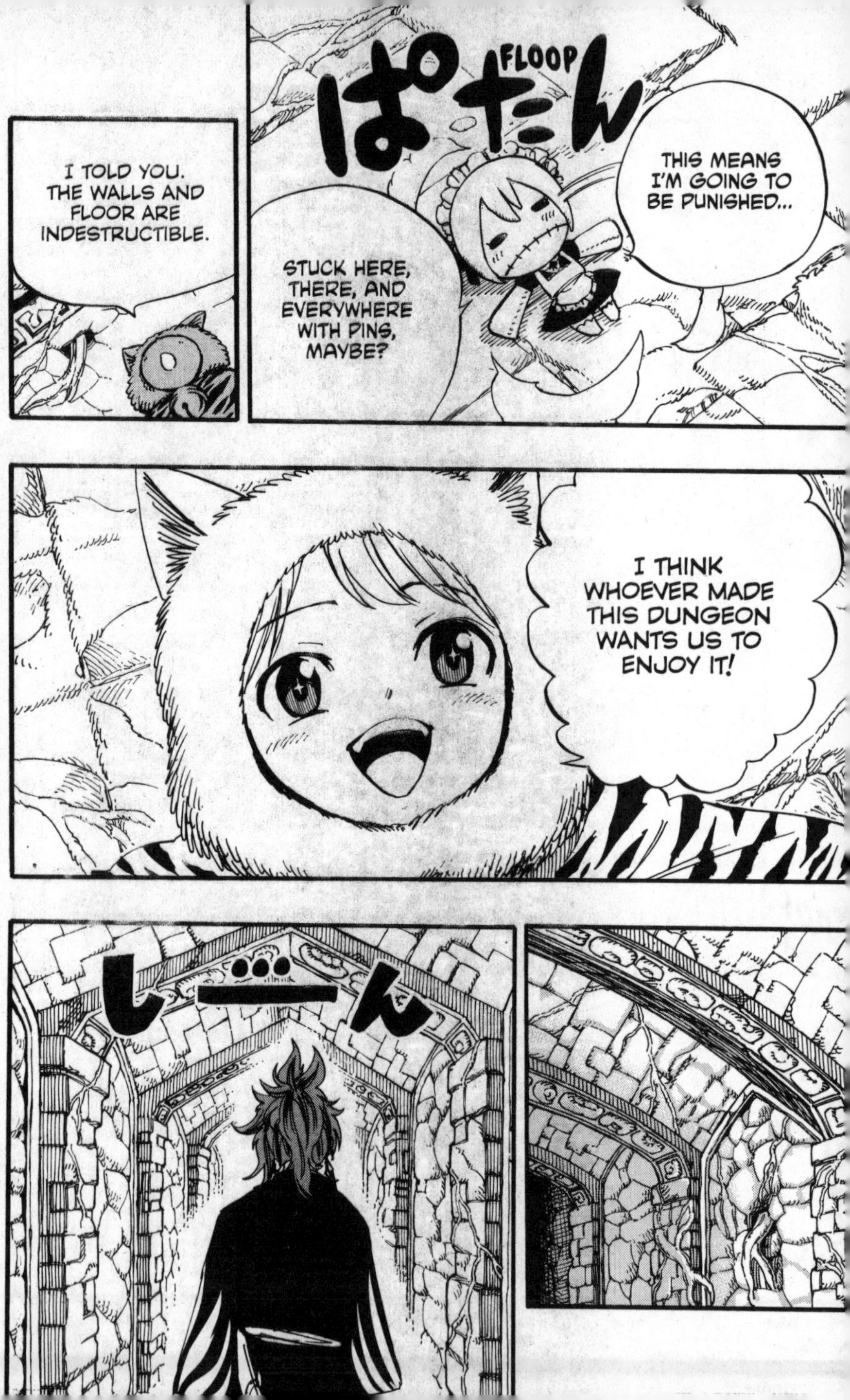
ぱたん
FLOOP
THIS MEANS I'M GOING TO BE PUNISHED...
STUCK HERE, THERE, AND EVERYWHERE WITH PINS, MAYBE?
I TOLD YOU. THE WALLS AND FLOOR ARE INDESTRUCTIBLE.
I THINK WHOEVER MADE THIS DUNGEON WANTS US TO ENJOY IT!
し…ーん

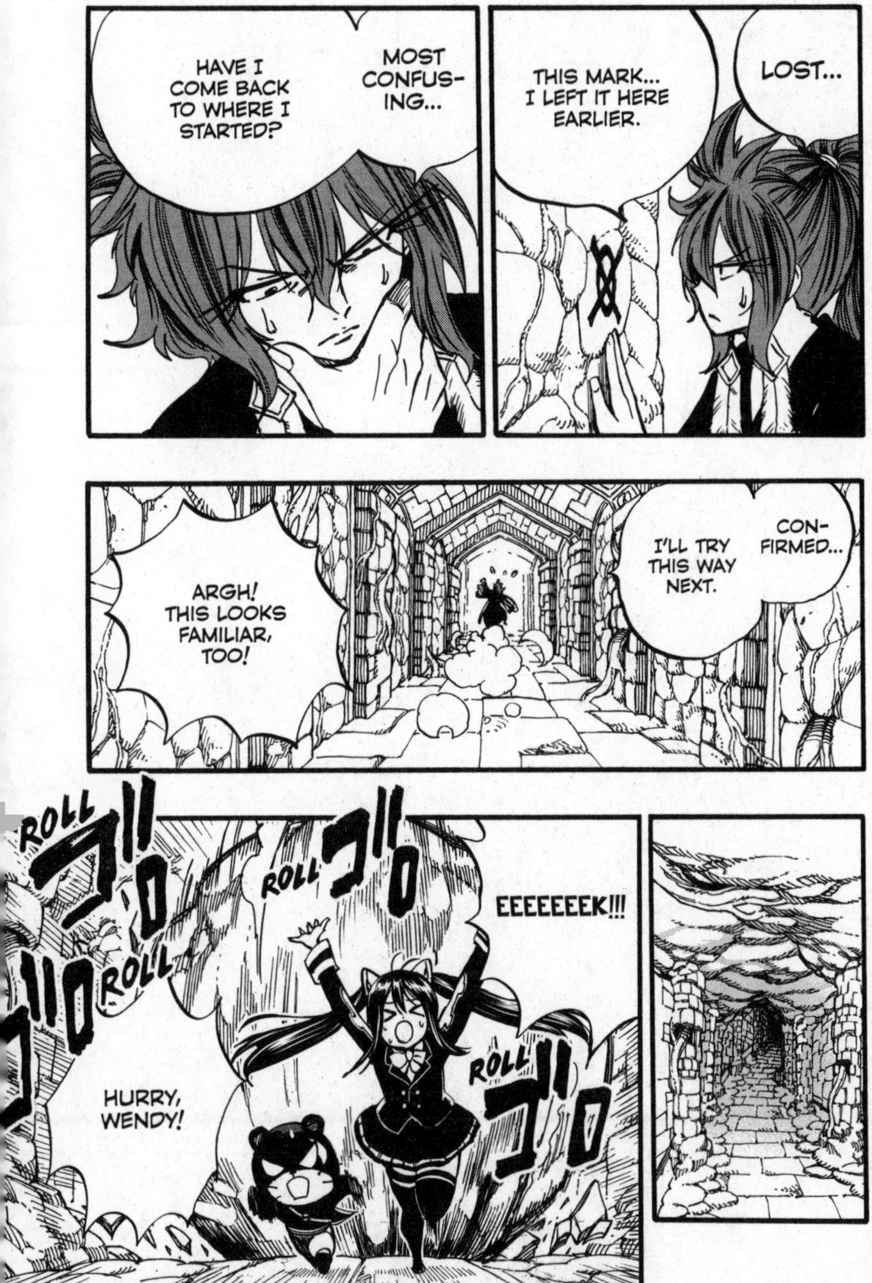
LOST...
THIS MARK... I LEFT IT HERE EARLIER.
MOST CONFUS-ING...
HAVE I COME BACK TO WHERE I STARTED?
CON-FIRMED...
I'LL TRY THIS WAY NEXT.
ARGH! THIS LOOKS FAMILIAR, TOO!
EEEEEEEK!!!
ROLL
ROLL
ROLL
ROLL
HURRY, WENDY!

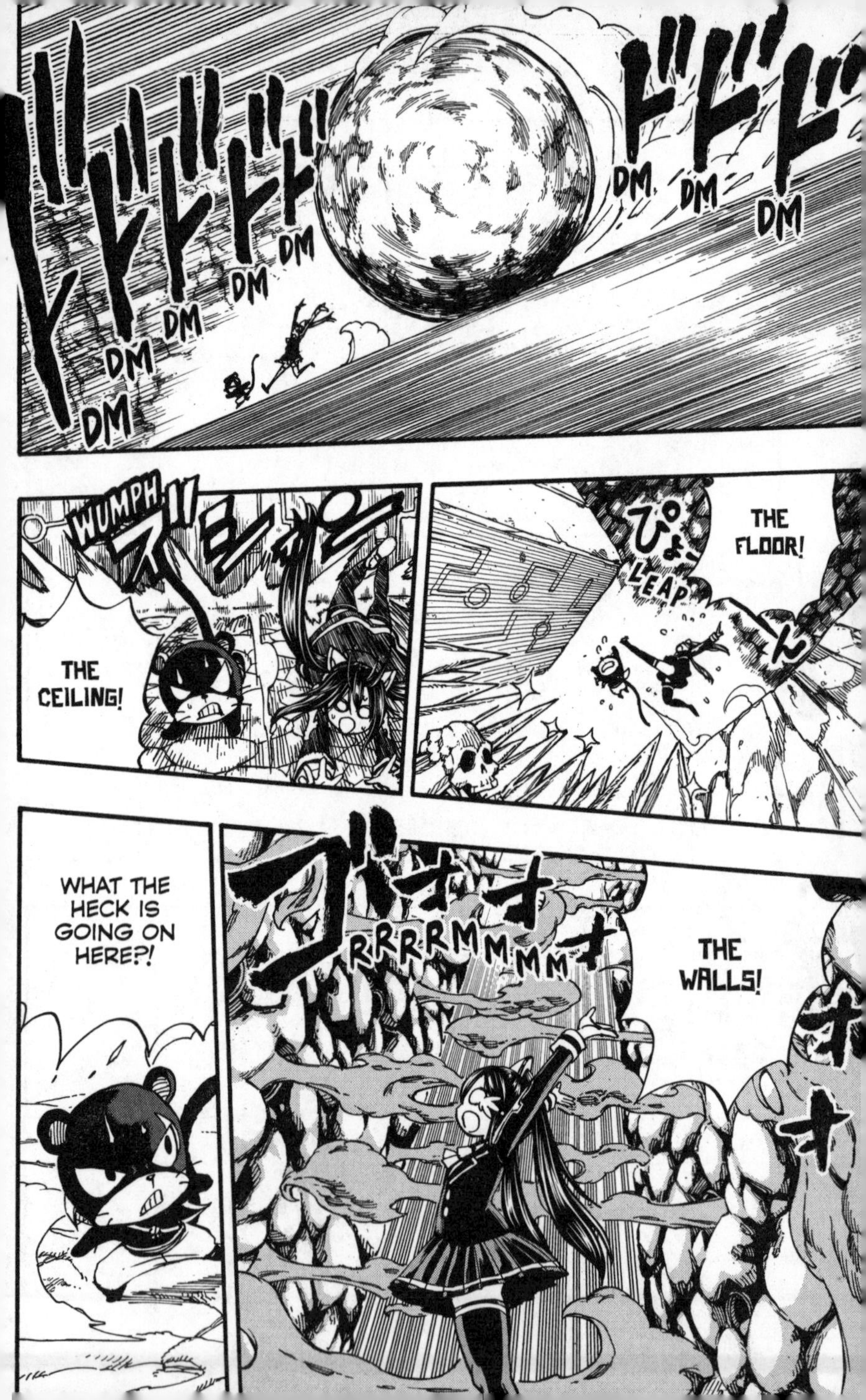
DM DM DM
DM DM DM DM DM DM
THE FLOOR!
ぴょ
LEAP
WUMPH
THE CEILING!
THE WALLS!
RRRRMMMMM
WHAT THE HECK IS GOING ON HERE?!

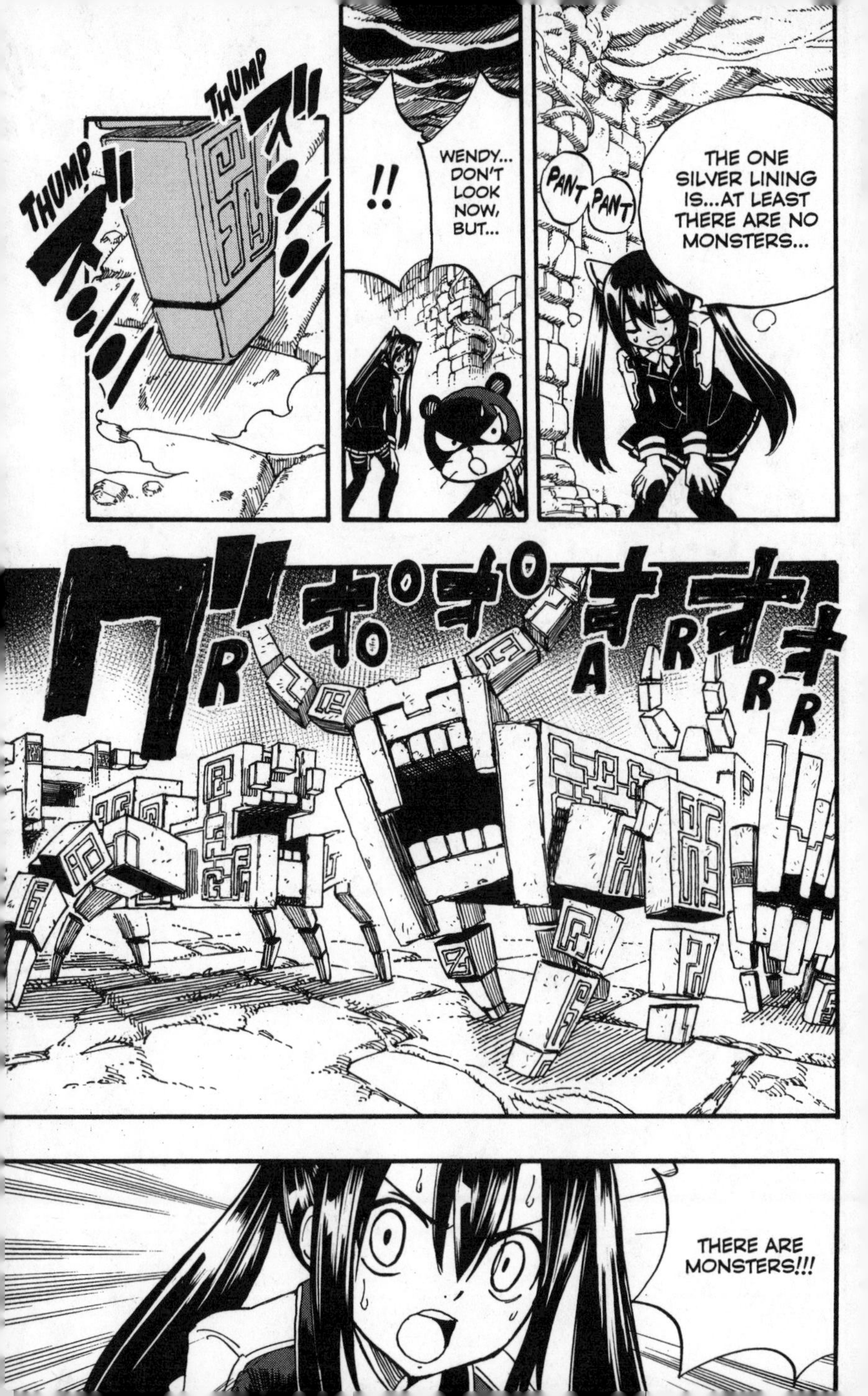
THE ONE SILVER LINING IS...AT LEAST THERE ARE NO MONSTERS...
PANT PANT
WENDY... DON'T LOOK NOW, BUT...
!!
THUMP
THUMP
RRARRR
THERE ARE MONSTERS!!!

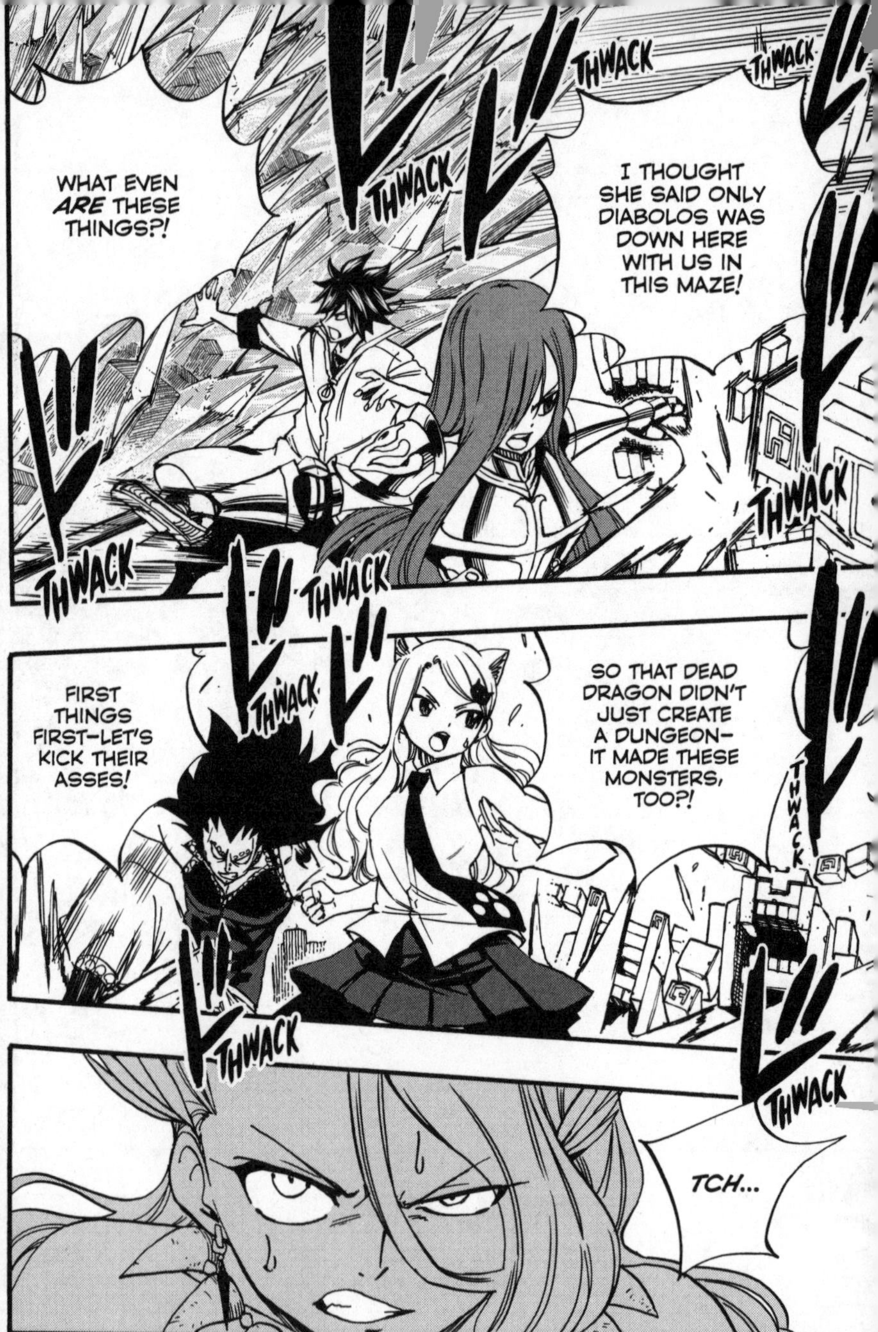
THWACK
THWACK
I THOUGHT SHE SAID ONLY DIABOLOS WAS DOWN HERE WITH US IN THIS MAZE!
THWACK
WHAT EVEN *ARE* THESE THINGS?!
THWACK
THWACK
THWACK
THWACK
SO THAT DEAD DRAGON DIDN'T JUST CREATE A DUNGEON—IT MADE THESE MONSTERS, TOO?!
THWACK
FIRST THINGS FIRST—LET'S KICK THEIR ASSES!
THWACK
THWACK
THWACK
TCH...

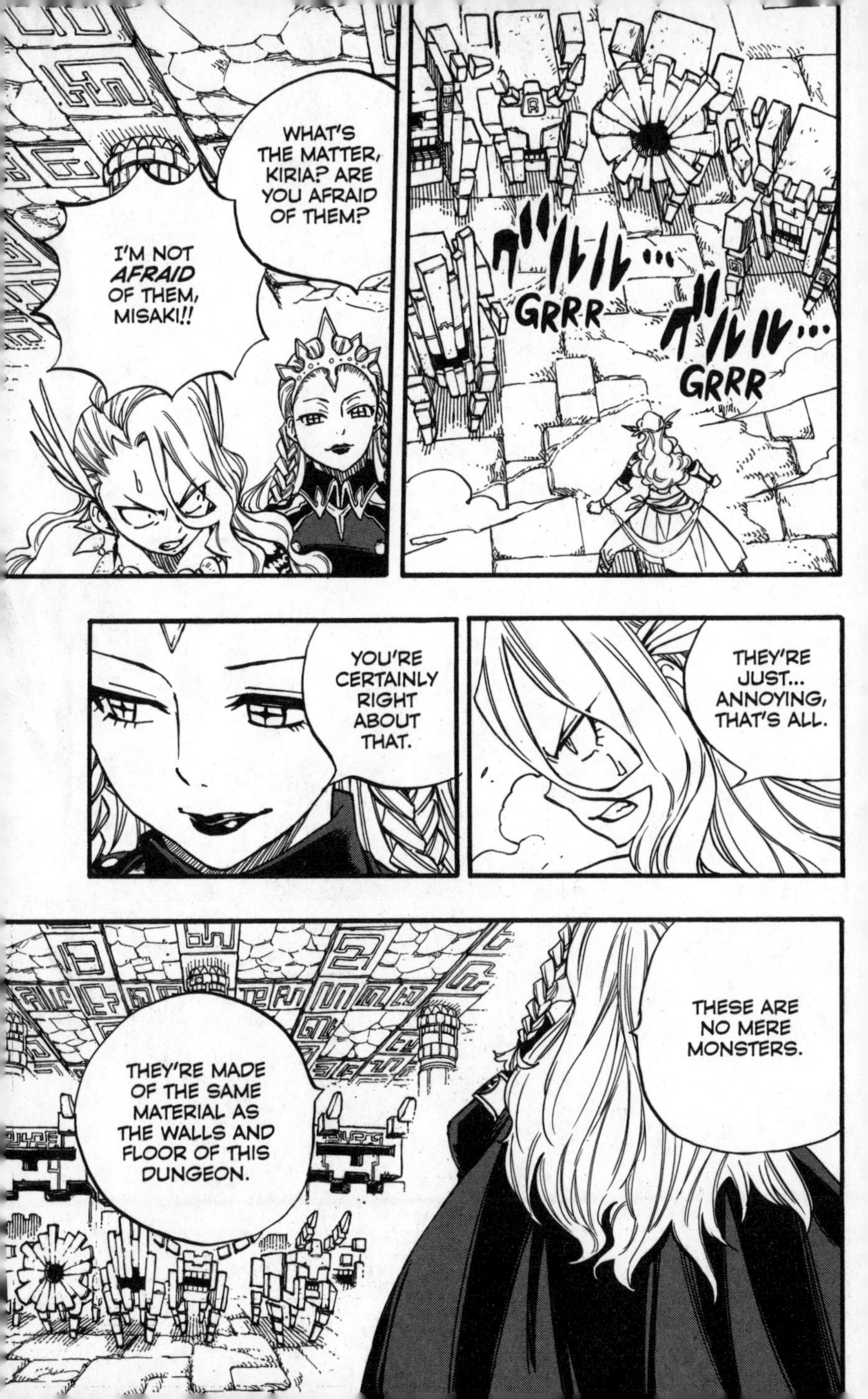
GRRR
GRRR
WHAT'S THE MATTER, KIRIA? ARE YOU AFRAID OF THEM?
I'M NOT *AFRAID* OF THEM, MISAKI!!
THEY'RE JUST... ANNOYING, THAT'S ALL.
YOU'RE CERTAINLY RIGHT ABOUT THAT.
THESE ARE NO MERE MONSTERS.
THEY'RE MADE OF THE SAME MATERIAL AS THE WALLS AND FLOOR OF THIS DUNGEON.

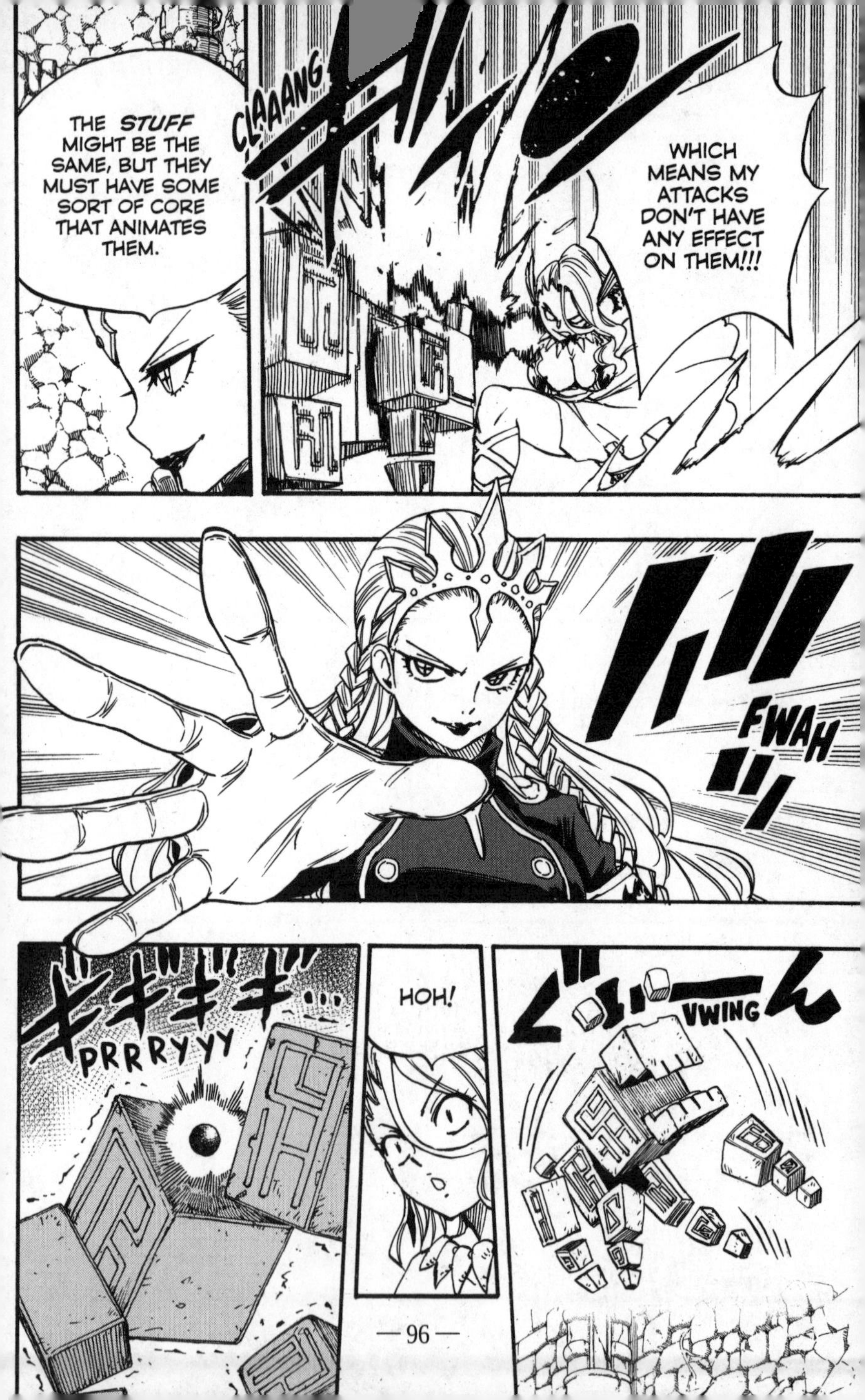
CLAAANG
WHICH MEANS MY ATTACKS DON'T HAVE ANY EFFECT ON THEM!!!
THE *STUFF* MIGHT BE THE SAME, BUT THEY MUST HAVE SOME SORT OF CORE THAT ANIMATES THEM.
FWAH
VWING
HOH!
PRRRYYY

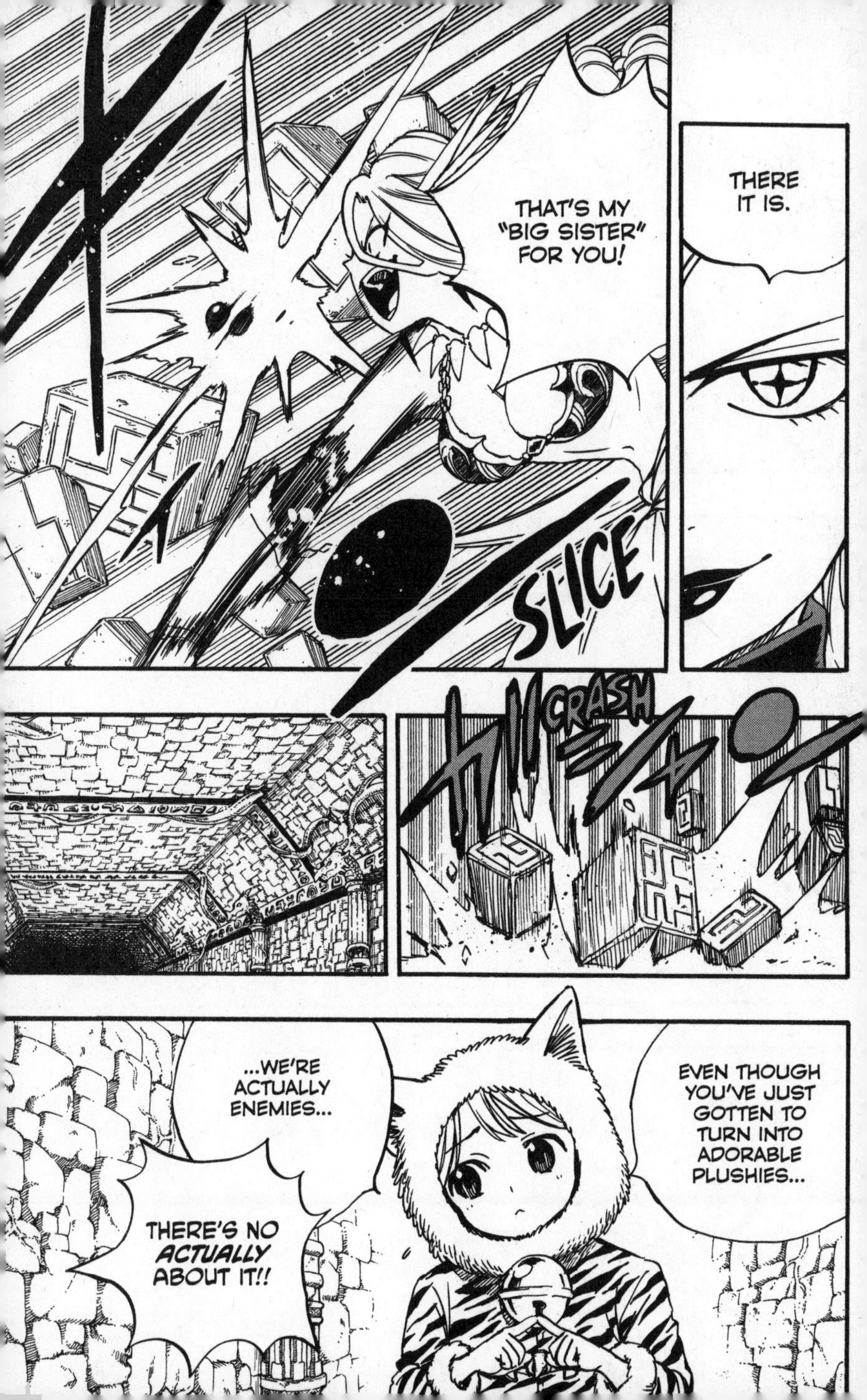
THERE IT IS.
THAT'S MY "BIG SISTER" FOR YOU!
SLICE
CRASH
EVEN THOUGH YOU'VE JUST GOTTEN TO TURN INTO ADORABLE PLUSHIES...
...WE'RE ACTUALLY ENEMIES...
THERE'S NO *ACTUALLY* ABOUT IT!!

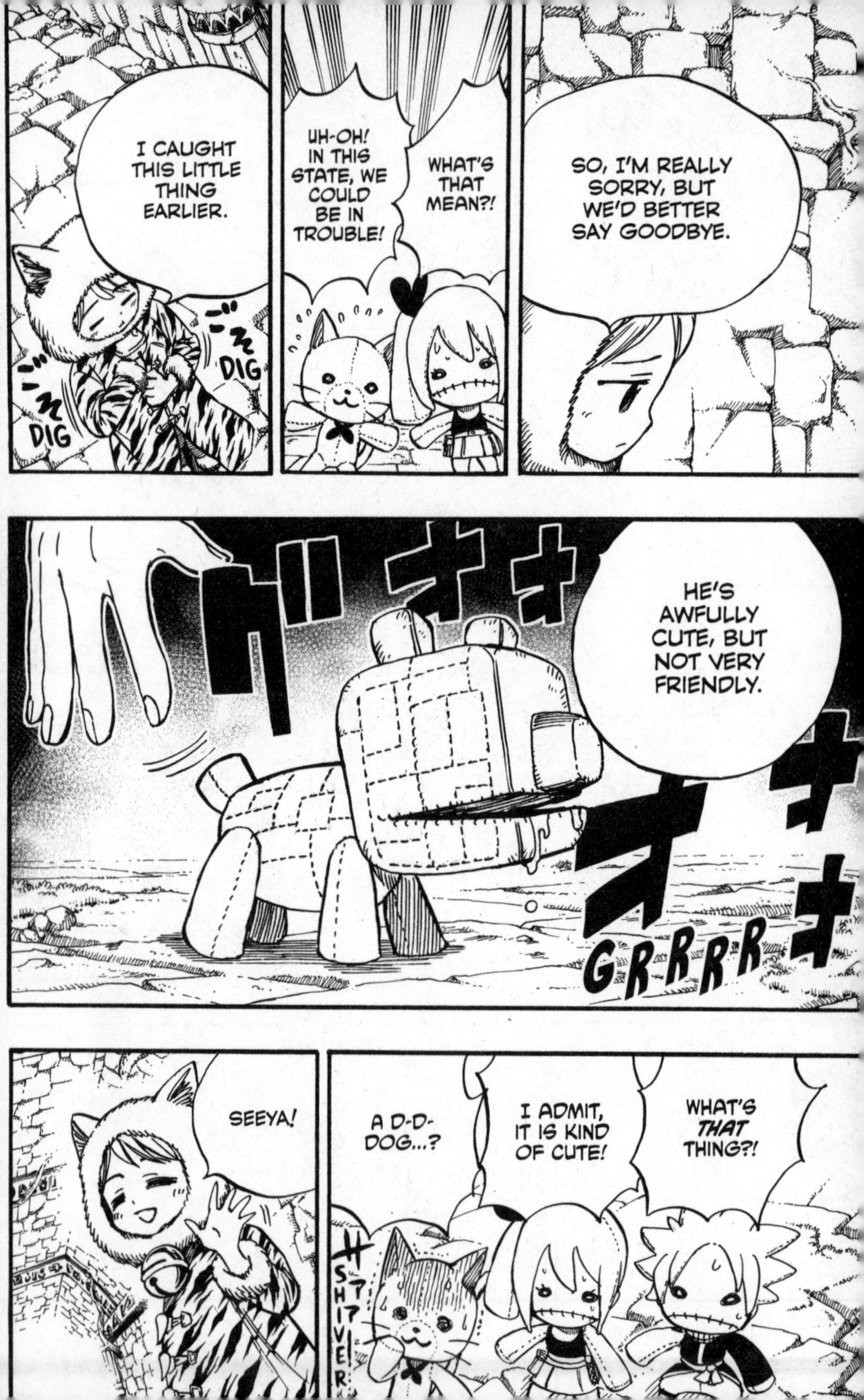
SO, I'M REALLY SORRY, BUT WE'D BETTER SAY GOODBYE.
WHAT'S THAT MEAN?!
UH-OH! IN THIS STATE, WE COULD BE IN TROUBLE!
I CAUGHT THIS LITTLE THING EARLIER.
DIG
DIG
HE'S AWFULLY CUTE, BUT NOT VERY FRIENDLY.
GRRRR
WHAT'S *THAT* THING?!
I ADMIT, IT IS KIND OF CUTE!
A D-D-DOG...?
SHIVER
SEEYA!

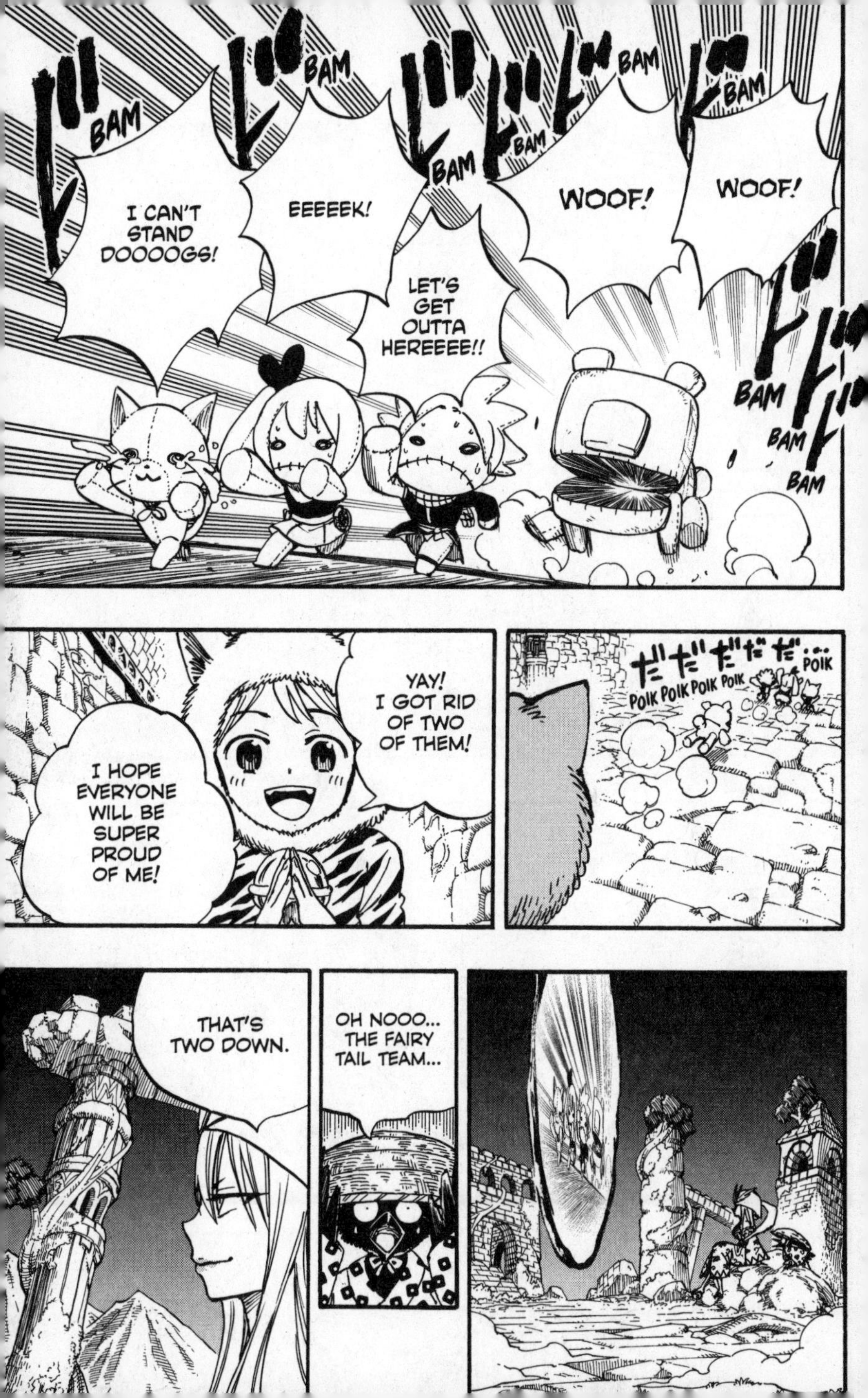
BAM
BAM
BAM
BAM
BAM
BAM
BAM
BAM
WOOF!
WOOF!
LET'S GET OUTTA HEREEEE!!
EEEEEK!
I CAN'T STAND DOOOOGS!
だだだだだ...
POIK POIK POIK POIK POIK
YAY! I GOT RID OF TWO OF THEM!
I HOPE EVERYONE WILL BE SUPER PROUD OF ME!
OH NOOO... THE FAIRY TAIL TEAM...
THAT'S TWO DOWN.

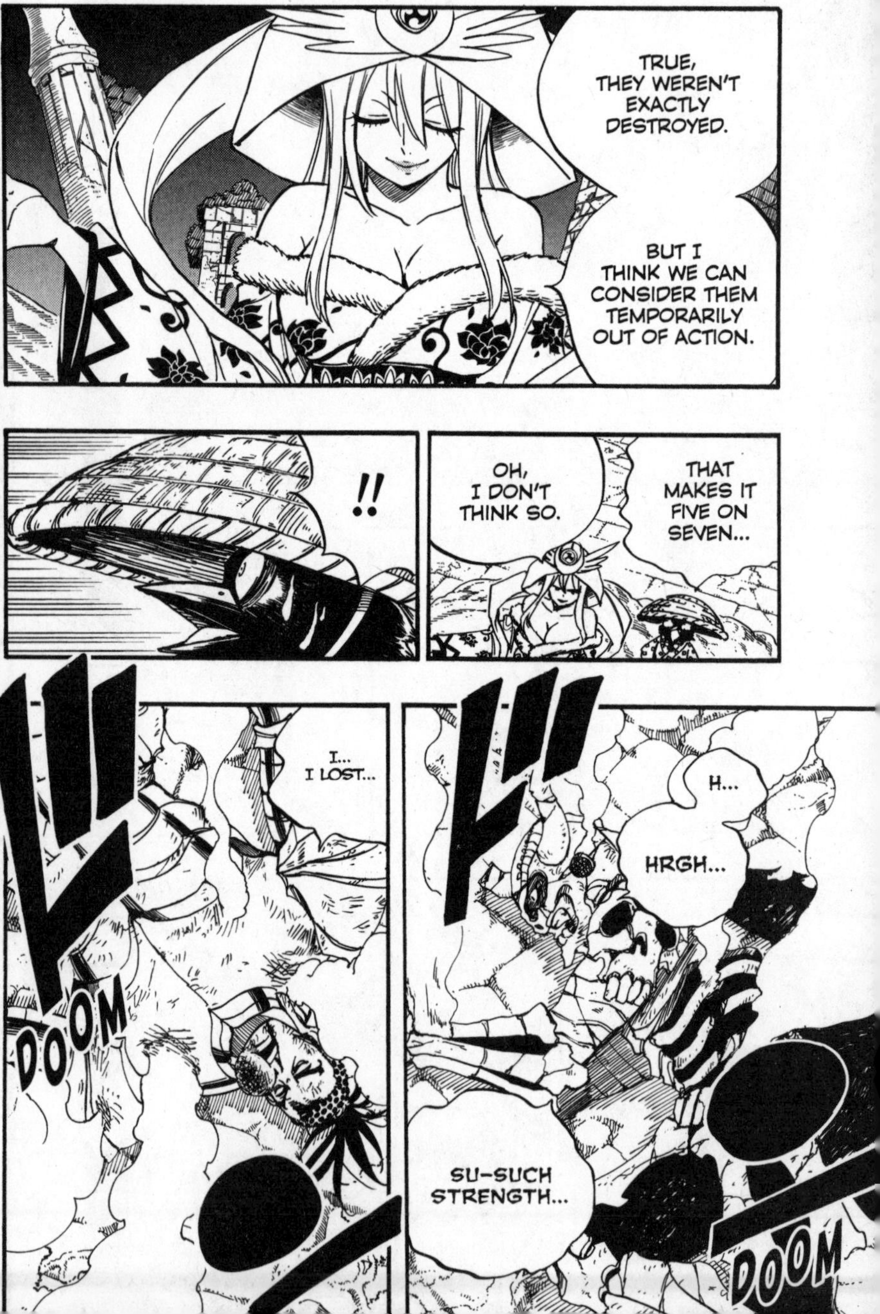
TRUE, THEY WEREN'T EXACTLY DESTROYED.
BUT I THINK WE CAN CONSIDER THEM TEMPORARILY OUT OF ACTION.
THAT MAKES IT FIVE ON SEVEN...
OH, I DON'T THINK SO.
!!
H...
HRGH...
SU-SUCH STRENGTH...
DOOM
I... I LOST...
DOOM

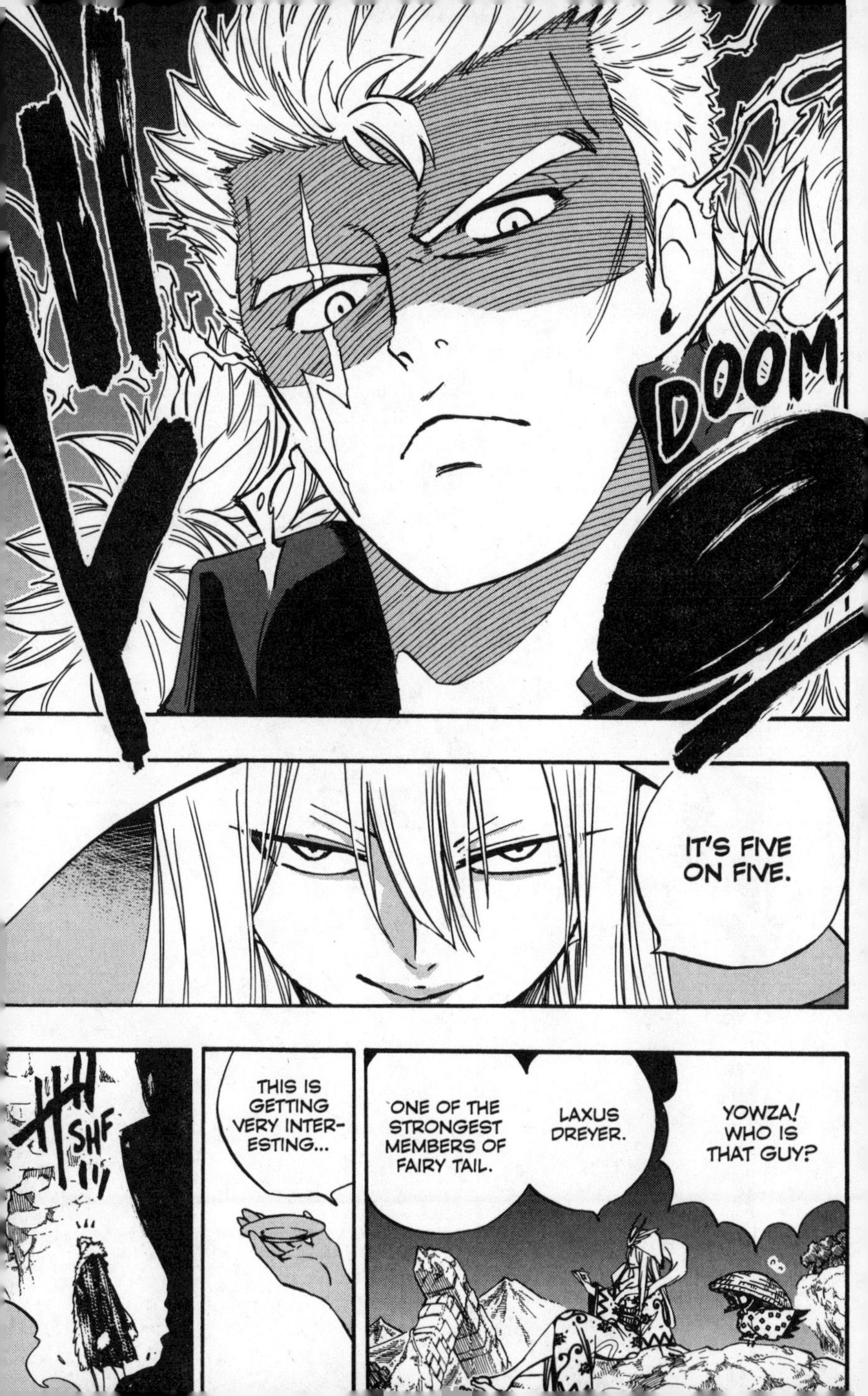
DOOM
IT'S FIVE ON FIVE.
YOWZA! WHO IS THAT GUY?
LAXUS DREYER.
ONE OF THE STRONGEST MEMBERS OF FAIRY TAIL.
THIS IS GETTING VERY INTER-ESTING...
SHF

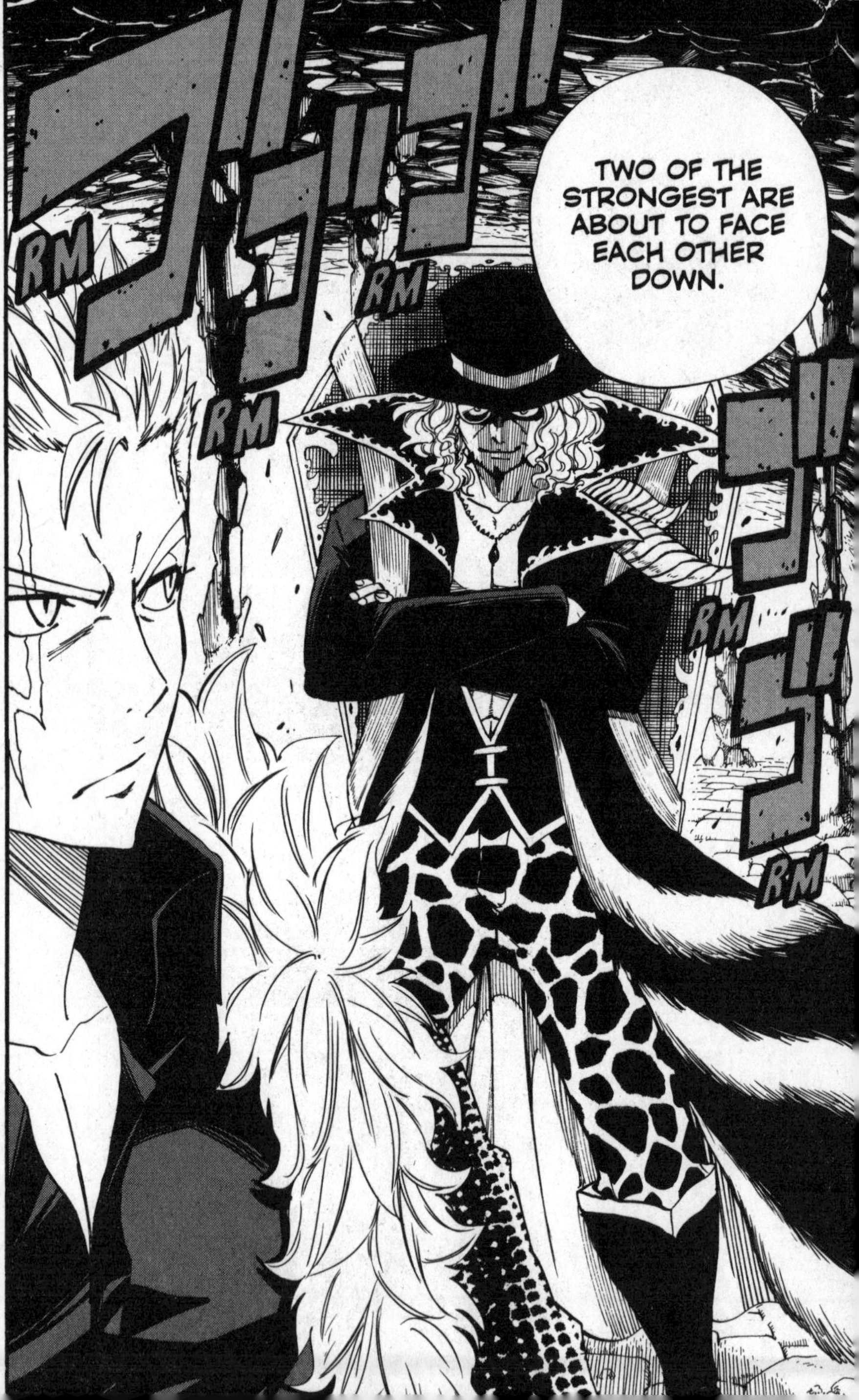
TWO OF THE STRONGEST ARE ABOUT TO FACE EACH OTHER DOWN.
RM
RM
RM
RM
RM
RM

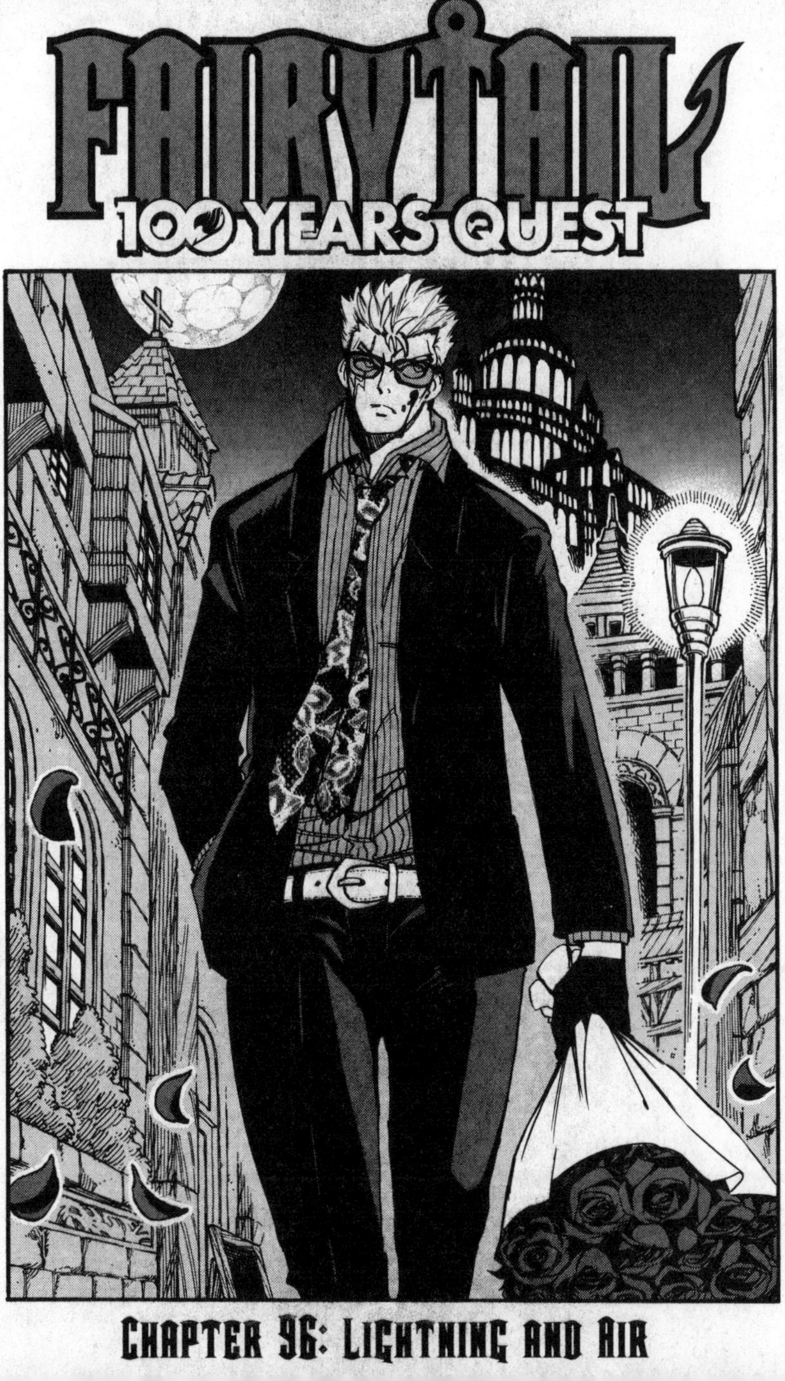
FAIRY TAIL
100 YEARS QUEST

CHAPTER 96: LIGHTNING AND AIR

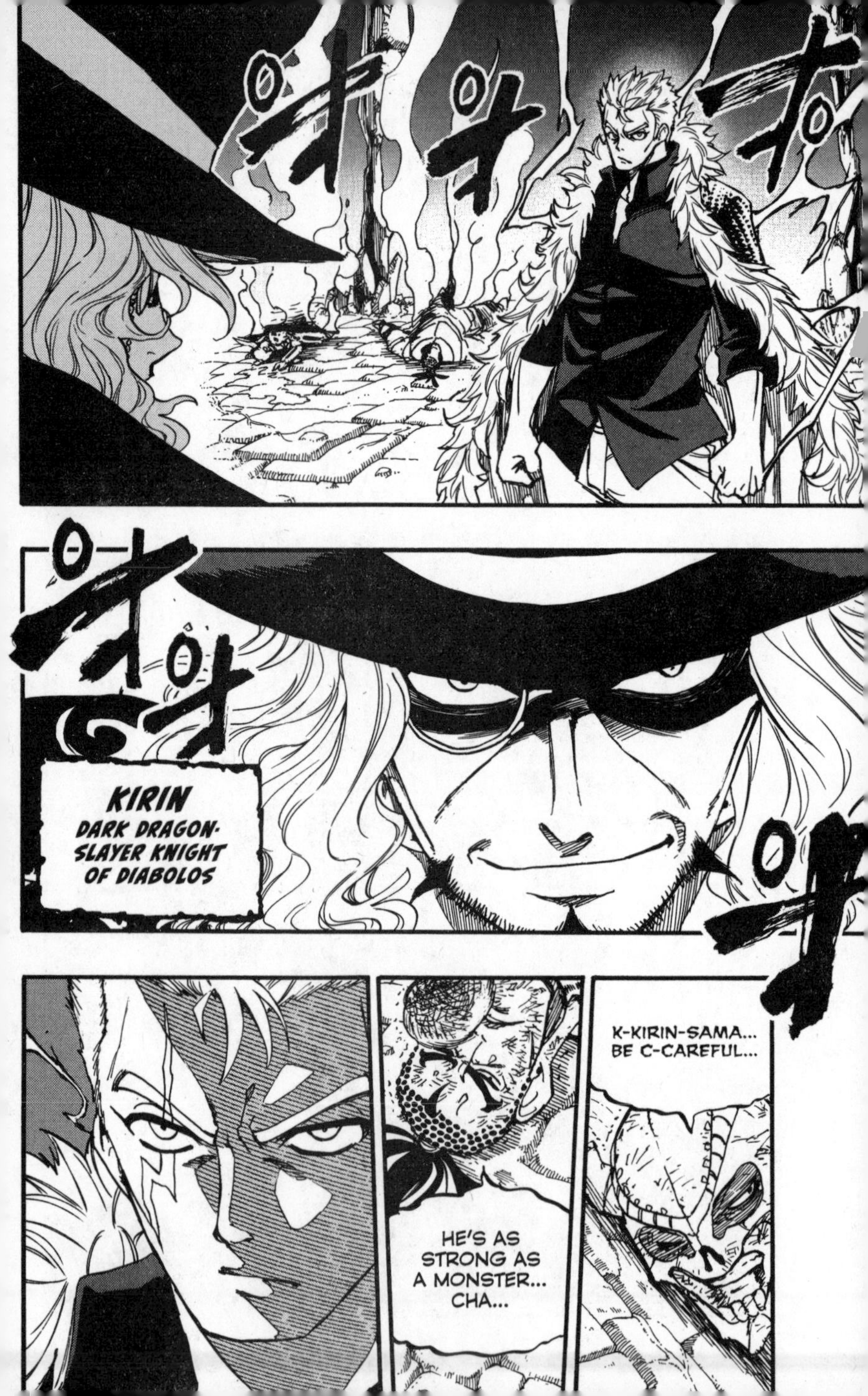
KIRIN
DARK DRAGON-SLAYER KNIGHT OF DIABOLOS
K-KIRIN-SAMA... BE C-CAREFUL...
HE'S AS STRONG AS A MONSTER... CHA...

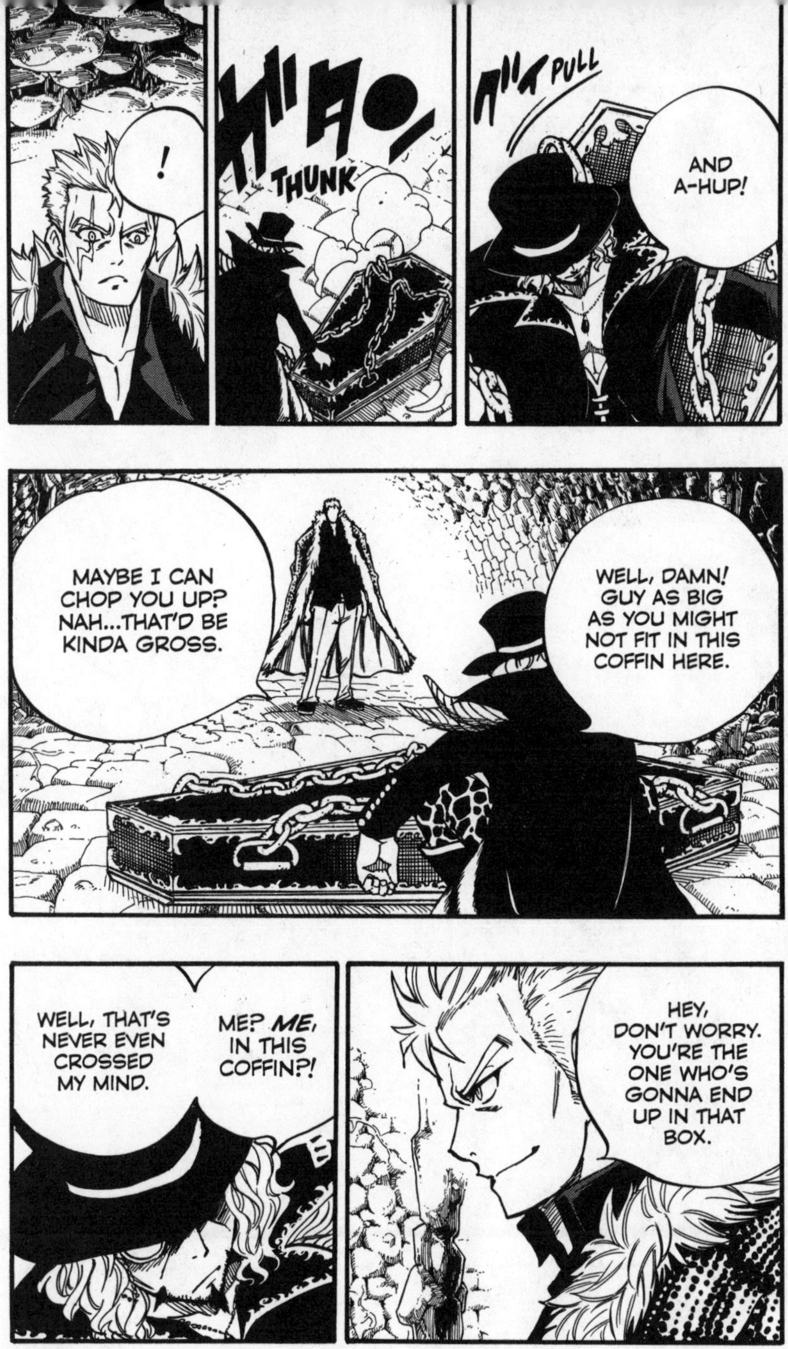
PULL
AND A-HUP!
THUNK
!
WELL, DAMN! GUY AS BIG AS YOU MIGHT NOT FIT IN THIS COFFIN HERE.
MAYBE I CAN CHOP YOU UP? NAH...THAT'D BE KINDA GROSS.
HEY, DON'T WORRY. YOU'RE THE ONE WHO'S GONNA END UP IN THAT BOX.
ME? *ME*, IN THIS COFFIN?!
WELL, THAT'S NEVER EVEN CROSSED MY MIND.

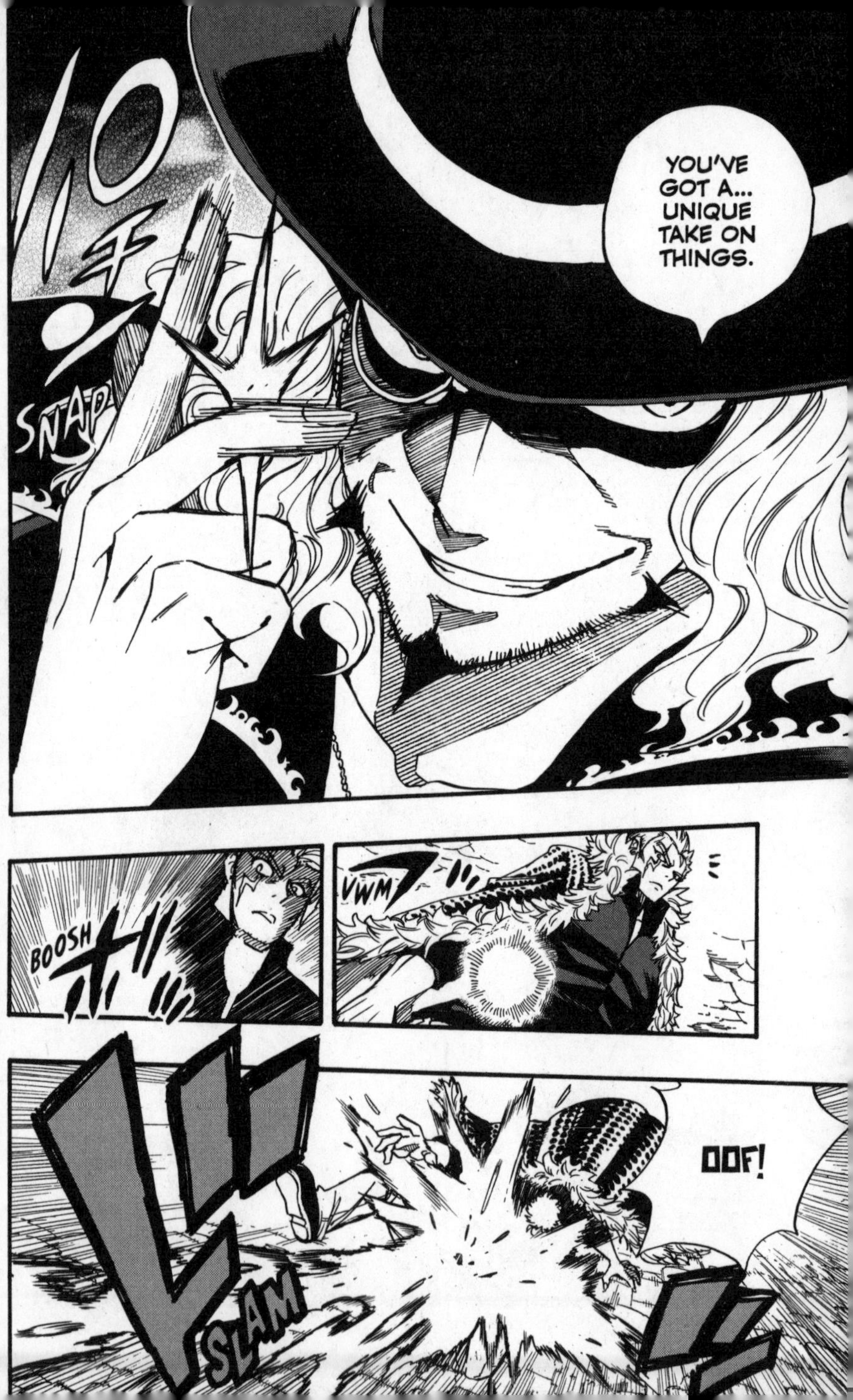
YOU'VE GOT A... UNIQUE TAKE ON THINGS.
SNAP
VWM
BOOSH
OOF!
SLAM

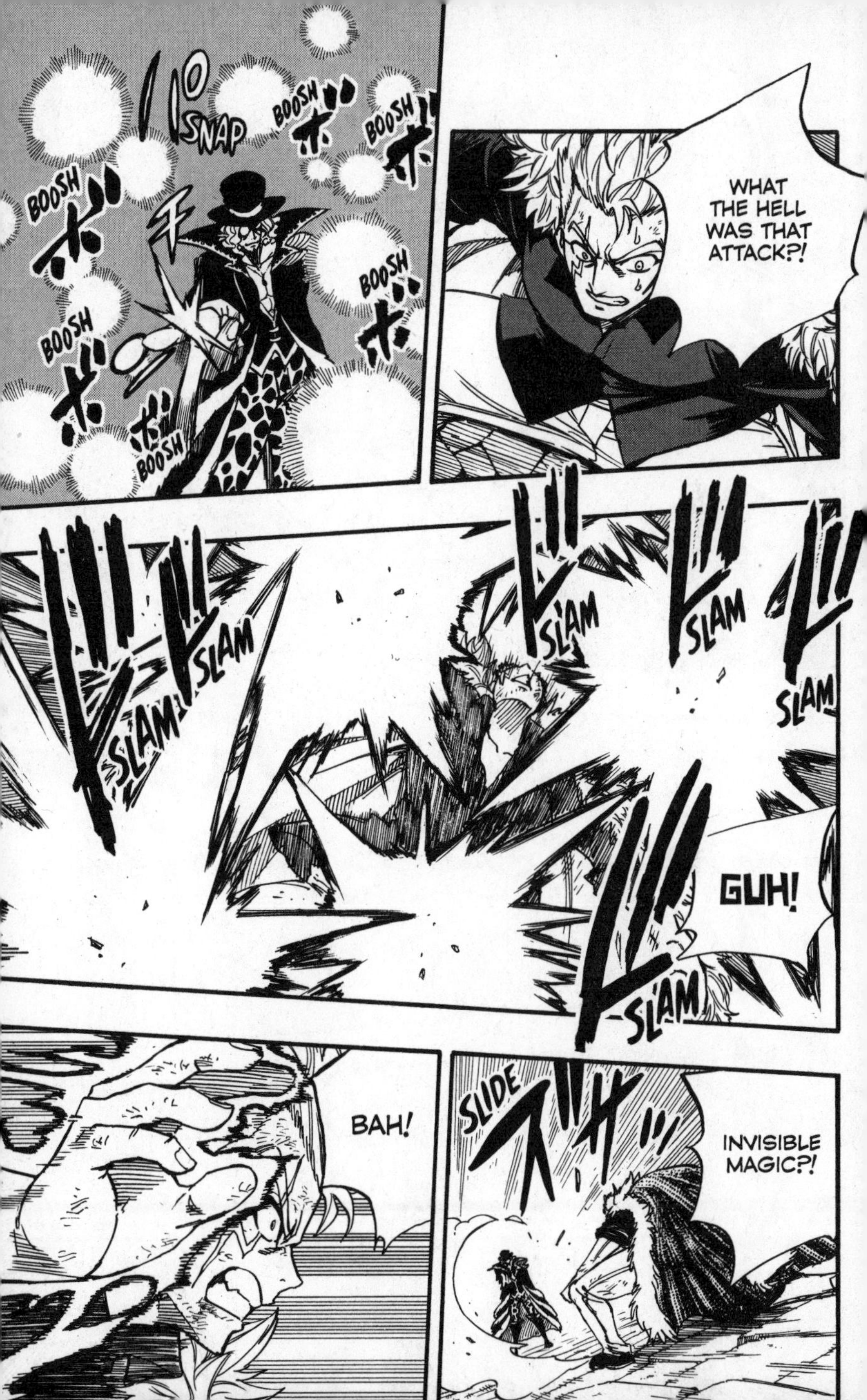

WHAT THE HELL WAS THAT ATTACK?!
BOOSH
BOOSH
SNAP
BOOSH
BOOSH
BOOSH
BOOSH
SLAM
SLAM
SLAM
GUH!
SLAM
SLAM
SLAM
SLIDE
INVISIBLE MAGIC?!
BAH!

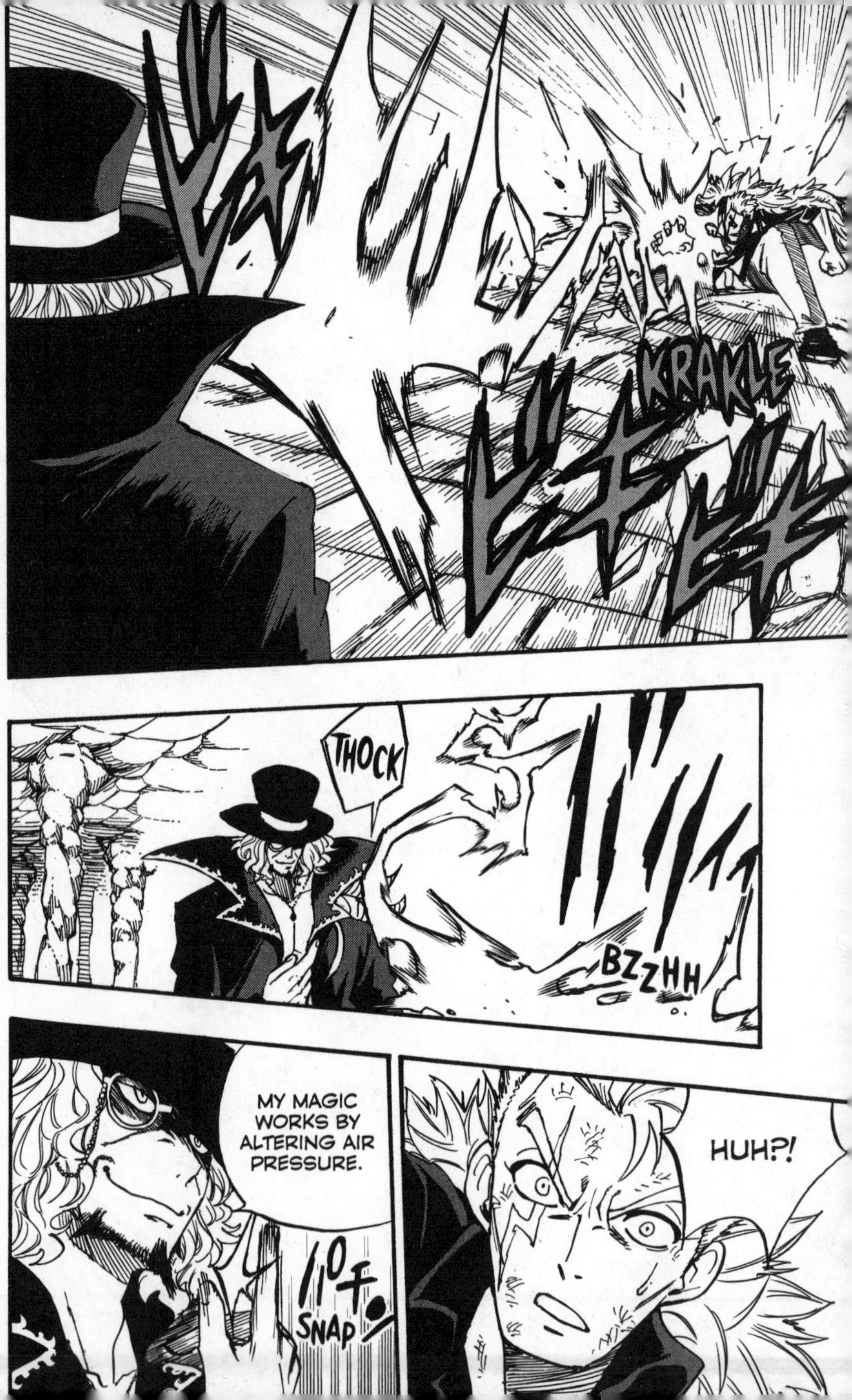
KRAKLE
THOCK
BZZHH
HUH?!
MY MAGIC WORKS BY ALTERING AIR PRESSURE.
SNAP

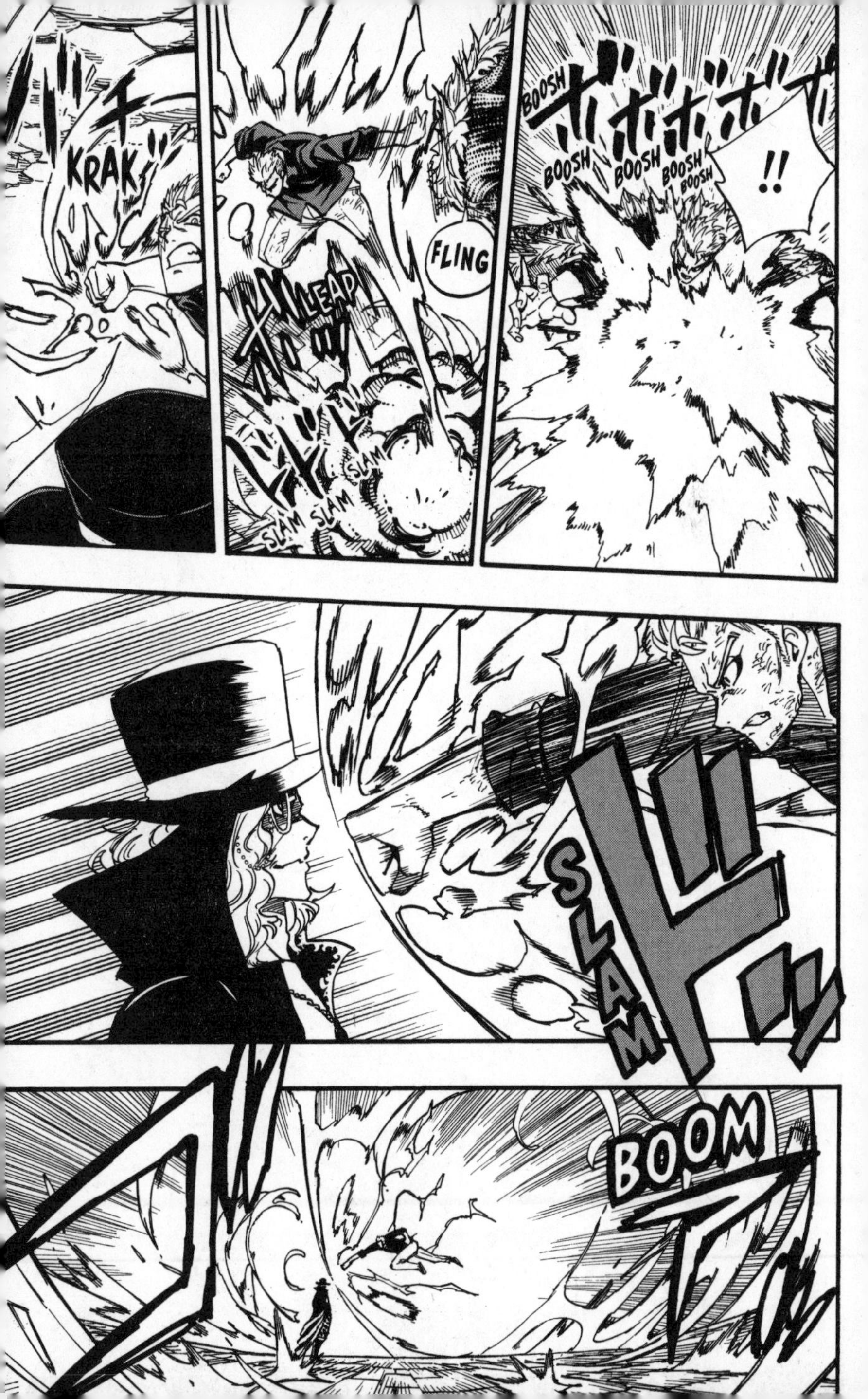
BOOSH
BOOSH
BOOSH
BOOSH
BOOSH
!!
FLING
LEAP
SLAM
SLAM
SLAM
KRAK
SLAM
BOOM

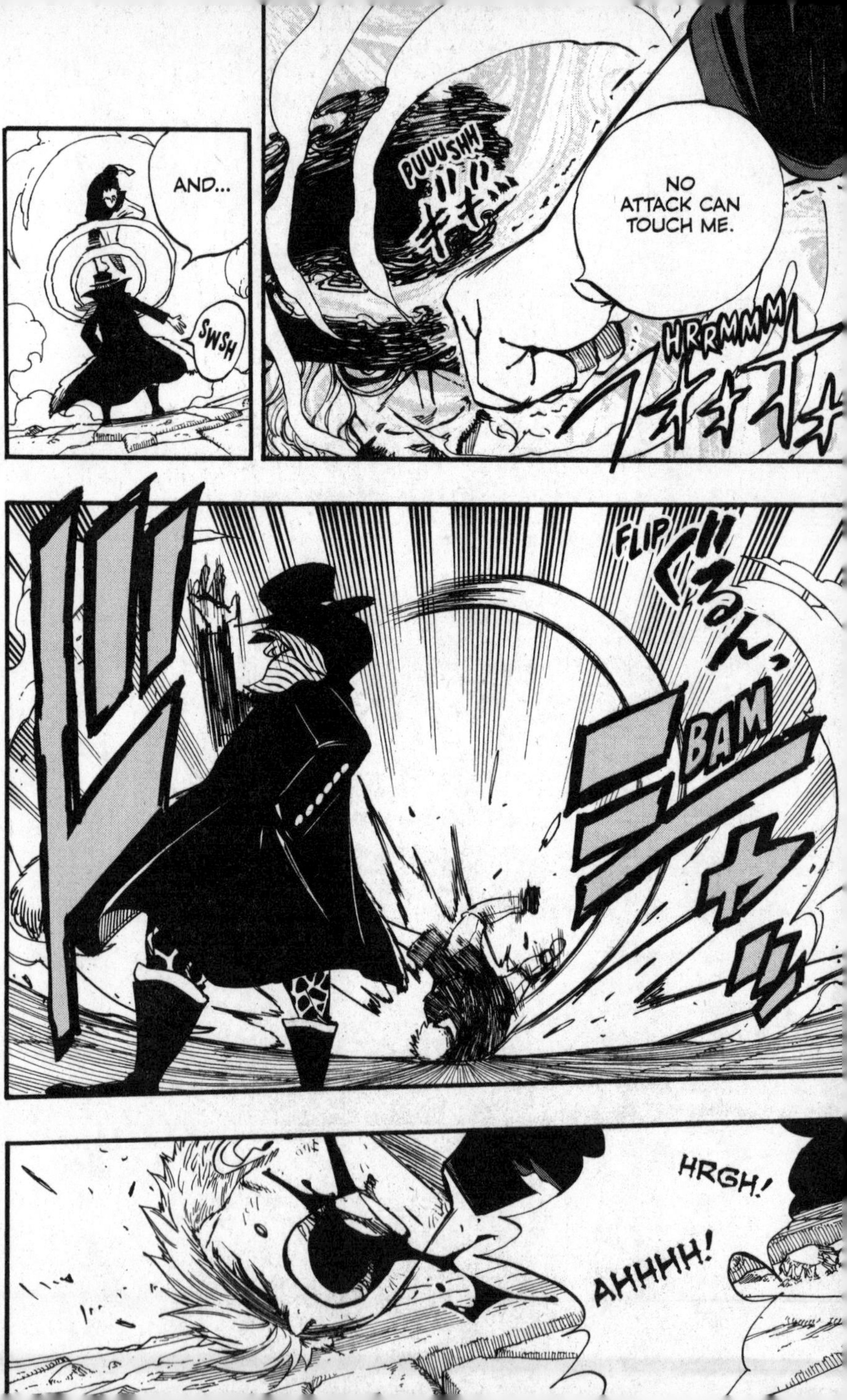
NO ATTACK CAN TOUCH ME.
PUUUSHH
HRRMMM
AND...
SWSH
FLIP
BAM
HRGH!
AHHHH!

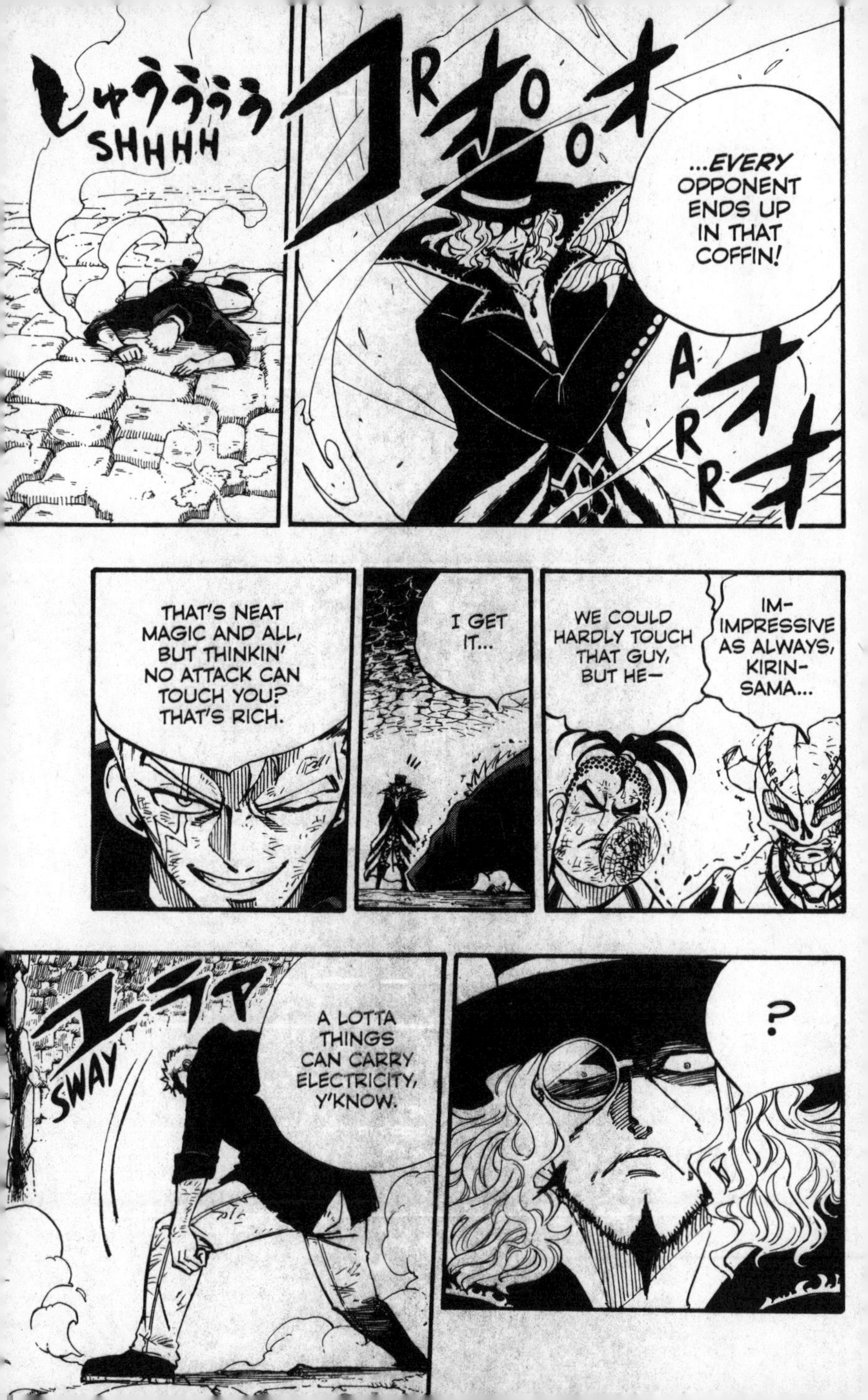
コオ
ROO
...EVERY OPPONENT ENDS UP IN THAT COFFIN!
オオ
ARR
ひゅうううう
SHHHH
IM-IMPRESSIVE AS ALWAYS, KIRIN-SAMA...
WE COULD HARDLY TOUCH THAT GUY, BUT HE—
I GET IT...
THAT'S NEAT MAGIC AND ALL, BUT THINKIN' NO ATTACK CAN TOUCH YOU? THAT'S RICH.
?
A LOTTA THINGS CAN CARRY ELECTRICITY, Y'KNOW.
ユラァ
SWAY

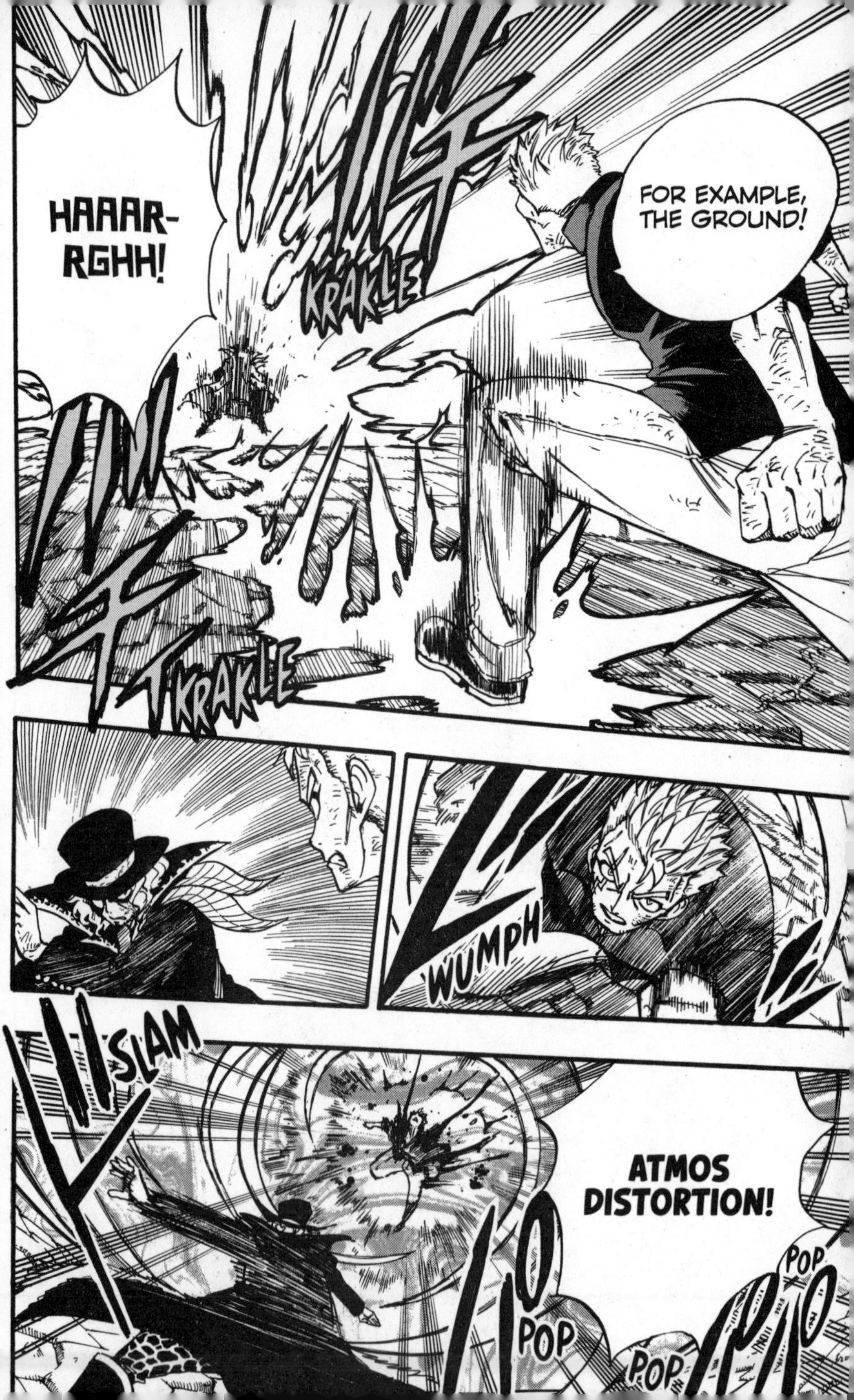
FOR EXAMPLE, THE GROUND!
HAAAR-RGHH!
KRAKLE
KRAKLE
WUMPH
ATMOS DISTORTION!
SLAM
POP
POP
POP
POP

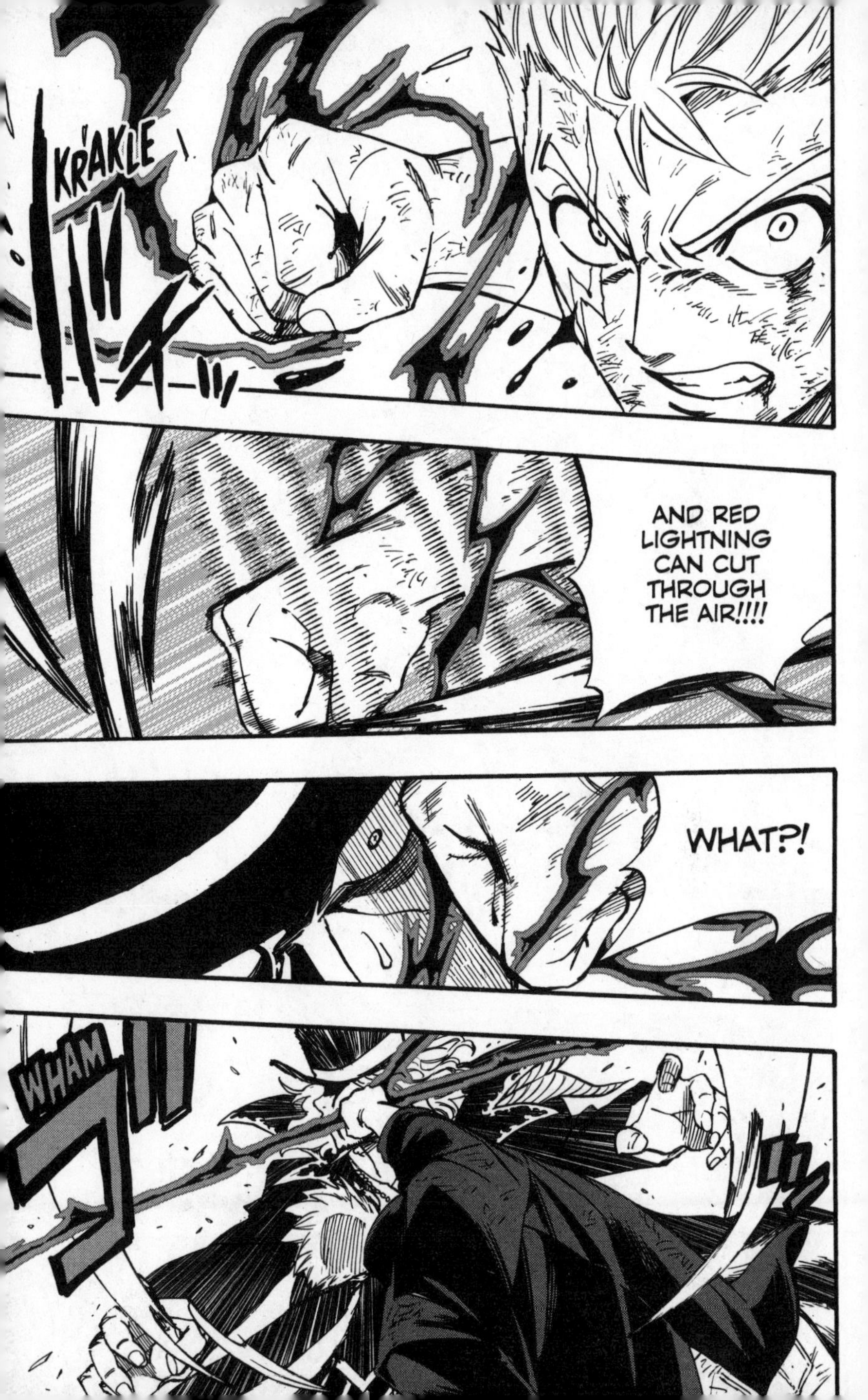
KRAKLE
AND RED LIGHTNING CAN CUT THROUGH THE AIR!!!!
WHAT?!
WHAM

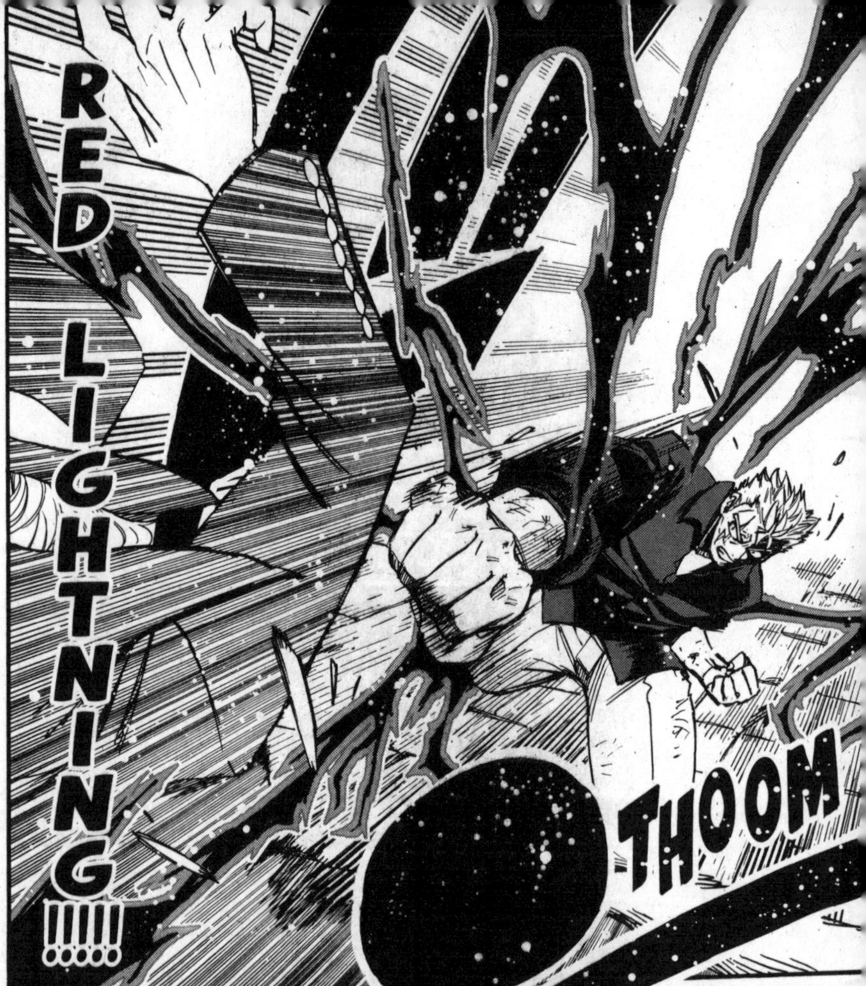
RED LIGHTNING!!!!!
THOOM
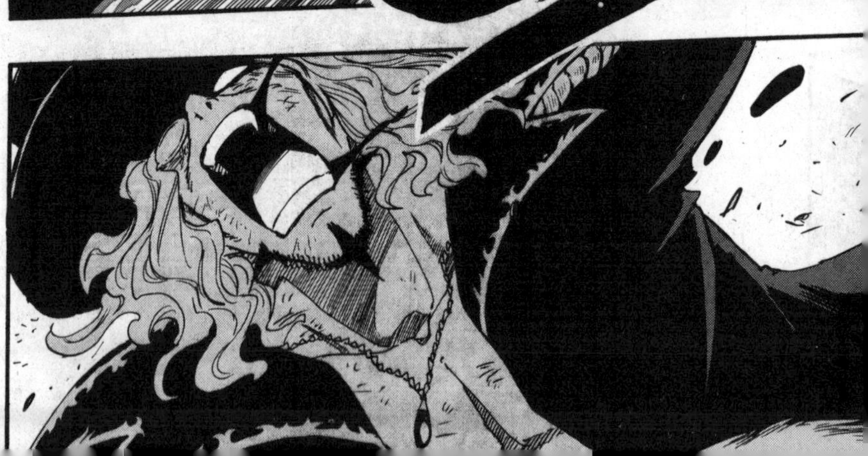

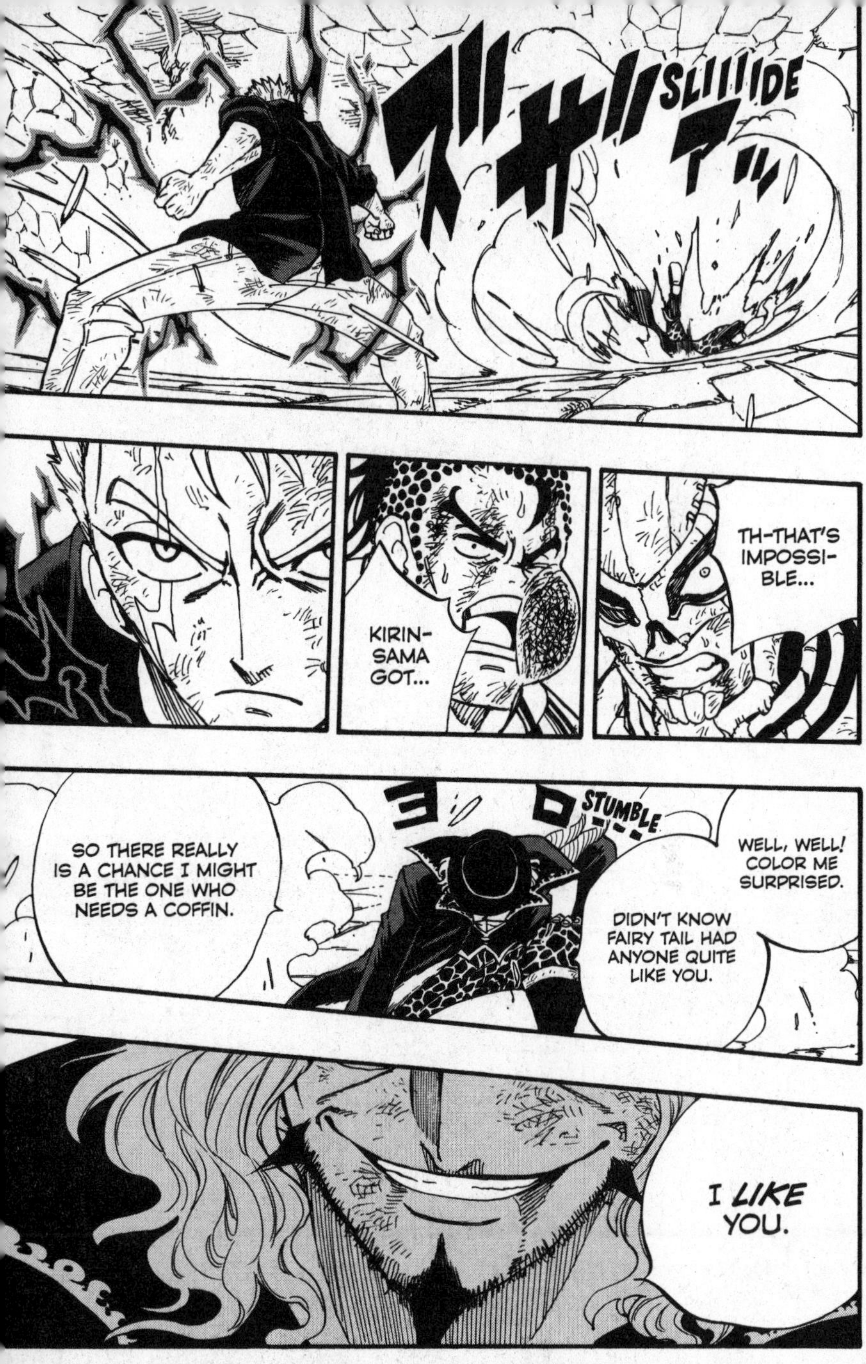

SLIIIIIDE
TH-THAT'S IMPOSSI-BLE...
KIRIN-SAMA GOT...
WELL, WELL! COLOR ME SURPRISED.
DIDN'T KNOW FAIRY TAIL HAD ANYONE QUITE LIKE YOU.
STUMBLE
SO THERE REALLY IS A CHANCE I MIGHT BE THE ONE WHO NEEDS A COFFIN.
I *LIKE* YOU.

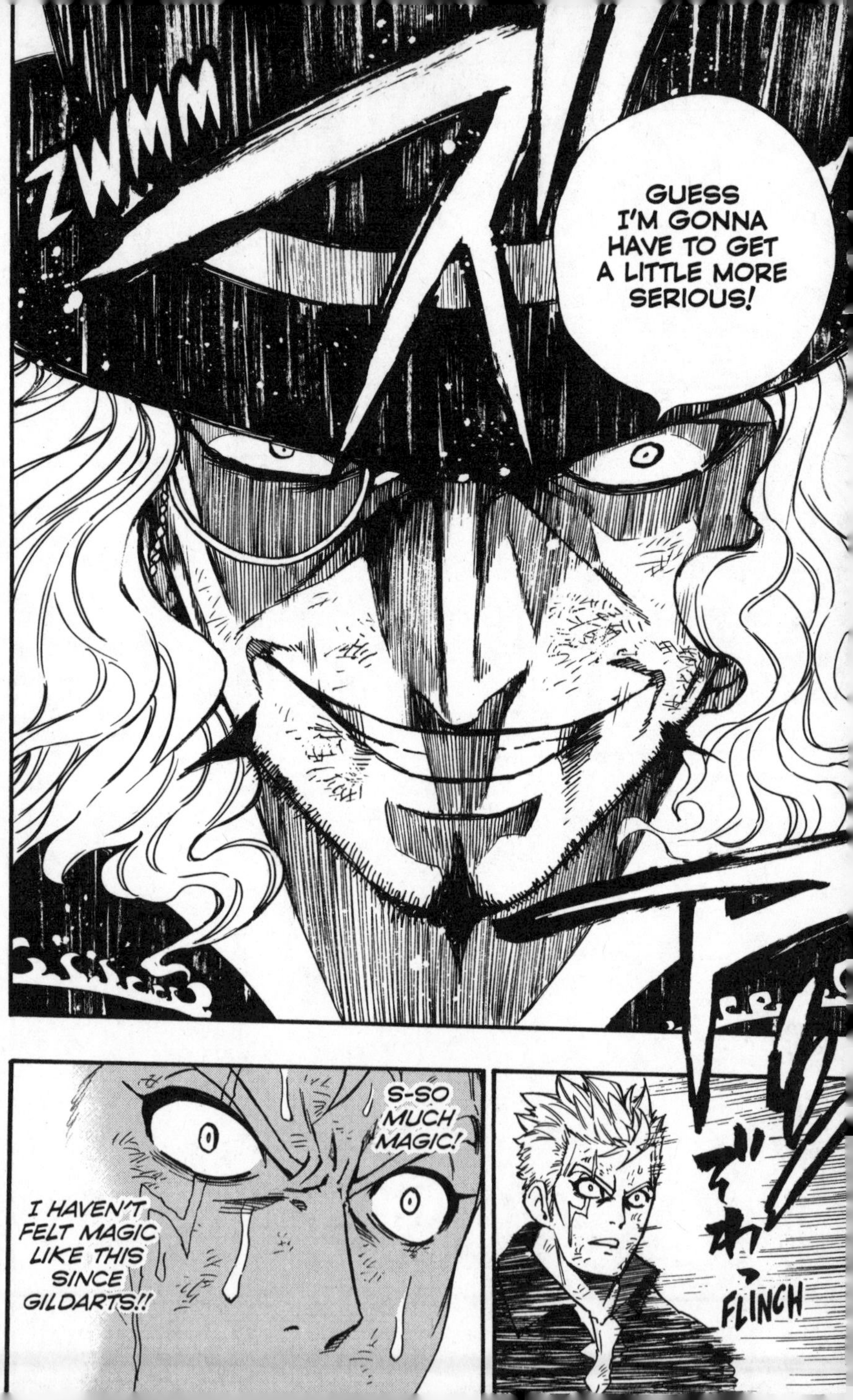
ZWMM
GUESS I'M GONNA HAVE TO GET A LITTLE MORE SERIOUS!
ざわっ
FLINCH
S-SO MUCH MAGIC!
I HAVEN'T FELT MAGIC LIKE THIS SINCE GILDARTS!!

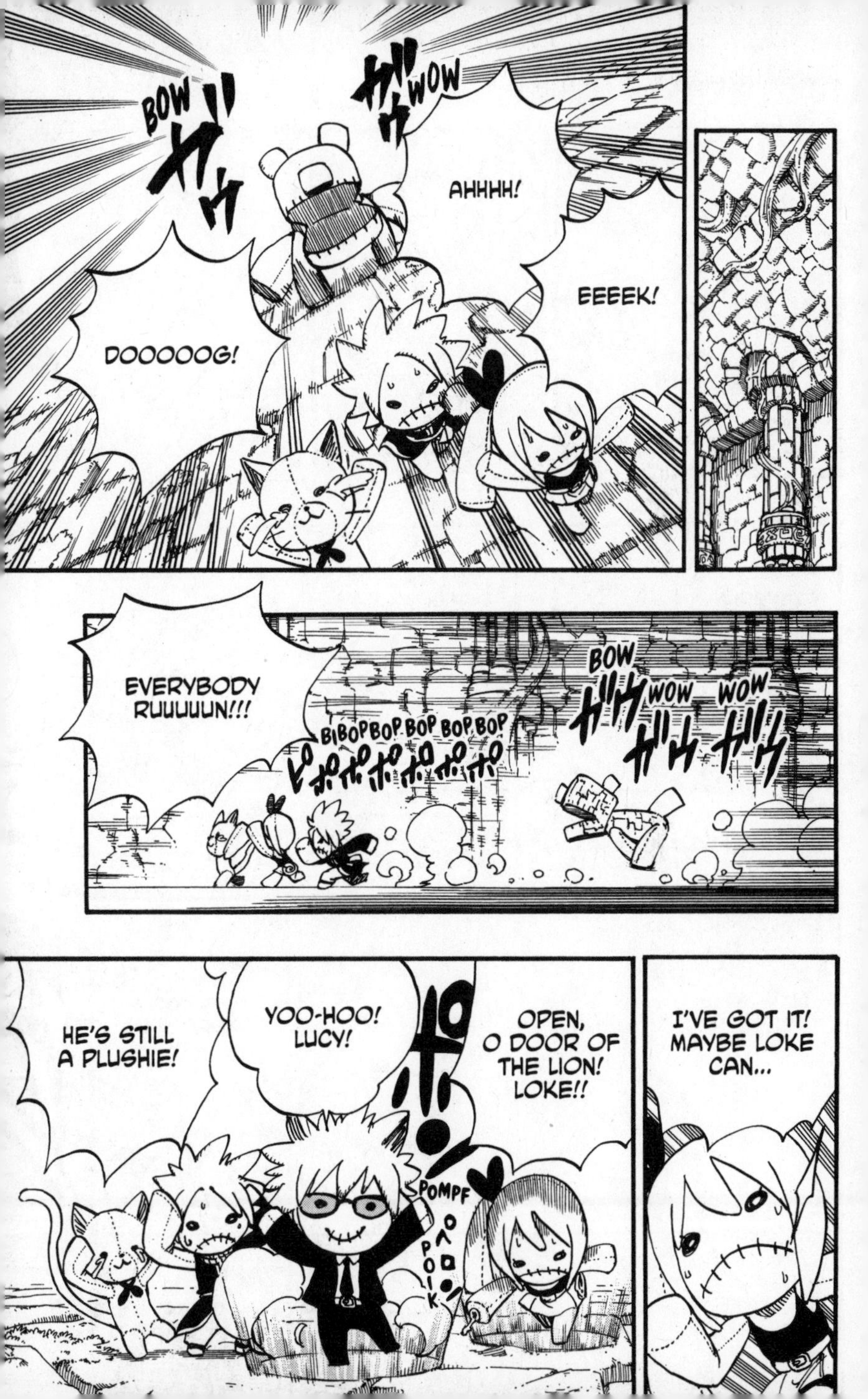
WOW
BOW
AHHHH!
EEEEK!
DOOOOOG!
BOW WOW WOW
BIBOPBOPBOPBOPBOP
EVERYBODY RUUUUUN!!!
I'VE GOT IT! MAYBE LOKE CAN...
OPEN, O DOOR OF THE LION! LOKE!!
POMPF
POIK
YOO-HOO! LUCY!
HE'S STILL A PLUSHIE!

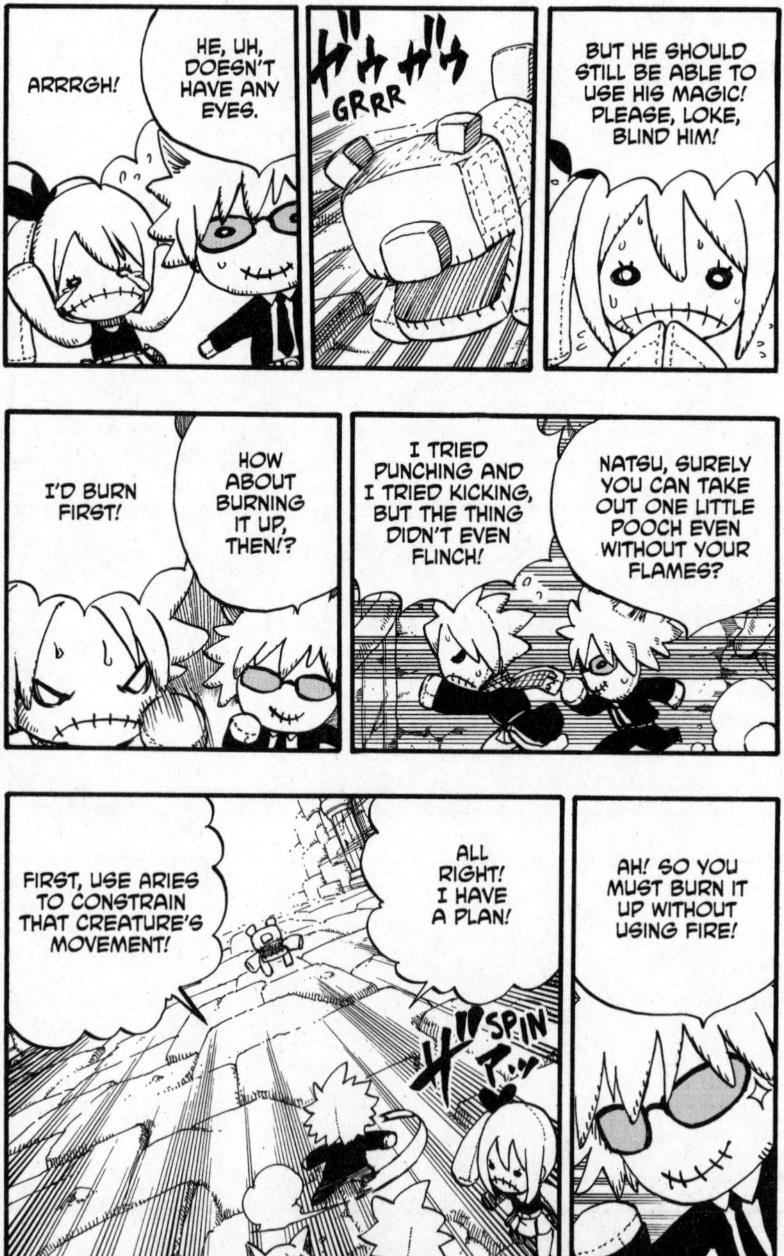
BUT HE SHOULD STILL BE ABLE TO USE HIS MAGIC! PLEASE, LOKE, BLIND HIM!
ガウガウ
GRRR
HE, UH, DOESN'T HAVE ANY EYES.
ARRRGH!
NATSU, SURELY YOU CAN TAKE OUT ONE LITTLE POOCH EVEN WITHOUT YOUR FLAMES?
I TRIED PUNCHING AND I TRIED KICKING, BUT THE THING DIDN'T EVEN FLINCH!
HOW ABOUT BURNING IT UP, THEN!?
I'D BURN FIRST!
AH! SO YOU MUST BURN IT UP WITHOUT USING FIRE!
ALL RIGHT! I HAVE A PLAN!
SPIN
FIRST, USE ARIES TO CONSTRAIN THAT CREATURE'S MOVEMENT!

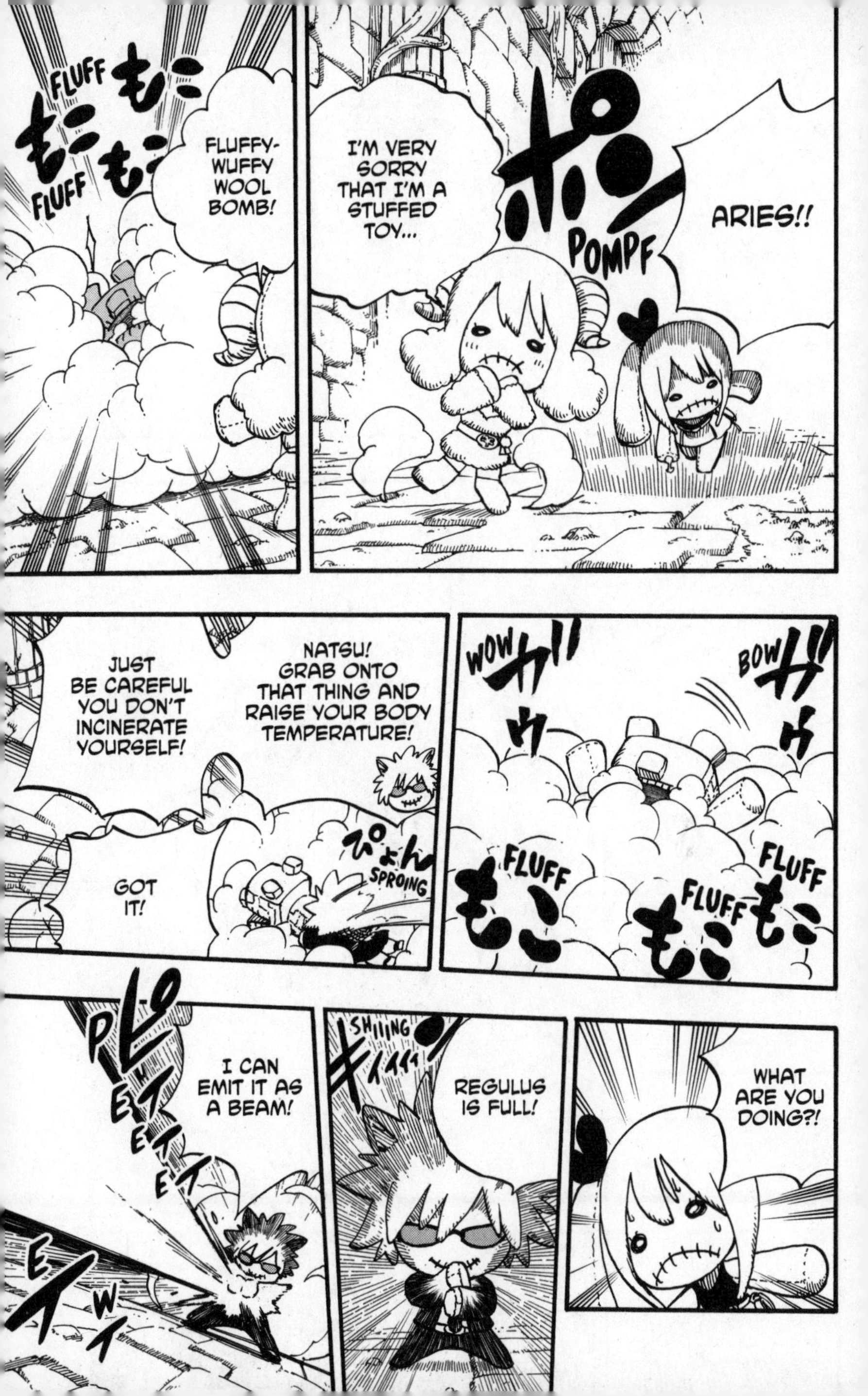
ポン
POMPF
ARIES!!
I'M VERY SORRY THAT I'M A STUFFED TOY...
FLUFFY-WUFFY WOOL BOMB!
もこ
FLUFF
もこ
FLUFF
BOW
ガウ
WOW
ガウ
FLUFF
もこ
FLUFF
もこ
FLUFF
もこ
NATSU! GRAB ONTO THAT THING AND RAISE YOUR BODY TEMPERATURE!
JUST BE CAREFUL YOU DON'T INCINERATE YOURSELF!
ぴょん
SPROING
GOT IT!
WHAT ARE YOU DOING?!
SHIIING
キィィ
REGULUS IS FULL!
I CAN EMIT IT AS A BEAM!
ピーイイイ

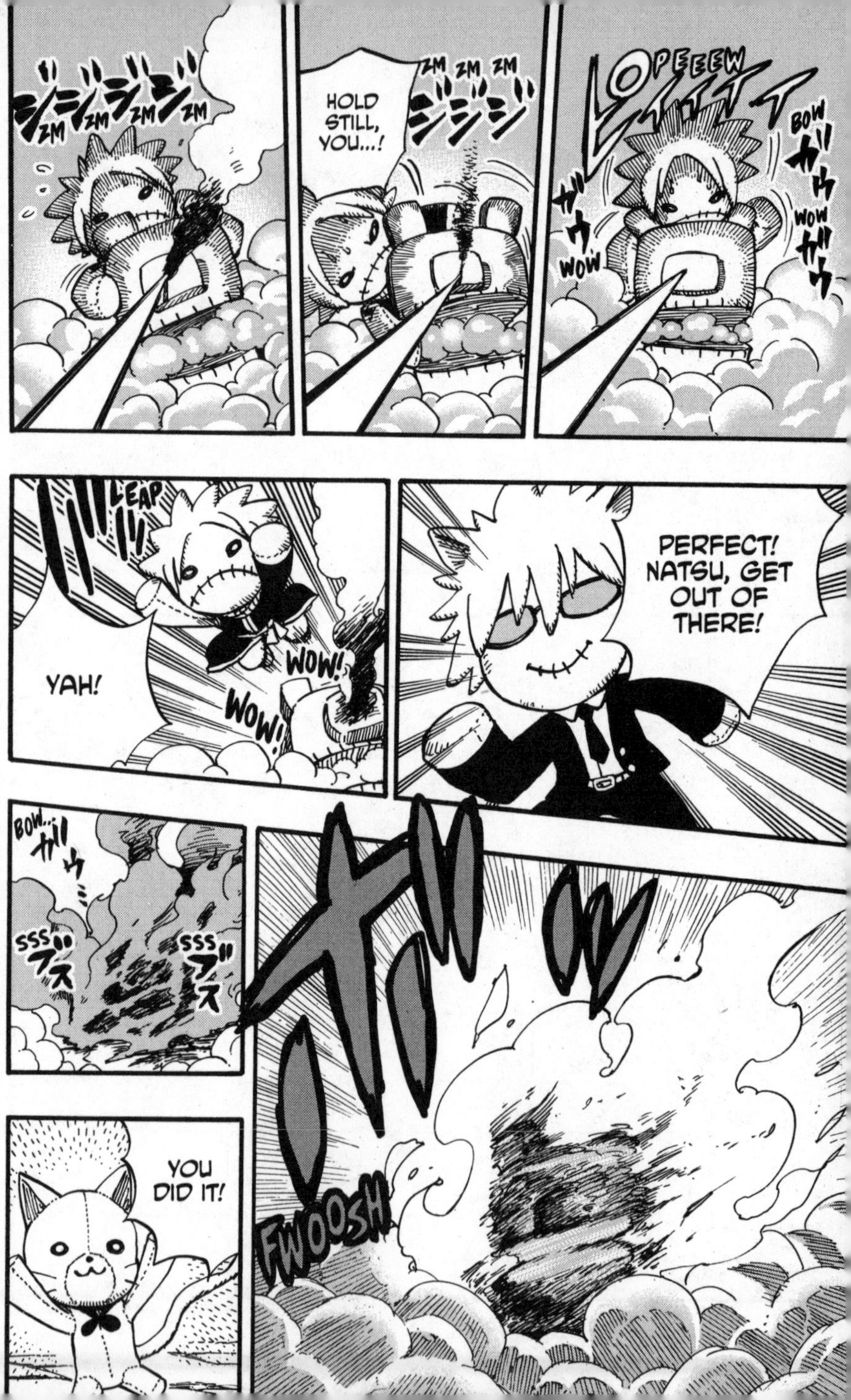
PEEEEW
BOW
WOW
WOW
ZM ZM ZM
HOLD STILL, YOU...!
ZM ZM ZM ZM ZM
PERFECT! NATSU, GET OUT OF THERE!
LEAP
YAH!
WOW!
WOW!
FWOOSH
BOW...
SSS
SSS
YOU DID IT!

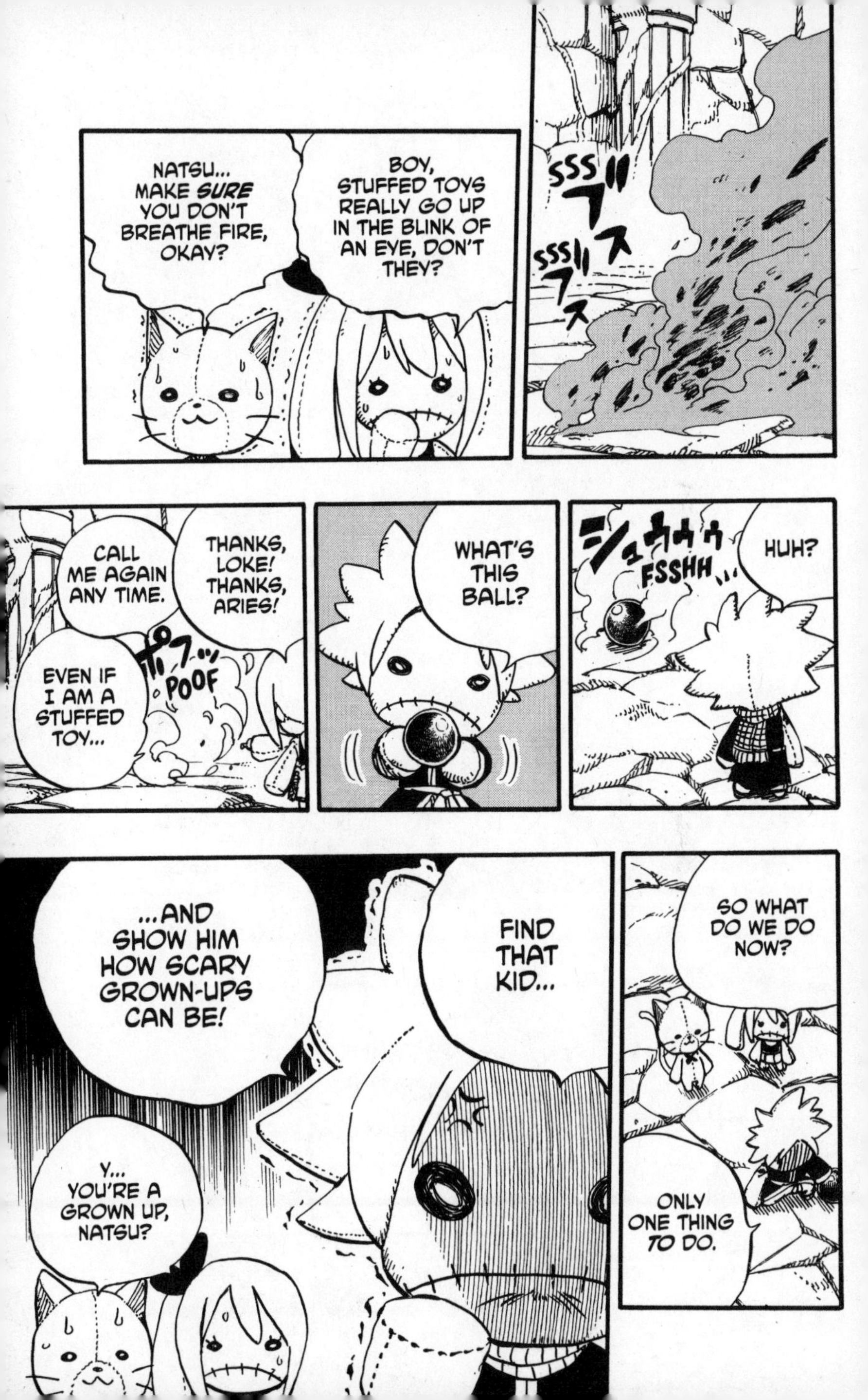
SSS
SSS
BOY, STUFFED TOYS REALLY GO UP IN THE BLINK OF AN EYE, DON'T THEY?
NATSU... MAKE *SURE* YOU DON'T BREATHE FIRE, OKAY?
FSSHH
HUH?
WHAT'S THIS BALL?
THANKS, LOKE! THANKS, ARIES!
CALL ME AGAIN ANY TIME.
POOF
EVEN IF I AM A STUFFED TOY...
SO WHAT DO WE DO NOW?
ONLY ONE THING *TO* DO.
FIND THAT KID...
...AND SHOW HIM HOW SCARY GROWN-UPS CAN BE!
Y... YOU'RE A GROWN UP, NATSU?

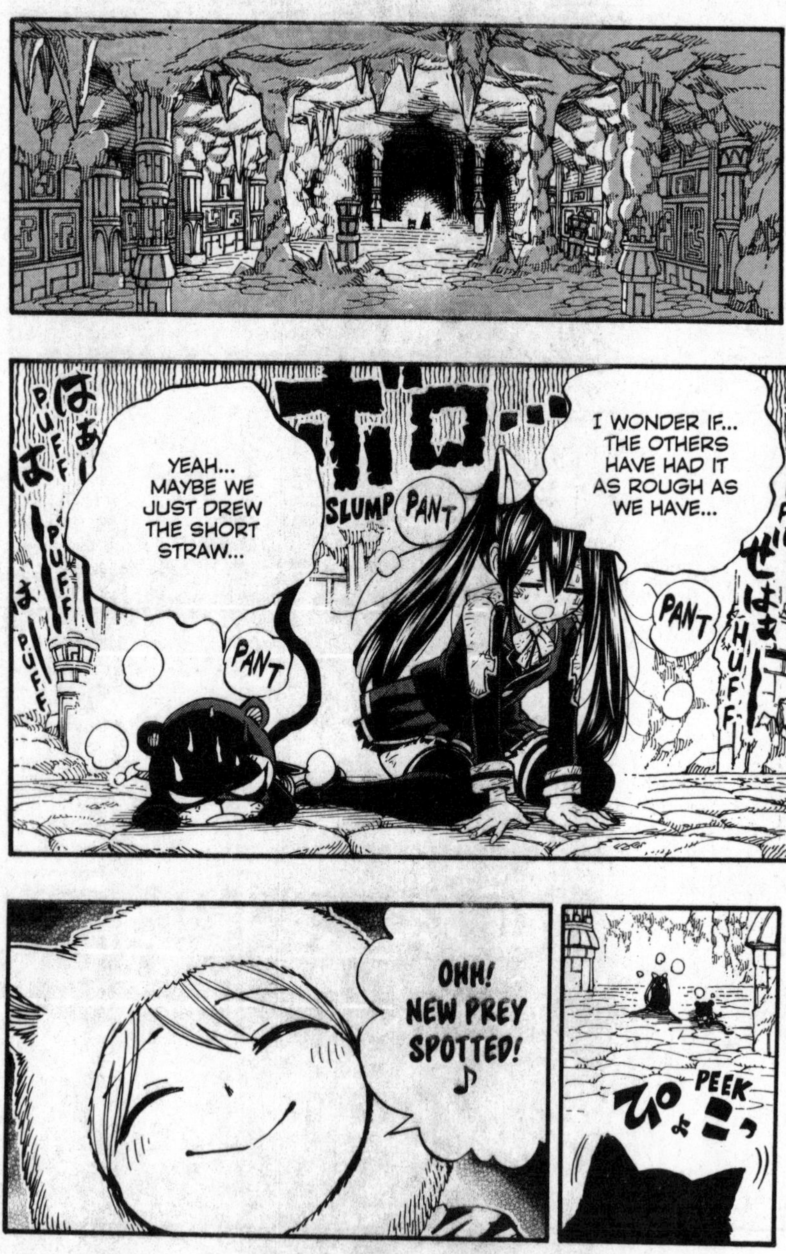
HUFF HUFF
HUFF HUFF
I WONDER IF... THE OTHERS HAVE HAD IT AS ROUGH AS WE HAVE...
PANT
SLUMP
PANT
YEAH... MAYBE WE JUST DREW THE SHORT STRAW...
PANT
PUFF PUFF
PUFF
PEEK
ぴょこっ
OHH! NEW PREY SPOTTED! ♪

FAIRY TAIL

100 YEARS QUEST

Chapter 97: Haku, the White-Tiger Dragon

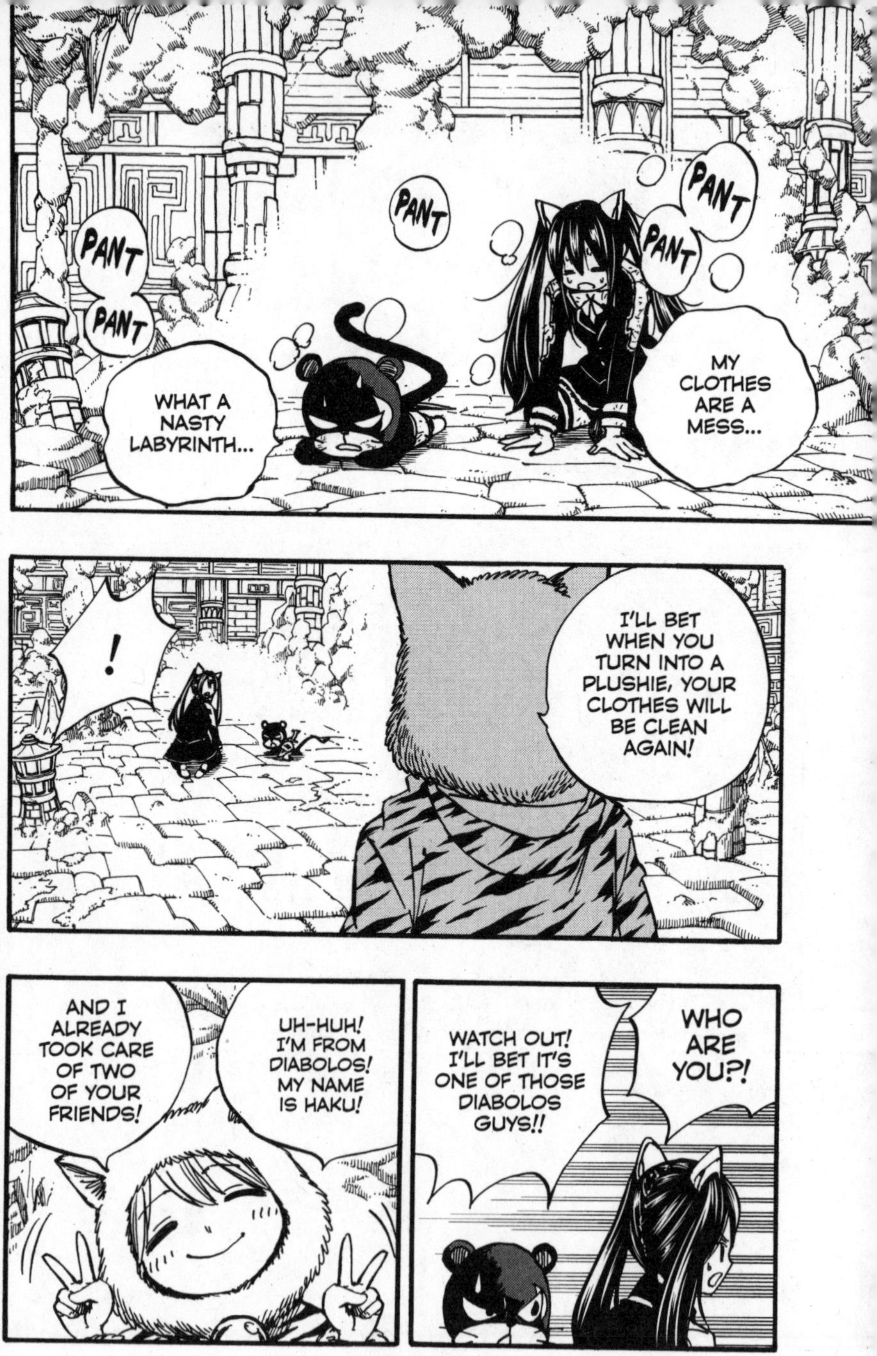
PANT
PANT
MY CLOTHES ARE A MESS...
PANT
PANT
PANT
WHAT A NASTY LABYRINTH...
I'LL BET WHEN YOU TURN INTO A PLUSHIE, YOUR CLOTHES WILL BE CLEAN AGAIN!
!
WHO ARE YOU?!
WATCH OUT! I'LL BET IT'S ONE OF THOSE DIABOLOS GUYS!!
UH-HUH! I'M FROM DIABOLOS! MY NAME IS HAKU!
AND I ALREADY TOOK CARE OF TWO OF YOUR FRIENDS!

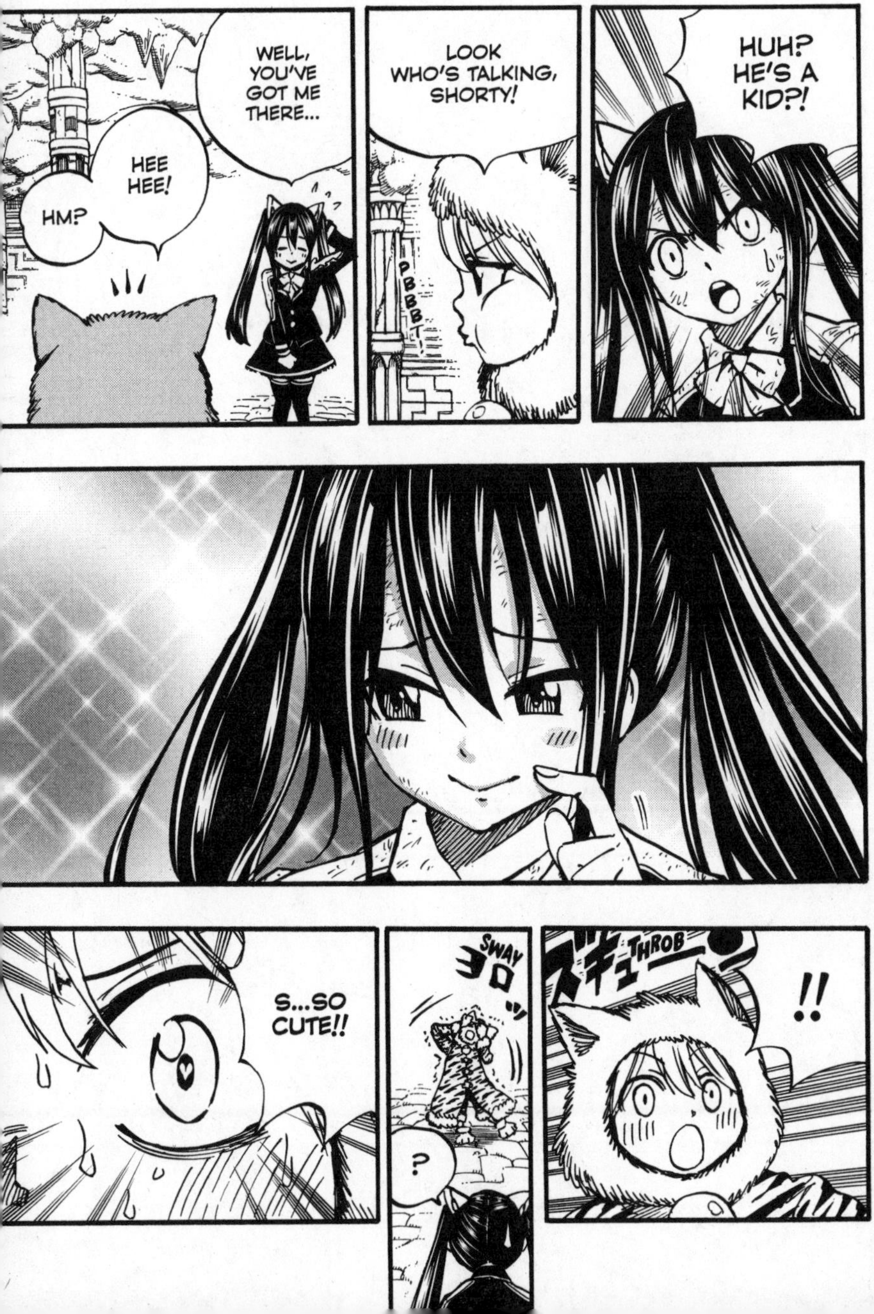
HUH? HE'S A KID?!
LOOK WHO'S TALKING, SHORTY!
PBBBT!
WELL, YOU'VE GOT ME THERE...
HEE HEE!
HM?
ズキュ
THROB
!!
ヨロ
SWAY
?
S...SO CUTE!!

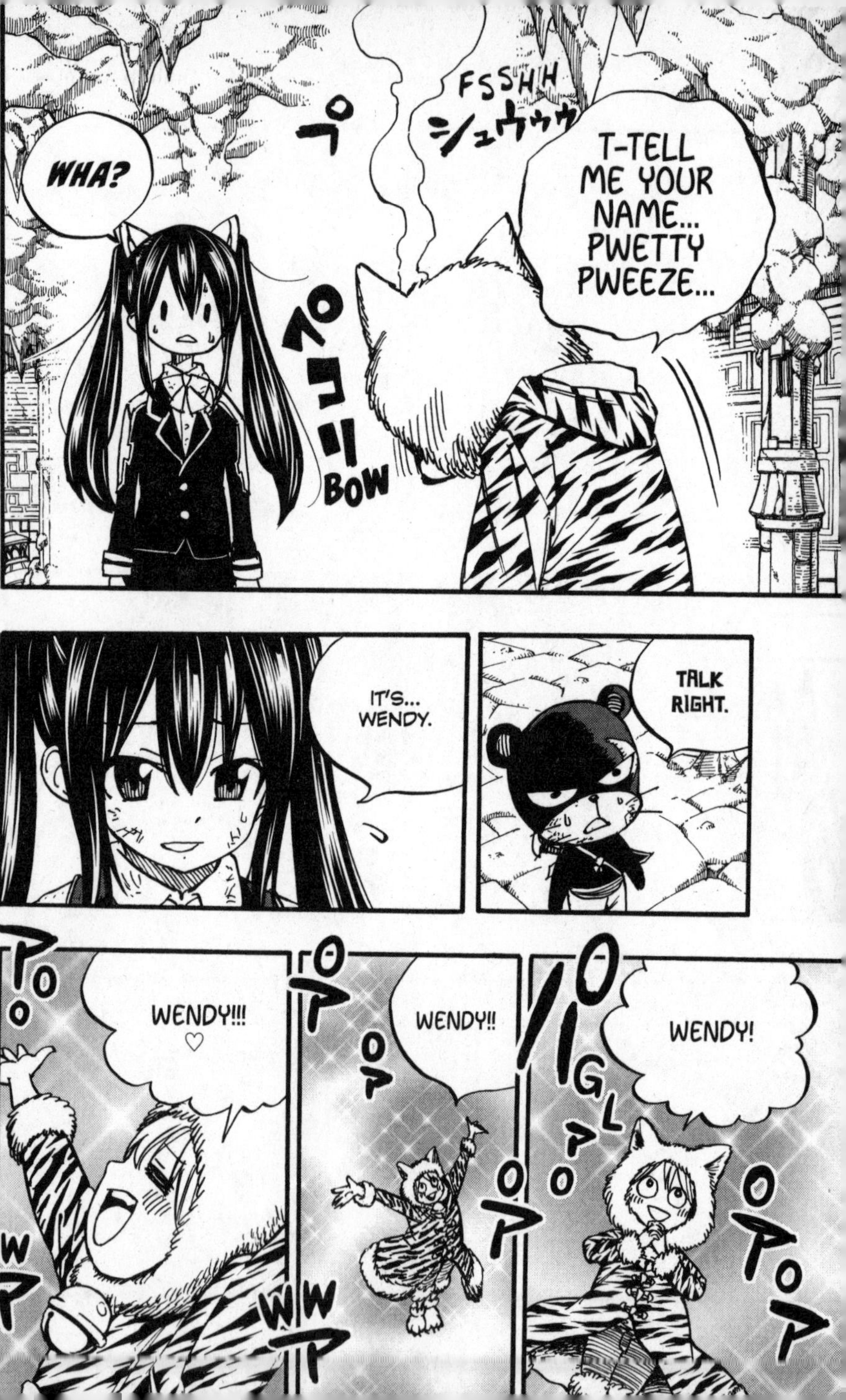
FSSHH
シュウウウ
T-TELL ME YOUR NAME... PWETTY PWEEZE...
プ
WHA?
ペコリ
BOW
TALK RIGHT.
IT'S... WENDY.
WENDY!
WENDY!!
WENDY!!! ♡

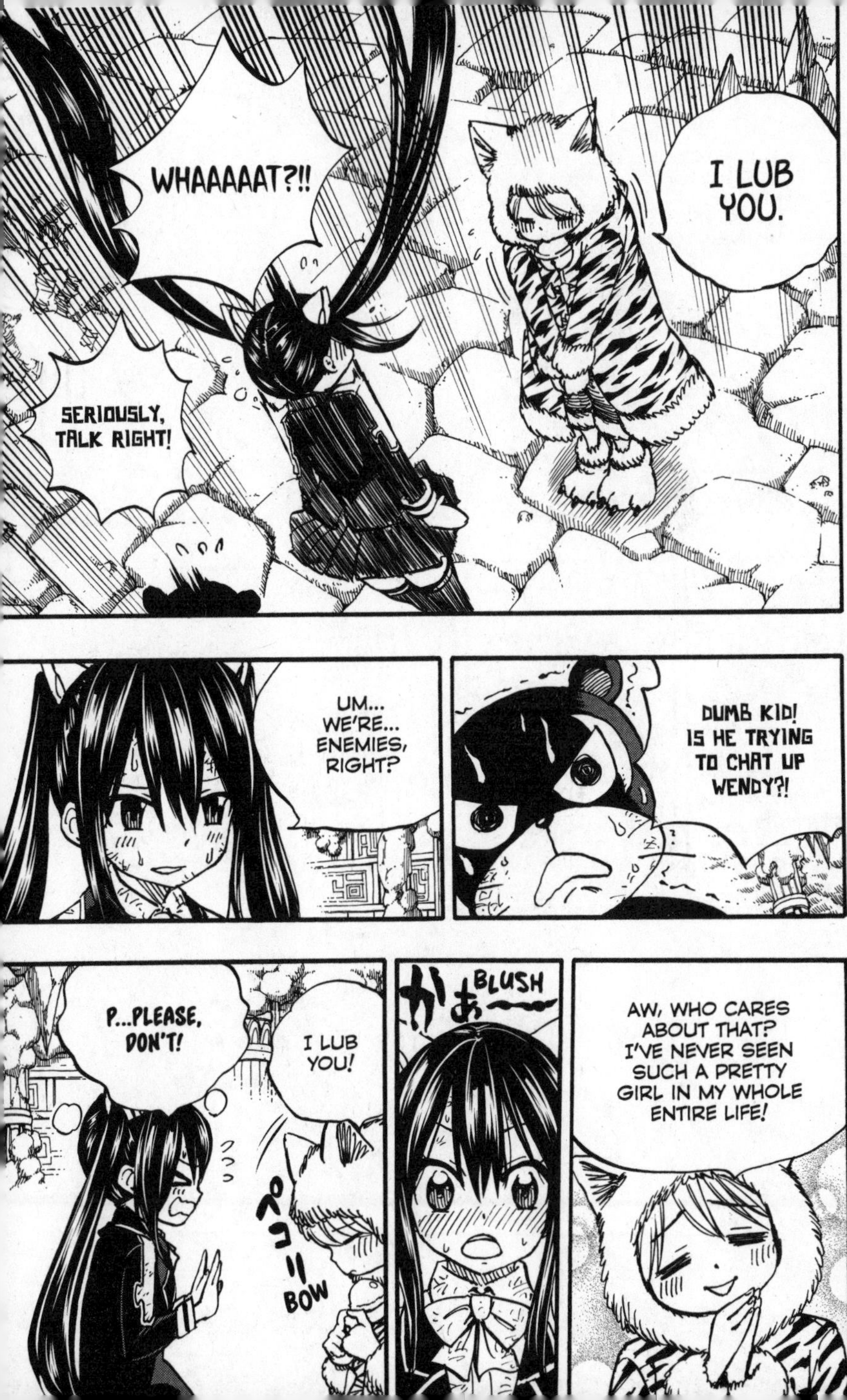
I LUB YOU.
WHAAAAAT?!!
SERIOUSLY, TALK RIGHT!
DUMB KID! IS HE TRYING TO CHAT UP WENDY?!
UM... WE'RE... ENEMIES, RIGHT?
AW, WHO CARES ABOUT THAT? I'VE NEVER SEEN SUCH A PRETTY GIRL IN MY WHOLE ENTIRE LIFE!
かぁ~~~ BLUSH
I LUB YOU!
ペコリ BOW
P...PLEASE, DON'T!

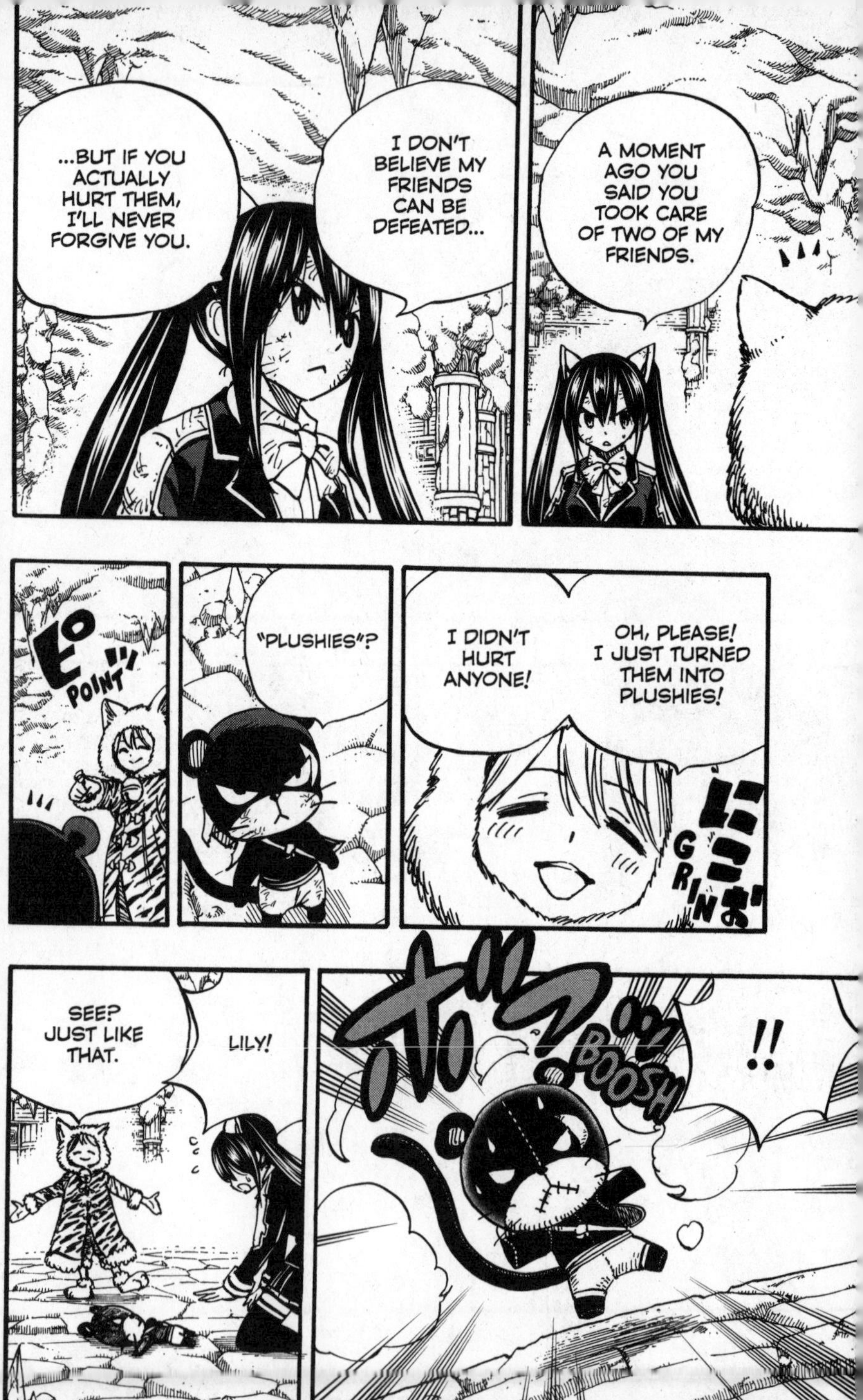
A MOMENT AGO YOU SAID YOU TOOK CARE OF TWO OF MY FRIENDS.
I DON'T BELIEVE MY FRIENDS CAN BE DEFEATED...
...BUT IF YOU ACTUALLY HURT THEM, I'LL NEVER FORGIVE YOU.
OH, PLEASE! I JUST TURNED THEM INTO PLUSHIES!
I DIDN'T HURT ANYONE!
GRIN
"PLUSHIES"?
POINT
!!
BOOSH
LILY!
SEE? JUST LIKE THAT.

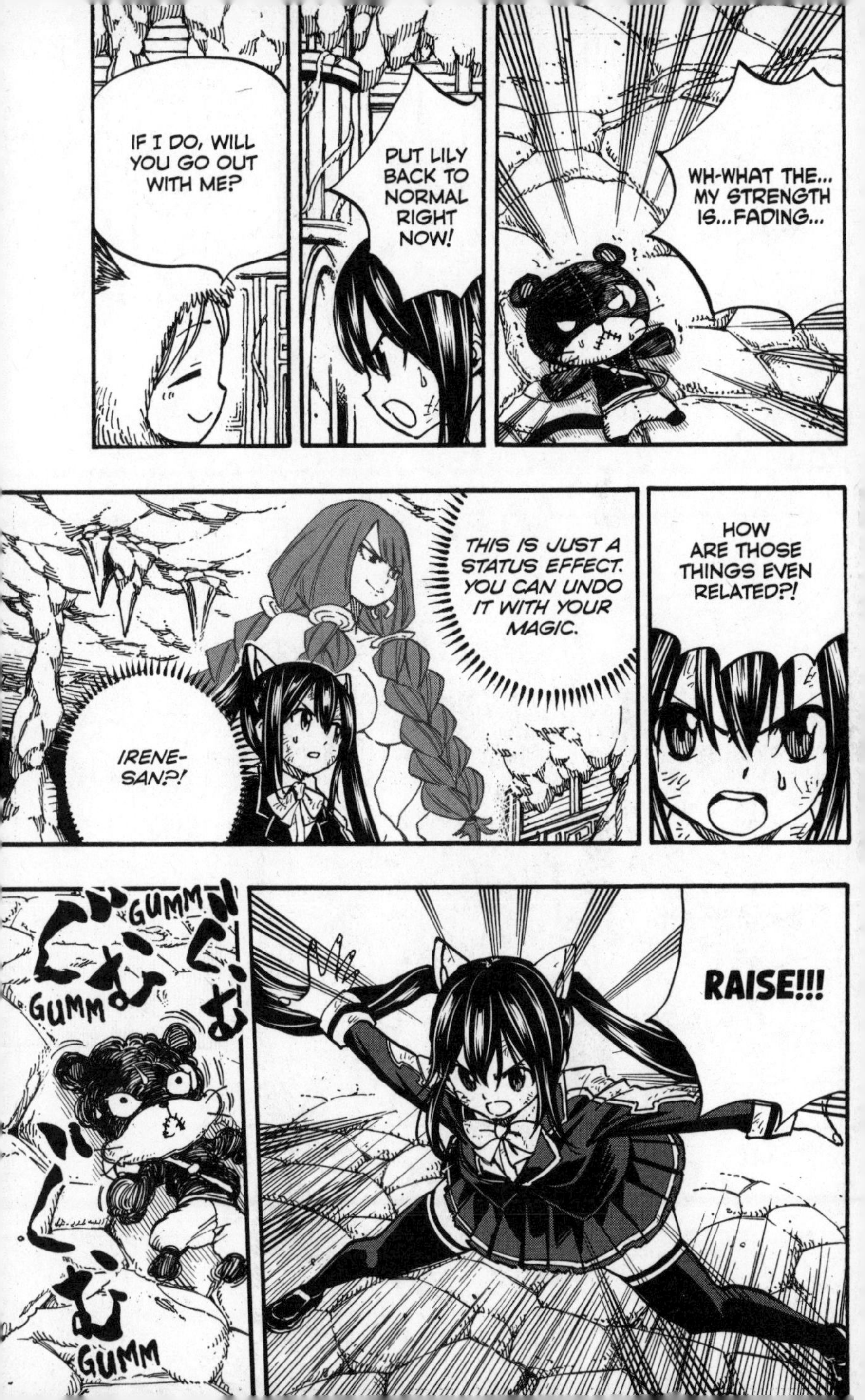
WH-WHAT THE... MY STRENGTH IS...FADING...
PUT LILY BACK TO NORMAL RIGHT NOW!
IF I DO, WILL YOU GO OUT WITH ME?
HOW ARE THOSE THINGS EVEN RELATED?!
THIS IS JUST A STATUS EFFECT. YOU CAN UNDO IT WITH YOUR MAGIC.
IRENE-SAN?!
RAISE!!!
GUMM
GUMM
GUMM

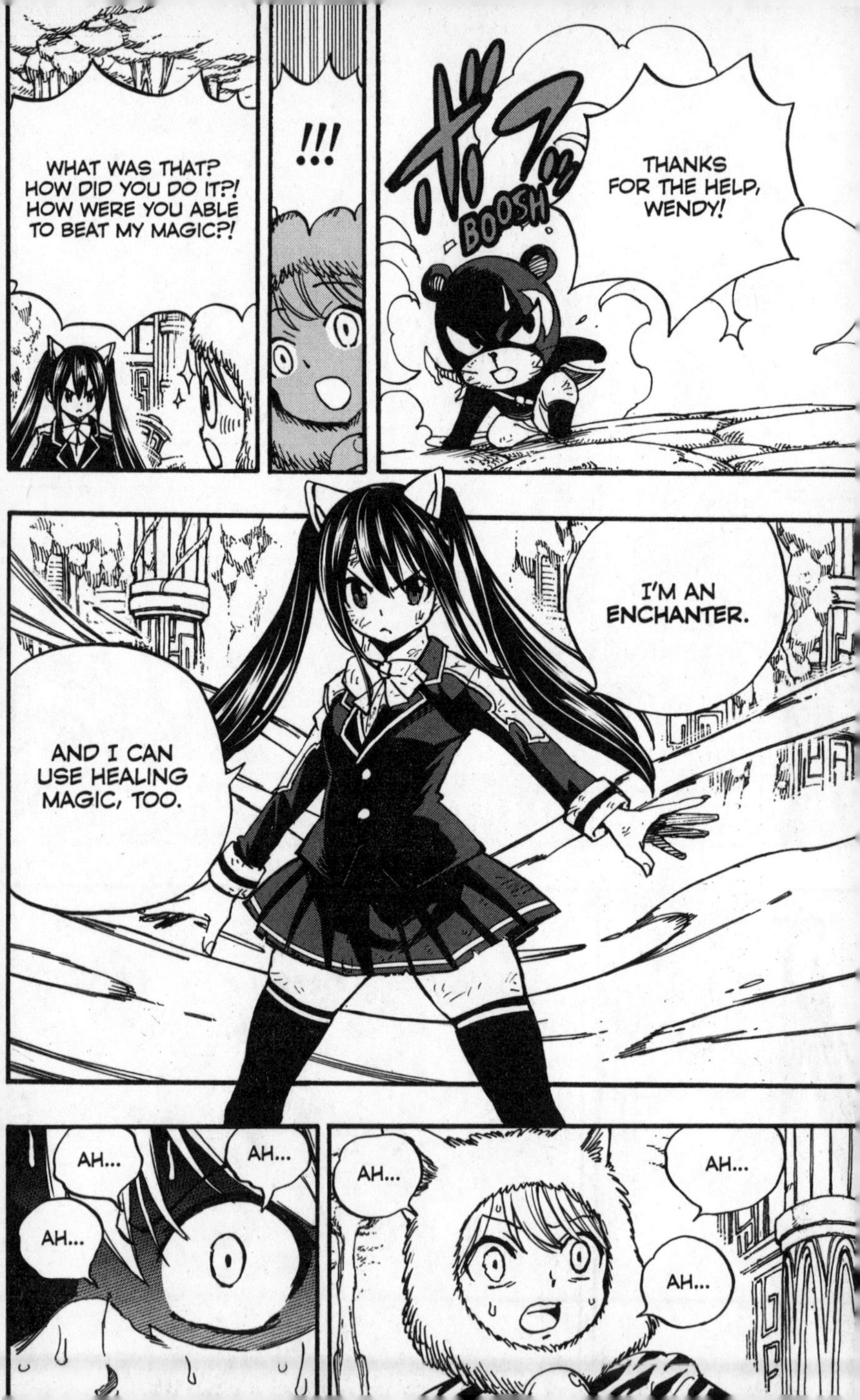
BOOSH
THANKS FOR THE HELP, WENDY!
!!!
WHAT WAS THAT? HOW DID YOU DO IT?! HOW WERE YOU ABLE TO BEAT MY MAGIC?!
I'M AN ENCHANTER.
AND I CAN USE HEALING MAGIC, TOO.
AH...
AH...
AH...
AH...
AH...
AH...

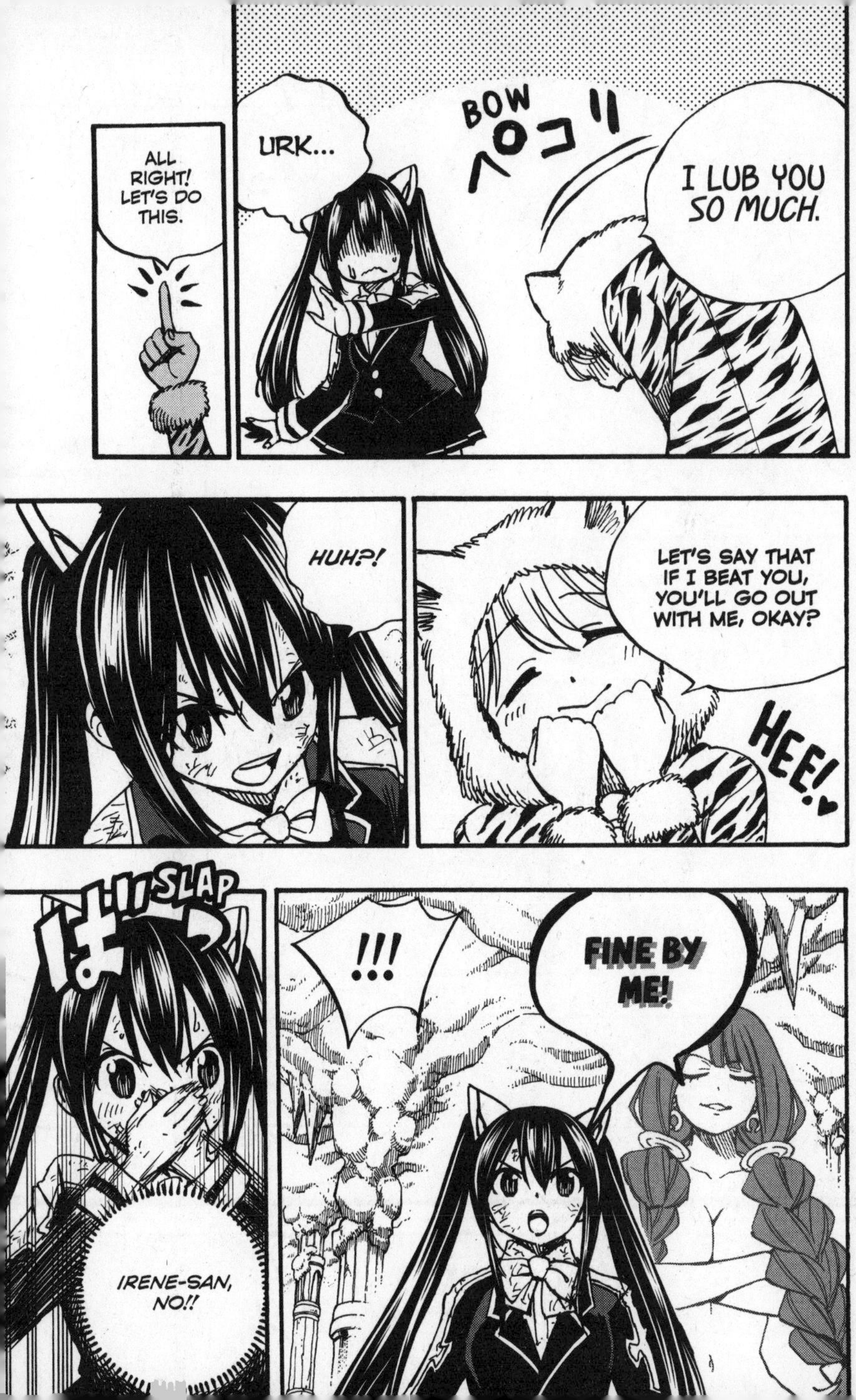
I LUB YOU SO MUCH.
BOW
URK...
ALL RIGHT! LET'S DO THIS.
LET'S SAY THAT IF I BEAT YOU, YOU'LL GO OUT WITH ME, OKAY?
HEE!♥
HUH?!
FINE BY ME!
!!!
SLAP
IRENE-SAN, NO!!

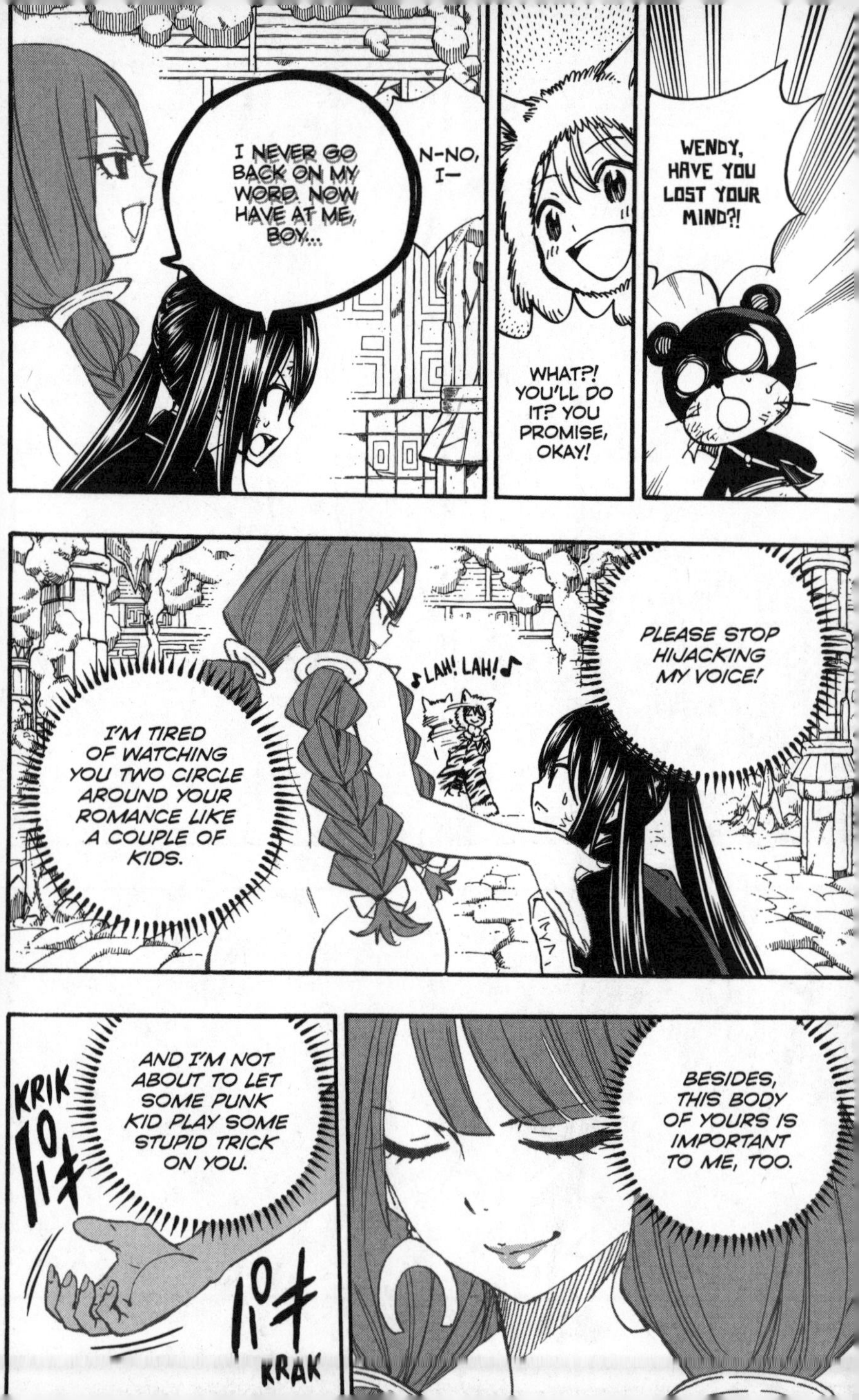
WENDY, HAVE YOU LOST YOUR MIND?!
WHAT?! YOU'LL DO IT? YOU PROMISE, OKAY!
N-NO, I—
I NEVER GO BACK ON MY WORD. NOW HAVE AT ME, BOY...
PLEASE STOP HIJACKING MY VOICE!
♪LAH! LAH!♪
I'M TIRED OF WATCHING YOU TWO CIRCLE AROUND YOUR ROMANCE LIKE A COUPLE OF KIDS.
BESIDES, THIS BODY OF YOURS IS IMPORTANT TO ME, TOO.
AND I'M NOT ABOUT TO LET SOME PUNK KID PLAY SOME STUPID TRICK ON YOU.
KRIK
KRAK

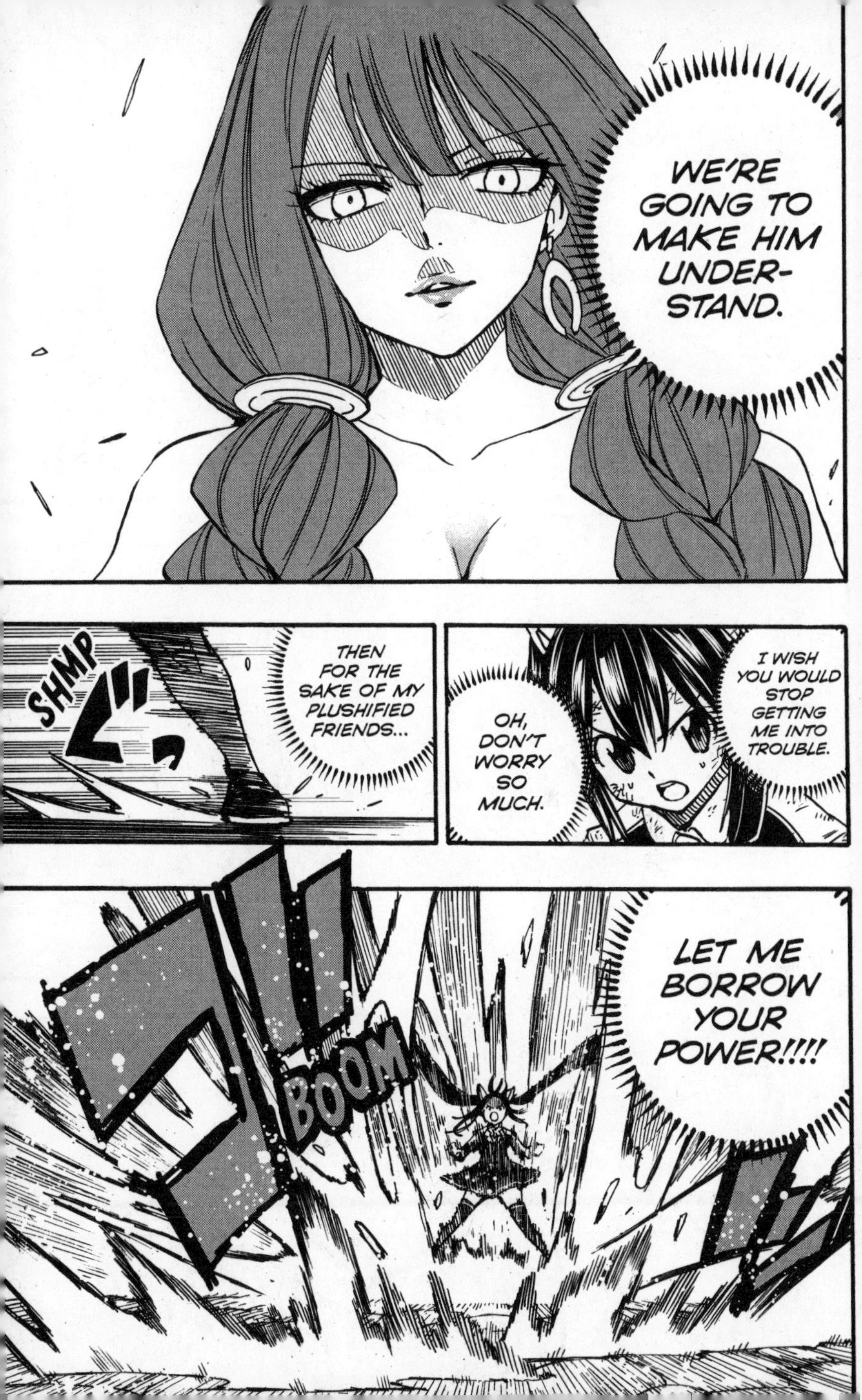
WE'RE GOING TO MAKE HIM UNDER-STAND.
I WISH YOU WOULD STOP GETTING ME INTO TROUBLE.
OH, DON'T WORRY SO MUCH.
THEN FOR THE SAKE OF MY PLUSHIFIED FRIENDS...
SHMP
LET ME BORROW YOUR POWER!!!!
BOOM

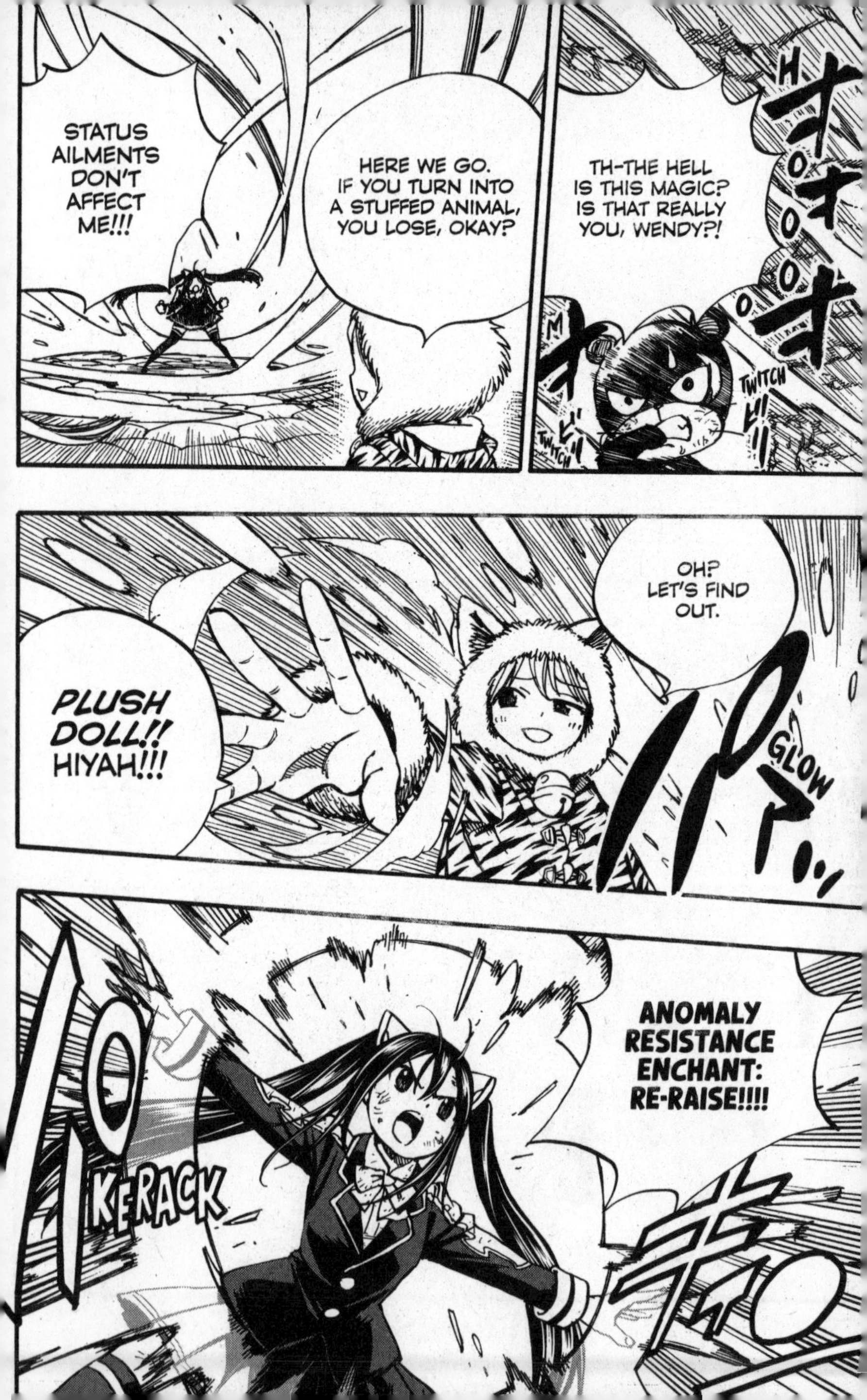
TH-THE HELL IS THIS MAGIC? IS THAT REALLY YOU, WENDY?!
TWITCH
TWITCH
HERE WE GO. IF YOU TURN INTO A STUFFED ANIMAL, YOU LOSE, OKAY?
STATUS AILMENTS DON'T AFFECT ME!!!
OH? LET'S FIND OUT.
GLOW
PLUSH DOLL!! HIYAH!!!
ANOMALY RESISTANCE ENCHANT: RE-RAISE!!!!
KERACK

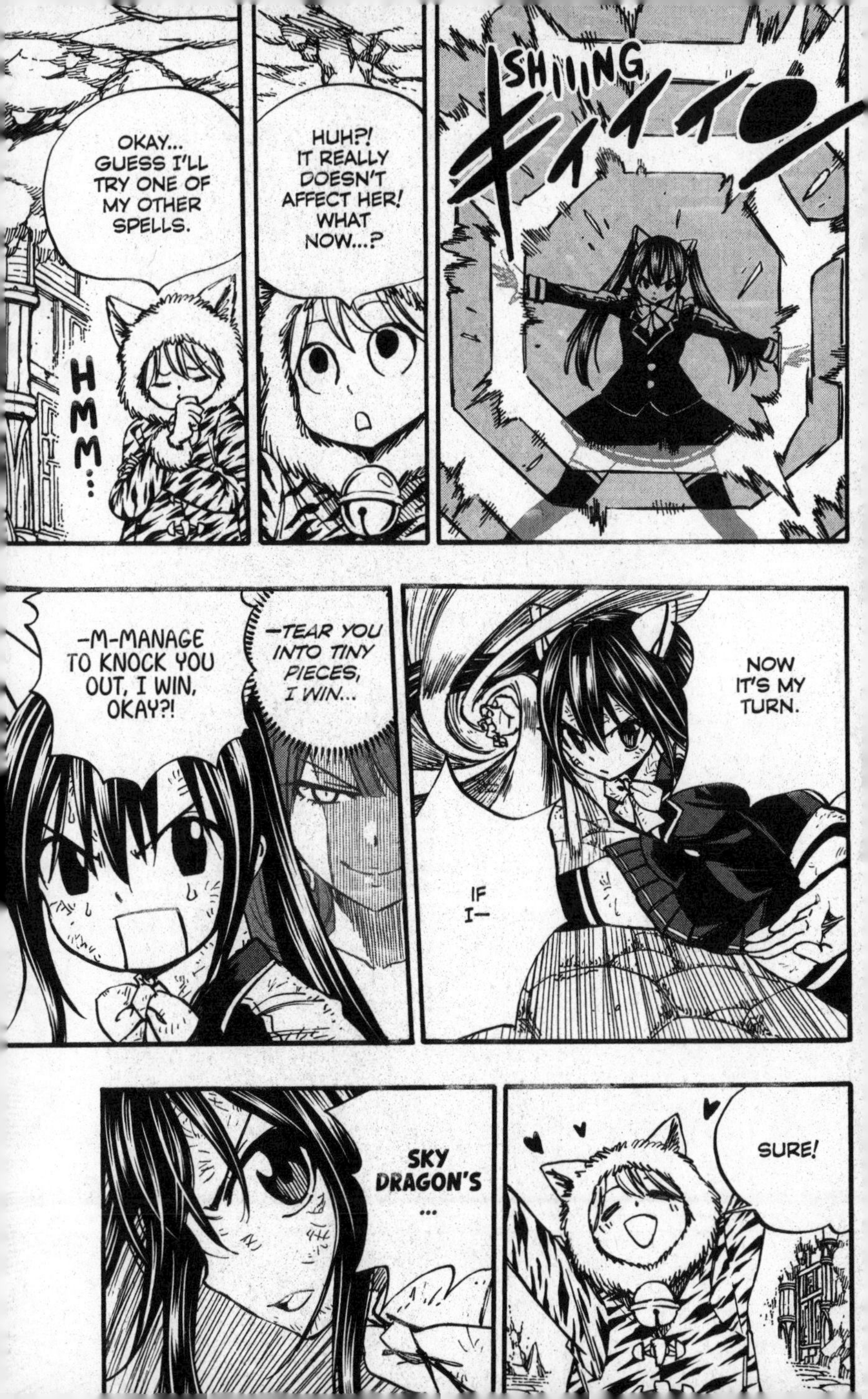
SHIIING
HUH?! IT REALLY DOESN'T AFFECT HER! WHAT NOW...?
OKAY... GUESS I'LL TRY ONE OF MY OTHER SPELLS.
HMM...
NOW IT'S MY TURN.
IF I—
—TEAR YOU INTO TINY PIECES, I WIN...
-M-MANAGE TO KNOCK YOU OUT, I WIN, OKAY?!
SURE!
SKY DRAGON'S ...

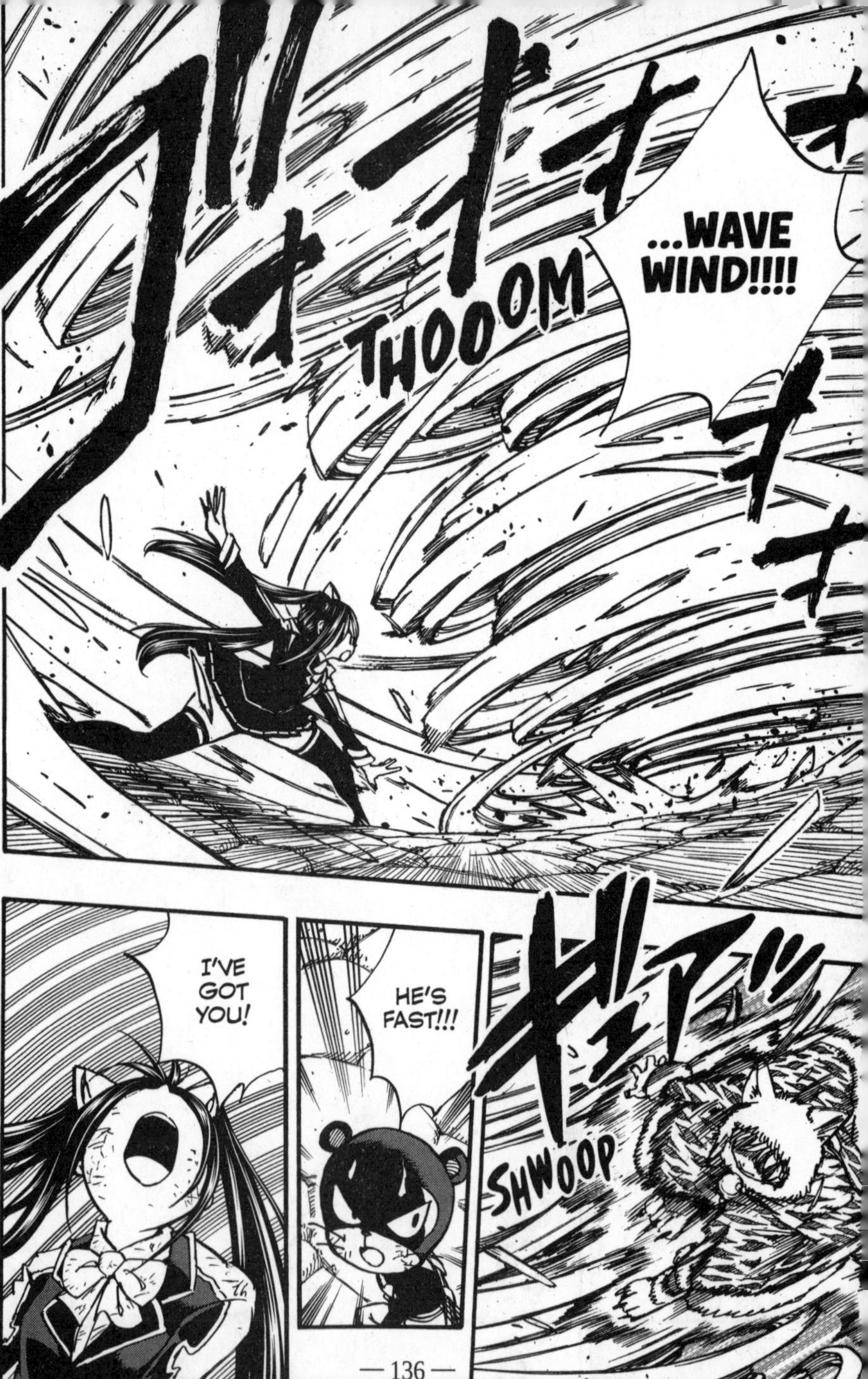
...WAVE WIND!!!!
THOOOM
SHWOOP
HE'S FAST!!!
I'VE GOT YOU!

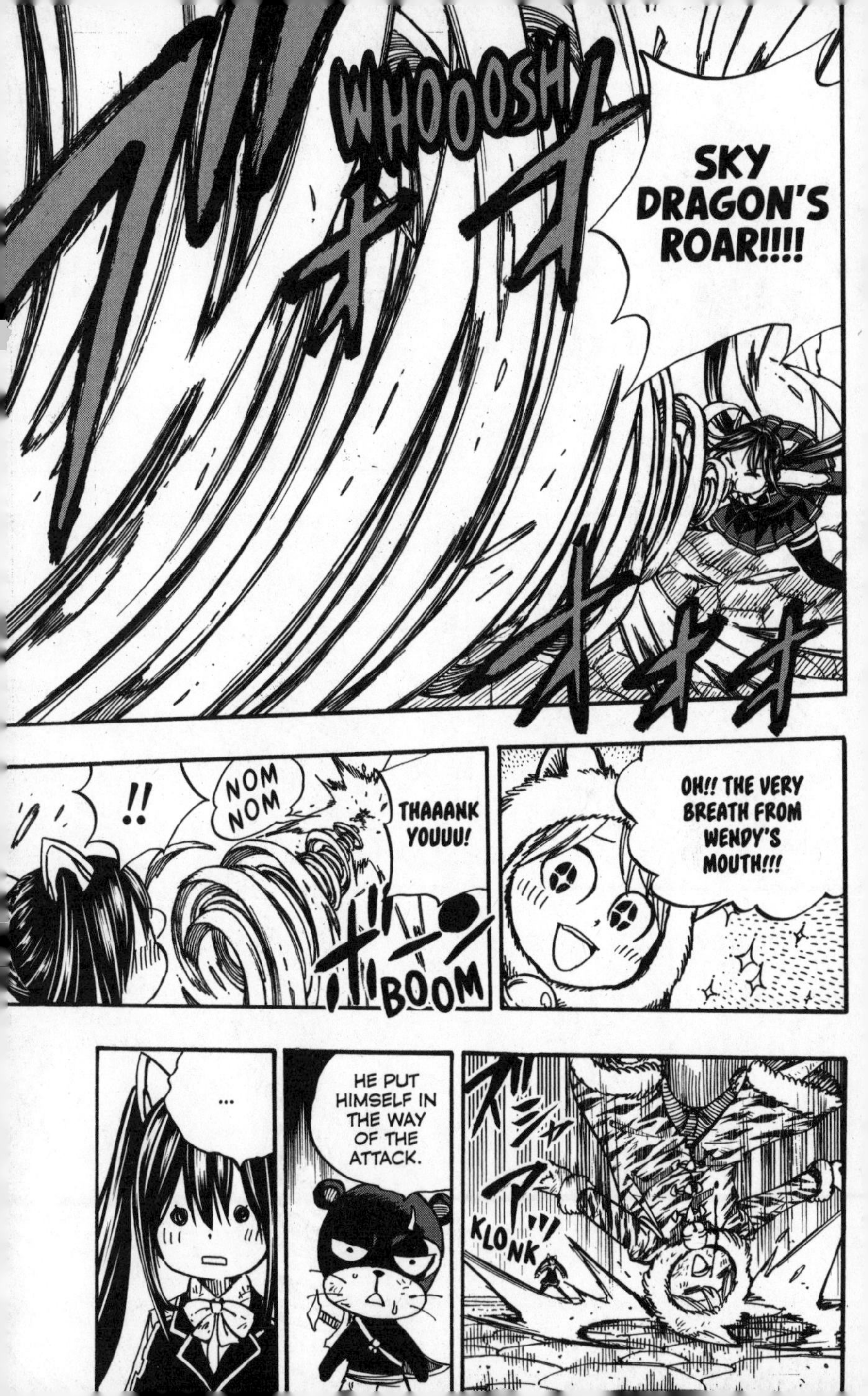
SKY DRAGON'S ROAR!!!!
WHOOOSH
OH!! THE VERY BREATH FROM WENDY'S MOUTH!!!
THAAANK YOUUU!
NOM NOM
!!
BOOM
KLONK
HE PUT HIMSELF IN THE WAY OF THE ATTACK.
...

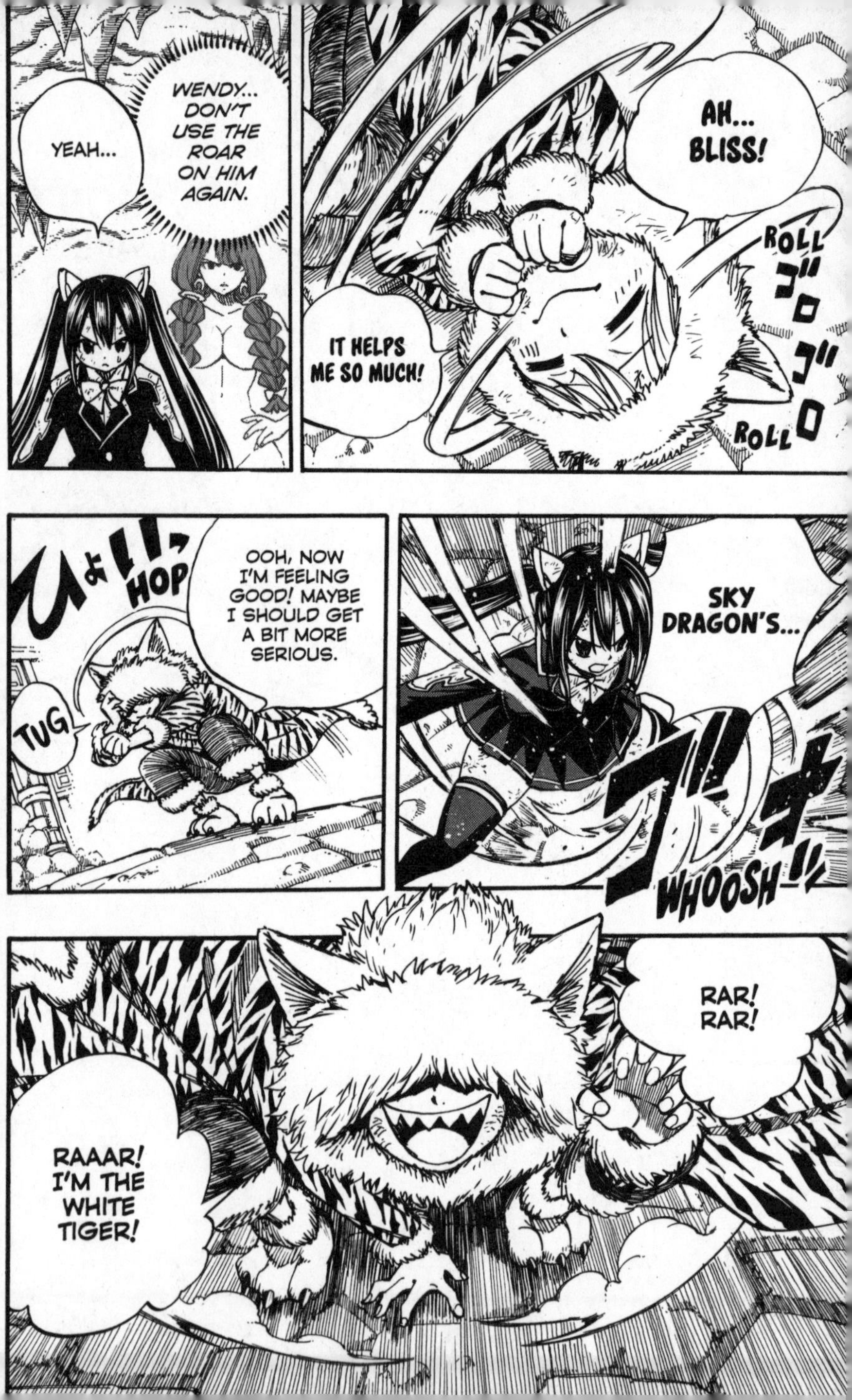
AH... BLISS!
ROLL ゴロ
ROLL ゴロ
IT HELPS ME SO MUCH!
WENDY... DON'T USE THE ROAR ON HIM AGAIN.
YEAH...
SKY DRAGON'S...
WHOOSH!!
OOH, NOW I'M FEELING GOOD! MAYBE I SHOULD GET A BIT MORE SERIOUS.
HOP
TUG
RAR! RAR!
RAAAR! I'M THE WHITE TIGER!

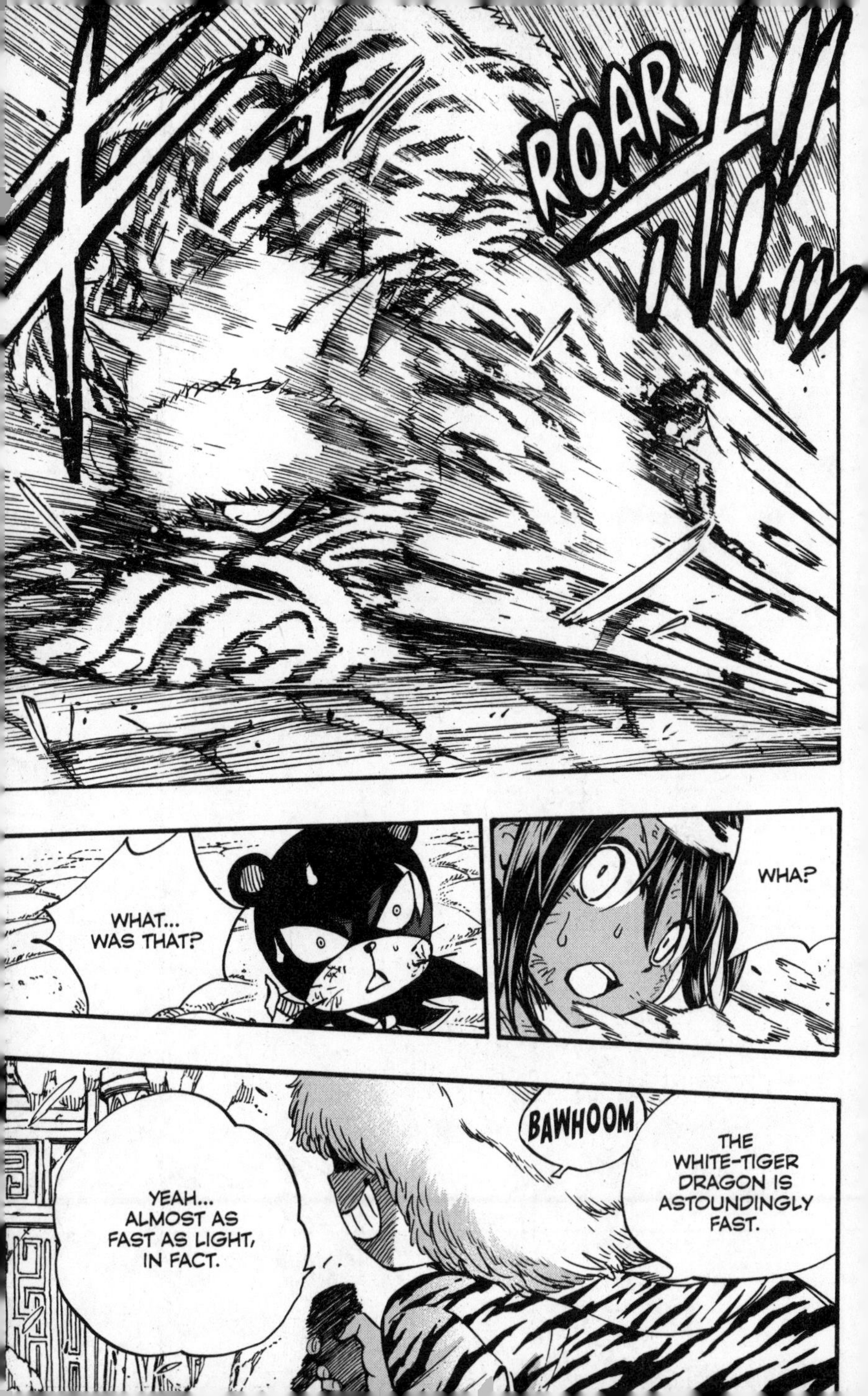
ROAR
WHA?
WHAT... WAS THAT?
BAWHOOM
THE WHITE-TIGER DRAGON IS ASTOUNDINGLY FAST.
YEAH... ALMOST AS FAST AS LIGHT, IN FACT.

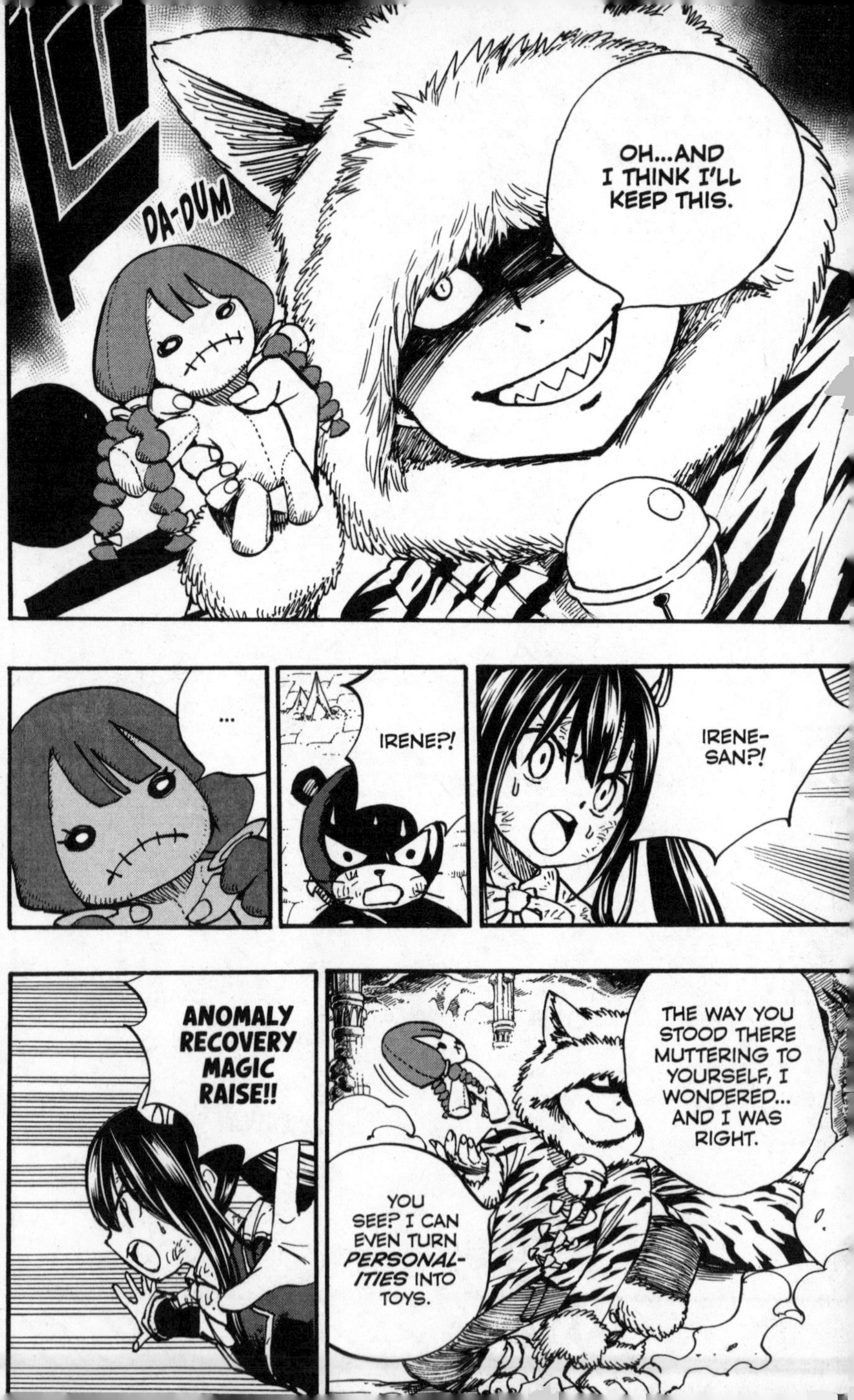
OH...AND I THINK I'LL KEEP THIS.
DA-DUM
IRENE-SAN?!
IRENE?!
...
THE WAY YOU STOOD THERE MUTTERING TO YOURSELF, I WONDERED... AND I WAS RIGHT.
YOU SEE? I CAN EVEN TURN *PERSONALITIES* INTO TOYS.
ANOMALY RECOVERY MAGIC RAISE!!

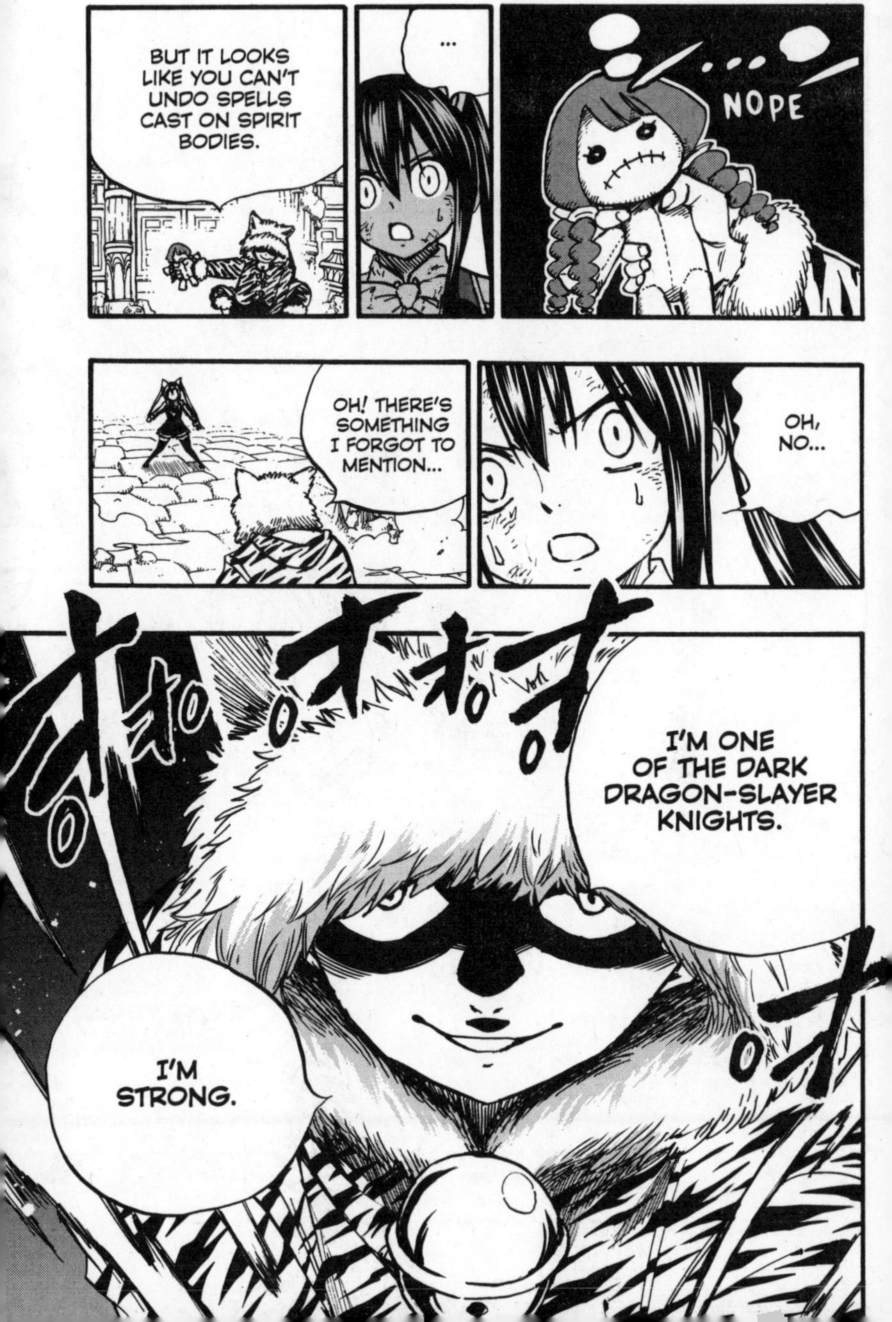
...
NOPE
...
BUT IT LOOKS LIKE YOU CAN'T UNDO SPELLS CAST ON SPIRIT BODIES.
OH, NO...
OH! THERE'S SOMETHING I FORGOT TO MENTION...
I'M ONE OF THE DARK DRAGON-SLAYER KNIGHTS.
I'M STRONG.

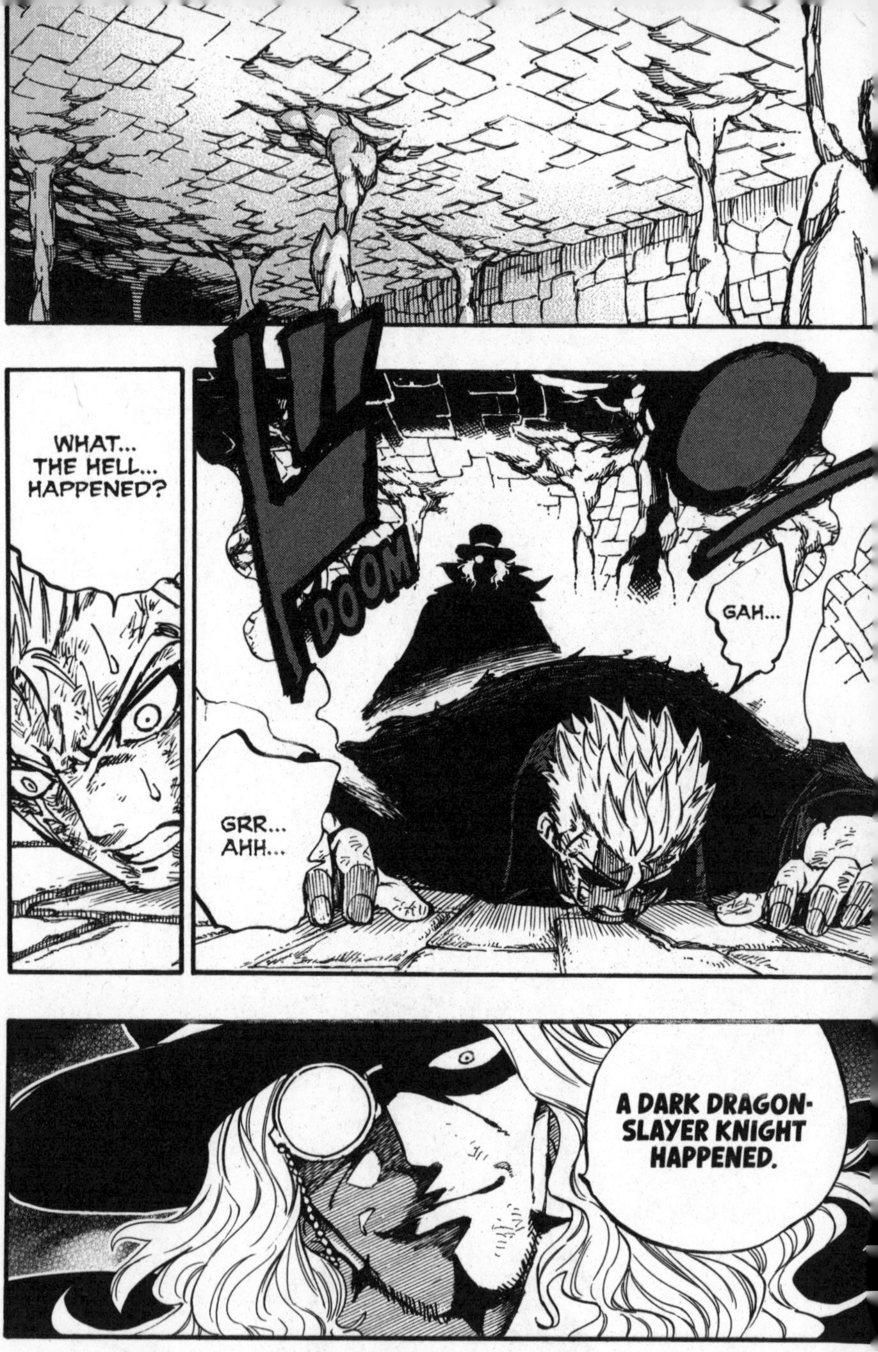
DOOM
GAH...
GRR... AHH...
WHAT... THE HELL... HAPPENED?
A DARK DRAGON-SLAYER KNIGHT HAPPENED.

FAIRY TAIL 100 YEARS QUEST

2022

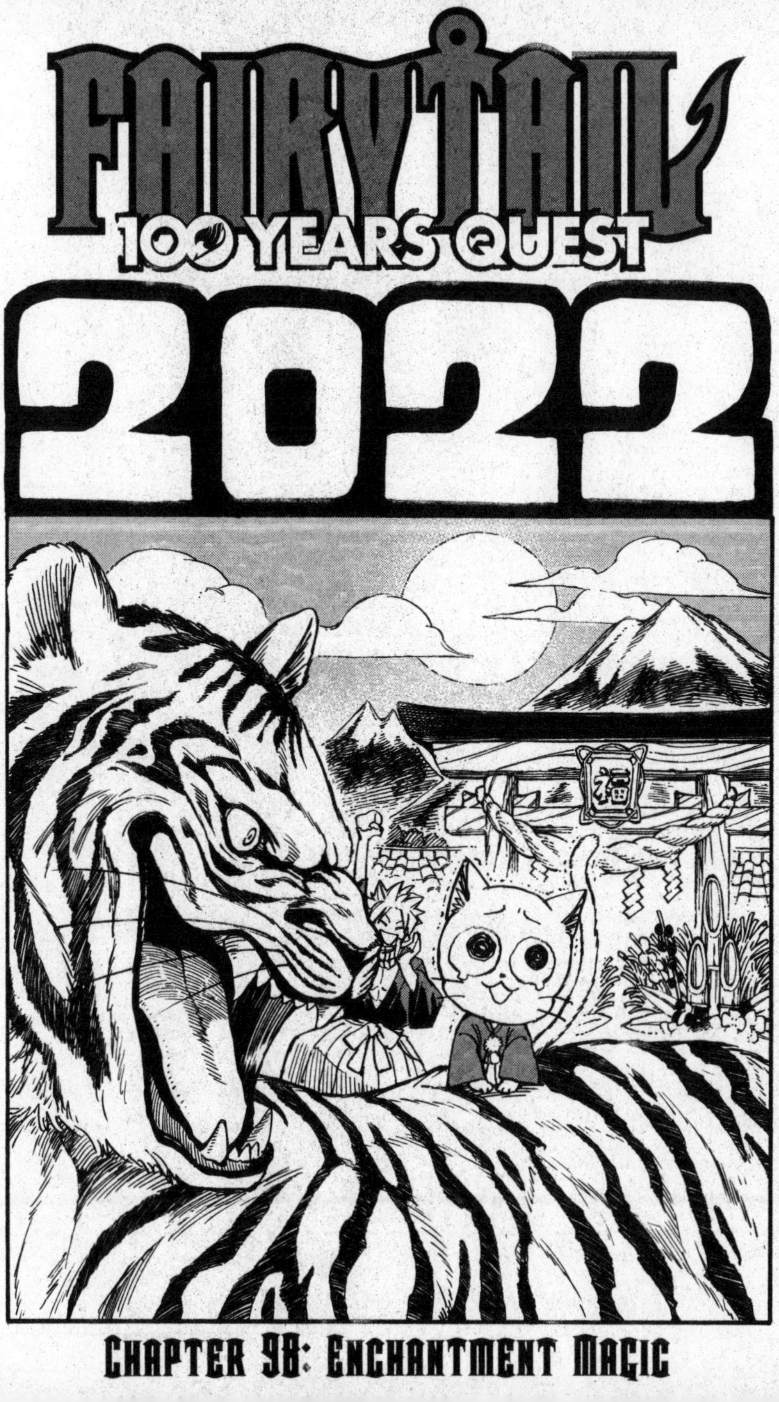
福

Chapter 98: Enchantment Magic

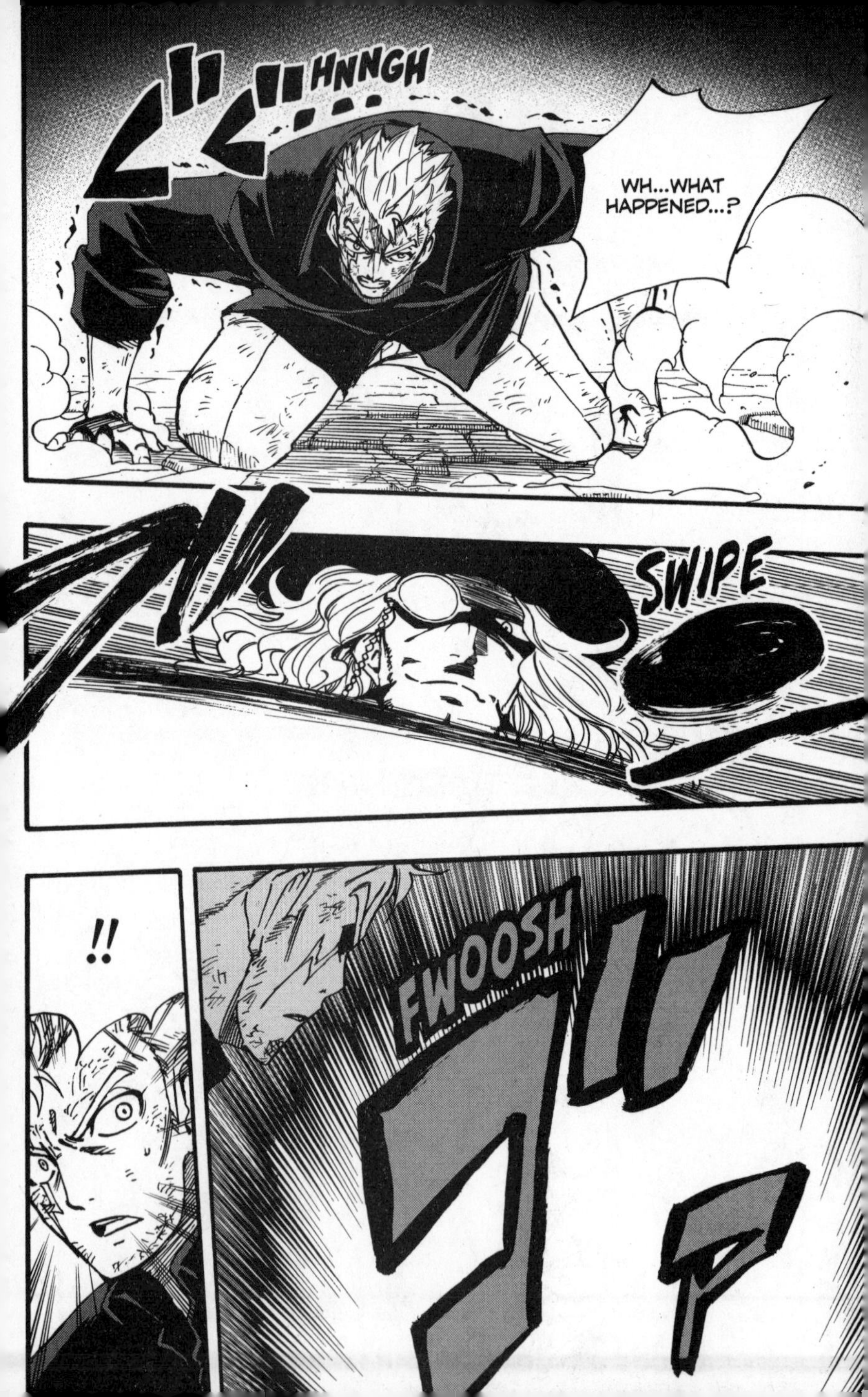
HNNGH
WH...WHAT HAPPENED...?
SWIPE
FWOOSH
!!

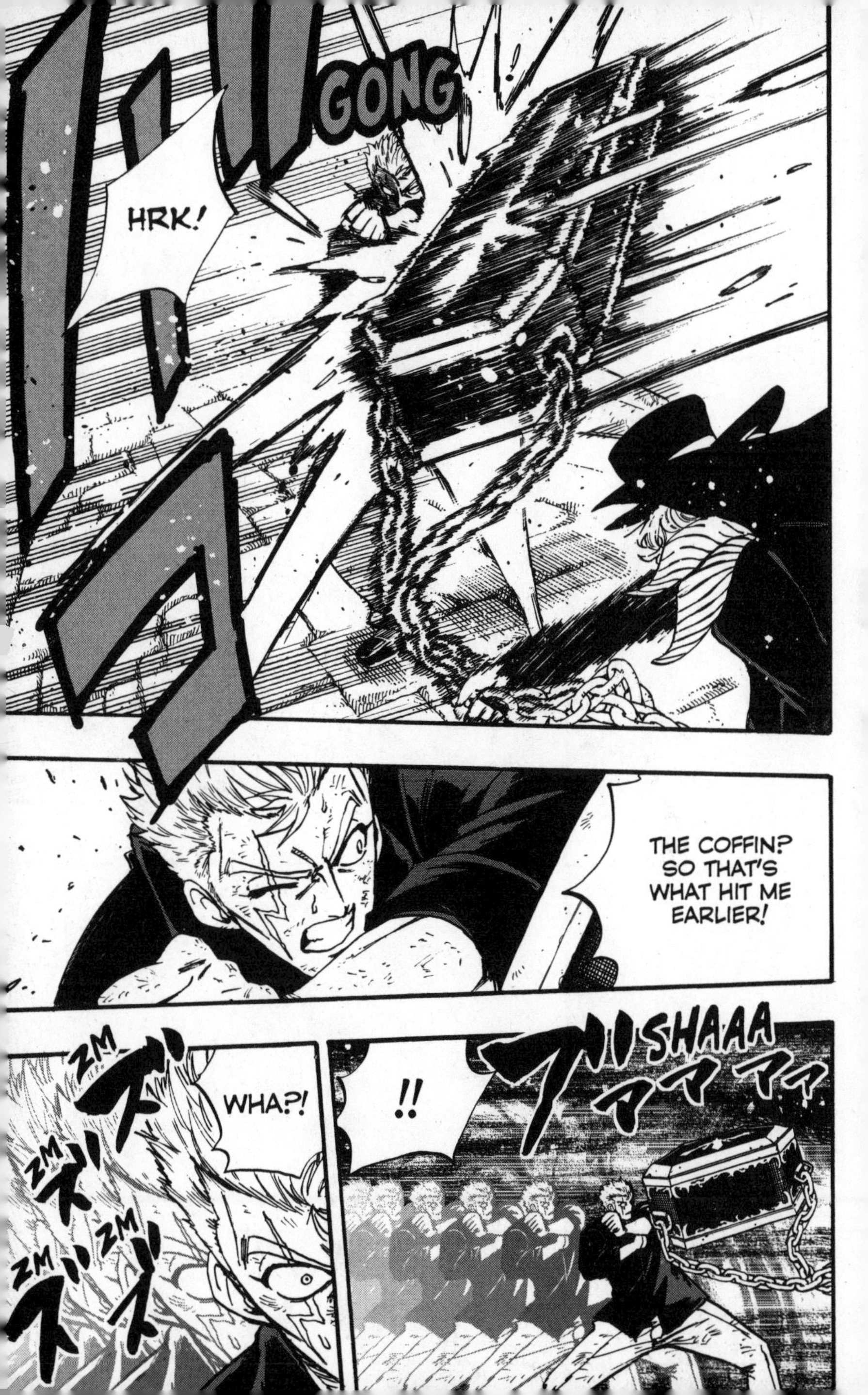
GONG
HRK!
THE COFFIN? SO THAT'S WHAT HIT ME EARLIER!
SHAAA
!!
WHA?!
ZM
ZM
ZM
ZM

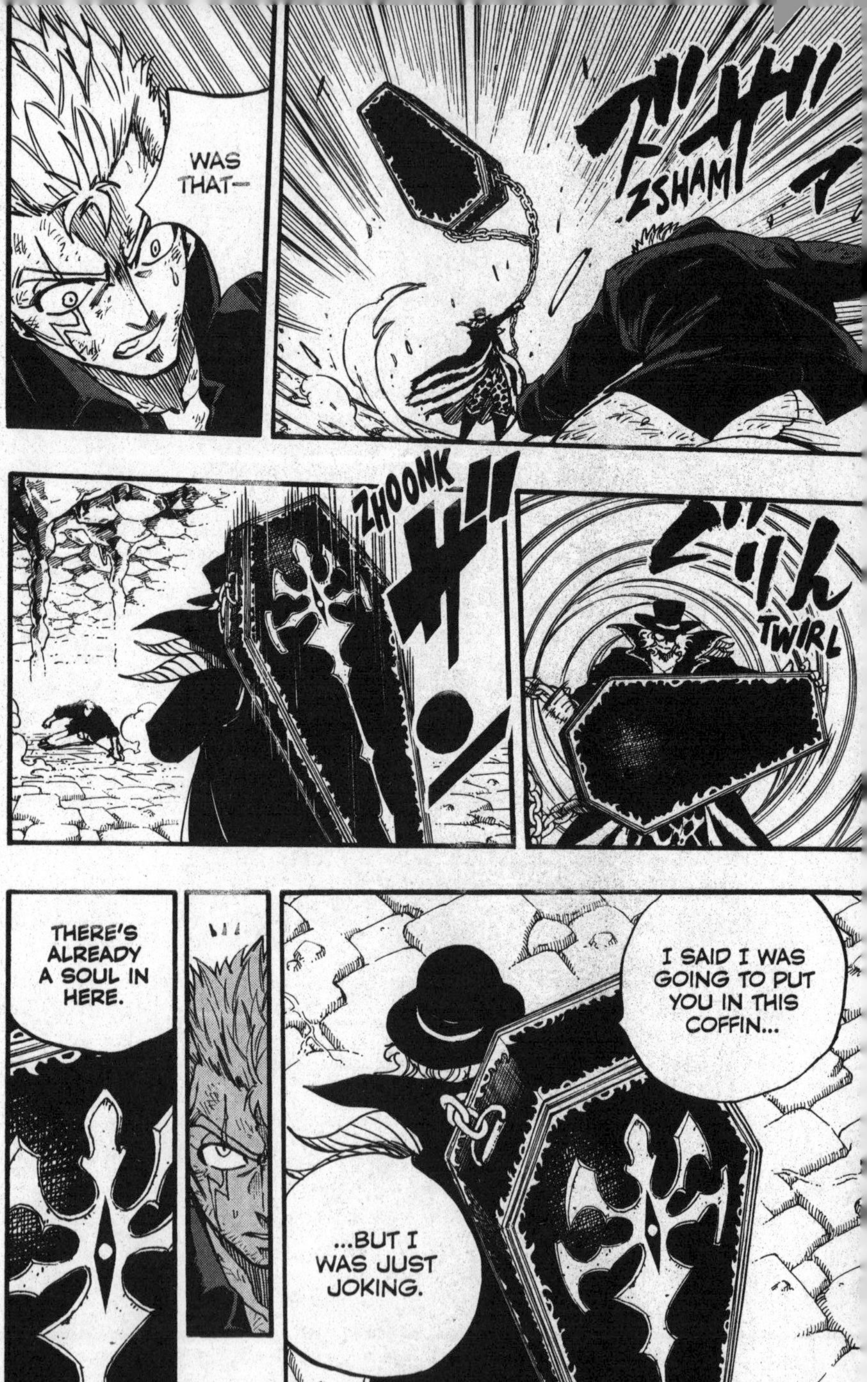
ZSHAM
WAS THAT—
TWIRL
ZHOONK
I SAID I WAS GOING TO PUT YOU IN THIS COFFIN...
...BUT I WAS JUST JOKING.
THERE'S ALREADY A SOUL IN HERE.

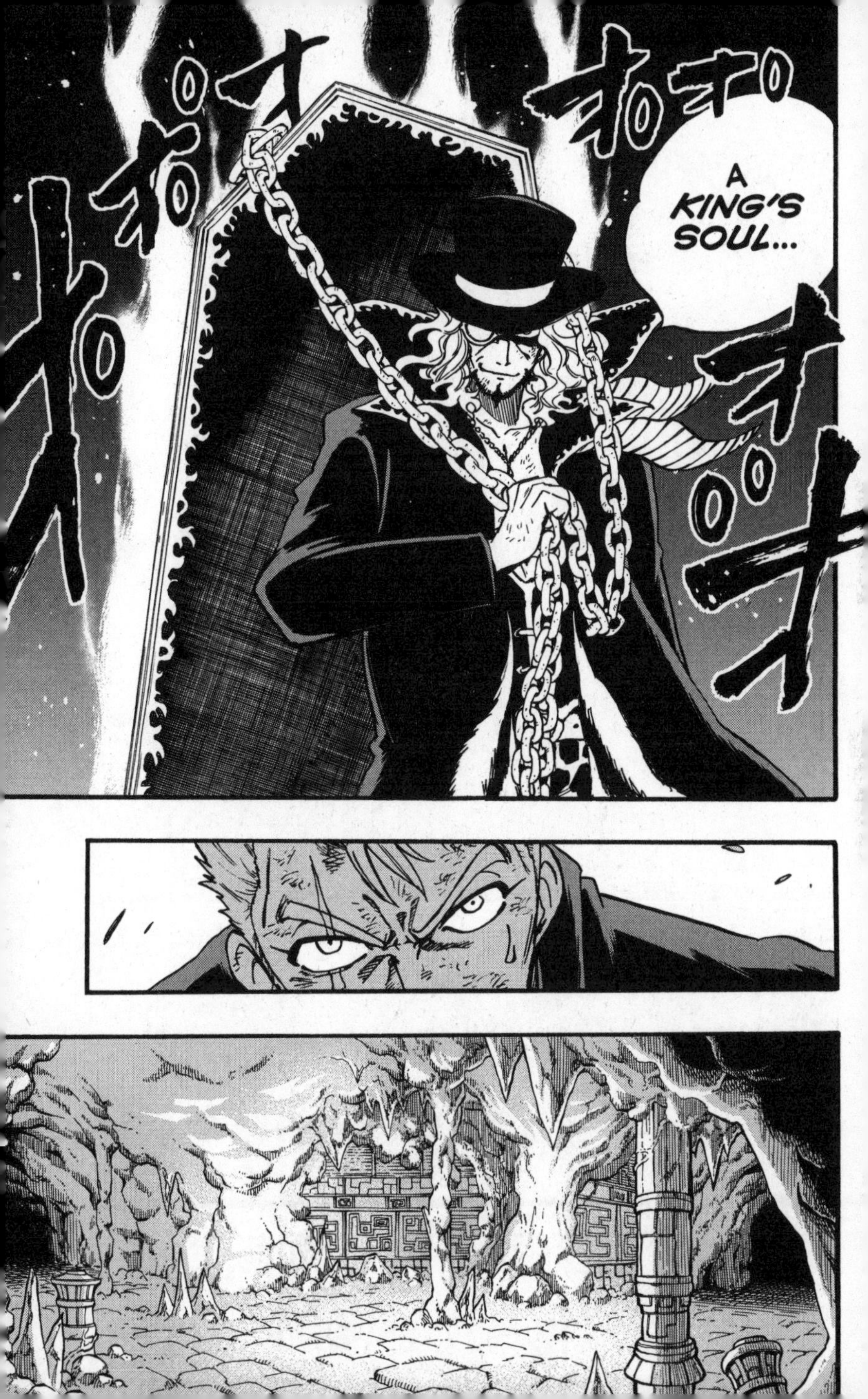

A KING'S SOUL...

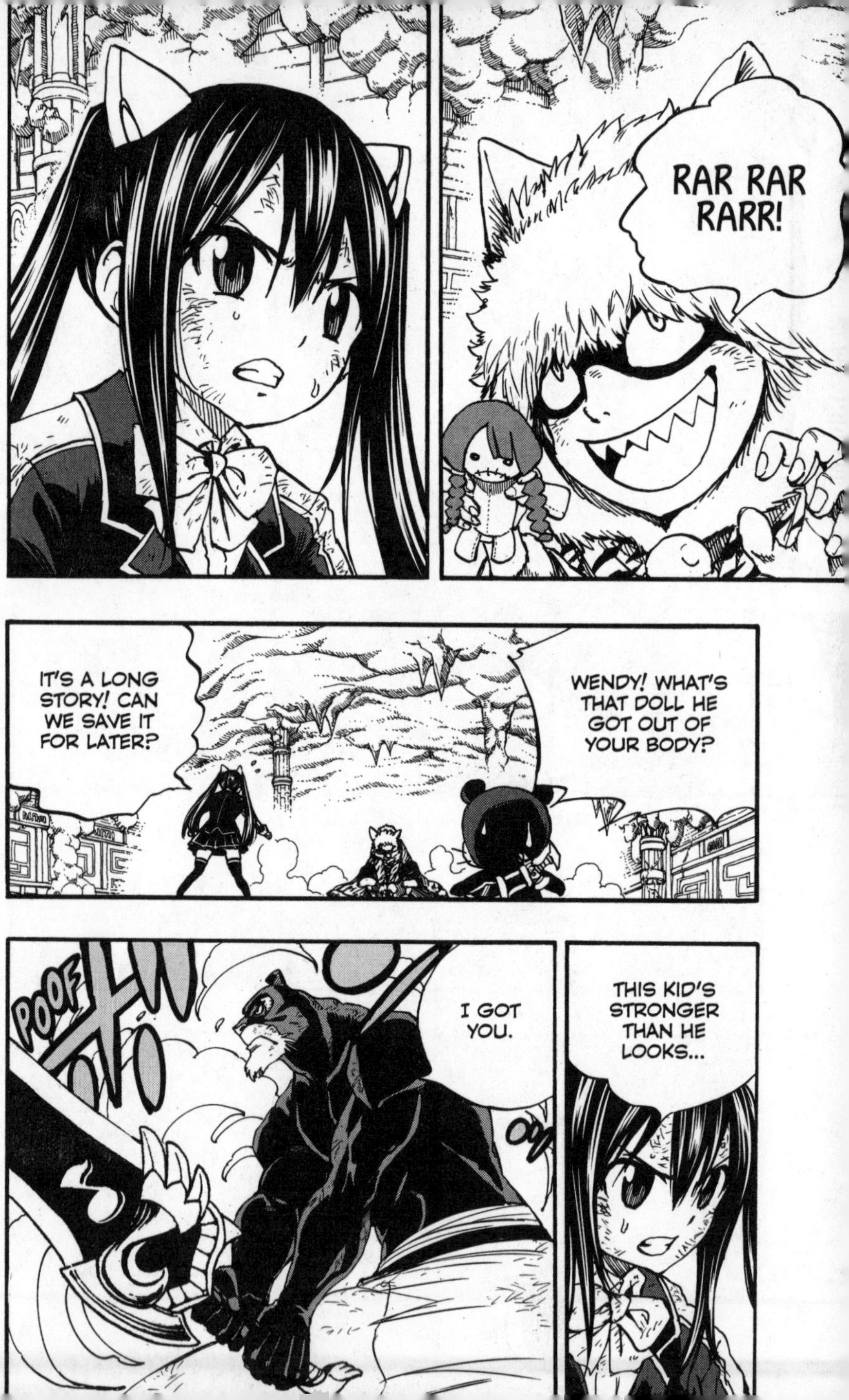
RAR RAR RARR!
WENDY! WHAT'S THAT DOLL HE GOT OUT OF YOUR BODY?
IT'S A LONG STORY! CAN WE SAVE IT FOR LATER?
THIS KID'S STRONGER THAN HE LOOKS...
I GOT YOU.
POOF

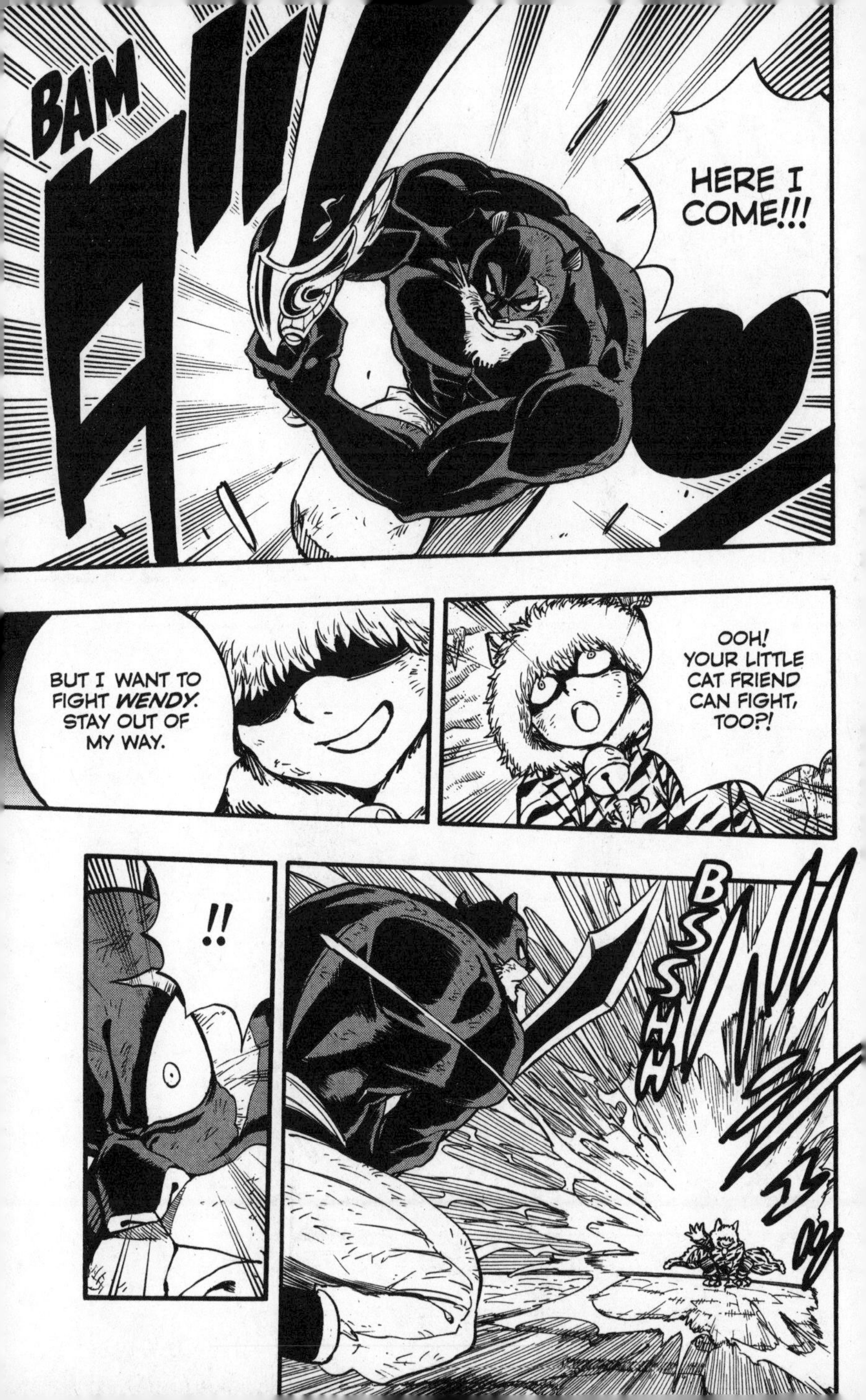
HERE I COME!!!
BAM
OOH! YOUR LITTLE CAT FRIEND CAN FIGHT, TOO?!
BUT I WANT TO FIGHT *WENDY*. STAY OUT OF MY WAY.
BSSHH
!!

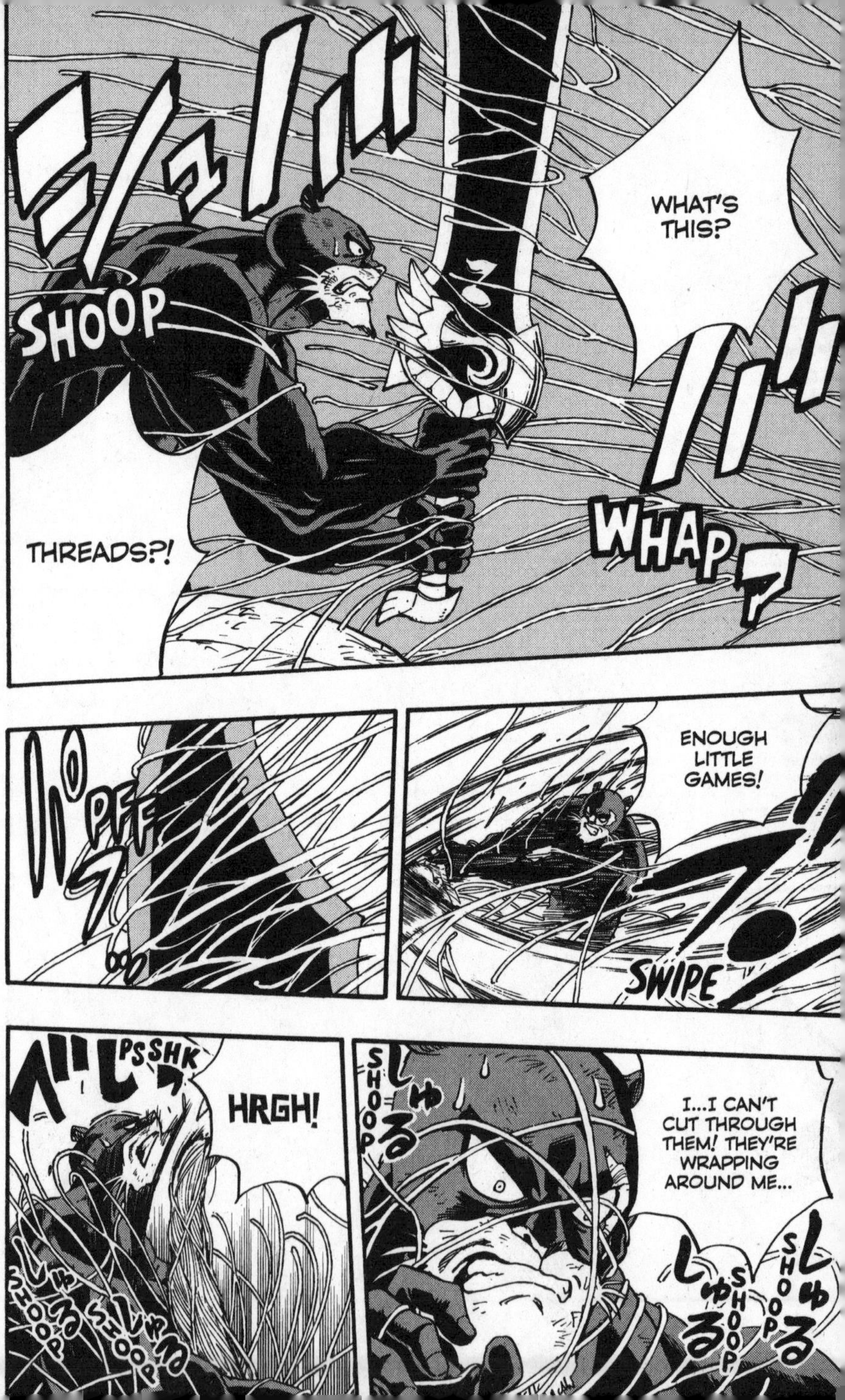
WHAT'S THIS?
WHAP
SHOOP
THREADS?!
ENOUGH LITTLE GAMES!
SWIPE
PFF
I...I CAN'T CUT THROUGH THEM! THEY'RE WRAPPING AROUND ME...
SHOOP
SHOOP
SHOOP
SHOOP
PSSHK
HRGH!
SHOOP
SHOOP

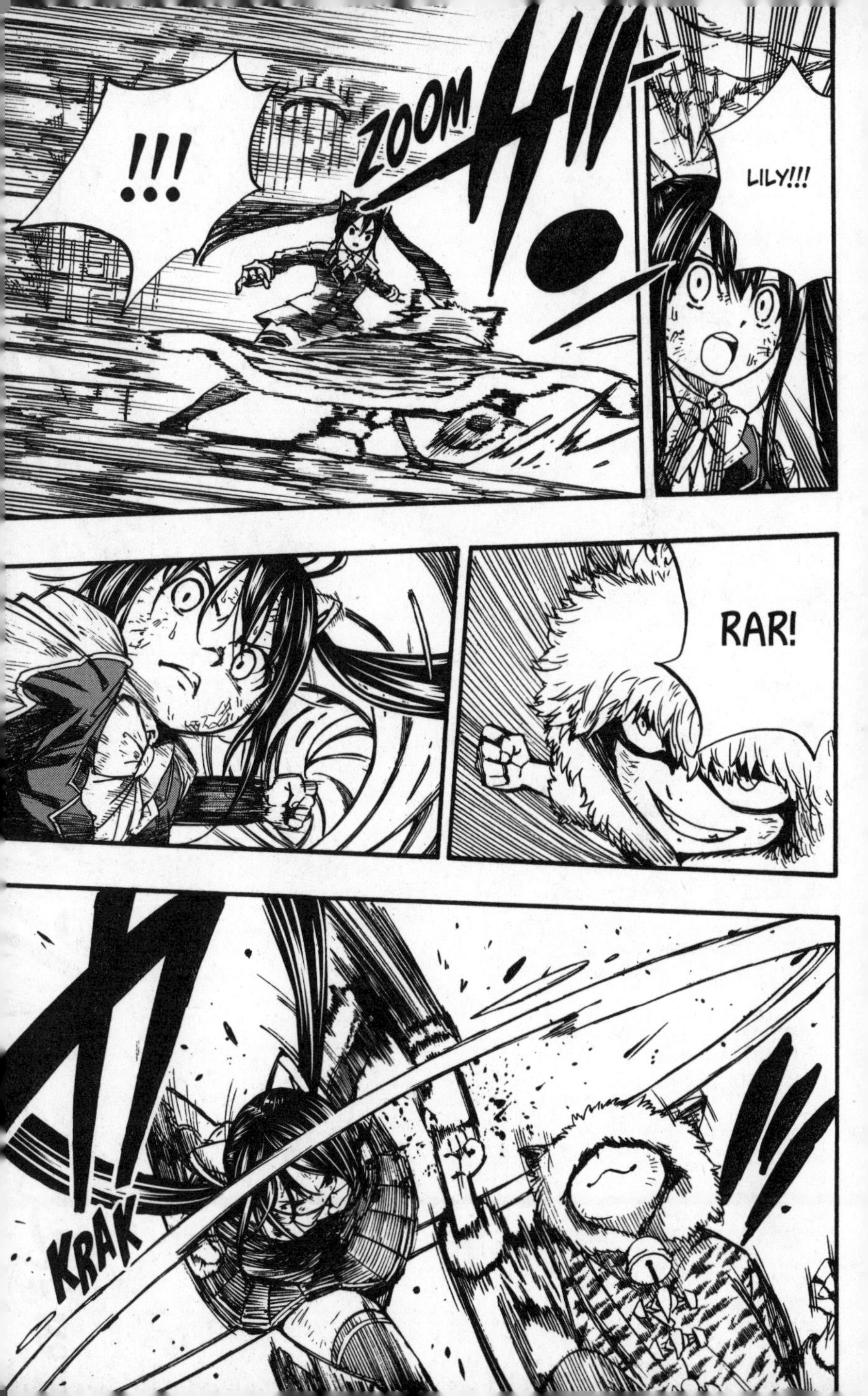
LILY!!!
ZOOM
!!!
RAR!
KRAK

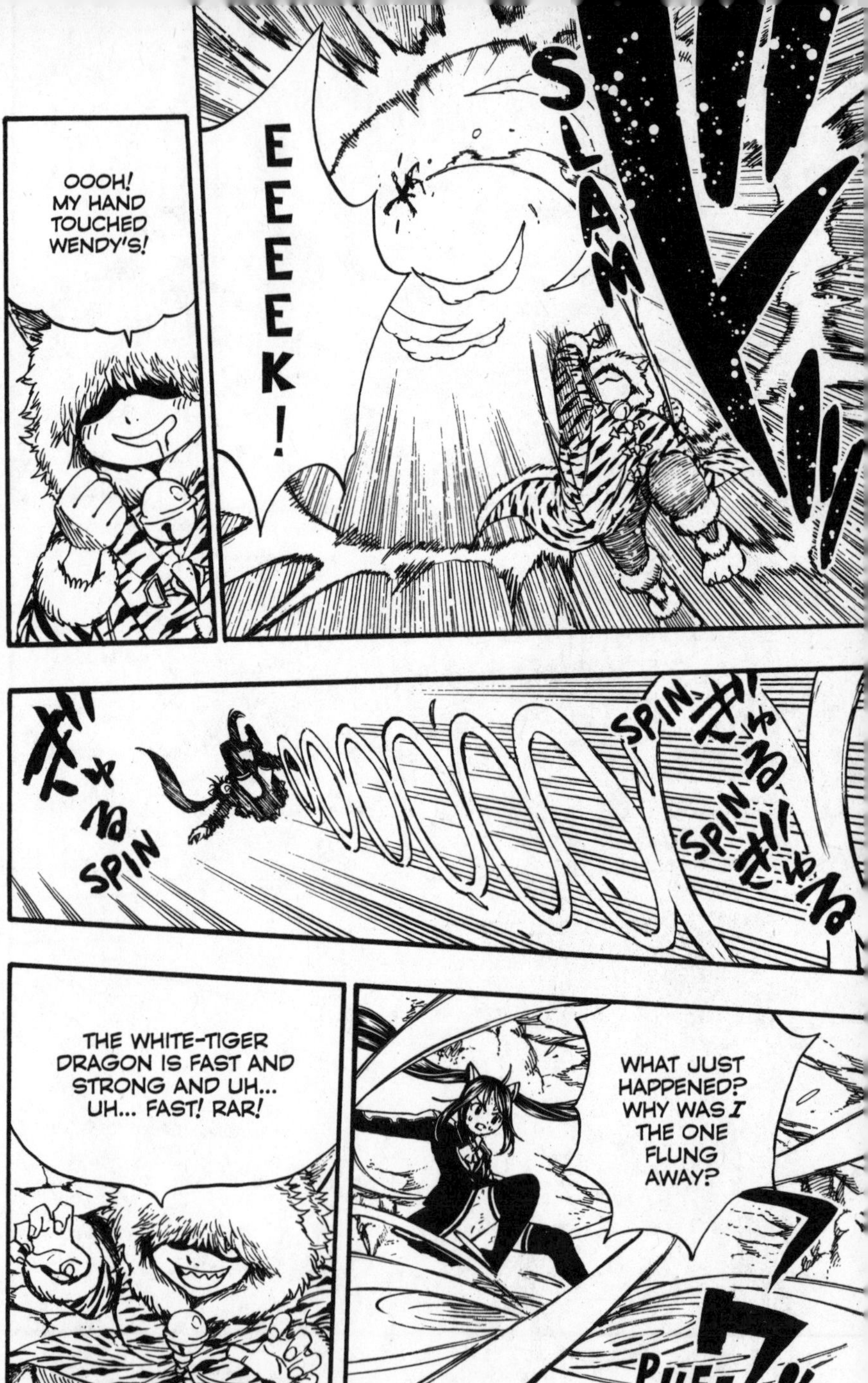
SLAM
EEEEK!
OOOH! MY HAND TOUCHED WENDY'S!
SPIN
SPIN
SPIN
WHAT JUST HAPPENED? WHY WAS *I* THE ONE FLUNG AWAY?
PUFF
THE WHITE-TIGER DRAGON IS FAST AND STRONG AND UH... UH... FAST! RAR!

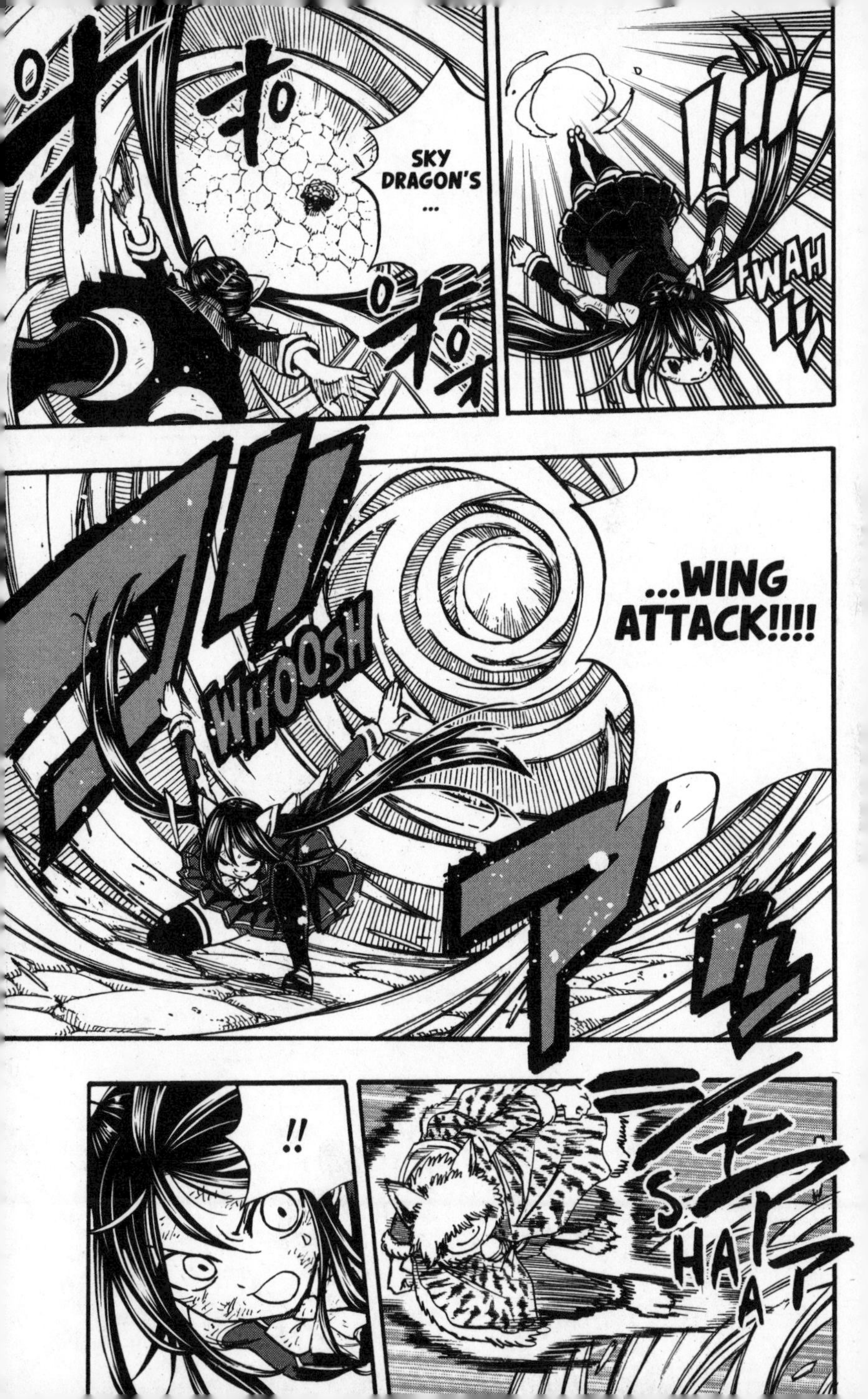
FWAH
SKY DRAGON'S ...
WHOOSH
...WING ATTACK!!!!
SHA
!!

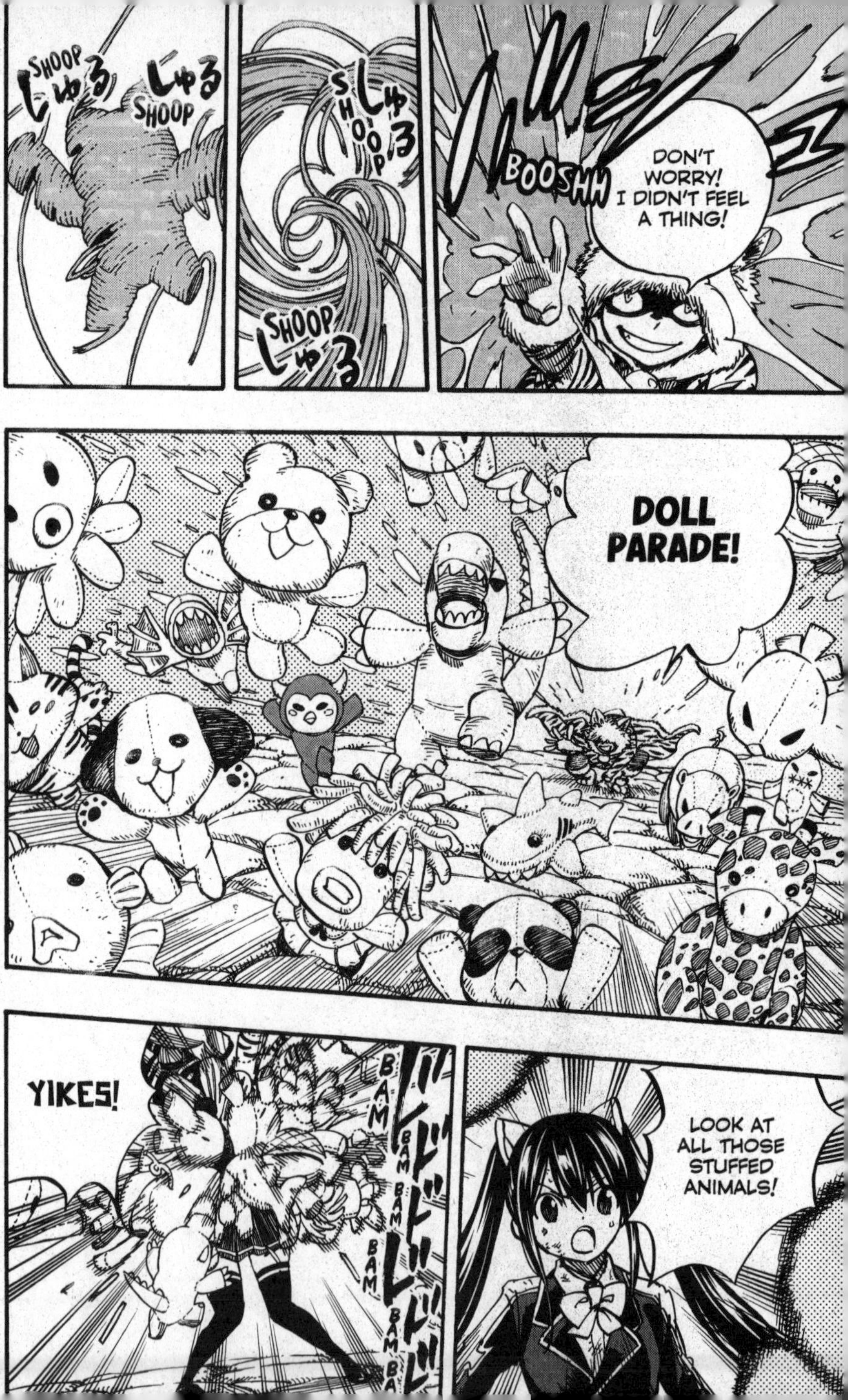
BOOSHH
DON'T WORRY! I DIDN'T FEEL A THING!
SHOOP しゅる
SHOOP しゅる
SHOOP しゅる
しゅる SHOOP
DOLL PARADE!
LOOK AT ALL THOSE STUFFED ANIMALS!
YIKES!
BAM BAM BAM BAM BAM

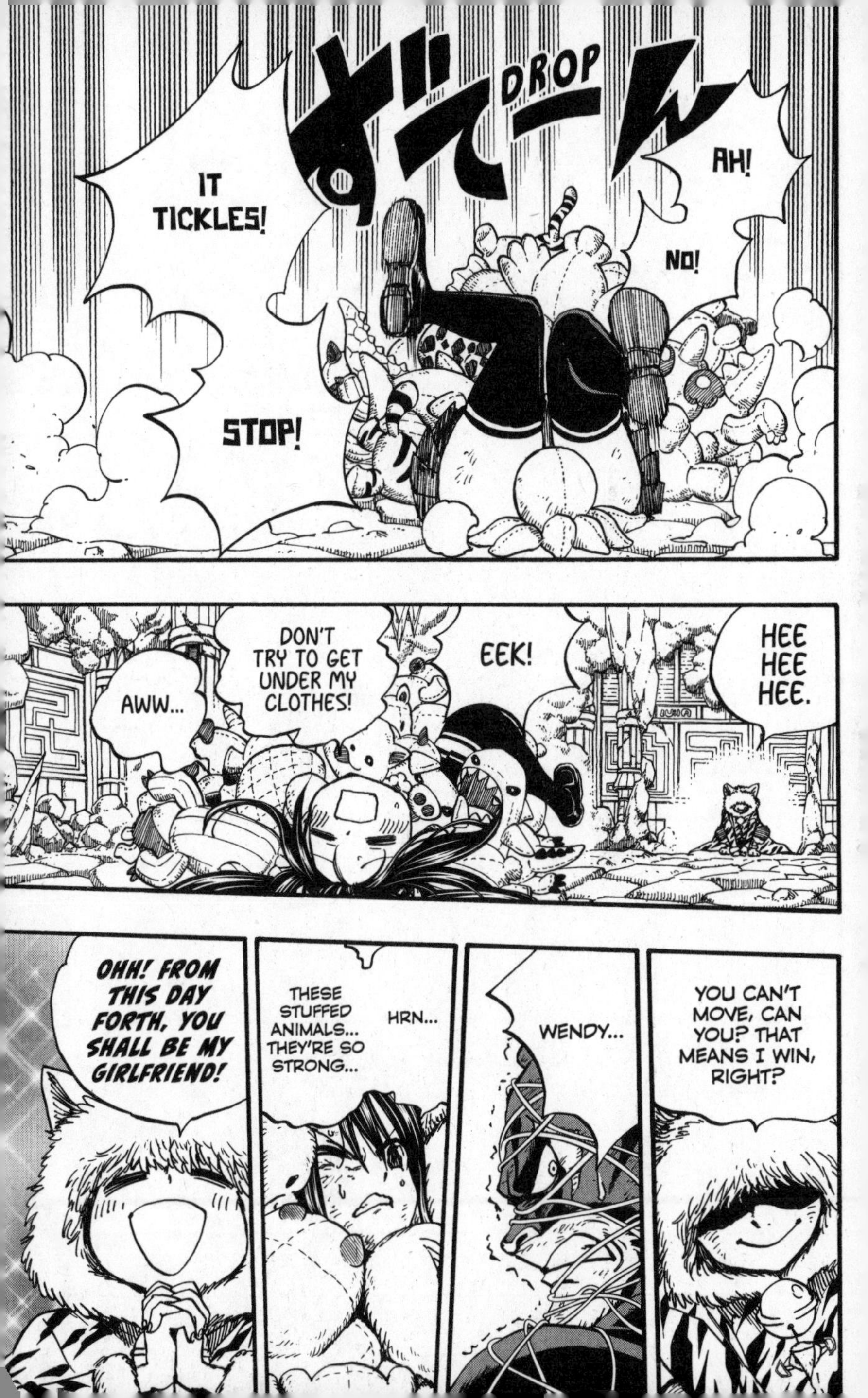
DROP
AH!
NO!
IT TICKLES!
STOP!
HEE HEE HEE.
EEK!
DON'T TRY TO GET UNDER MY CLOTHES!
AWW...
YOU CAN'T MOVE, CAN YOU? THAT MEANS I WIN, RIGHT?
WENDY...
HRN...
THESE STUFFED ANIMALS... THEY'RE SO STRONG...
OHH! FROM THIS DAY FORTH, YOU SHALL BE MY GIRLFRIEND!

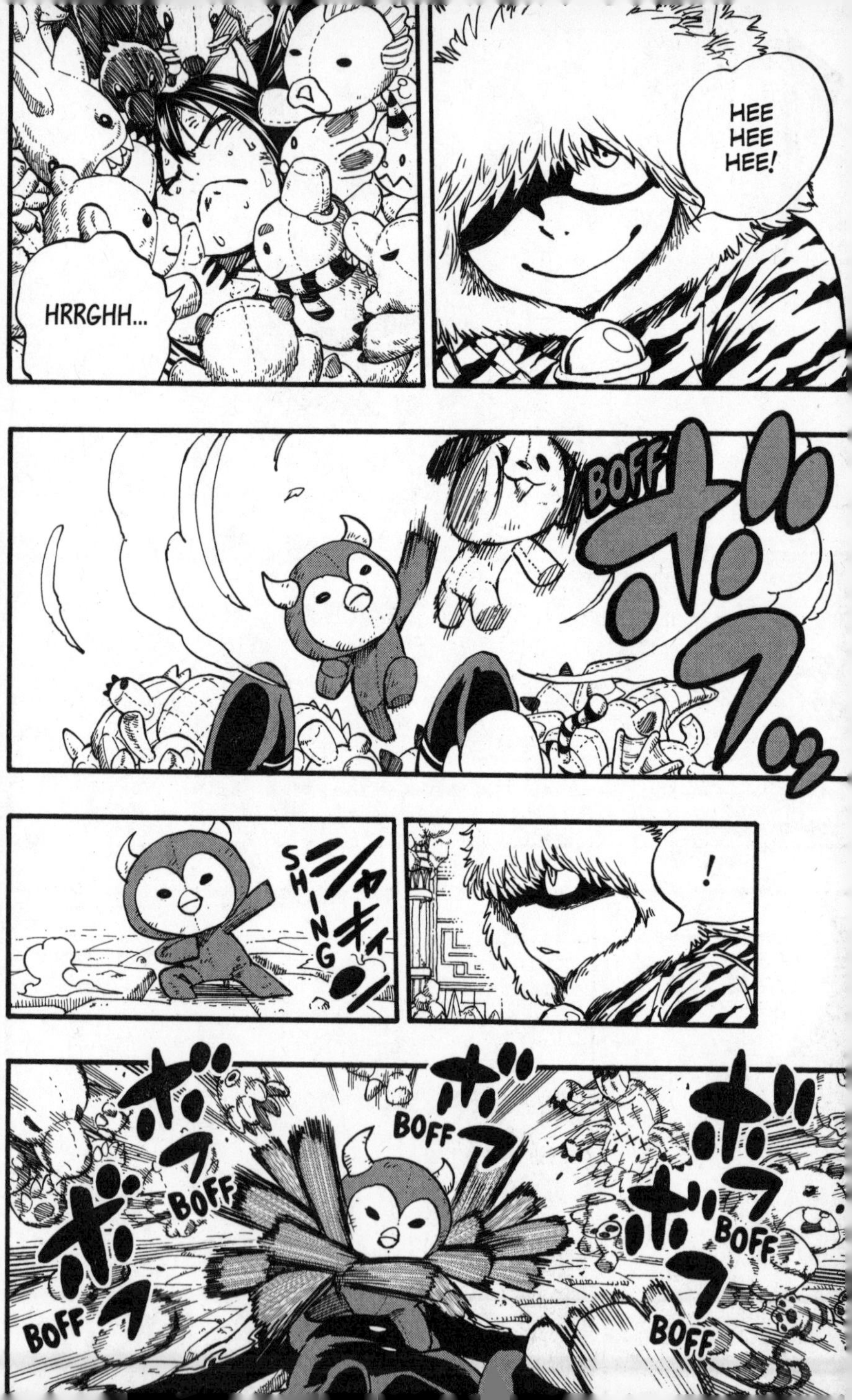
HEE HEE HEE!
HRRGHH...
BOFF
!
SHING
BOFF
BOFF
BOFF
BOFF
BOFF
BOFF

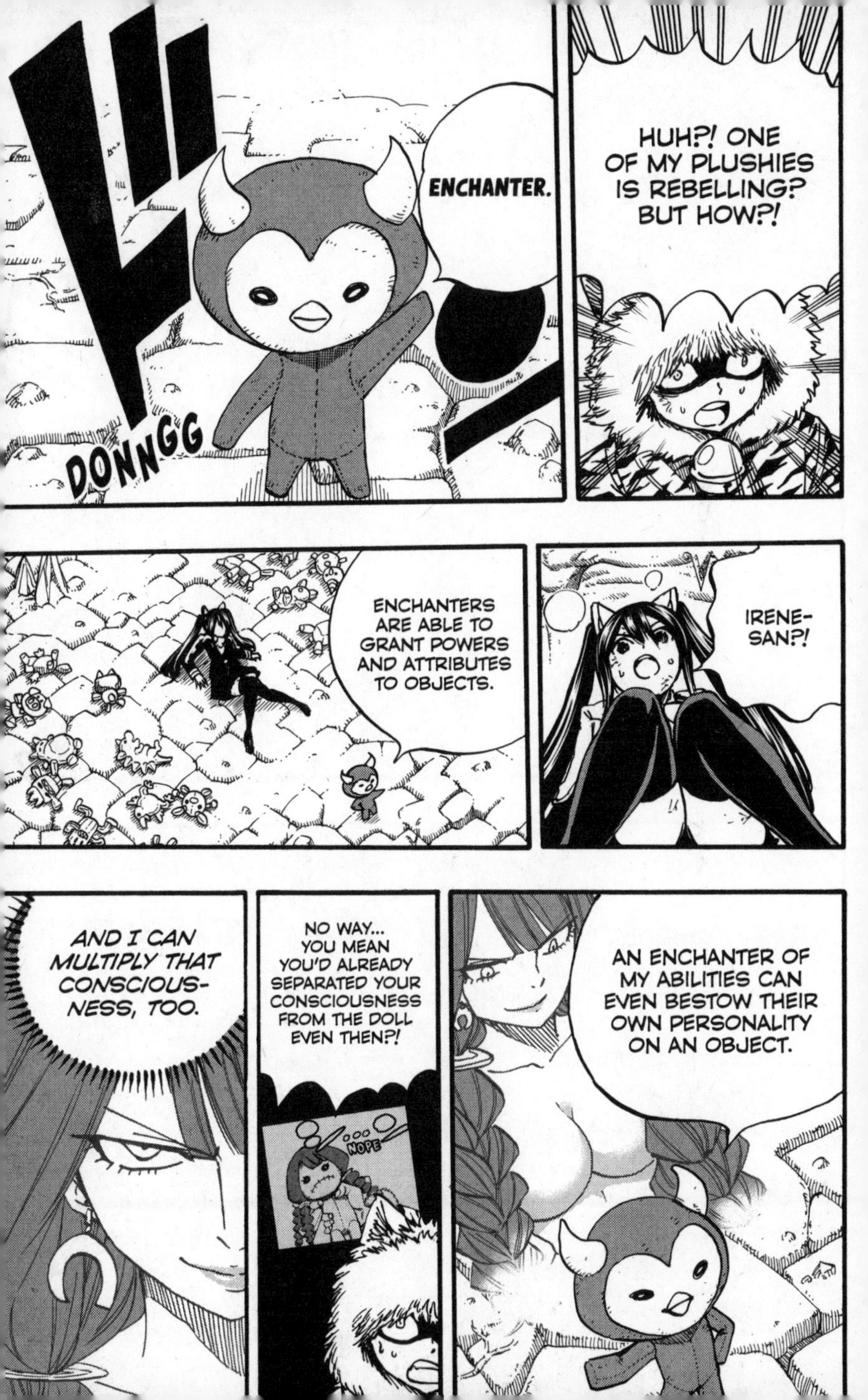
HUH?! ONE OF MY PLUSHIES IS REBELLING? BUT HOW?!
ENCHANTER.
DONNGG
IRENE-SAN?!
ENCHANTERS ARE ABLE TO GRANT POWERS AND ATTRIBUTES TO OBJECTS.
AN ENCHANTER OF MY ABILITIES CAN EVEN BESTOW THEIR OWN PERSONALITY ON AN OBJECT.
NO WAY... YOU MEAN YOU'D ALREADY SEPARATED YOUR CONSCIOUSNESS FROM THE DOLL EVEN THEN?!
NOPE
AND I CAN MULTIPLY THAT CONSCIOUS-NESS, TOO.

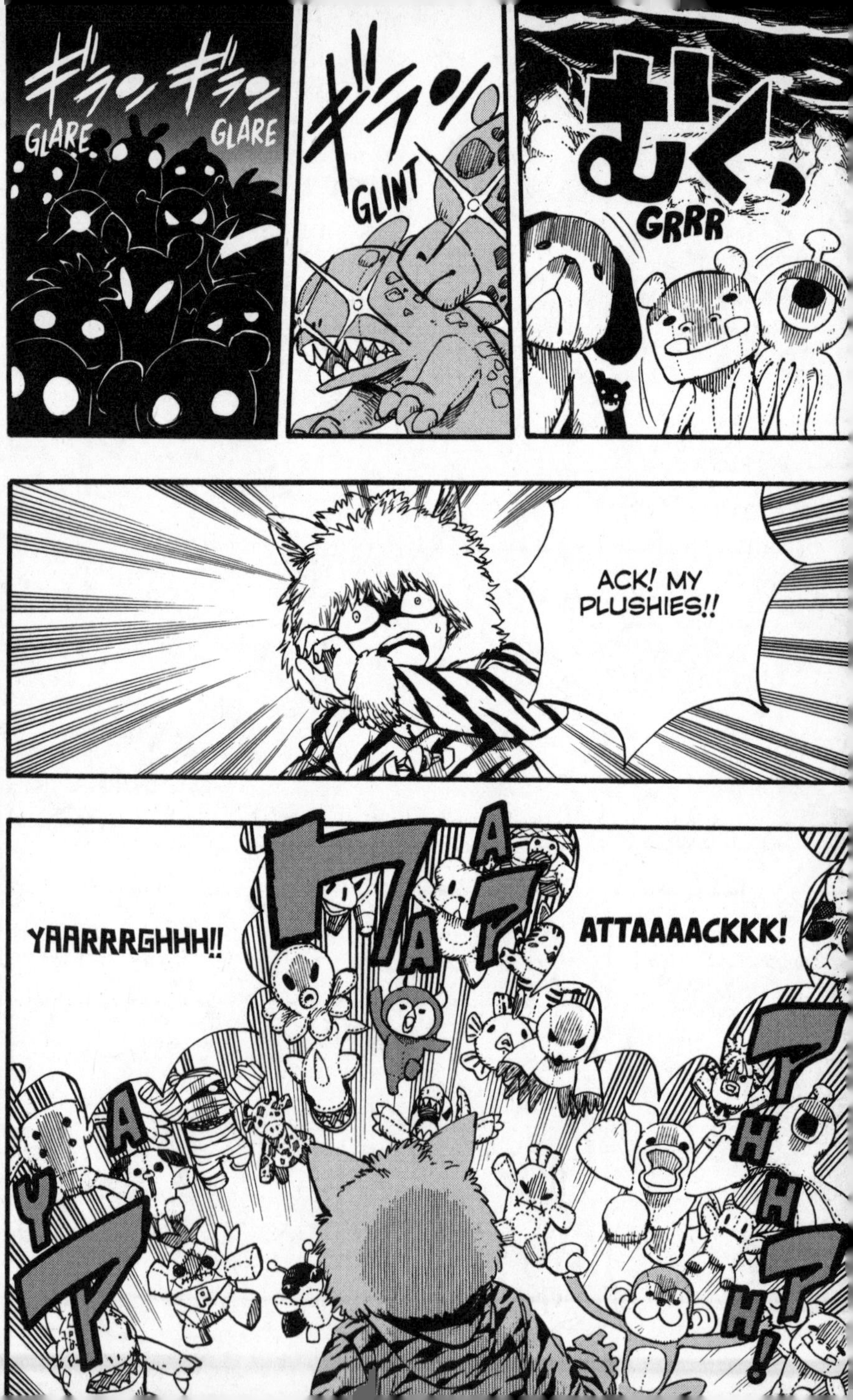
むくっ
GRRR
ギラッ
GLINT
ギラン ギラン
GLARE
GLARE
ACK! MY PLUSHIES!!
ATTAAAACKKK!
YAARRRGHHH!!

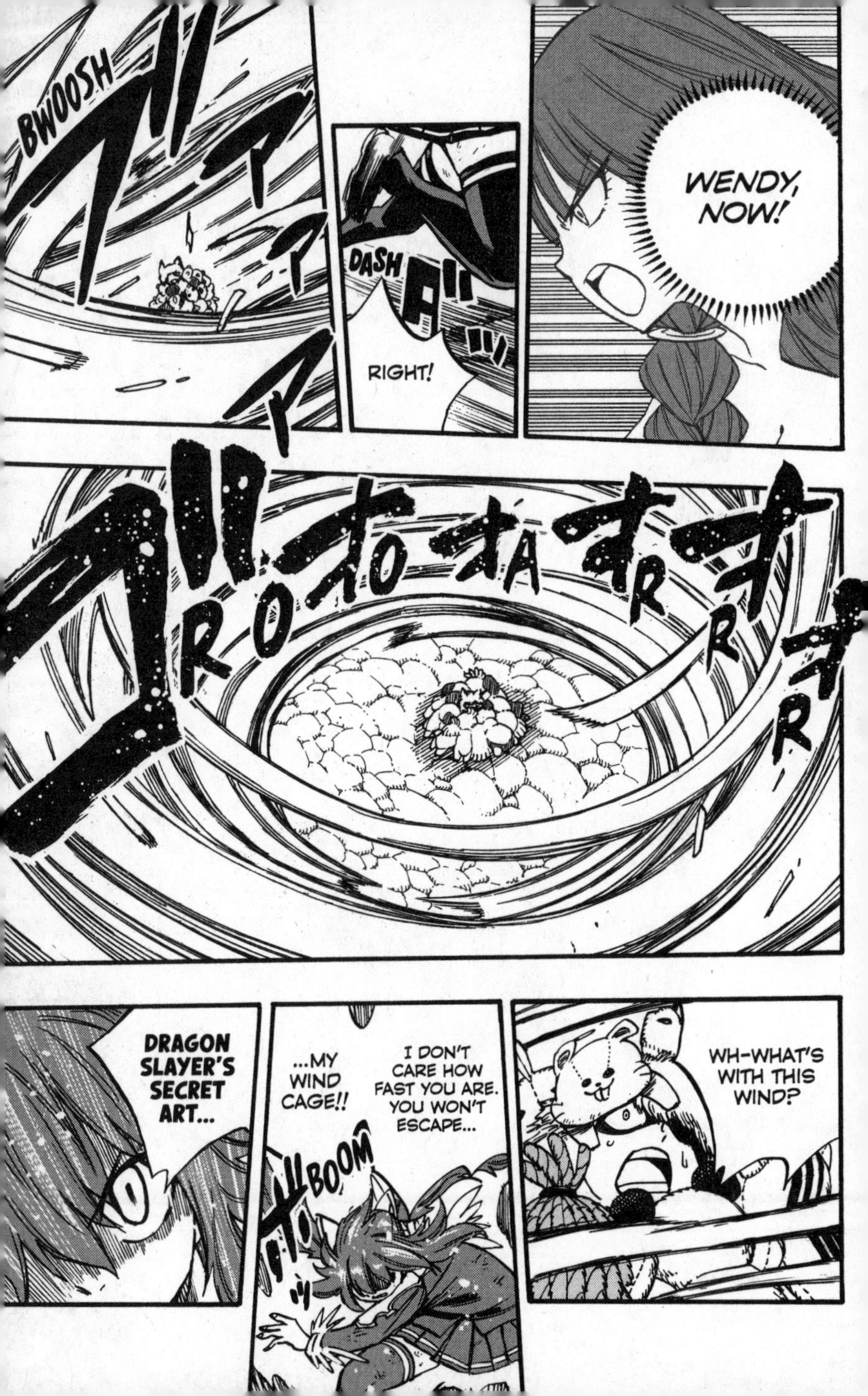
WENDY, NOW!
DASH
RIGHT!
BWOOSH
ROARRR
WH-WHAT'S WITH THIS WIND?
I DON'T CARE HOW FAST YOU ARE. YOU WON'T ESCAPE...
...MY WIND CAGE!!
BOOM
DRAGON SLAYER'S SECRET ART...

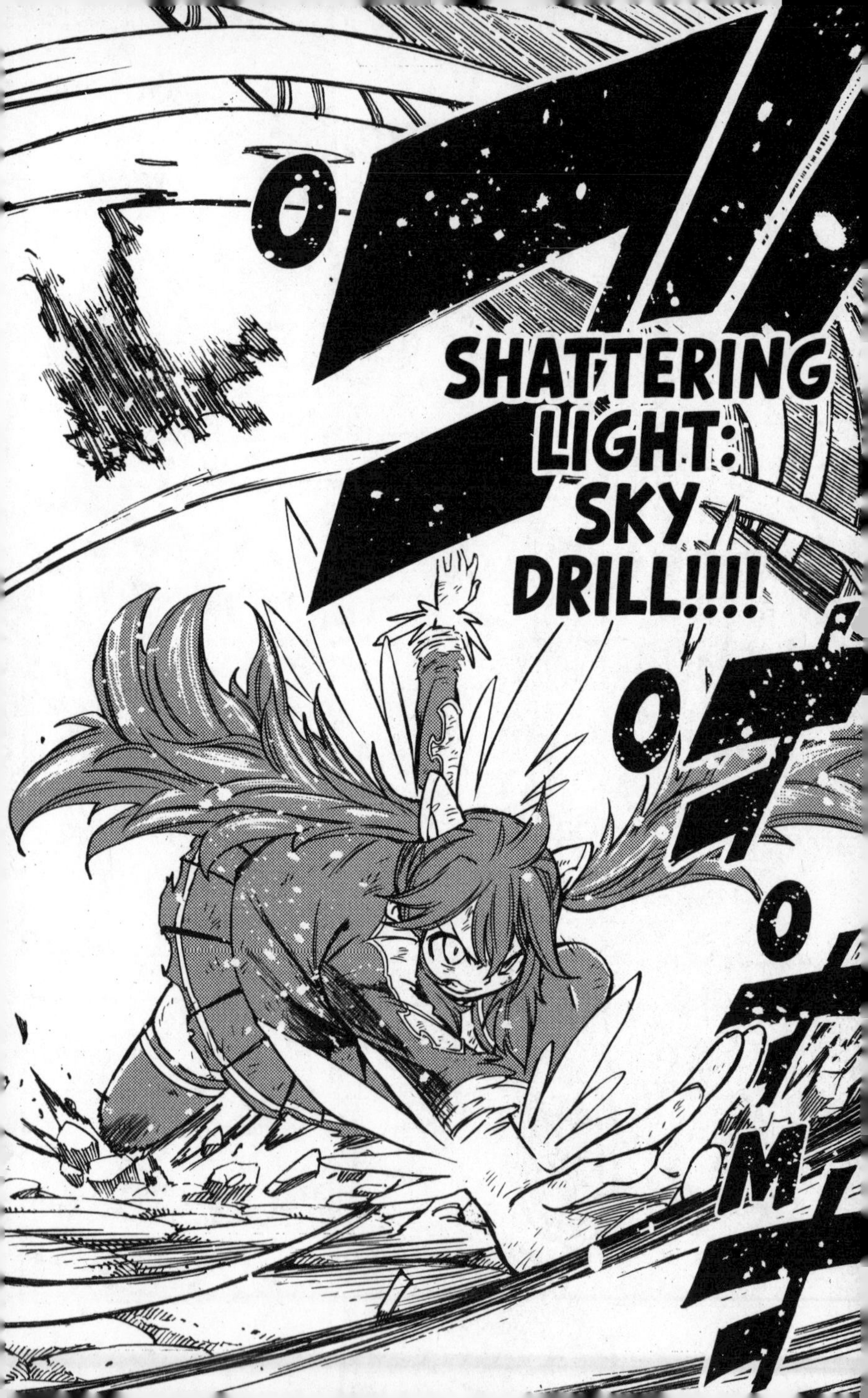
SHATTERING LIGHT: SKY DRILL!!!!

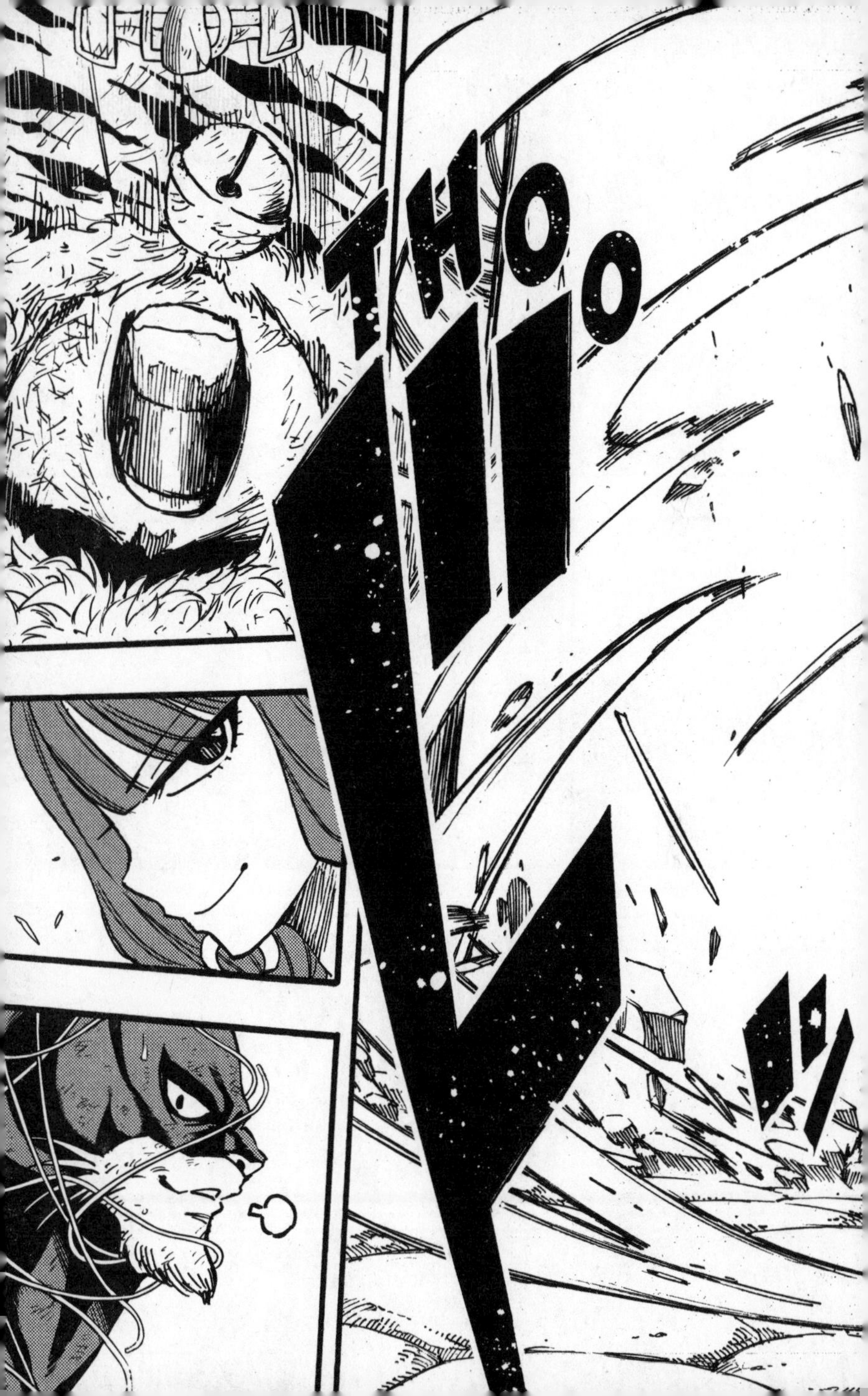
THOO

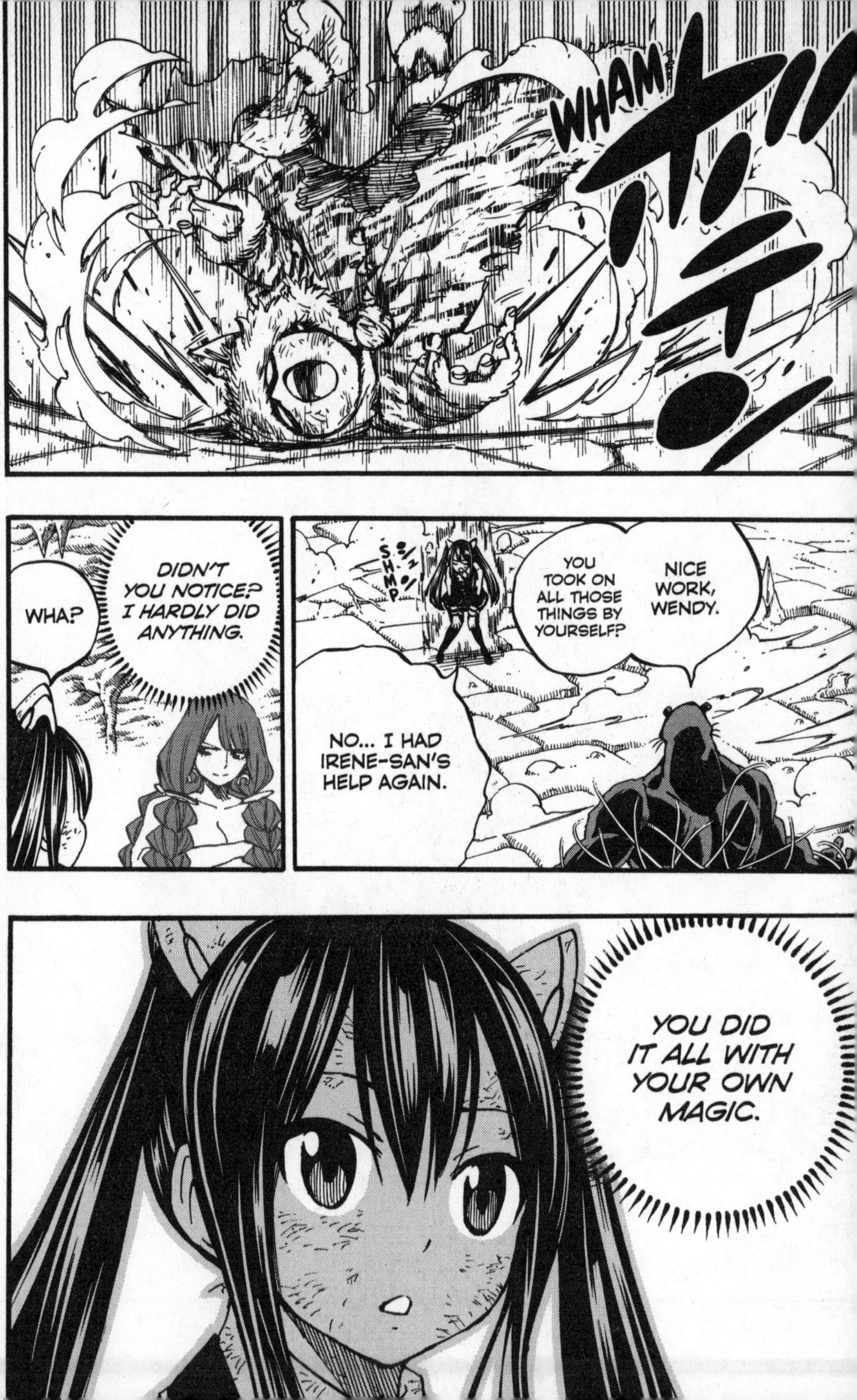
WHAM
SHMP
NICE WORK, WENDY.
YOU TOOK ON ALL THOSE THINGS BY YOURSELF?
NO... I HAD IRENE-SAN'S HELP AGAIN.
DIDN'T YOU NOTICE? I HARDLY DID ANYTHING.
WHA?
YOU DID IT ALL WITH YOUR OWN MAGIC.

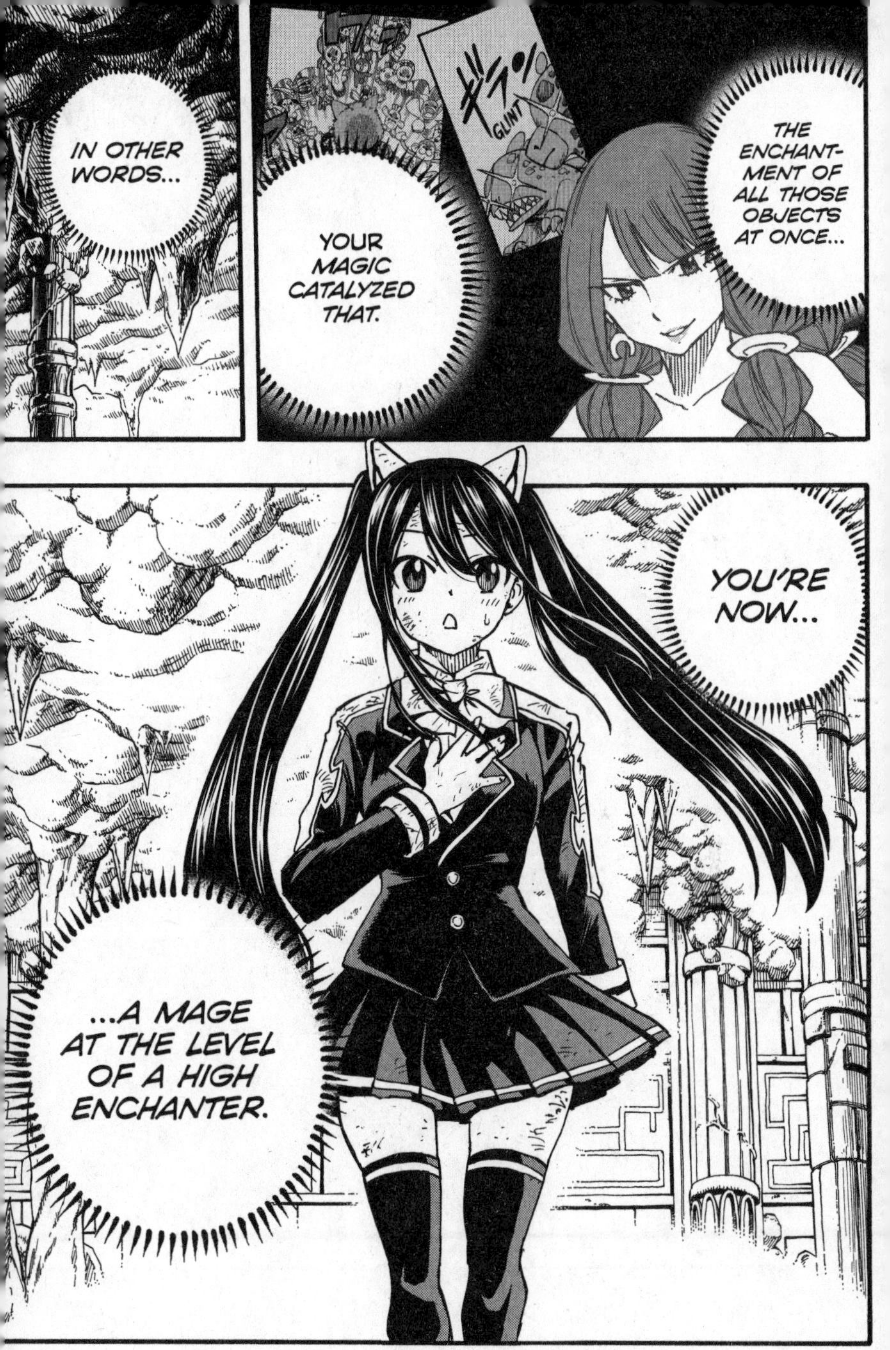
GLINT
THE ENCHANTMENT OF ALL THOSE OBJECTS AT ONCE...
YOUR MAGIC CATALYZED THAT.
IN OTHER WORDS...
YOU'RE NOW...
...A MAGE AT THE LEVEL OF A HIGH ENCHANTER.

FAIRY TAIL
100 YEARS QUEST

FAIRY TAIL
100 YEARS QUEST

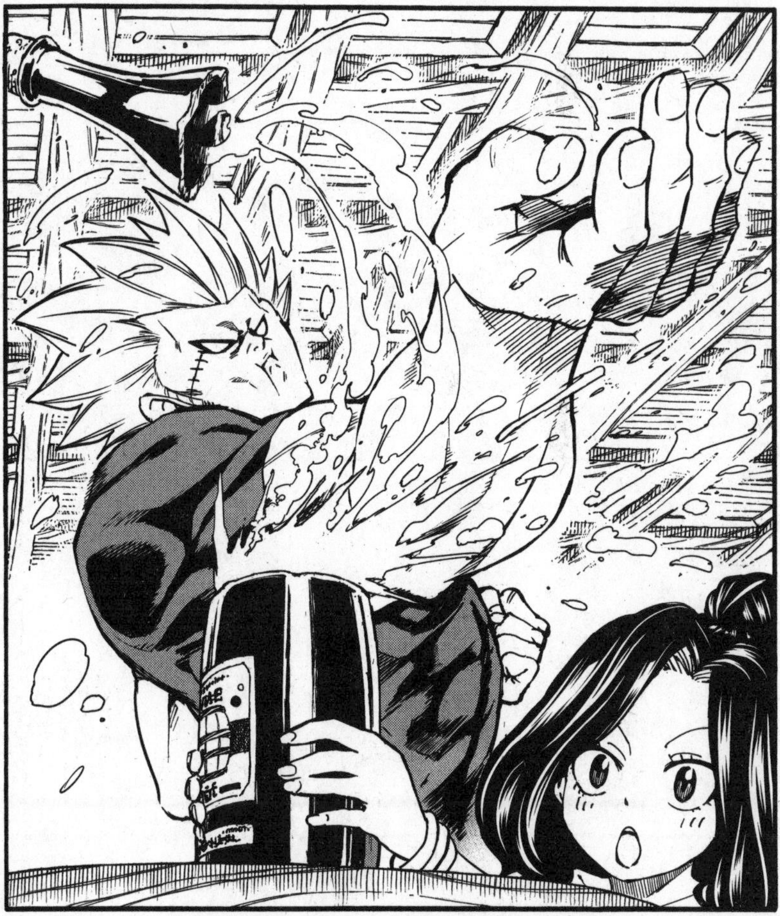

Chapter 99: Scarlet Rage

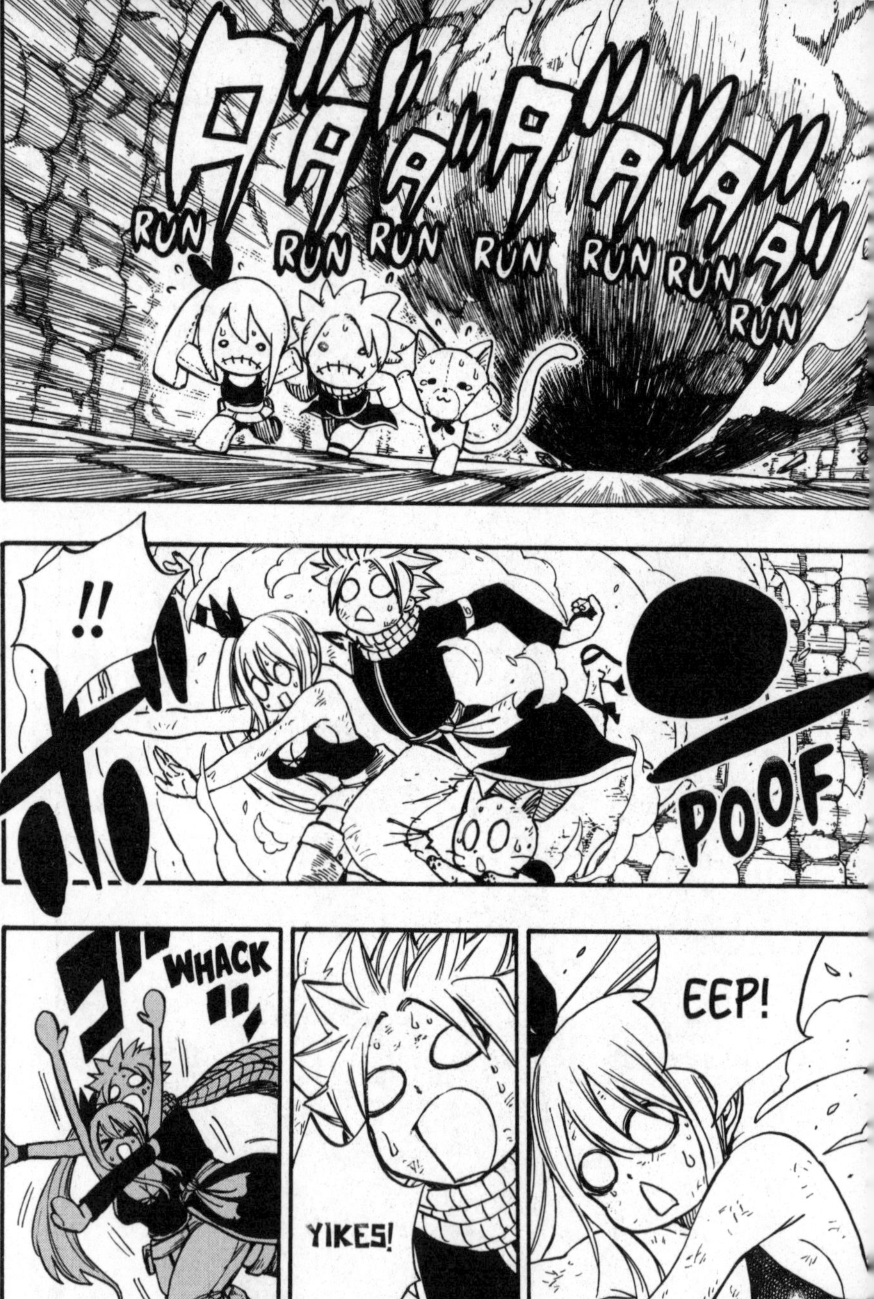
RUN
RUN
RUN
RUN
RUN
RUN
RUN
POOF
!!
EEP!
YIKES!
WHACK

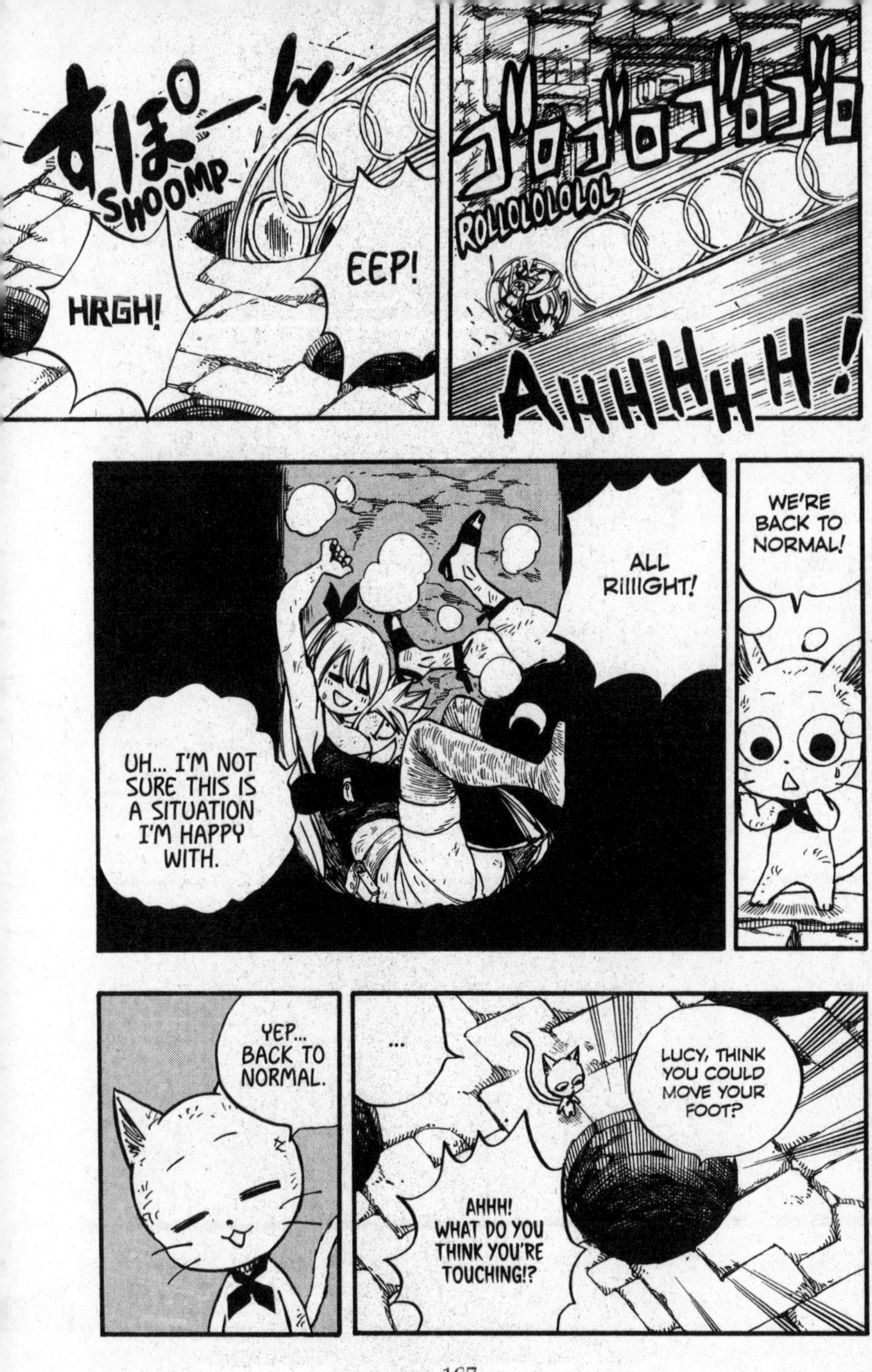

ゴロッゴロゴロッゴロ
ROLLOLOLOLOL
AHHHHHH!
すぽーん
SHOOMP
EEP!
HRGH!
WE'RE BACK TO NORMAL!
ALL RIIIIGHT!
UH... I'M NOT SURE THIS IS A SITUATION I'M HAPPY WITH.
LUCY, THINK YOU COULD MOVE YOUR FOOT?
...
AHHH! WHAT DO YOU THINK YOU'RE TOUCHING!?
YEP... BACK TO NORMAL.

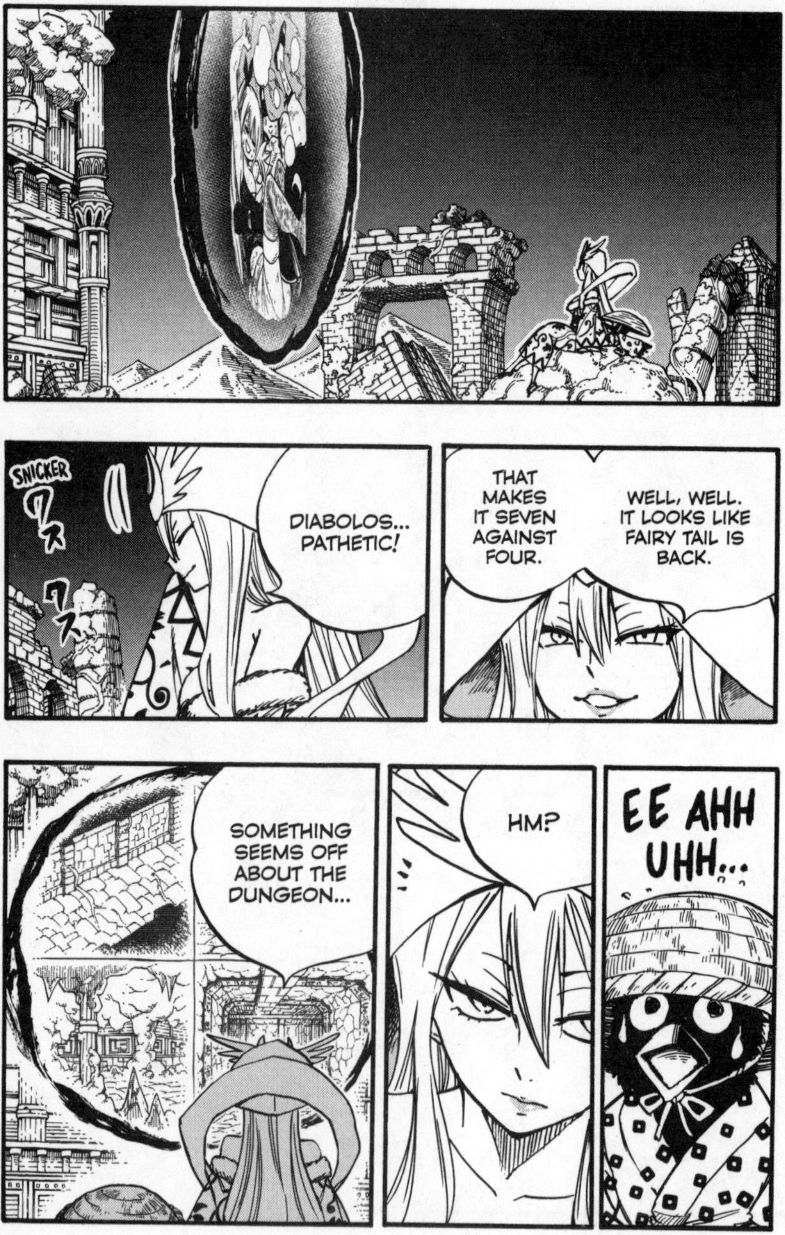
WELL, WELL. IT LOOKS LIKE FAIRY TAIL IS BACK.
THAT MAKES IT SEVEN AGAINST FOUR.
DIABOLOS... PATHETIC!
SNICKER
EE AHH UHH...
HM?
SOMETHING SEEMS OFF ABOUT THE DUNGEON...

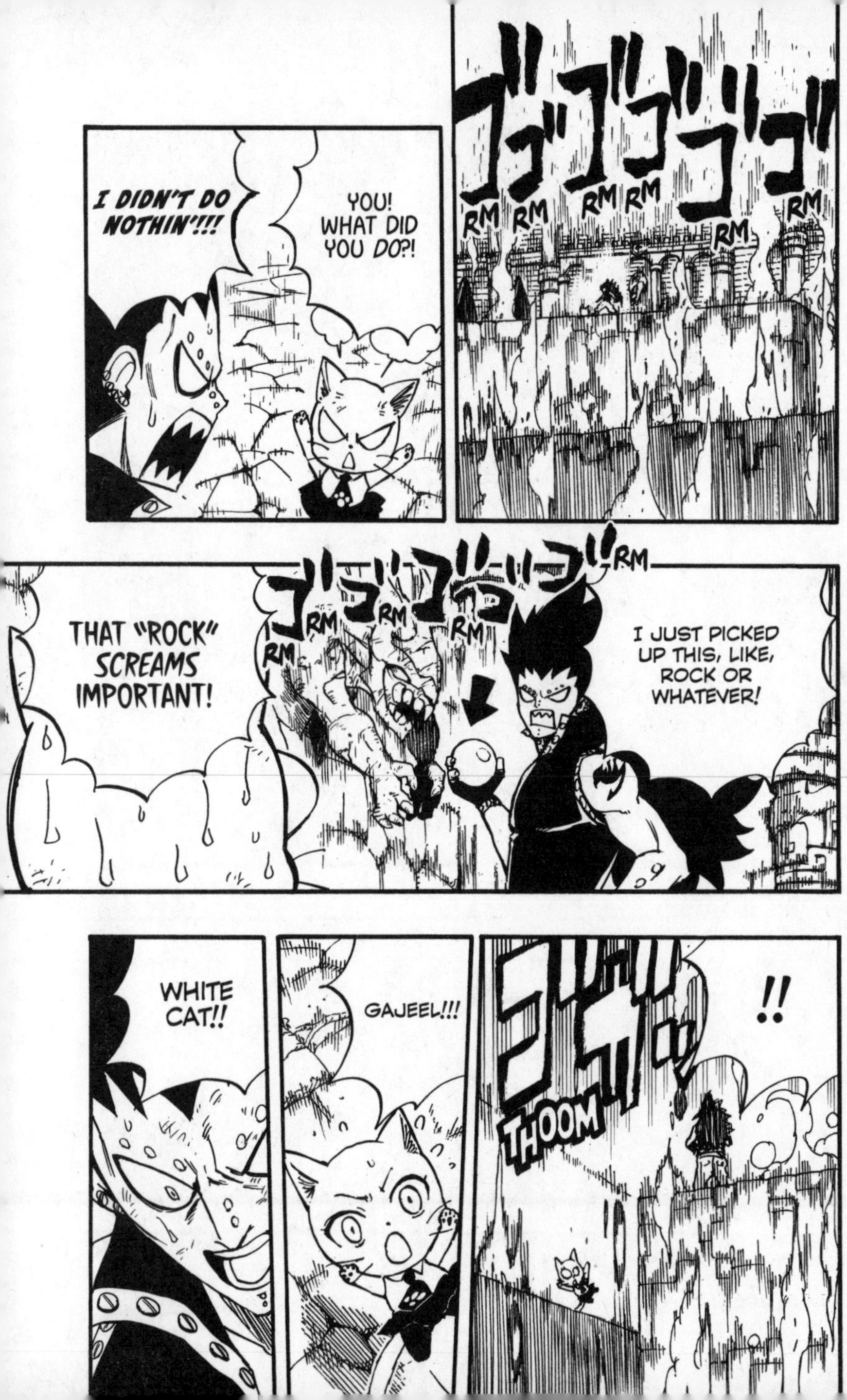
RM RM RM RM RM RM RM
YOU! WHAT DID YOU DO?!
I DIDN'T DO NOTHIN'!!!
RM RM RM RM RM
I JUST PICKED UP THIS, LIKE, ROCK OR WHATEVER!
THAT "ROCK" SCREAMS IMPORTANT!
THOOM
!!
GAJEEL!!!
WHITE CAT!!

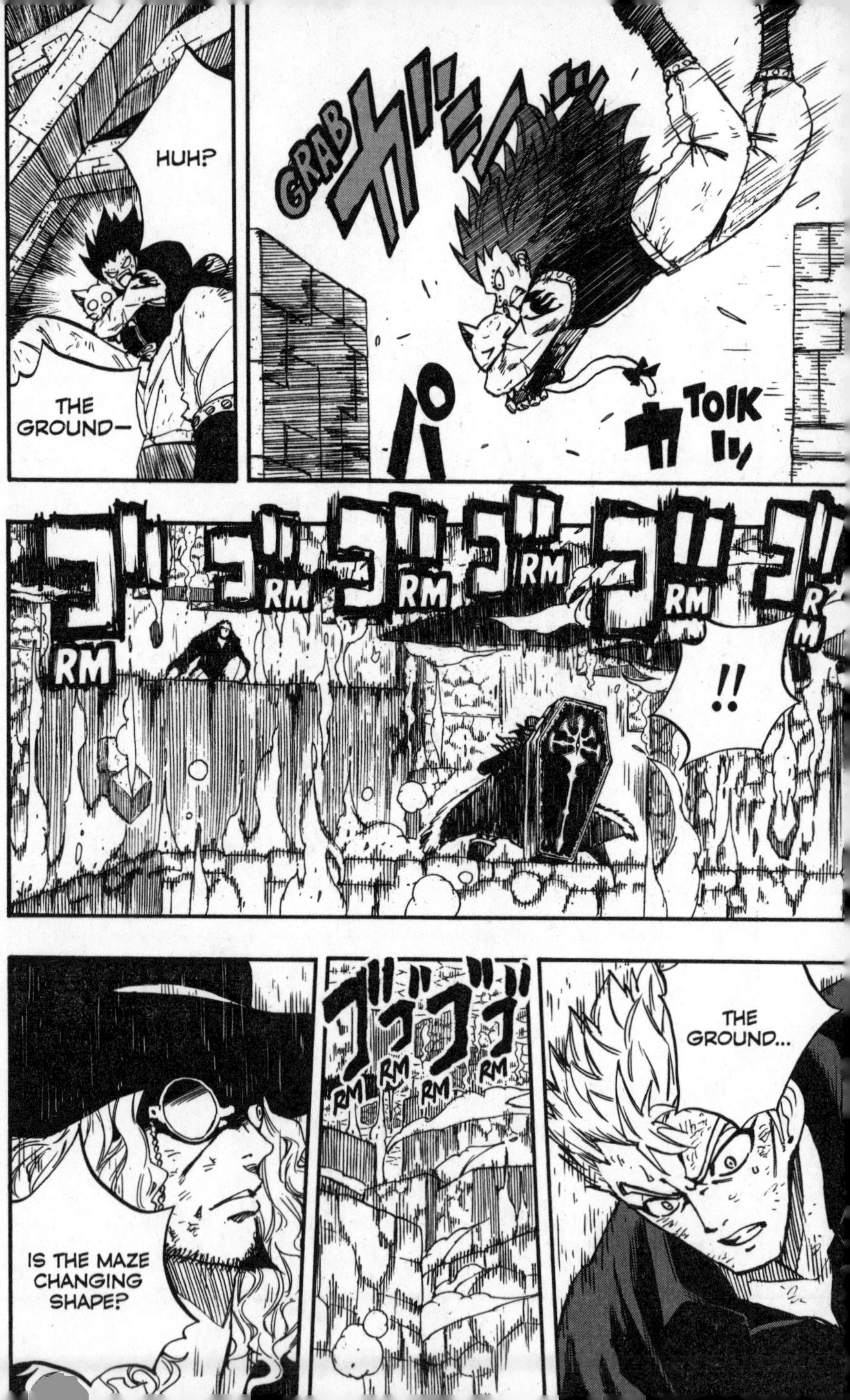
GRAB
TOIK
HUH?
THE GROUND—
RM RM RM RM RM RM
!!
THE GROUND...
RM RM RM RM
IS THE MAZE CHANGING SHAPE?

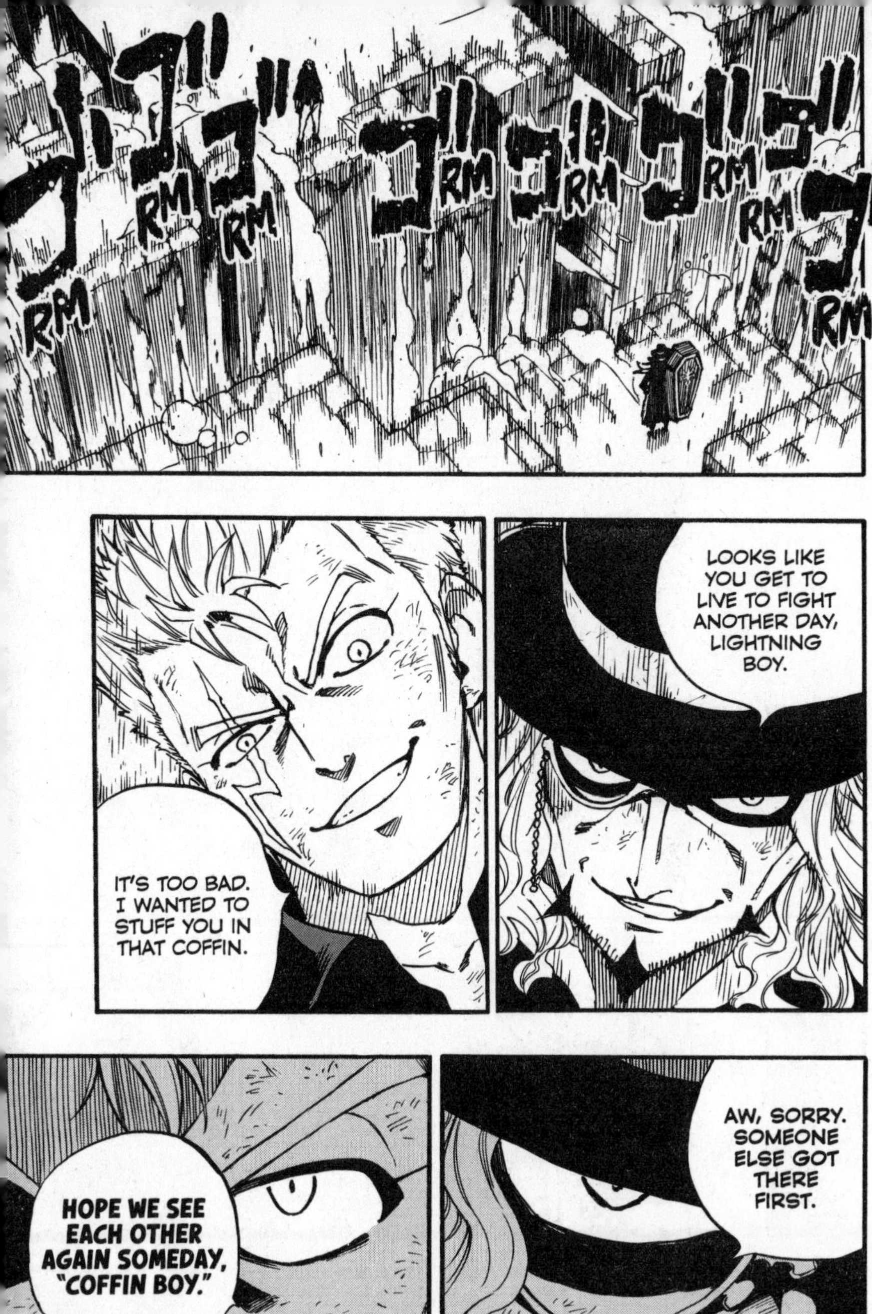
RM RM RM RM RM RM RM RM
LOOKS LIKE YOU GET TO LIVE TO FIGHT ANOTHER DAY, LIGHTNING BOY.
IT'S TOO BAD. I WANTED TO STUFF YOU IN THAT COFFIN.
AW, SORRY. SOMEONE ELSE GOT THERE FIRST.
HOPE WE SEE EACH OTHER AGAIN SOMEDAY, "COFFIN BOY."

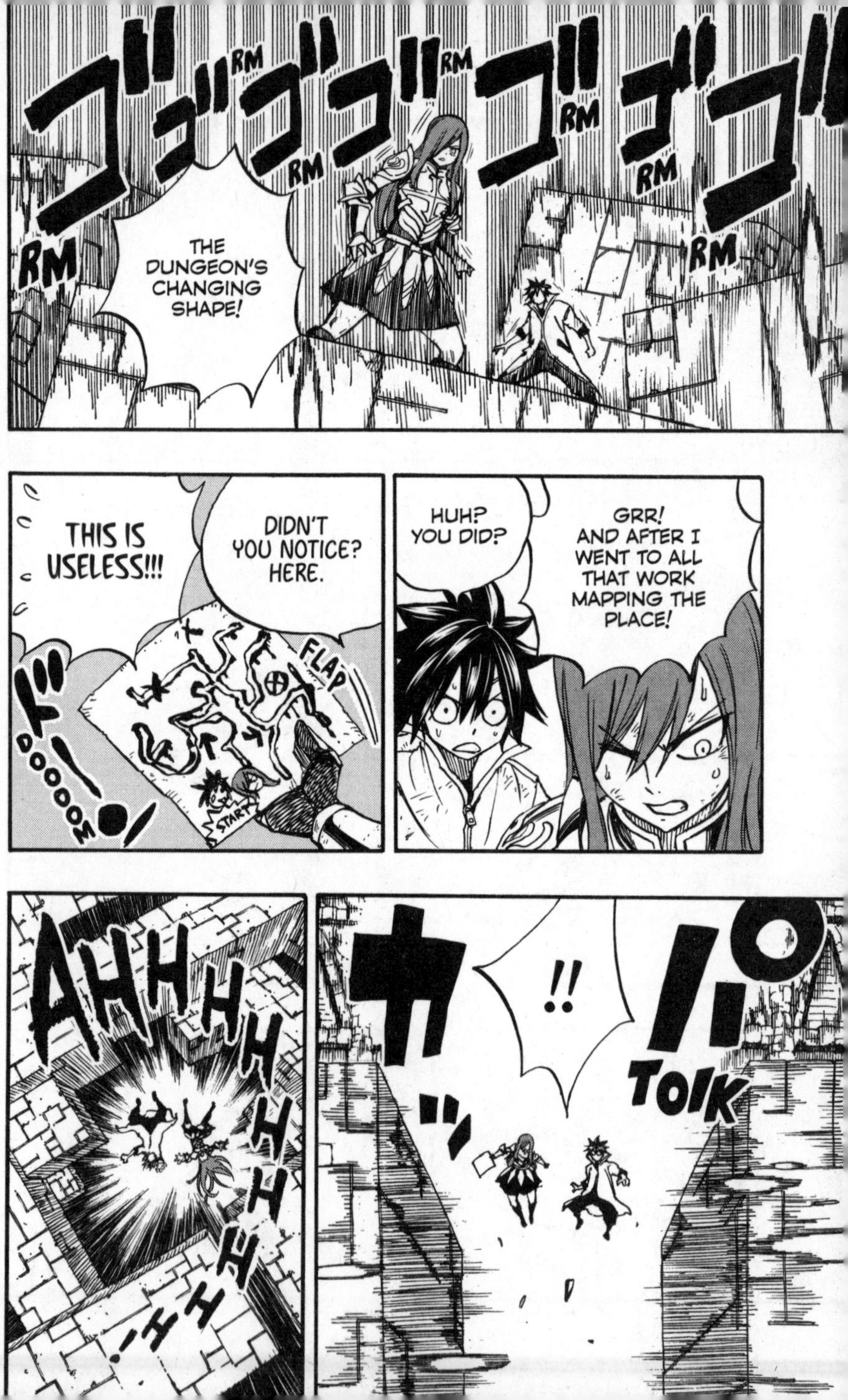
RM
RM
RM
RM
RM
RM
RM
THE DUNGEON'S CHANGING SHAPE!
GRR! AND AFTER I WENT TO ALL THAT WORK MAPPING THE PLACE!
HUH? YOU DID?
DIDN'T YOU NOTICE? HERE.
THIS IS USELESS!!!
FLAP
START
DOOOOOM
!!
TOIK
AHHHHHHHH

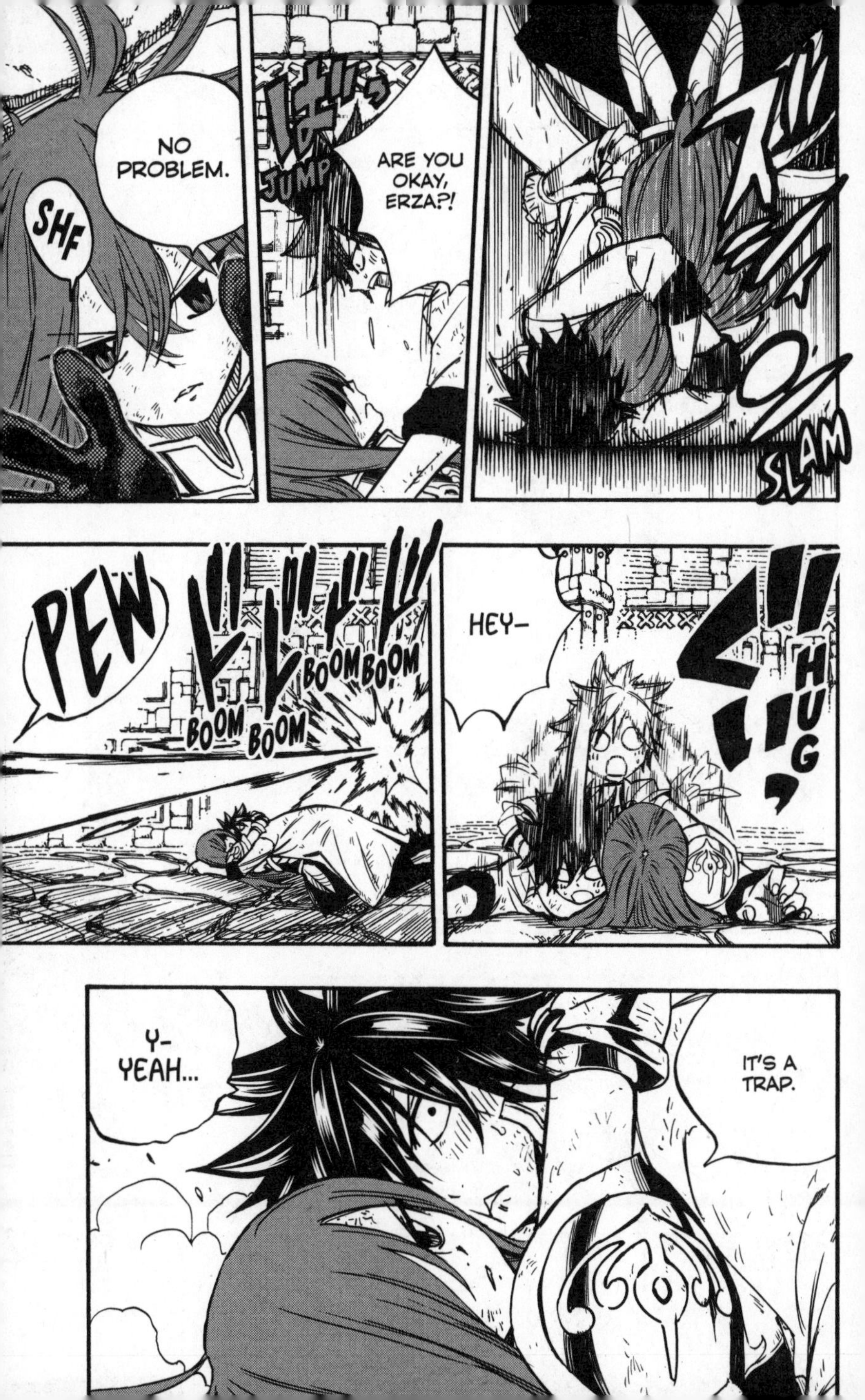
SLAM
JUMP
ARE YOU OKAY, ERZA?!
NO PROBLEM.
SHF
HEY-
HUG
PEW
BOOM
BOOM
BOOM
BOOM
IT'S A TRAP.
Y-YEAH...

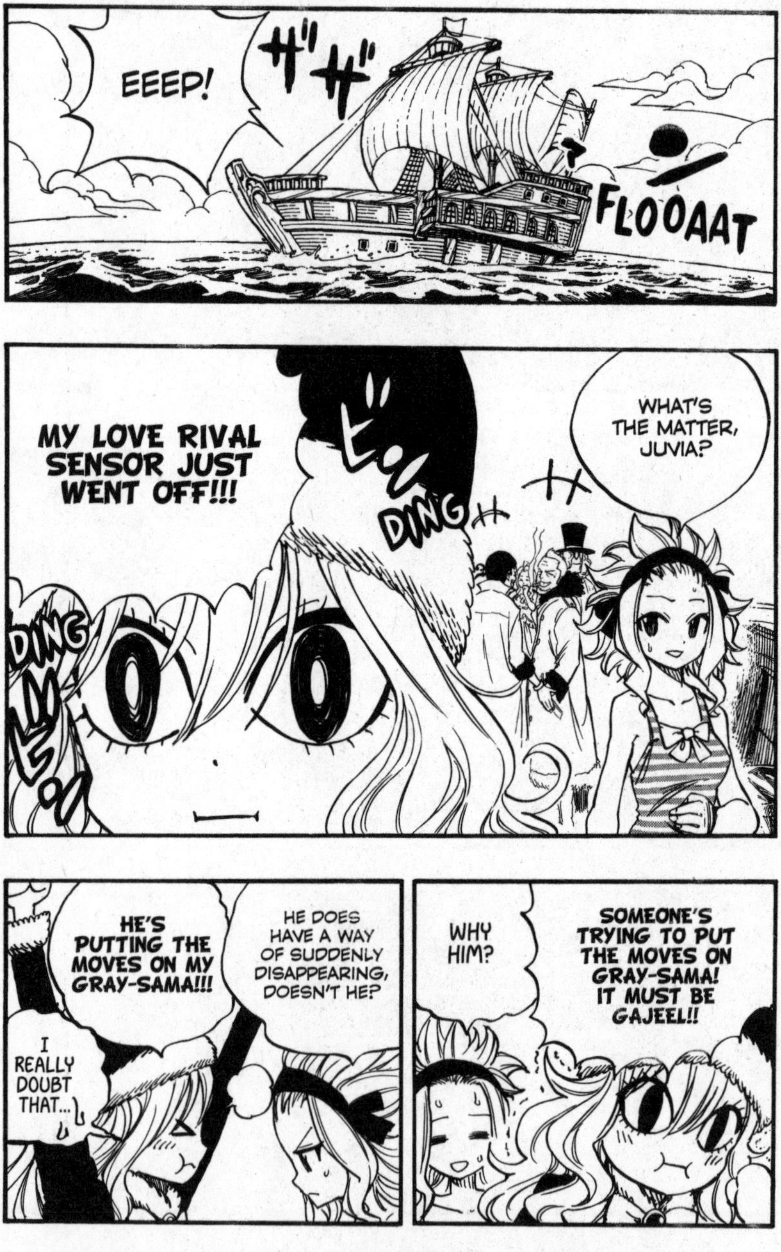
ザザ
EEEP!
FLOOAAT
WHAT'S THE MATTER, JUVIA?
DING
MY LOVE RIVAL SENSOR JUST WENT OFF!!!
DING
SOMEONE'S TRYING TO PUT THE MOVES ON GRAY-SAMA! IT MUST BE GAJEEL!!
WHY HIM?
HE DOES HAVE A WAY OF SUDDENLY DISAPPEARING, DOESN'T HE?
HE'S PUTTING THE MOVES ON MY GRAY-SAMA!!!
I REALLY DOUBT THAT...

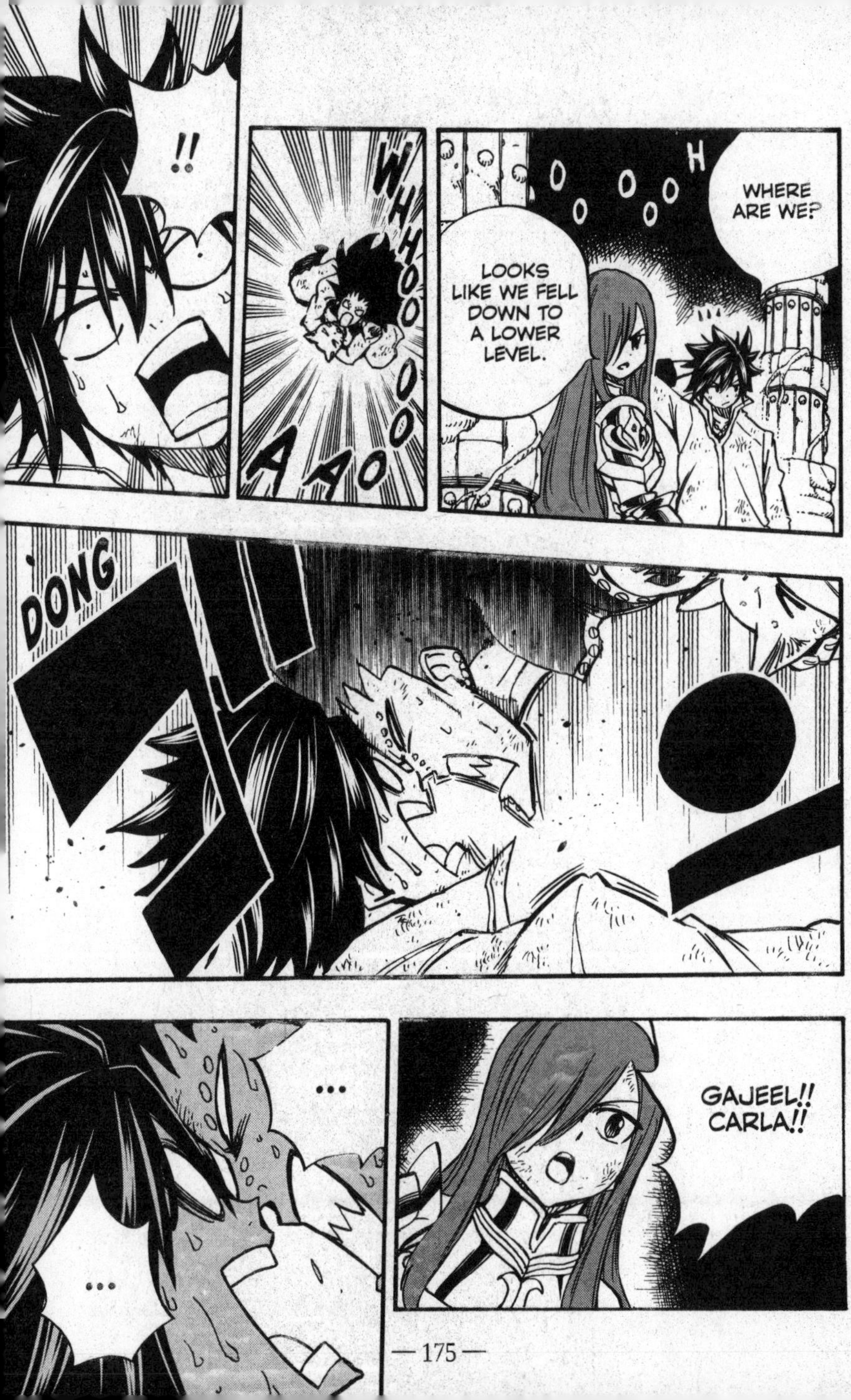
WHERE ARE WE?
OOOOOH
LOOKS LIKE WE FELL DOWN TO A LOWER LEVEL.
WHHOOOOOOOAA
!!
DONG
GAJEEL!! CARLA!!
...
...

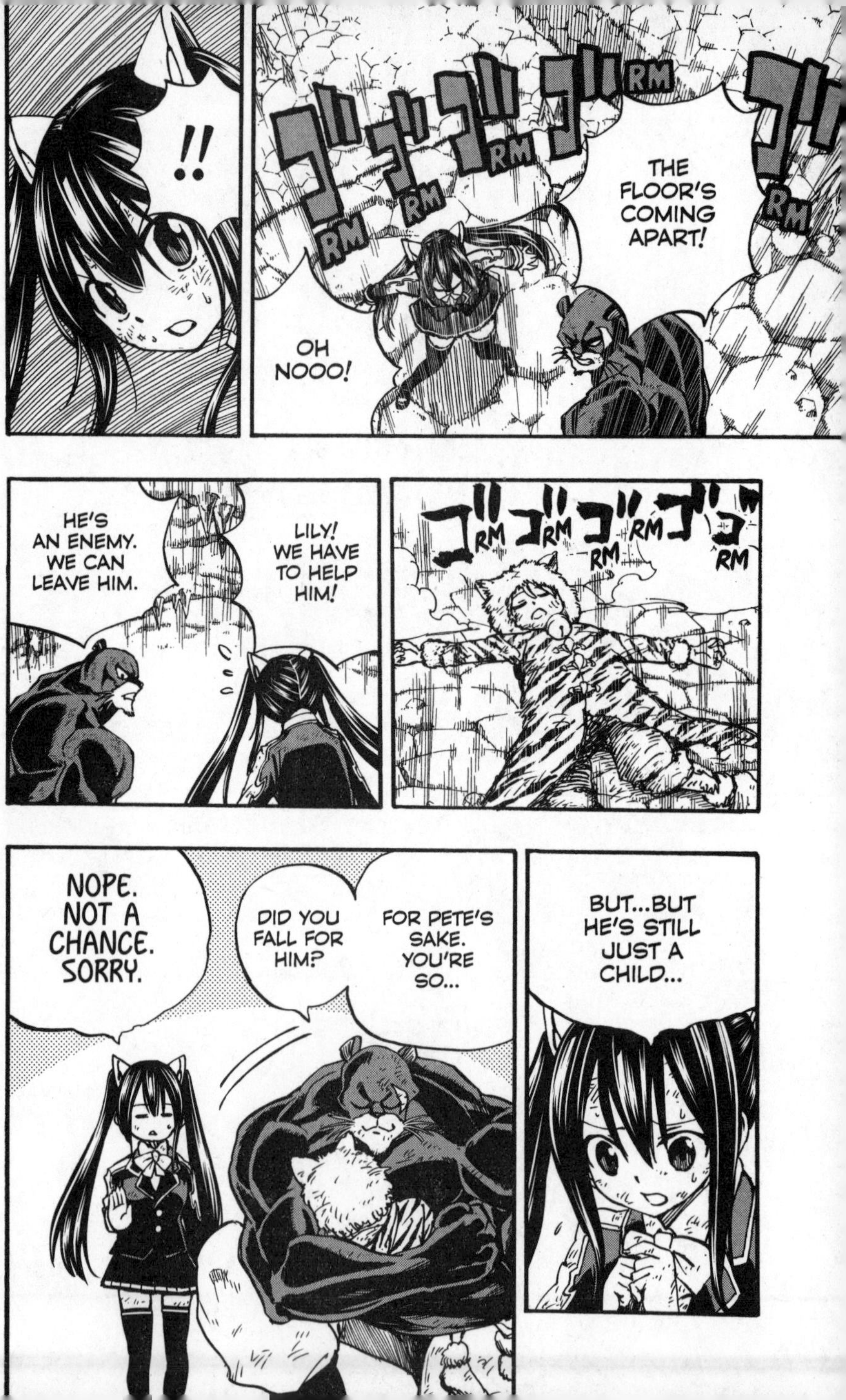

RM
RM
RM
RM
RM
RM
THE FLOOR'S COMING APART!
OH NOOO!
!!
RM
RM
RM
RM
RM
RM
RM
LILY! WE HAVE TO HELP HIM!
HE'S AN ENEMY. WE CAN LEAVE HIM.
BUT...BUT HE'S STILL JUST A CHILD...
FOR PETE'S SAKE. YOU'RE SO...
DID YOU FALL FOR HIM?
NOPE. NOT A CHANCE. SORRY.

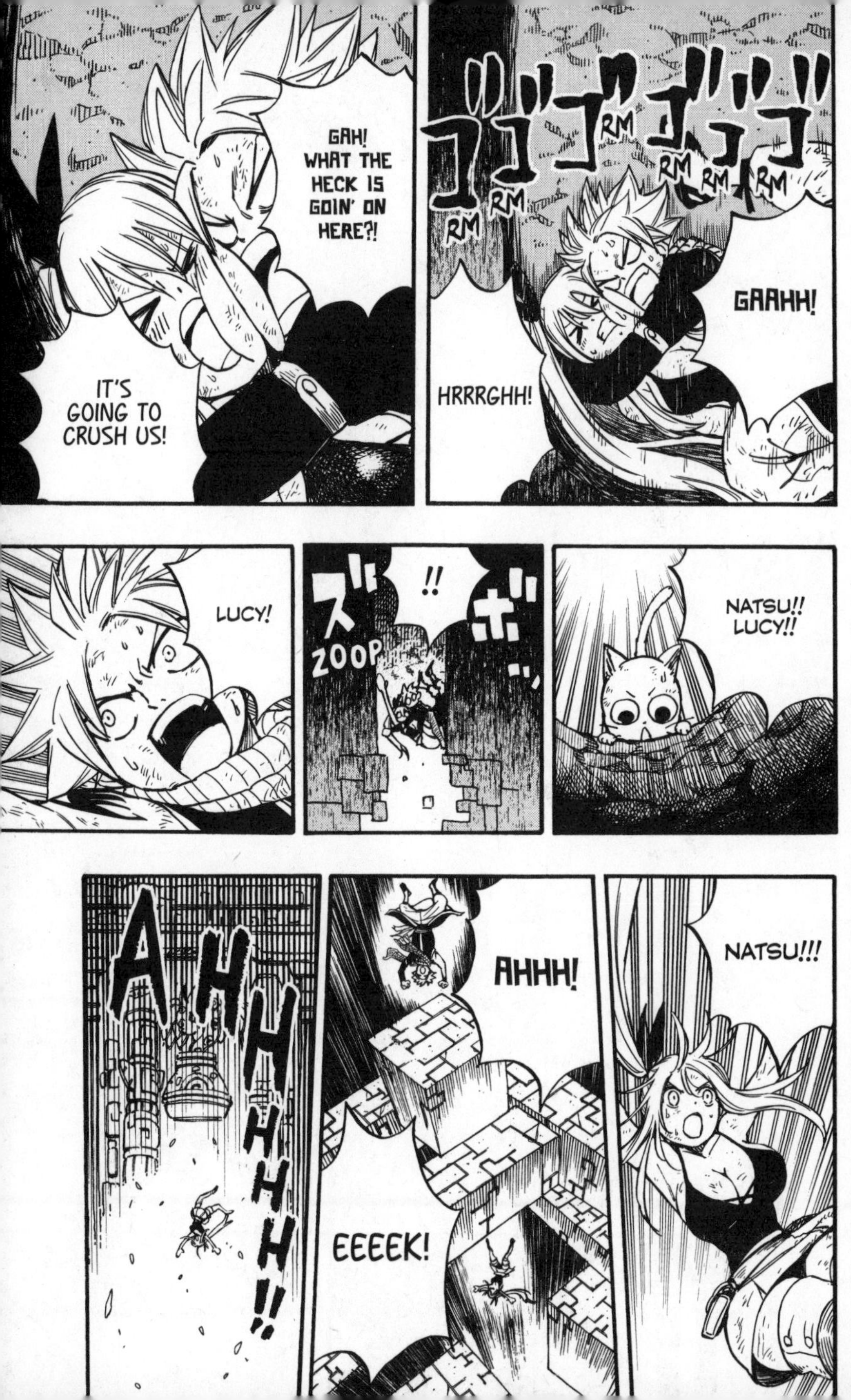
RM RM RM RM RM RM
GAAHH!
HRRRGHH!
GAH! WHAT THE HECK IS GOIN' ON HERE?!
IT'S GOING TO CRUSH US!
NATSU!! LUCY!!
!!
ZOOP
LUCY!
NATSU!!!
AHHH!
EEEEK!
AHHHHHH!!

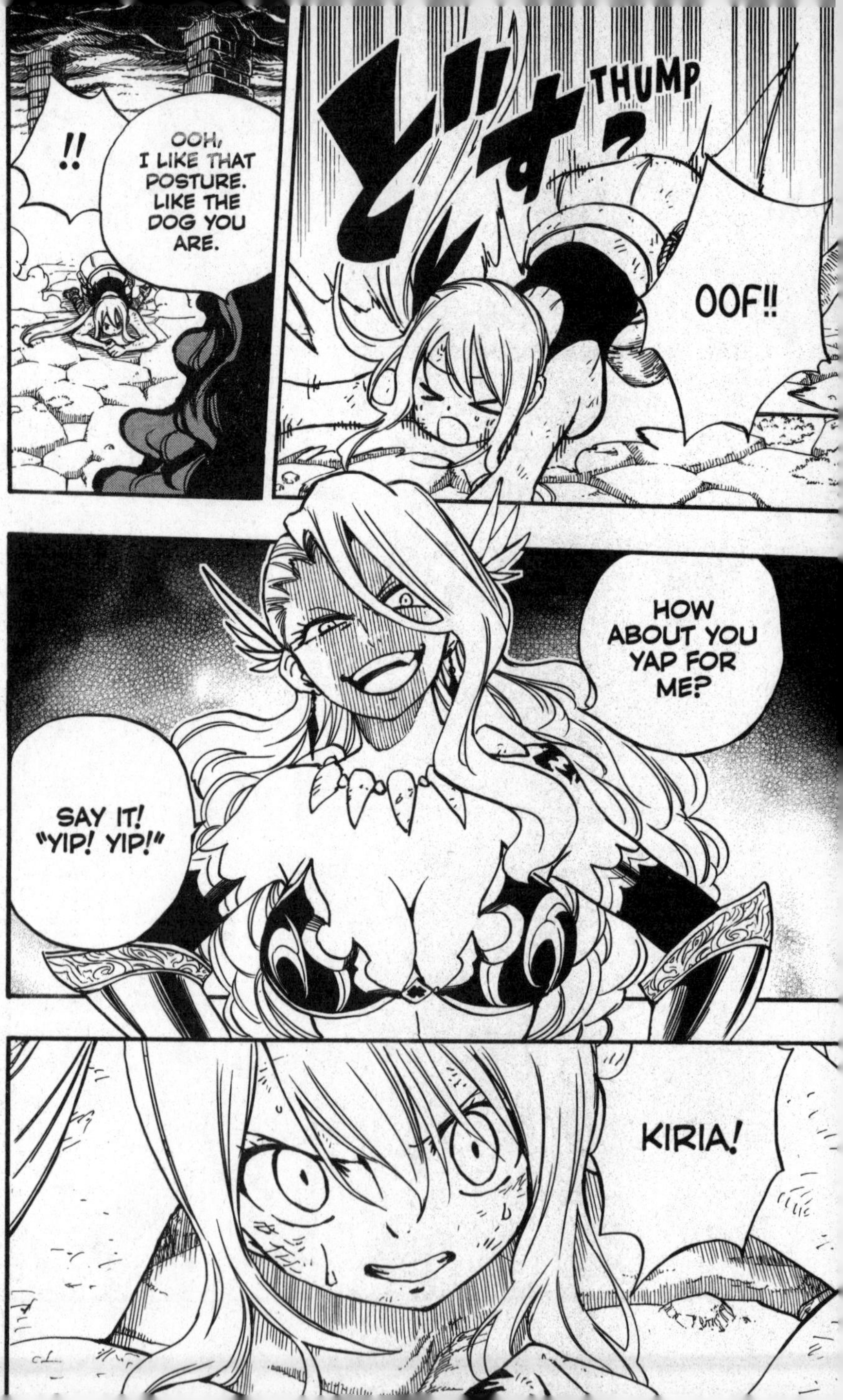
THUMP
OOF!!
!!
OOH, I LIKE THAT POSTURE. LIKE THE DOG YOU ARE.
HOW ABOUT YOU YAP FOR ME?
SAY IT! "YIP! YIP!"
KIRIA!

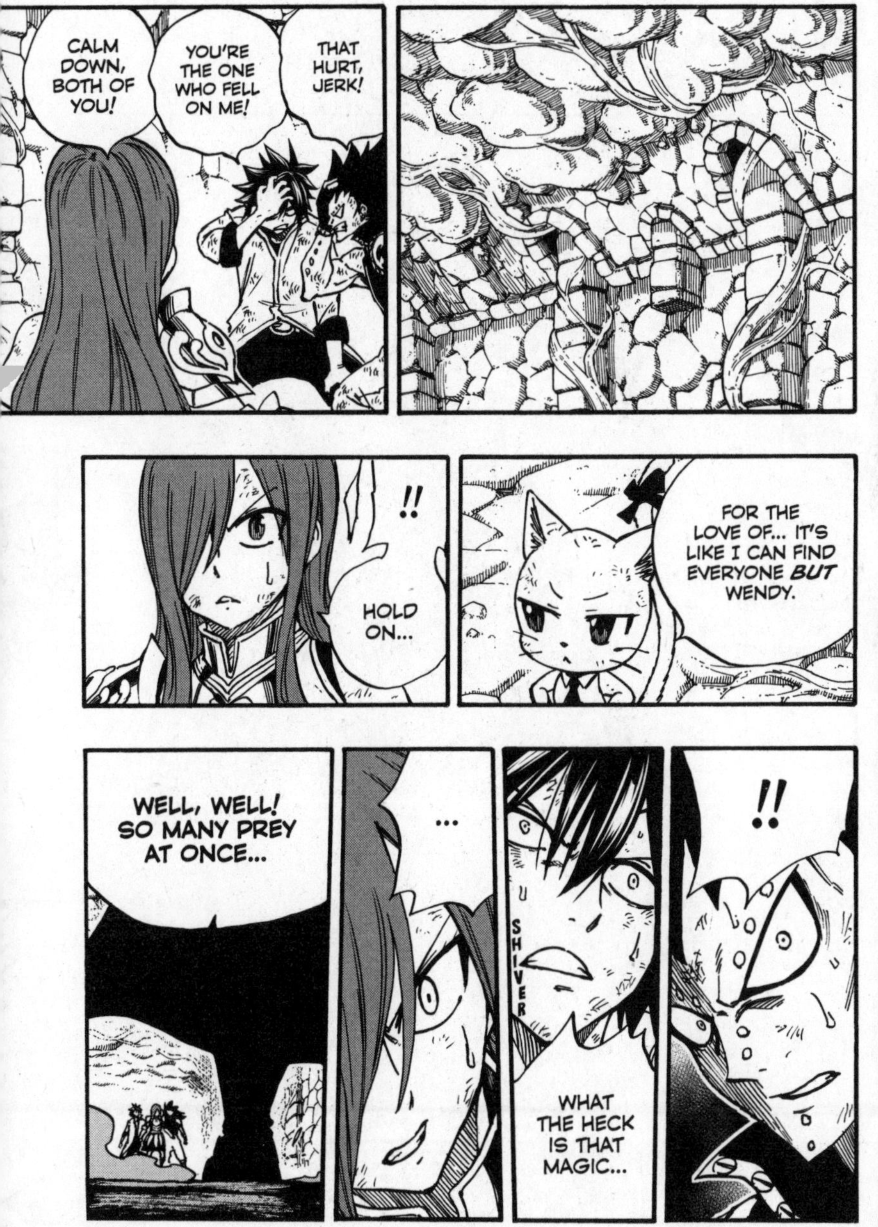
THAT HURT, JERK!
YOU'RE THE ONE WHO FELL ON ME!
CALM DOWN, BOTH OF YOU!
FOR THE LOVE OF... IT'S LIKE I CAN FIND EVERYONE *BUT* WENDY.
!!
HOLD ON...
!!
SHIVER
WHAT THE HECK IS THAT MAGIC...
...
WELL, WELL! SO MANY PREY AT ONCE...

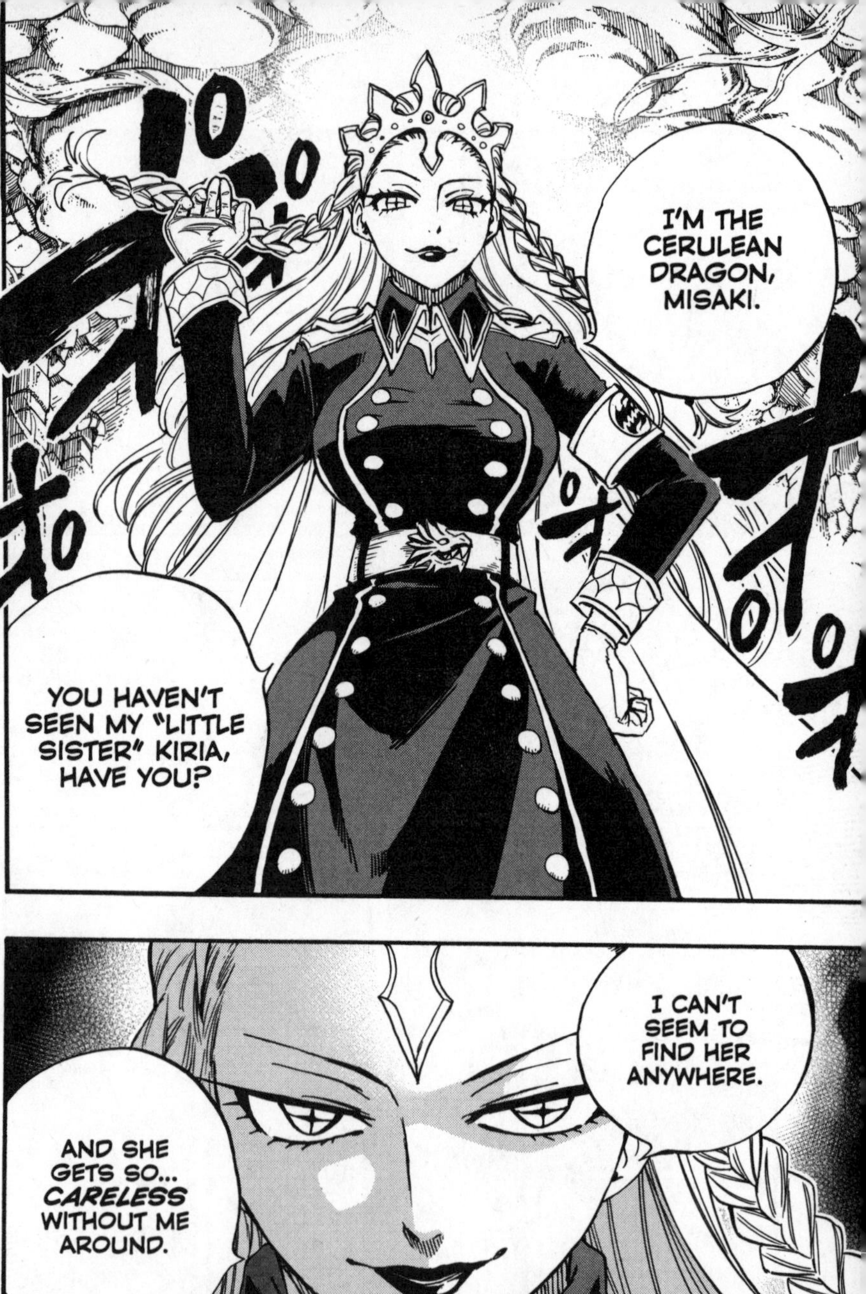
I'M THE CERULEAN DRAGON, MISAKI.
YOU HAVEN'T SEEN MY "LITTLE SISTER" KIRIA, HAVE YOU?
I CAN'T SEEM TO FIND HER ANYWHERE.
AND SHE GETS SO... *CARELESS* WITHOUT ME AROUND.

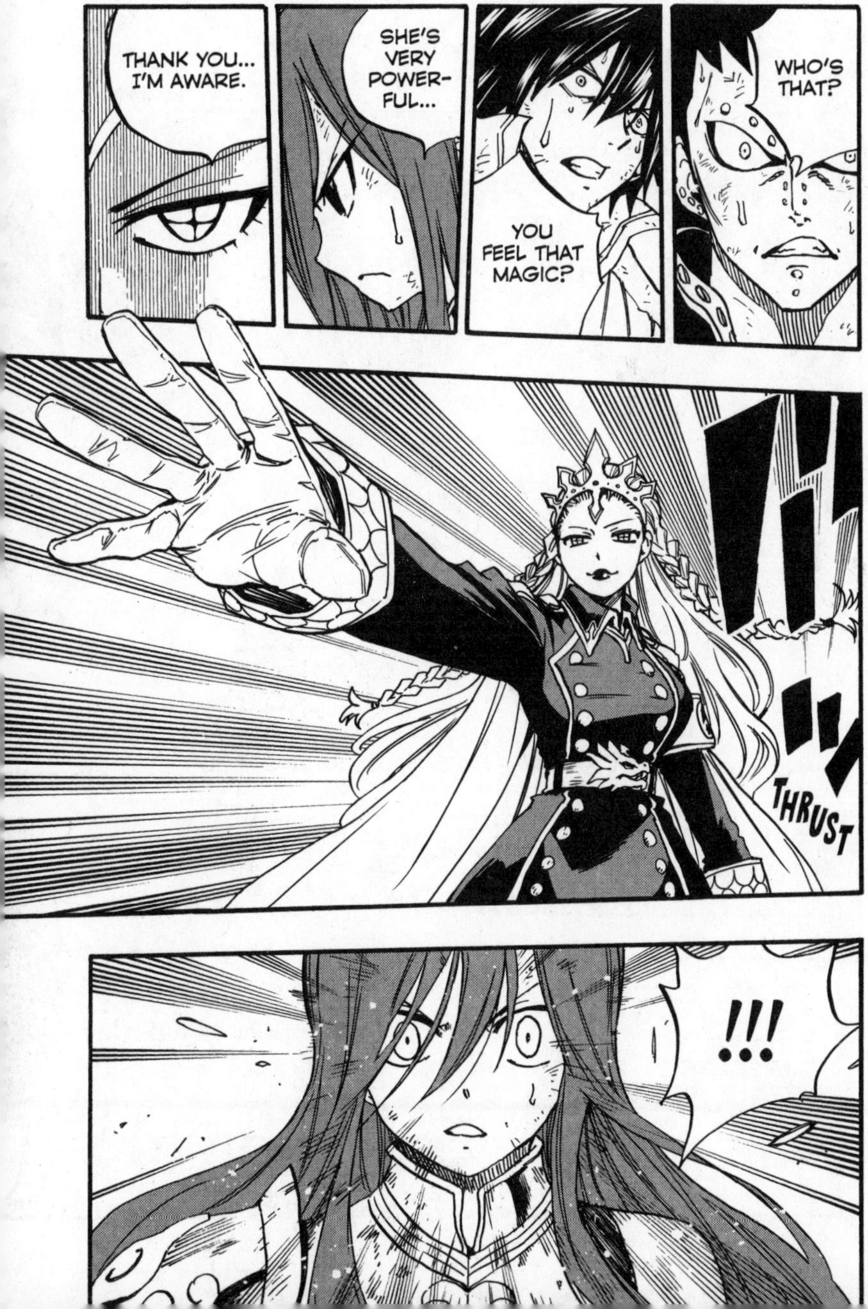
WHO'S THAT?
YOU FEEL THAT MAGIC?
SHE'S VERY POWER-FUL...
THANK YOU... I'M AWARE.
THRUST
!!!

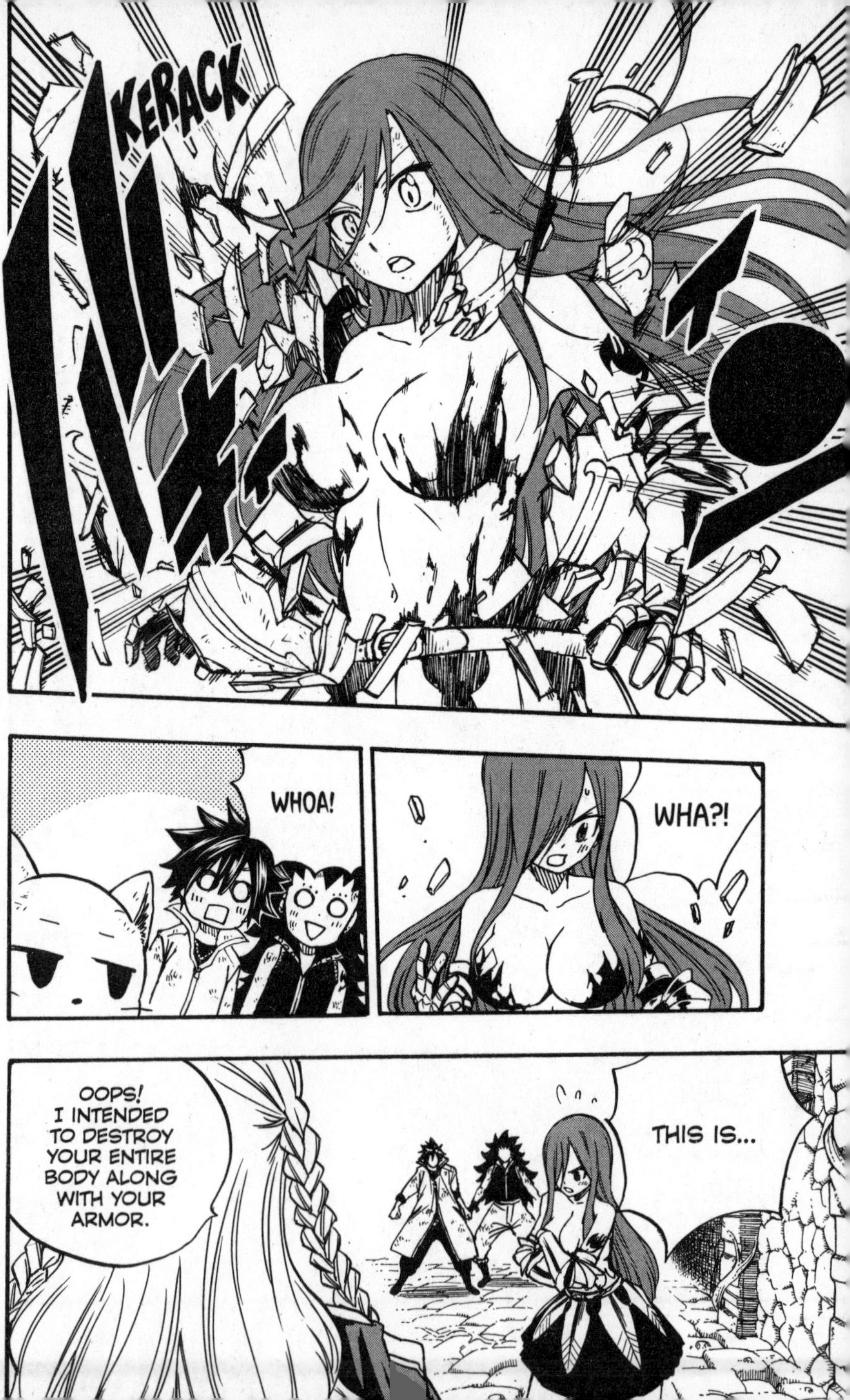
KERACK
WHA?!
WHOA!
THIS IS...
OOPS! I INTENDED TO DESTROY YOUR ENTIRE BODY ALONG WITH YOUR ARMOR.

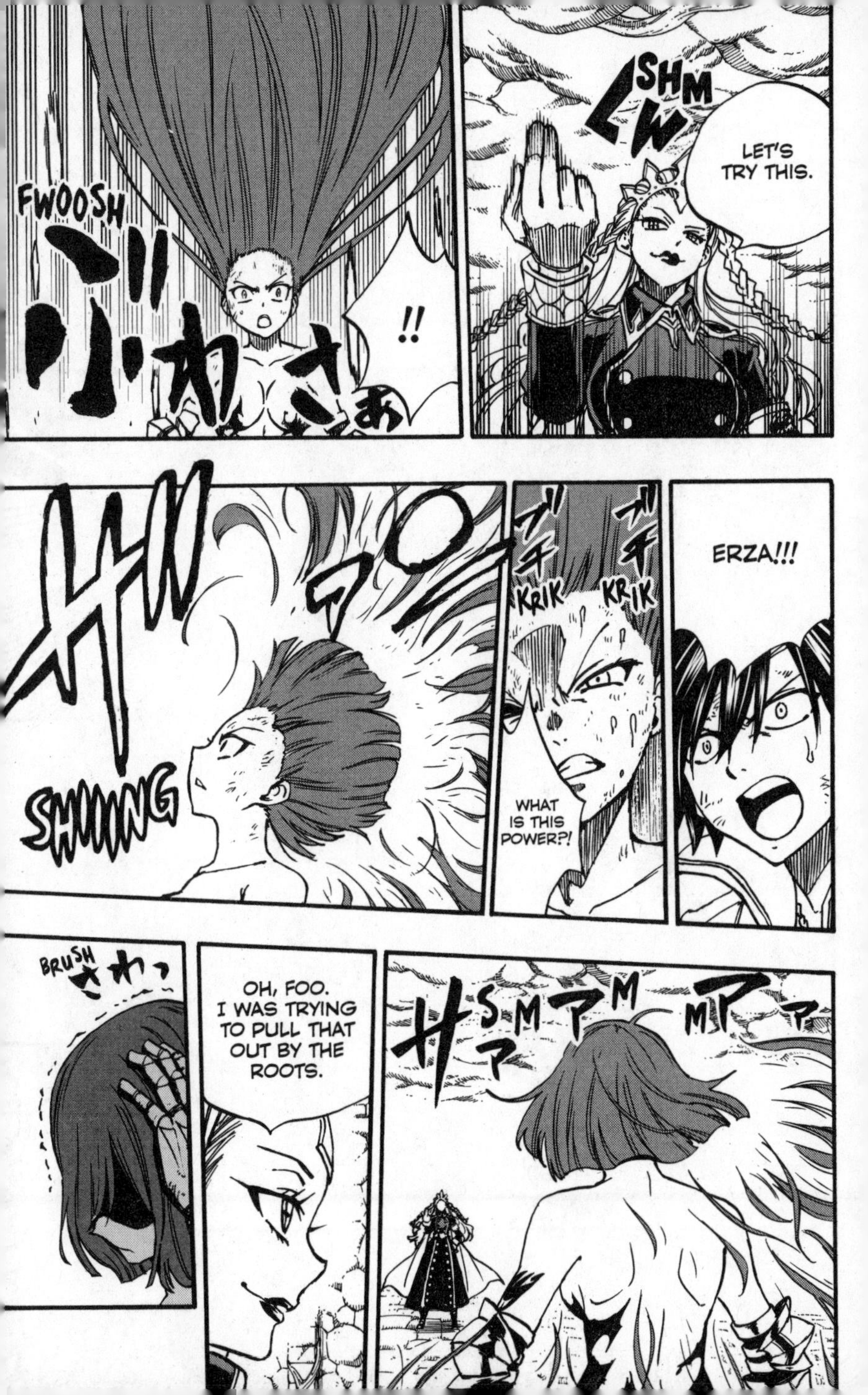
SHM
LET'S TRY THIS.
FWOOSH
!!
ERZA!!!
KRIK KRIK
WHAT IS THIS POWER?!
SHIING
SMMM MM
OH, FOO. I WAS TRYING TO PULL THAT OUT BY THE ROOTS.
BRUSH

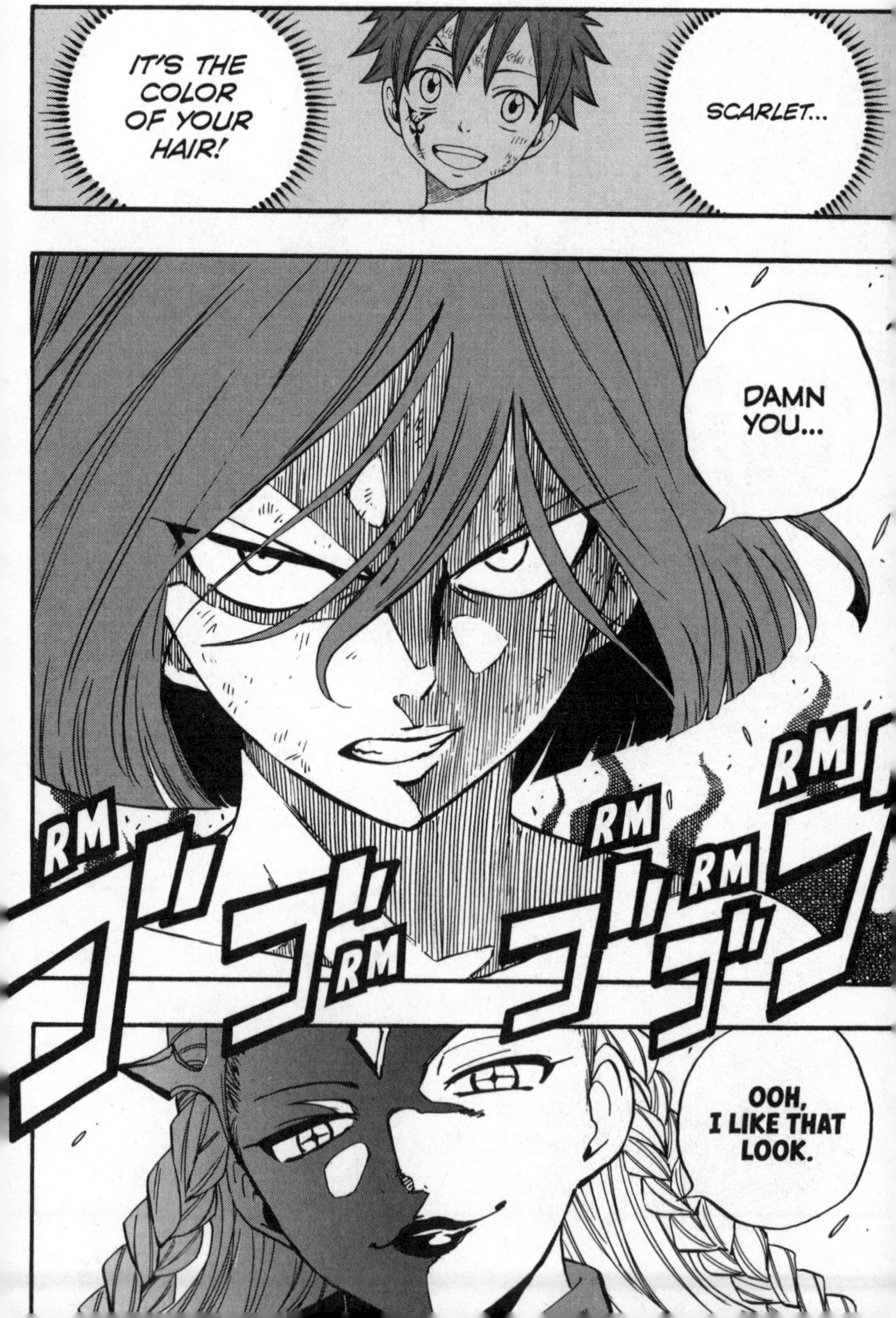
SCARLET...
IT'S THE COLOR OF YOUR HAIR!
DAMN YOU...
RM RM RM RM RM RM
OOH, I LIKE THAT LOOK.

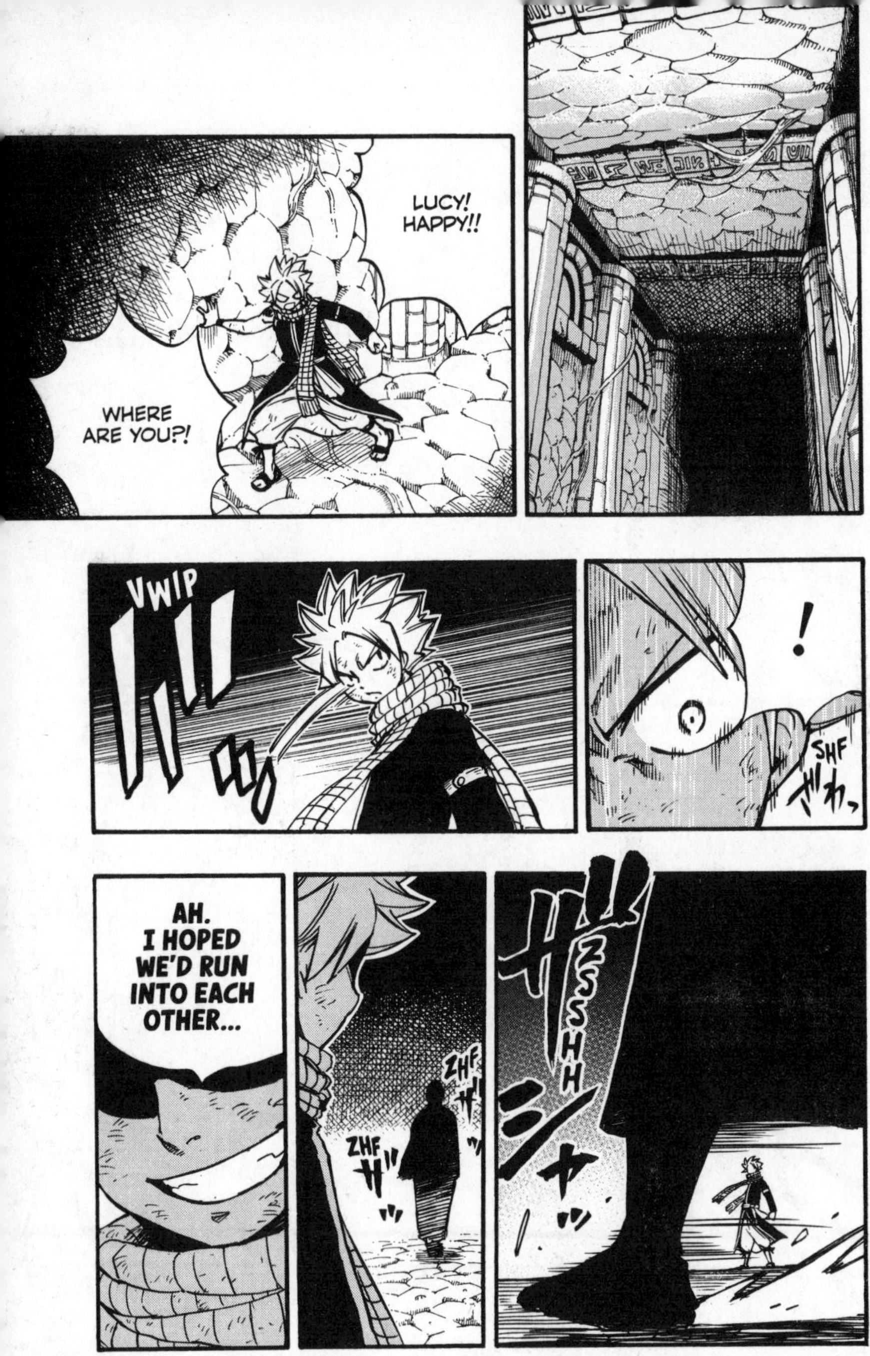
LUCY! HAPPY!!
WHERE ARE YOU?!
!
SHF
VWIP
ZSSHH
ZHF
ZHF
AH. I HOPED WE'D RUN INTO EACH OTHER...

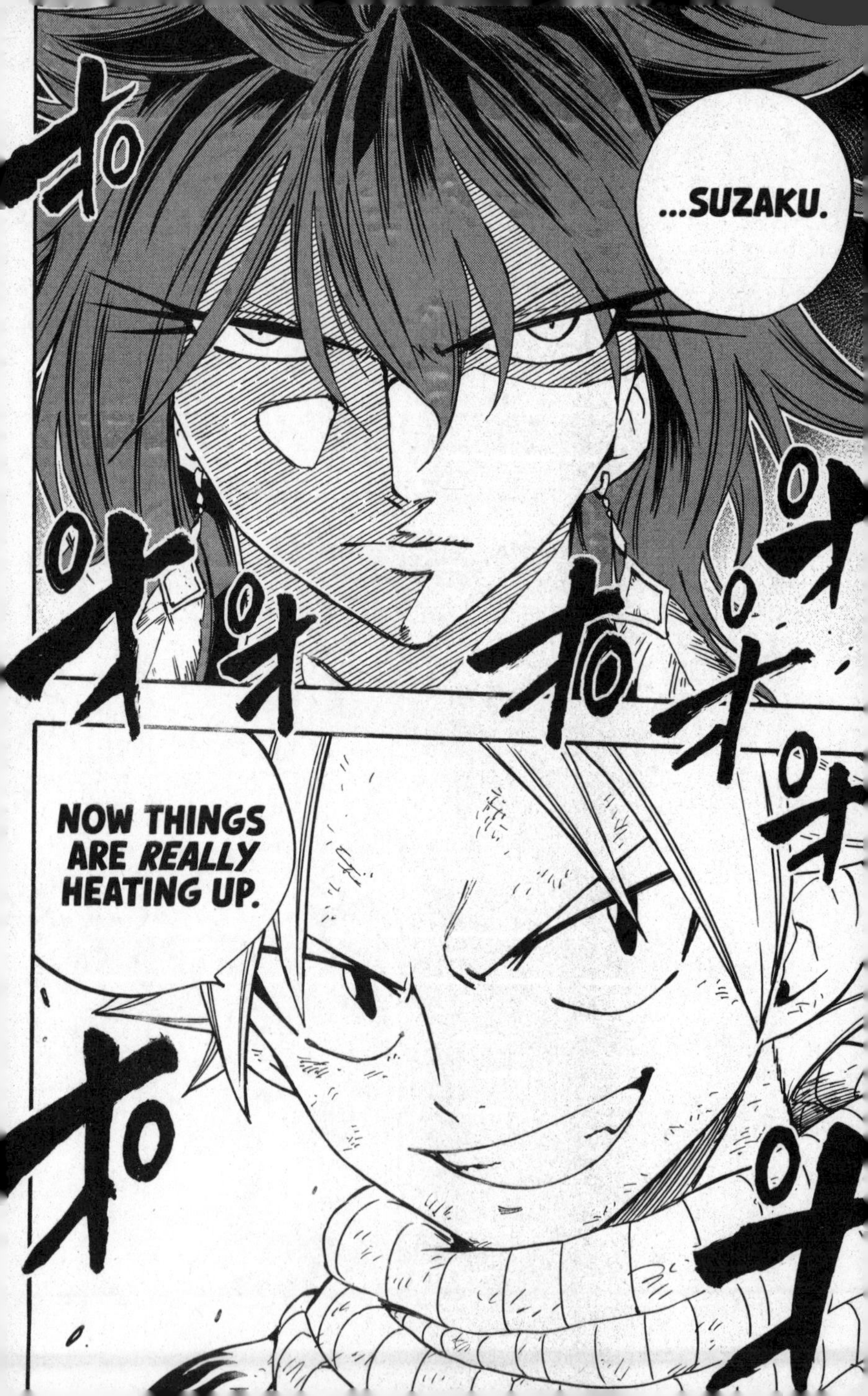
...SUZAKU.
NOW THINGS ARE *REALLY* HEATING UP.

SPEAK NOT OF IT

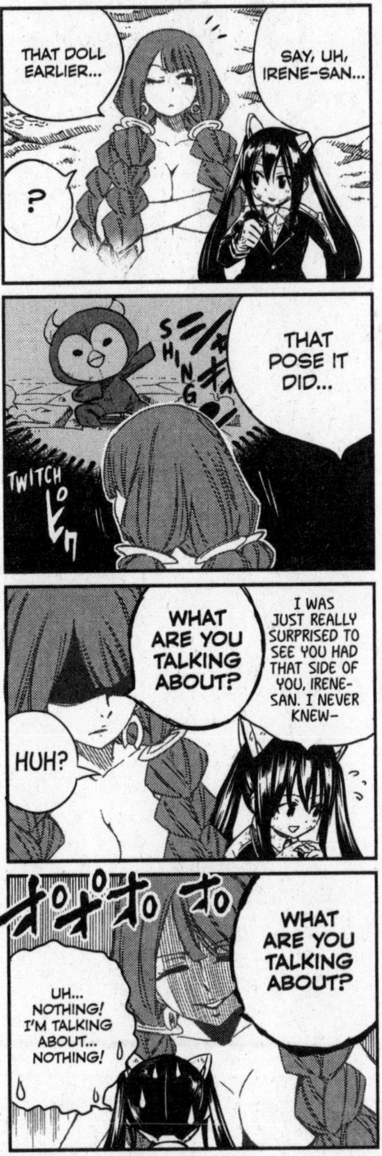
SAY, UH, IRENE-SAN...
THAT DOLL EARLIER...
?
THAT POSE IT DID...
SHING
TWITCH
I WAS JUST REALLY SURPRISED TO SEE YOU HAD THAT SIDE OF YOU, IRENE-SAN. I NEVER KNEW-
WHAT ARE YOU TALKING ABOUT?
HUH?
WHAT ARE YOU TALKING ABOUT?
UH... NOTHING! I'M TALKING ABOUT... NOTHING!

DE ART RETURNS

(FUKUSHIMA PREFECTURE I LOVE SIEGHART & SATORU GOJO & BL ♡)

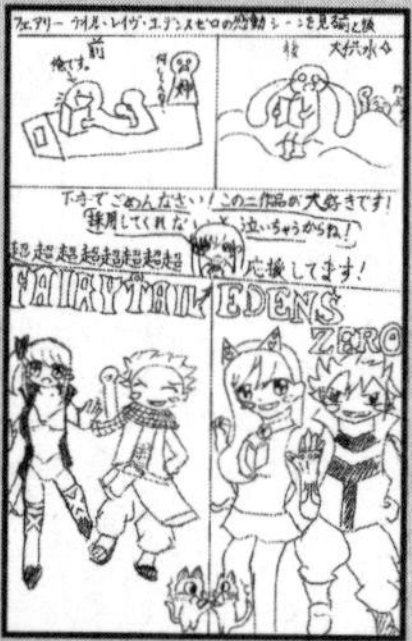
下手でごめんなさい！この二作品が大好きです！
採用してくれないと泣いちゃうからね！
超超超超超超超超応援してます！
FAIRY TAIL
EDENS ZERO

▲ THANKS FOR YOUR ENCOURAGEMENT ON BOTH THESE SERIES!

(FUKUSHIMA PREFECTURE SHUN ARAKAWA)

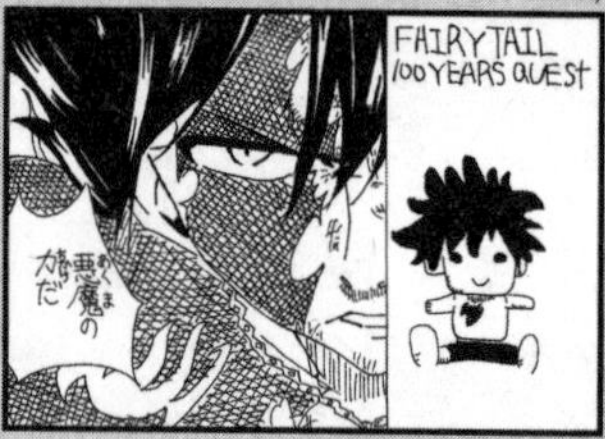
FAIRY TAIL
100 YEARS QUEST
悪魔の力だ

▲ THE BALANCE OF COOLNESS AND CUTENESS IS GREAT!

(OITA PREFECTURE RIMURU)

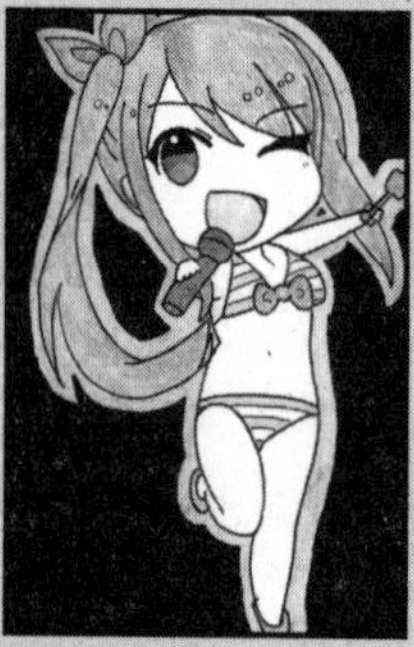

▲ I LOVE HOW SHE LOOKS LIKE SHE'S HAVING FUN!

(SHIZUOKA PREFECTURE TIA)

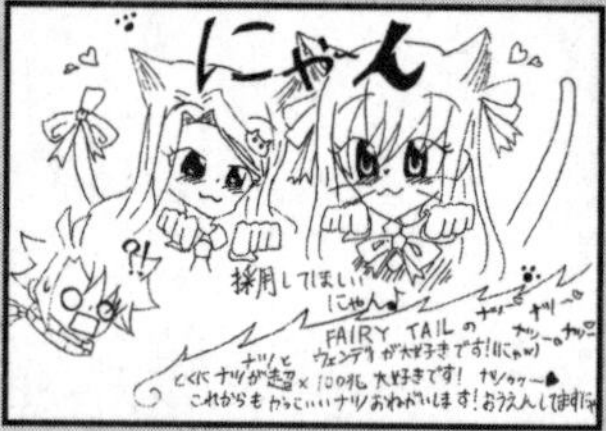
にゃん
採用してほしいにゃん
FAIRY TAIL

▶ THEY'RE BOTH MEOWY CUTE!

(AOMORI PREFECTURE SAKURAMARU)

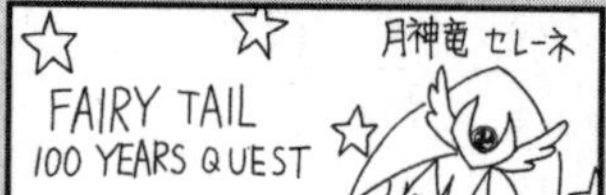
月神竜 セレーネ
FAIRY TAIL
100 YEARS QUEST
アニメ化決定
おめでとうございます！

▲ CHIBI-SELENE... IT'S TOO CUTE...

(SHIGA PREFECTURE SUZAKUN)

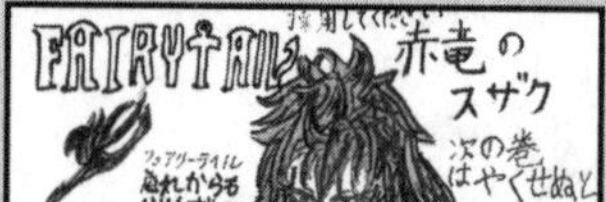
FAIRYTAIL
赤竜のスザク
100 YEARS QUEST
困惑…

▲ EXCELLENT... FOR THE POWER COMES THROUGH THE TEXT.

FAIRY TAIL 100 YEARS QUEST GUILD

(HYOGO PREFECTURE KIUMI MIYAMOTO)

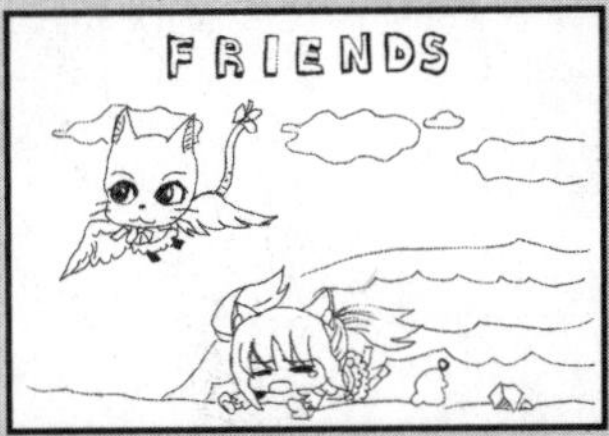
FRIENDS

▲ MAY THEIR FRIENDSHIP ENDURE FOREVER.

(SHIZUOKA NASUY)

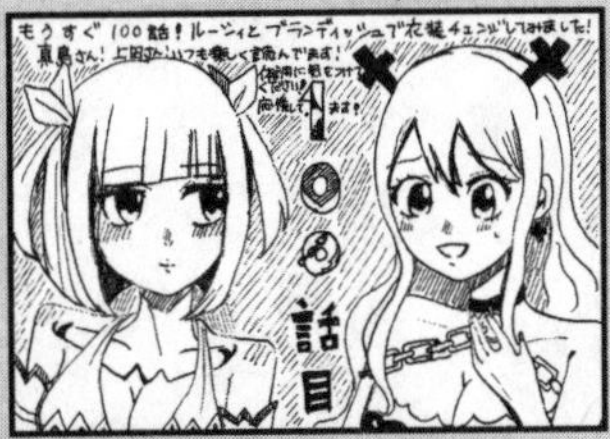
話
目

▲ A CHANGE OF CLOTHES CAN BRING A WHOLE NEW PERSPECTIVE. GREAT!

(TOKYO PREFECTURE RIKA ARAI)

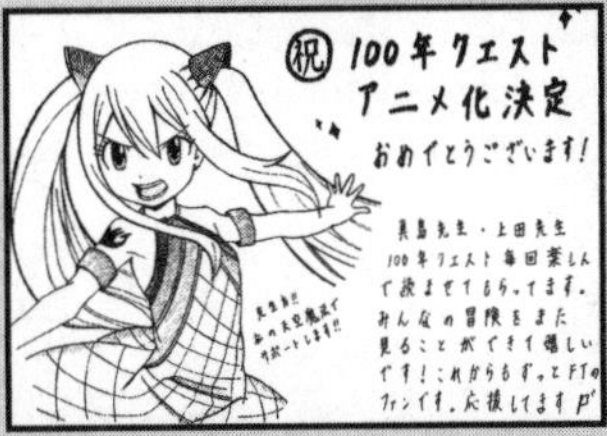
祝 100年クエスト
アニメ化決定
おめでとうございます!
真島先生・上田先生
100年クエスト毎回楽しんで読ませてもらってます。
みんなの冒険をまた見ることができて嬉しいです!これからもずっとFTのファンです。応援してます

▲ WENDY GROWS UP SO FAST. I FEEL LIKE A PROUD DAD.

(TAIWAN LAI ENCAN)

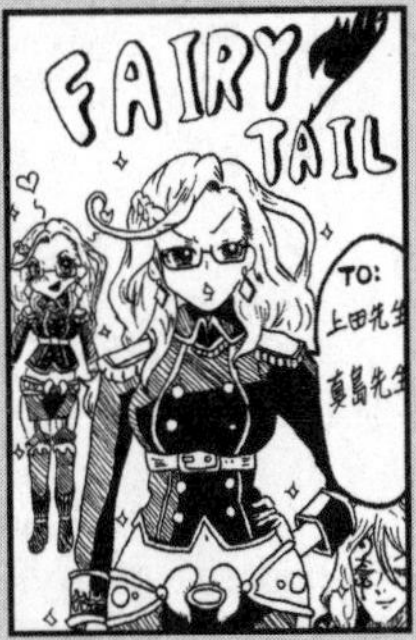
FAIRY TAIL
TO:
上田先生
真島先生

▲ THANKS FOR THIS GORGEOUS PICTURE!

FAIL CORNER

(IWATE PREFECTURE MARIBO BEANS)

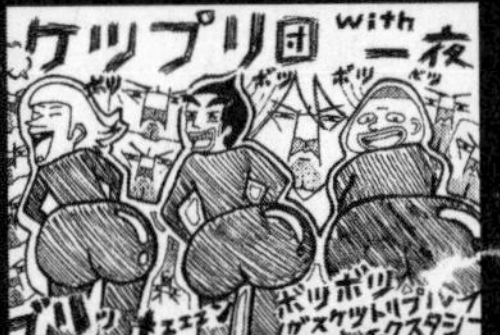
ケツプリ団 with 一夜

▲ THREE BUTTS I THINK I'M GOING TO BE SEEING IN MY DREAMS...

EDITOR'S NOTE: DRAWING SUBMISSIONS LIMITED TO JAPAN.

TRANSLATION NOTES

The Dark Dragon-Slayer Knights, page 40

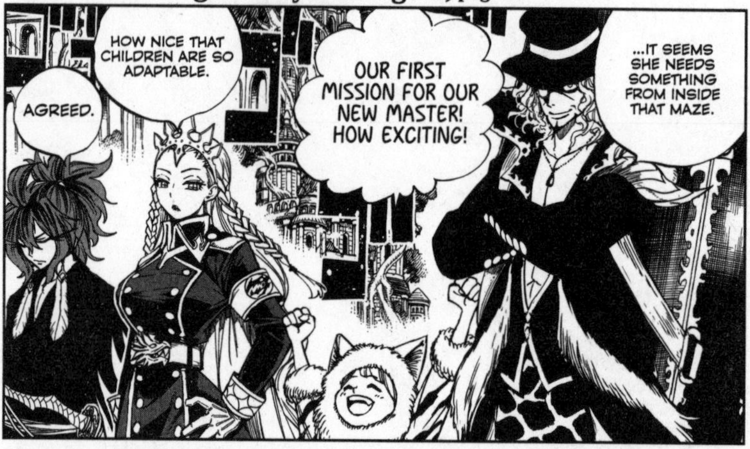
...IT SEEMS SHE NEEDS SOMETHING FROM INSIDE THAT MAZE.
OUR FIRST MISSION FOR OUR NEW MASTER! HOW EXCITING!
HOW NICE THAT CHILDREN ARE SO ADAPTABLE.
AGREED.

The names of the Dark Dragon-Slayer Knights are each culturally significant; they're largely (though not entirely) based on the Four Beasts of Chinese mythology.

Suzaku is the name of the "scarlet bird" and one of the Four Beasts; this is presumably why Suzaku is the Scarlet Dragon. The "cerulean dragon" (*qinglong*) is another of these creatures, although its name in Japanese is Seiryu. (Notice the dragon-head buckle on Misaki's belt.) "Misaki" is a term for a collection of spirits that serve somewhere below the highest levels of the divine *kami*.

Haku's name means "white," and is related to his identification as the *byakko-ryuu* or "Byakko dragon." Byakko is the Japanese name of the third of the Four Beasts, and translates to "White Tiger." Although this makes his name the odd one out in terms of styling, the "tiger" identity relates to both his outfit and some of his behavior.

Finally, Kirin is the *qilin* or unicorn. Although the last of the Four Beasts is traditionally Genbu (a tortoise, associated with the color black), some catalogs of these creatures also include the Yellow Dragon and/or Qilin as a fifth beast, associated with the center "direction" (in the way that Suzaku is associated with the south, the cerulean dragon with the east, and the white tiger with the west). However, in Japanese, *kirin* is also the word for giraffe (perhaps because of a slight resemblance to the mythical animal) – which might explain the pattern on this character's outfit.

Fuku, page 143

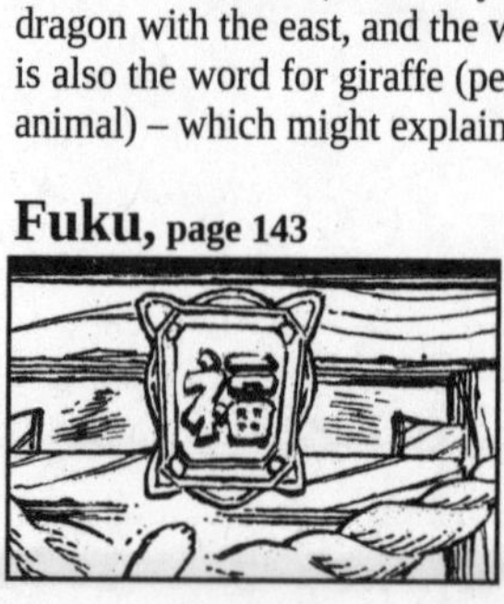
福

The kanji character on the torii shrine gate (roughly in the center of the illustration) reads fuku, "blessing." (It can also more generally represent a wish for good fortune.) 2022 is the Year of the Tiger according to the Chinese zodiac, hence the animal in the illustration.

FAIRY TAIL
100 YEARS QUEST

A Kodansha Comics Trade Paperback Original
FAIRY TAIL: 100 Years Quest 11 copyright © 2022 Hiro Mashima/Atsuo Ueda
English translation copyright © 2022 Hiro Mashima/Atsuo Ueda

Published in the United States by Kodansha Comics, an imprint of
Kodansha USA Publishing, LLC, New York.

Publication rights for this English edition arranged through
Kodansha Ltd., Tokyo.

First published in Japan in 2022 by Kodansha Ltd., Tokyo.

ISBN 978-1-64651-573-8

Original cover design by Hisao Ogawa (Blue in Green)

Printed in the United States of America.

www.kodansha.us

1st Printing
Translation: Kevin Steinbach
Lettering: Phil Christie
Editing: David Yoo
Kodansha Comics edition cover design by Phil Balsman

Publisher: Kiichiro Sugawara

Director of Publishing Services: Ben Applegate
Director of Publishing Operations: Dave Barrett
Associate Director of Publishing Operations: Stephen Pakula
Publishing Services Managing Editors: Madison Salters, Alanna Ruse, with Grace Chen
Senior Production Manager: Angela Zurlo